Benchmark Papers
in Human Physiology

Series Editor: L. L. Langley
School of Medicine
University of Missouri, Kansas City

Benchmark Papers
in Human Physiology / 11

A BENCHMARK® Books Series

AGING

Edited by

GERALDINE M. EMERSON

**University of Alabama in
Birmingham**

Dowden, Hutchinson
& Ross, Inc.

STROUDSBURG, PENNSYLVANIA

Copyright © 1977 by **Dowden, Hutchinson & Ross, Inc.**
Benchmark Papers in Human Physiology, Volume 11
Library of Congress Catalog Card Number: 77-4340
ISBN: 0-87933-296-4

79 78 77   1 2 3 4 5
Manufactured in the United States of America.

LIBRARY OF CONGRESS CATALOGING IN PUBLICATION DATA

Main entry under title:
Aging.
    (Benchmark papers in human physiology ; 11)
    English, French, or German.
    Bibliography: p.
    Includes indexes.
    1. Aging—Addresses, essays, lectures. 2. Longevity—Addresses,
essays, lectures. I. Emerson, Geraldine M.
QP86.A358   612.6'7   77-4340
ISBN 0-87933-296-4

Exclusive Distributor: **Halsted Press**
A Division of John Wiley & Sons, Inc.
ISBN: 0-470-99266-2

SERIES EDITOR'S FOREWORD

This is the eleventh volume in the Benchmark Papers on Human Physiology series. This series began with a consideration of homeostasis, one of the most basic concepts in physiology and has included volumes on contraception, circulation, temperature regulation, infant nutrition, and respiration. It now continues with this volume on aging by Dr. Emerson.

Aging probably has concerned man since the beginning of time. One would think, therefore, that the literature would be so terribly extensive as to defy pruning to fit into the limitations of this volume. To be sure, aging has been written about endlessly but of all that has been written, there is remarkably little that can justifiably be called science, at least, the science of physiology. To separate fact from fiction, physiology from philosophy, the meaningful from the myth, requires a scholar who has been concerned with the problem for a very long period of time and with a true oneness of purpose during that period. That is why I asked Dr. Emerson to undertake the task.

I met and helped recruit Dr. Jack Emerson and his wife, Geraldine, in 1952. Jack became a faculty member in our department at the University of Alabama School of Medicine and Gerry quickly settled in to complete her doctorate requirements. I have thus had the opportunity of following a fruitful career from its inception. As Dr. Emerson says, she was introduced to the subject of aging by her husband and together they formed an inseparable, tireless team. Their goal was to learn as much as two people could in a lifetime about a single subject and they achieved that goal. Unfortunately Dr. Jack Emerson died much too prematurely but Gerry has continued their work and shows no signs of having her purpose diverted.

As the articles she has selected for this volume make clear, the end is not in sight—the underlying mechanisms involved in aging still are poorly understood. Yet, by bringing together what is known, Dr. Emerson has provided a distinct service and provided a timely foundation from which to carry on the search.

L. L. LANGLEY

PREFACE

In a book whose primary purpose is the reprinting of outstanding articles in an area of interest, the biggest problem faced is making the selection from a vast array of meritorious writings. I have chosen to include a few examples of thinking in the realm of aging during a one hundred and twenty-five year period, both by gerontologists and others. So very much in our concepts of aging depends upon the thoughts of the diverse members of society as a whole that to be representative, I am including quotes from some writers that reflect, in many instances, the scientific opinions on the subject of aging.

I am indebted to all those whose works in gerontology I have read since being introduced to the subject thirty years ago by the late Dr. Jack D. Emerson. We felt during our quarter century of working together the thrilling challenge in seeking the basis of aging (even though fundamental understanding comes slowly) and ways to circumvent its despoliation. This many others (cited and uncited in this book) have done and are doing, not only under the umbrella of aging but in other endeavors. It is my feeling that the "secret of aging" is locked in with our understanding both of differentiation and the neoplastic process.

The indulgence of one of my former physiology professors, and this series editor, Lee Langley, is gratefully acknowledged. Thanks are due to Dowden, Hutchinson & Ross, Inc. for wanting to publish in this subject.

The resources of the Lister Hill Library of the Health Sciences of the Medical Center of the University of Alabama in Birmingham made my task possible and the resource personnel of this library made it easier.

For checking my French translations I am indebted to my friend Laura Wingo. For assistance in typing, Mary Hamaker, Charlotte Enis, and Maggie Green were invaluable. To my student assistant Dwight Barron goes a general service recognition with thanks.

GERALDINE M. EMERSON

CONTENTS

Contents

Contents

CONTENTS BY AUTHOR

AGING

INTRODUCTION

Aging has probably been, along with reproduction and sleep, a subject of concern to the thinking man from antiquity. Probably it has always been less well defined than the other two and probably more individual variation has always accompanied it.

Aging has many different connotations in the English lanuage: as used herein aging means processes occurring in individuals who are well beyond the average chronological age for that species as differentiated from the processes of growth and maturation, which occur before the average chronological age is attained. Aging is the province of the science of gerontology. We deal in operational definitions of aging; mine—aging is a consequence of the inability of the organism to restore homeostasis after perturbations (which in one's earlier years was easily restored) so that dependence on extracorporeal measures becomes more and more necessary for survival to continue.

I have chosen to include articles from some representative areas of mid-twentieth century thinking, without being inclusive, since twentieth century literature is so much more readily available from libraries. Each of us operates from a somewhat different vantage point and my selections obviously will reflect my own overview of gerontology. I have chosen to translate a few French language articles as well as include the original so that those who prefer to read the one or the other will have it readily available. One of the greatest values in reading thoughts of our predecessors is to put us back into the right perspective as to how far we have progressed in our thinking in the area. It is very interesting to read some of these papers of the mid-1800s. If the places or language were just slightly modified, they would appear to have been written in 1976.

A recurrent idea among gerontologists is that the functioning of the endocrine glands is importantly involved in some yet obscure metabolic manner in the aging process for the obvious reasons so clearly stated in the reproduced papers. Further, as most of the general papers indicate, much of geriatric good health depends on lifelong good diet and exercise. I have included some of the classic papers which have demonstrated in experimental animal studies that life can be prolonged by dietary restriction (Papers 27, 28, 29, and 30). Neither those authors nor I believe that this represents a desirable or feasible way to increase the vigor of man's later years. *And* increase in the number of years is not my interest; rather to be an able participant in activities both mental and physical is the desideratum. In fact, when so many decry the quality of life even for our young people, I find the preoccupation (of some) with trying to find ways to increase man's years of life enigmatic and incompatile. In fairness, many believe that an understanding of the factors involved in longevity and life-shortening will give insight into the basic etiology of aging. Without absolute criteria of aging, the obvious association of debility and death are bases in experimental animal work and in human geriatrics that use longevity as one of the (or the only) objective criterion.

There is also the fact of human interest in those persons who are outstanding in some manner from the average. Venerability or longevity has long been admired. Incompatibilities among gerontologists in the meaning of the term longevity exist. Most mean those truly older members of our society who maintain a special status because of their mature years and their continuing contributions to those with whom they associate; however, a few of us confuse the "Fountain of Youth" concept with the concept of longevity. That perhaps, just perhaps, aging could be prevented or reversed is also a fairly old idea of man—Ponce de Leon and the Fountain of Youth* is an outstanding example reminding all those who visit St Augustine, Florida.

In terms of looks, no one yet knows why ten persons of the same chronological age do not appear to an observer to be of the same age (physiological age). This is probably a fruitful lead to pursue in searching for those biochemical parameters which underlie

* The concept is said to come from mythology. Jupiter transformed the nymph Juventas into a fountain which conferred youth upon whoever therein plunged.

the differential rate of aging. Although investigations into the nature of biochemical changes in gerontology have been productive, still there is nothing which can be used as a measure of physiological age (although I am optimistic that such an index will be found). I believe that such an objective measure of physiological aging will give the obvious therapeutic advantage in indicating the time for institution of therapy for maintaining geriatric health.

I have specifically excluded theories of aging. I have included a few additional readings (Bullough, 1973; Linn, 1975) for those who want to pursue this topic.

This book is not primarily concerned with therapy, yet the preponderance of the papers have that as their theme. For further reading in this subject I refer you to the reference list and additional readings.

Always be prepared for much value judgment by any of us: since we have so little solid scientific knowledge, there are less constraints on our imaginations. For instance, as it has raged since the first published report, there is much controversy on the subject of replacement therapy in the human female climacterium. As one leading text said a few years ago, in effect, let us not interfere with God's purpose by giving females replacement and preventing their growing old gracefully; others continue the objection to replacement by finding some correlation with another disease entity and so on in the continuum to the concept, justified by years of human therapy, that gonadal insufficiency should be as vigorously treated as any other hormonal deficiency (be it insulin, glucocorticoid, etc.) and as vigorously as any infectious disease.

One area only briefly touched is either nature- or human-produced models of aging. Although material is grouped by subject, it also falls partially at least in chronological sequence.

What is Youth and What is Age?
    It is the years one's lived or is it the state
    of life?—one's outlook and approach?
    This is a subject that we often broach.
    In the US 1970 census report
    We are given some sort of retort
    The questions posed—the answer, we
    May or may not, wish to see.
    Of our 204 million population
    The gap is at least several generations
    The "oldsters" 65 years and beyond
    Account for 20 million US sons.
    Of this number but a few
        can claim
            the fame
                of centenarians—
    15,000 is their number
    But there are the somewhat younger
        Nonagenarians (235,000)
    Leaving the 65-90 group represented
        By 19 and ½ million "resented"
    Are they old fogies? just in the way?
    Their own and every one else's? —SAY,
    Let's do the job to make them healthy, sturdy, strong!
    Relieve the disabled, disgrunted, debilitated—throng.

                              G. M. Emerson, 1971

Part I

MAN'S THOUGHTS ON AGING AS EXPRESSED BY POETS, PHILOSOPHERS, AND OTHERS

Editor's Comments
on Paper 1

1   ROYKO

A Vote for Old Riggs, Victim of Social Injustice

In any geriatric setting the attitudes of the patients toward their years is an important factor. This obviously is influenced to some extent by the abilities and faculties remaining with the patient. Nonetheless, two otherwise equal individuals may have quite different mental attitudes as shown in the following:

W. S. Landor, in "To Age" (1852) said:

> "He who hath braved youth's dizzy heat
> Dreds not the frost of Age"

In "A Satire Against Mankind" (1675), John Wilmont, Earl of Rochester, wrote:

> "Then Old Age and Experience, hand in hand,
> Lead him to death, and make him understand,
> After a search so painful and so long,
> That all his life he has been in the wrong."

Walt Whitman expresses it in "Youth, Day, Old Age and Night" (1885), in *Leaves of Grass I*:

> "Youth, large, lusty, loving—Youth, full of grace,
>   force, fascination.
> Do you know that Old Age may come after you, with equal
>   grace, force, fascination?"

And to conclude the poems, the whimsey of George Arnold's (1834–1865) "Age":

> "Youth hath many charms,
> —Hath many joys, and much delight;
> Even its doubts, and vague alarms,
> —By contrast make it bright!
> And yet—and yet—forsooth,
> —I love Age as well as Youth!
>
> Well, since I love them both,
> —The good of both I will combine,
> In women, I will look for Youth,
> —And look for Age, in wine:
> And then—and then—I'll bless
> —This twain that gives me happiness!"

Paper 1 gives yet another approach, in which Mr. Royko turned the sex battle of the century into a "youth" (Billie Jean King, female) versus an "oldster" (Bobby Riggs, male) contest. Mike Royko indeed makes one aware that things are often not what they appear to be!

1

Reprinted from *The Birmingham News*, September 21, 1973, p. 10

A vote for old Riggs, victim of social injustice

BY MIKE ROYKO

CHICAGO

About halfway through the match, I started pulling for Bobby Riggs, even though my money was on Billie Jean King.

It was when his legs got heavy and all those perky smile-lines in his face started sagging into creases of age.

And up in the TV booth, a female commentator was snarling as if she wouldn't be satisfied until he turned blue and pitched over on his face.

SITTING A COUPLE of stools down from me was a young sports writer, trim and fit in his mod clothing. He chortled: "He had it coming, the big mouth. He asked for it and he got it.

"Nah," I said, "he's just a guy who sees 60 around the corner and he doesn't like it."

The young man snorted: "Then an old guy like him ought to sit down and shut up."

That's when I realized what the real issue was on that tennis court. And it wasn't the hoked-up battle of the sexes that had captured the limited imagination of the sports experts.

I saw that if there was a victim of social injustice in the game, Mrs. King wasn't the only one.

BOBBY RIGGS represents many men who have somehow been deprived of the traditional rewards for honorable service to their country — including the right to a graceful old age.

Take a man of 55. Not necessarily Riggs, but any men about that age.

When they became teenagers — a privileged term not even used then — they found themselves in the worst depression we ever had. Everybody ate potato pancakes and was nervous.

By the time they were young men, the Depression ended — just in time for the biggest war we've ever been in.

NEXT CAME a deluge of social changes, bigger, faster and more complex than any we've gone through.

And what was their reward for struggling from one troubled decade to another and another? Were they permitted to enter their mature, mellow years with respect for a job well-intentioned, if not always well-done? Could they take their places as pillars of society, admired for the wisdom of their years?

Of course not. They woke up one day and found themselves being pounded on the head with surfboards and accused of having goofed everything up because they were insensitive, materialistic and their values were all wrong.

They hardly got over the shock of that, when something even worse happened: the youth cult came along and they were made to feel ashamed of the natural aging process.

INSTEAD OF being permitted to develop a respectable case of gout, or to sit back and become prosperously fat, they had to get out there and jog. In order to remain vigorous and vital!

Everytime they picked up a paper, there was a headline for a new series that said something like:

"Can a man over 40 ever find work again?"

Or: "How to prevent your husband from being depressed after he loses his job and has his first cardiac."

Everytime they turned on the TV, that damned Tommy Harmon and his wife were leaping around the patio, telling them how to avoid getting another day older by eating Munchy-Wunchies.

MANY MEN remained calm and, quite reasonably, said: "Go to hell. Mean and old is beautiful."

But many others didn't. Under the barrage of stay-young propaganda, they began wolfing down powdered goat horns (for virility), vitamin J (to ward off red nose veins), extract of shark liver (for even more virility), and vitamin Q (for a rakish grin).

They had their hernias corrected, slipped into their body shirts, hot-combed their eyebrows up over their naked scalps, and went frugging and hip-hugging into the swinging Now Society. They grabbed at the new values because the old were gone, flattened under the tires of a thousand Hondas.

Thus, a generation that muscled its way out of a Depression and axed the Axis, also produced the nation's biggest crop of silly old men.

SO THERE WAS Bobby Riggs, who should have been in a tweed jacket, puffing a pipe, sipping his brandy and walking his trusted dog through the autumn countryside while humming "September Song."

Instead, he combed his hair into a pixie-prune style and took to nuzzling California staylets.

And with the world watching, he pointed his racket at Billie Jean and boasted: "I can still do it!"

But he couldn't. She even called him an old creep. It couldn't have been more humiliating if his false choppers had fallen out in Butch McGuire's dating bar.

I tried to explain all of this to the chortling young sports writer. He just sneered. But someday he'll have a prostate problem, and I'll send him a get-worse card.

—CDN service

Part II

EARLY ACCOUNTS OF LONGEVITY

Editor's Comments
on Papers 2 Through 9

Some recent statistics compiled in the United States by the Department of Health, Education and Welfare (Wilder, 1971) indicate that the sixty-five year and older age group averages over four visits per year to a physician's office. Of the civilian noninstitutionalized population: 205/1,000 persons in this age group have visual impairments compared with 47/1,000 for all ages; hearing impairments occur in 231/1,000 of the 65–74 year group and 399/1,000 in the 75 year and older group, whereas for all ages the rate is 72/1,000.

In Paper 2 details of diseases of more than 360 persons whom Dr. Purdon had observed during the years 1850–1867 are given. The 64/217 deaths observed during this period were due to "Decay of Nature" or "Senile Marasmus" (malnutrition due either to lack of nutritious food or failure of proper digestion and assimilation of nutritional food). The patients complained of loss of appetite. "Mental faculties [are] clear and unclouded till the last," Dr. Purdon reported. The least frequent "diseases" were stomach ulcer, chronic eczema, necrotic maxillary lesion, and "suddenly." Apparently in contrast to all others, where diagnosed illness preceded it, the last entry is explained "one death occurred *suddenly* probably from heart disease." In directing his attention to treatment of these diseases, Dr. Purdon gave a detailed recipe for a soup, and suggested arrowroot and cod liver oil for "Decay of Nature." Even though he said medicines were of little use, he lists recipes for treatment of the various conditions existing in these elderly patients.

The 1869 *Boston Medical and Surgical Journal* contains a report by "R. D." (Paper 3) giving a short vivid account of the activities of an old man in his 110 years and beyond.

In 1875 a New York newspaper article concerned itself with centenarians, which became the subject of an editorial in the fifth volume of *The Medical Record*. The details, given in Paper 4, are quite specific.

Chaillé, in the *New Orleans Medical and Surgical Journal* of 1859 (Paper 5), is critiquing the proposal of Ed. Robin, a chemist who believes senility and death are due to accumulation of alkaline residues of diet in the soft tissues (calcification or ossification of soft tissues). "I whole heartedly approved of Robin's proposed research." Chaillé then cites evidence of some people who have lived a much longer time than the average with maintenance of their physical and mental capabilities. He also points out that persons residing in the South live longer than those in other parts of the United States. Although supportive of those seeking causes of longevity, he concludes with a quotation from Fluorens:

> Just as the duration of growth, multiplied a certain number of times, say five times, gives the ordinary duration of life, so does this ordinary duration, multiplied a certain number of times, say twice, give the extreme duration. A first century of ordinary life, and almost a second century, half a century (at least) of extraordinary life, is then the prospect science holds out to man! We leave it for those who love it, more than the undersigned to say, Amen.

Dr. Cutler (Paper 6) also believes in the notion of Robin, as stated by Dr. Chaillé. Clogging of the metabolic machinery by mineralized matter occurs, rendering an otherwise good diet inadequate, because of accumulation of the elements of food that cannot enter into oxidation (p. 97). "It might be asked, why the cells become clogged with mineral matter as age advances? Could we give the answer, the mystery of old age, if not life itself, would be solved."

In so many instances, whenever an author is discussing those persons who have had particularly long life, the name of Thomas Parr crops up. He is the person described by Sir William Harvey, referred to in Paper 7 by Dr. Maximin LeGrand and by Chaillé (Paper 5). Another recurrent theme is the concept of mineralization of soft tissues of the old, which is not seen in soft tissues of young persons (see also Cutler, Paper 6). LeGrand's remedy is the administration of lactic acid to reverse the mineralization of soft tissues and therefore alleviate some of the problems of aging. In justifying Robin's experiments, LeGrand says, "Toute qualite qui apparait exceptionnellement en une espece est l'endice d'une regle nouvelle a laquelle cette espece peut etre soumise." Therefore, if there are macrobiotes or centenarians in the human species, macrobiosis is compatible with the human organism. There is always a cause with effect relationship and what remains here is for us to discover it.

LeGrand recounts about fifteen cases of lifetimes in excess of 100 years during the 1700s and 1800s. Looking for a common thread, all he finds is diversity. He ends as follows:

> And thus be it as related; we would add only a couple of words namely *first* that the preceding were published for the first time in February 1853 and *second* that Harvey gave us the curious details of Thomas Parr; upon whom he performed the autopsy. He was married at 120 years of age; at 130 years he was summoned before the House of Commons on morals charges. Harvey was said to have been an eye witness to sexual intercourse engaged in by Thomas Parr at 140 years of age. 'On n'est pas un grand anatomiste sans être posséde du demon de curiosité!'

In Paper 8 George Harris gives a brief historical account of observations on comparative longevity. On page 75 he says, "The late Dr. Monro went so far as to maintain, in his anatomical lectures, that 'as far as he could observe the human body, as a machine, was perfect; that it bore within itself no marks by which we could possibly predicate its decay; that it was apparently calculated to go on forever; and that we learned only by experience that it would not do so'."

Harris then asks, "Is it altogether irrational to suppose that some principle analogous to that of vaccination, or to that supposed to be contained in the very tree of life itself, may at some distant period in the progress of science be brought to light by which the animal frame may be revigorated and rescued from decay, and so fitted to endure, I will not presume to say for ever, but to an age corresponding with that to which we are told that both the patriarch and many animals have attained?"

Further, according to Harris (p. 76), "People in reality die of old age, not when they have lived so many years, but when they are worn out—by the progress of waste and decay outstripping that of growth and renovation. As many therefore, die of old age, from being worn out, at eighteen as at eighty." Harris cautions us that an increase in average lifespan does not mean an increased longevity, "All that it proves is, not that men are longer-lived than they used to be, but that owing to increased attention to sanitary laws, they are less frequently cut off by diseases resulting from the neglect of sanitary precautions. It is very possible indeed, for mortality in a particular district to be very great, owing to the neglect of sanitary laws, and yet in the same district for remarkable instances of longevity to be found."

The last paper in this section, by Smith (Paper 9), touches on actuarial aspects of lifespan records and their validity and accuracy; additionally he cites changes in England which contributed to the increased average lifetime during the eighteenth century.

2

Reprinted from *Medical Mirror* 5:662–669 (1868)

STATISTICAL DETAILS OF THE DISEASES
OF ADVANCED LIFE

Henry Samuel Purdon, M.D.
Belfast

HAVING, at the Poor House and Infirmary of the Belfast Charitable Society (incorporated by Act of Parliament, 1771), an excellent field for observing the diseases of advanced life, the inmates, who were of the better class of society, such as tradesmen, servants, small shopkeepers, &c., being admitted for life when aged and unfit for further employment, and who are consequently for years under observation, it has occurred to me that the recording of such facts and peculiarities with regard to their diseases which I may have observed, may not be uninteresting. There is also attached to the institution a small ward for incurables, as well as an infirmary, into which, cases from the town are occasionally admitted. The number of aged inmates annually in the house is generally one hundred, and the number of deaths which has been recorded from November, 1850 till November, 1867, is 217. I have not been able to go further back than 1850, owing to the various report books not being forthcoming.

TABLE I.—*Annual number of Inmates admitted.*

Year.	Admitted.	Dismissed or left the House.	Number of Deaths.	Total Number during the year in the House.
1850	33	6	18	104
1851	29	5	13	115
1852	33	15	10	123
1853	21	6	16	120
1854	14	7	11	116
1855	15	7	7	103
1856	7	3	7	104
1857	19	6	17	100
1858	8	4	11	93
1859	21	10	5	99
1860	30	10	13	103
1861	20	10	15	100
1862	26	6	9	104
1863	4	3	9	92
1864	30	9	16	97
1865	21	8	16	94
1866	26	4	14	102
1867	12	3	10	100
	369	122	217	

TABLE II.—*Deaths which have occurred amongst the aged Inmates from November, 1850, till November, 1867.*

	Males.	Females.	Total.
Decay of Nature	33	31	64
Chronic Bronchitis	21	8	29
Paralysis	5	6	11
Apoplexy	5	5	10
Diarrhœa and Dysentery	5	9	14
Disease of the Heart (not specified)	8	26	34
Hypertrophy and Dilatation	2	3	5
Disease of Right Side of Heart	—	1	1
Fatty Degeneration of Heart	—	3	3
Pericarditis	1	—	1
Angina Pectoris	—	1	1
Gangrene of Leg	1	2	3
Gangrene of Penis	1	—	1
Gangrene of Back	—	1	1
Disease of the Brain	1	1	2
Obstruction of the Bowels and Constipation	4	1	5
Dropsy	2	2	4
Asthma	2	—	2
Phthisis	1	2	3
Erysipelas	1	—	1
Chronic Catarrh of Bladder	1	—	1
Scirrhus of Colon	—	1	1
,, Stomach	—	2	2
,, Uterus	—	2	2
,, Nipple	—	1	1
,, Breast	—	2	2
Disease of Liver	—	3	3
Inflammation of Bowels	—	2	2
Ulcer of Stomach	—	1	1
Chronic Eczema	—	1	1
Stricture of Œsophagus	—	1	1
Necrosis of Superior Maxillary	—	1	1
,, Inferior ,,	—	1	1
Chronic Rheumatism	—	1	1
Hernia	—	1	1
Suddenly	—	1	1

217

Decay of Nature, or *Senile Marasmus,* has the greatest number of deaths attributed to it, the number of males and females being nearly equal, viz,, 33 males and 31 females. Their ages vary from 69 to 96 years; one death at 69, two at 70, two at 71, three at 72, two at 73, five at 75, six at 76, two at 77, two at 78, three at 83, and six above 90 years, the oldest being aged 96. The inmates affected with this gradual wasting of the body, which approaches very slowly, have usually their mental faculties clear and unclouded till the last, but complain of loss of appetite, bowels costive, pulse small, quick, and weak, and sleepless nights, feel no pain, and look on death with seeming indifference and carelessness, in many cases as a happy release. With regard to treatment medicines are of little use. Latterly I have prescribed the syrup of the phosphate of quinia, strychnine, and iron, with benefit. In other cases benefit has been derived from the administration of ether, and stimulants, together with a good nutritious diet. The following soup will be found serviceable in these cases, as well as in some forms of dyspepsia :—Take of linseed half an ounce, fine bran one ounce, water one quart; boil for two hours and strain ; then add beef from half a pound to a pound, and make into a soup with vegetables, &c. The linseed in the above soup contains a large quantity of oil and nutritive matter for producing fat ; the bran is also very nutritious, containing what chemists call gluten, but which M. Mége Mouries has found to consist of a vegetable ferment, or metamorphic nitrogenous substance called *cerealin,* and another substance, *casein.* The former is an active ferment on starch and glucose, producing the lactic and butyric changes, a good tonic, as also stimulant to weakened digestion, in increasing to a remarkable extent the dissolving properties of pepsine, and the soup thus made according to the above formula is extremely palatable.

Another excellent article of diet in these cases is arrow-root, its chemical composition being $C_6 H_5 O_5$. Now, all amylaceous substances when taken into the animal economy go to form fat, and produce animal heat, by means of the consumption of the carbon and hydrogen that they contain, and arrow-root being one of the richest and most nutritious of these substances, it will be evident that in diseases accompanied by much emaciation, it will prove very serviceable. In senile maramus cod-liver oil is also useful.

Chronic Bronchitis.—In this disease we have nine deaths recorded as occurring between the ages of seventy and eighty years, one at sixty-six, and one at forty-two, the deaths usually taking place during the winter months, especially January, February, and March. Chronic bronchitis, or bronchorrhœa, is accompanied by a troublesome cough and expectoration of a yellowish tenacious sputa, usually in the morning after awakening. A feeling of oppression at the heart, and a sense of tightness across the chest are frequently complained of. The breathing is often gasping, and mucous râles in the chest apparent to a bystander exist. In the majority of cases there is more or less emphysema. On percussion, the thorax is clearer than natural, not so elastic on inspiration as it should be ; the skin dry and harsh ; patient emaciated ; pulse weak and slow ; appetite bad, and bowels generally costive. The treatment consists of the administration of stimulating expectorants, and one which I generally prescribe, consists in infusion of senega, carbonate of ammonia, tincture of squills, and tincture of opium with camphor, also mustard cataplasm to the chest; when the expectoration is very profuse, small doses of balsam of copaiba are of use. In the majority of cases of heart disease bronchitis is present, probably arising from venous congestion.

Paralysis.—The deaths from this disease occurred in five instances in males and six in females, the ages varying from forty-two till eighty years. In old persons, from ossification of the arteries and weakened nervous power, the heart is called on to do extra work, and frequently, some of the smaller vessels, especially of the brain, may be ruptured, and apoplexy or paralysis ensue.

Apoplexy.—The deaths from this complaint are ten in number, both sexes being equal, the ages varying from seventy-three till seventy-nine years.

Diarrhœa and Dysentery proved fatal in fourteen instances. The former is common during the months of August and September, one death being at the age of fifty-five, one at eighty-five, one at eighty-seven, the oldest case being aged ninety-six years. With regard to the treatment to be adopted in these cases, stimulants take the first place, the vital powers being easily exhausted. The following is the formula for the house " cholera mixture " :—

Take of ether 3j. ; Spt. Ammoniæ aromat. 3ij. ; Spt. lavandulæ co. 3ij. ; Tinct. capsici. 3j. ; Tinct. catechu 3ss. ; Tinct. opii, 3ij. ; Aquæ menth pip. 3vi. Misce. Dose, a dessert-spoonful.

Hot water jars to the feet, and turpentine stupes to the abdomen being always ordered. When the attack is slight, one of the following pills at night sometimes cuts the disease short. Take of Pulv. capsici, gr. vi ; Pulv. opii, gr. iii ; Pulv. camphoræ, gr. vj. ; Pil hydrargyri gr. xij. ; Ext. hæmatoxyli gr. xij. Misce. Div. in pil. xii.

Disease of the Heart.—The commonest affection of this organ met with is softening, the deaths being as follows :—One at fifty-five years, three at sixty-seven, and ten between seventy and eighty years. From softening of the heart its force of propelling the blood is weakened, venous congestion and dropsy are apt to ensue, manifested by swelling of the feet and ankles and eyelids. Palpitation of the heart after exertion is also common. In many cases the liver has become enlarged, hæmorrhoids likewise being present from congestion of the portal system. With regard to diagnosis, the duration of the complaint is to be taken into consideration. In functional palpitation, which is very common in old people from distension of the stomach with flatus, no organic disease can be discovered by either auscultation or percussion ; and again, functional palpitation may occur at any time, organic only after exercise or anger, and is relieved by rest. In softening of the heart the pulse is usually intermittent.

The excessive smoking of tobacco, which is a common habit amongst the aged inmates, is also a cause of palpitation ; and amongst the aged female inmates tea drinking to excess is very common ; the first symptoms that they usually complain of are pyrosis, bad appetite, costiveness, and palpitation of the heart. This organ becomes symptomatically affected by means of the semi-lunar ganglia of the sympathetic, the splanchnic nerves which form the ganglia communicating in the thorax with the cardiac nerves. The greater splanchnic also receives a small branch from the pneumogastric and phrenic. The communication existing between the phrenic and splanchnic nerves accounts for the pain which patients have sometimes described to me as passing from xiphoid cartilage towards the spine. The heart then communicates with the stomach by means of the pneumogastric and cardiac nerves, these nerves sending branches to the greater splanchnic, which eventually form the solar plexus that supplies the stomach and other abdominal viscera. The digestive functions of the stomach being impaired, the heart sympathises with it through its nervous connections, functional palpitations being the most usual symptom. With regard to treatment, the diffusible stimulants, as ether, aromatic spirit of ammonia, and anti-spasmodics, as tincture of assafœtida, are useful. If an arterial sedative is required, the tincture of veratrum viride is an excellent remedy. Hypertrophy with dilatation proved fatal in five instances. One died at the age of forty-two, one at sixty-four, another at seventy-six, and two at seventy-seven years. In this affection of the heart the impulse is increased in force, the apex of the heart striking against the thoracic walls. The muscular structure is also enlarged, and sometimes thinner than natural, The heart's action is slow and labouring, the area of dulness being enlarged to a considerable extent, and both the first and second sounds are increased in intensity. With valvular disease we have an organic murmur of either a blowing or a rasping sound, and which is intermittent in character, taking place at any part of the rhythm. Disease of the heart is usually situated at the left side : when at the right side it is rare, as during seventeen years we have had only one case, that of a female, which proved fatal at the age of seventy-eight years, and was accompanied by derangement of the portal system. Intermission of the pulse usually depends on imperfect contraction of the ventricles, valvular disease being usually present, and softening of the muscular structure. In long standing cases the lungs become congested, and difficulty of breathing is a common symptom. With regard to treatment, counter-irritants, as tartar emetic ointment, is useful ; in some cases anodyne applications answer better, and a very good one is emplastrum belladonna. The tincture of nux vomica is a valuable remedy in these cases. Three cases of fatty degeneration of the heart are recorded, which proved fatal at the ages of fifty-seven, sixty, and seventy-five. The arcus senilis was apparent in each case. Pericarditis was fatal in a male whose age is not stated, following an attack of rheumatic fever. Angina pectoris has one death recorded to it at the age of sixty. This affection is now looked on as a neuralgia of the heart, and the remedy of most service is the tincture of aconite.

Gangrene of leg proved fatal in three instances. Gangrene of the back, or mortification of this region, at seventy-six. A rare affection proved fatal in a male aged seventy, viz., gangrene of the penis. Opium was the remedy employed in each instance.

Disease of the brain was fatal in two cases, aged respectively seventy and seventy-nine years.

Constipation and obstruction of the bowels has five deaths recorded to it as having occurred between the ages of seventy and seventy-nine years. Constipation is a very common complaint, as also flatulence. The safest aperient is castor-oil. The following as recommended by Dr. Graves keeps the bowels regular :—

R Confect. sennæ, ʒij. ; Acidi potass tart., ʒj. ; Ferri carb. ʒij. ; Syrupi zincgil, ʒss. Sig. A small tea-spoonful occasionally.

For flatulence I have found the Pulvis. cretæ aromat an excellent remedy.

Dropsy, accompanied with disease of the kidneys, occurred in four instances, the sexes being equally represented, aged respectively forty-three, fifty-four, seventy-nine, and eighty-eight.

Asthma.—There is more or less difficulty of breathing in all cases of heart diseases. This disease was fatal in two instances aged seventy-three and seventy-eight. With regard to treatment, I have derived much benefit from the employment of the tincture of strammonium.

Phthisis proved fatal in three instances, aged respectively forty-two, forty-six, and fifty-six.

Erysipelas.— Idiopathic erysipelas only occurred once. Its situation is not stated. The patient was a male.

Chronic Catarrh of the Bladder has also one death recorded to it. Age not stated.

Scirrhus of Colon, which is a rare affection occurred once. The patient was a female, aged seventy-nine years. *Scirrhus of Stomach* has two deaths recorded to it, at the ages of forty-two and seventy. *Scirrhus of the Uterus* occurred twice, patients aged respectively forty-six and sixty-seven. Morphia suppositories afforded most relief. *Scirrhus of Breast* was fatal in two instances, aged sixty-eight and seventy. A rare cancerous affection occurred once, viz., scirrhus of the nipple ;

the patient was aged seventy-two years. In "Chelius' System of Surgery," edited by South, page 785, the following occurs : —"The nipple ulcerates, and is covered with a yellowish crust, which separates and forms afresh. More extensive ulceration follows, the nipple is destroyed, and a scirrhus substance is laid bare. The scirrhus spreads widely round the nipple, and the pain becomes more violent, but the diseased part is not tender to the touch." Cancer of the nipple begins at the root of this structure, and is hard, irregular, and painful. Brodie considers that a permanent cure may result from an operation when the disease is in the nipple, although doubtful when in the breast. We have at present a case of open cancer of the chin in a man aged seventy-eight years, and the best application that has yet been applied to it is chlorate of potash and opium dissolved in water. (This patient has died since the above was written, December, 1867.)

Disease of the Liver proved fatal in three instances. One died from jaundice, aged sixty-four ; two from hepatitis, aged respectively sixty-four and sixty-five.

Inflammation of the Bowels.—From chronic inflammation of the bowels one patient died, aged seventy-two ; from acute enteritis, another aged seventy-six.

Ulceration of the Stomach was fatal in one case, a female, aged seventy-three years. We have at present in the infirmary a case of this disease in which the hypodermic injection of morphia is being tried.

Chronic Eczema has one death recorded to it, that of a female, aged seventy-six. This affection, as well as eczematous ulcers of the lower extremities, are very common, but is rarely fatal. In healing a long-standing eruption a counter discharge ought to be made.

Stricture of the Œsophagus was fatal in one case, aged seventy-two.

Necrosis of the Superior Maxillary occurred once, the palate bone and nasal plate of the superior maxillary falling out. The patient died comatose. The breath was very offensive, and was somewhat relieved by gargles of "Condy's fluid." The patient was aged sixty-eight years.

Necrosis of the Inferior Maxillary also occurred once, and what was a curious fact, complete anchylosis of the condyles took place several weeks before death, the patient dying from inanition, aged seventy-one years.

Chronic Rheumatism has one death accorded to it, that of a female, aged fifty-two years. Rheumatic pains, especially lumbago, are very common amongst the aged inmates. The medicines that are generally used are iodide of potassium, tincture of actæ, racemosa, and the "Chelsea Pensioner."

Hernia.—One death took place from strangulated femoral hernia at the age of sixty-six years. Inguinal hernia is very common amongst the males, although rarely fatal ; the external and internal rings become approximated, the scrotum in several cases becoming of an enormous size. Occasionally uneasy symptoms are complained of, when a strong infusion of coffee is administered every half hour with the best results. Locally, cloths steeped in equal parts of vinegar and cold water are applied to the rupture.

One death occurred suddenly probably from heart disease.

Dyspepsia and gastric irritation are common affections amongst the aged inmates, and I may remark, *en passant*, that much benefit may be derived in the former complaint from the administration of charcoal in capsules ; in the latter from the hypophosphites of lime, soda, and potash. External hæmorrhoids are also common, and the treatment usually adopted in these cases is the application of gall ointment, to which the extract of belladonna has been added, the patient at the same time taking the confection of black pepper, the bowels being kept regular by gentle laxatives.

Diseases of the Teeth are rare. The teeth are certainly liable to fall out and become carious, and I have had one case of alveolar abscess, and one of extensive ulceration of the gums.

Interscapular Fracture of the Neck of the Thigh Bone is common, but as far as I am aware, has never proved fatal. During the last three years we have had about six cases of this accident.

3

Reprinted from *Boston Med. & Surg. J.* **80**:432 (1869)

SOME ACCOUNT OF JOHN GILLEY, WHO DIED IN AUGUSTA, ME., AT THE AGE OF 124 YEARS

by R. D.

IF you think that your readers would like to know something about this very old man, you can give the following notice of him a place in your JOURNAL.

The late Prof. R. D. Mussey visited him when he was 118 years old, and some years before his own death gave me some facts in regard to him, of which I made a note at the time, and which were essentially as follows :

He was an Irishman by birth, and had lived for many years in Augusta. His figure was small and erect ; and he could not have weighed over 100 lbs. Intellect quite *mediocre*. His diet consisted of animal and vegetable food, in about the usual proportion ; and he still retained seven of his teeth. His habits were and had been generally temperate in the use of liquor, and he did not habitually indulge in tobacco. Once he fractured his leg, but he had never been confined by a fit of sickness. It was upon a cold day in winter when Prof. M. called to see him, and he found him in his barn, taking care of his cattle. He had already cut all of his wood for the winter. When he was between 70 and 80 years of age he was married for the first time, and he took for his wife an Irish girl only 18 years old. By her he had eight children, all of whom had left him, though his wife was still living, and at the age of 60 years. Prof. M. had been informed that after the death of the old man she had said that his virility left him, and suddenly, when he was 120 years old.

4

Reprinted from *The Medical Record* 5:317–319 (1875)

CENTENARIANS

CENTENARIANS.—*The New York Times* of the 18th inst. publishes an interesting table, compiled by Dr. John T. Nagle, Deputy Registrar of Records of the Health Department of this city, which gives the names and conditions of ninety eight centenarians, whose deaths have been reported to the Board of Health since 1864, and which we reproduce, since the question has lately been raised whether authenticated cases exist of persons who have attained the age of one hundred years.

Mary Nixon, born in Ireland in 1765, died in this city, Aug. 26, 1873. She was attended in her last illness by Dr. John H. Wilson, who stated that she died of softening of the brain, nervous exhaustion, and old age, her memory and eyesight having completely failed previous to her death.

Patrick White, born in Ireland in 1771, emigrated to New York City in 1853, where he died, aged 102 years, July 25, 1873. Dr. J. R. MacGregor attended him in his last illness. Mr. White was married between the ages of forty-five and fifty. His occupation in Ireland was that of a farmer, and his diet while there consisted principally, according to his own statement, of potatoes and milk, with an addition sometimes of fish and eggs. He did not eat meat more than once or twice a week, and oftentimes not more than once a month. He drank liquor moderately, and after his arrival in this country performed no hard work.

NAME.	Date of Death.	Year.	Years.	Months	Days.	Condition.	Nativity.	How long a resident of this City.	Color.	Occupation.	Cause of Death.
Hulda Wood	Jan. 9	1864	100	3			New Jersey		Colored		Senile asthenia.
Bridget O'Brien	Jan. 8	1864	100				Ireland		White		Pneumonia.
Ira Cromwell	March 16	1864	104	6			Baltimore, Md		Colored		Senile asthenia.
Mary Buckley	March 21	1864	105				New York		Colored		Erysipelas.
Minte Thomas	May 27	1864	103				Maryland		Colored		Senile asthenia.
Elizabeth Price	May 31	1864	100				N. Carolina		Colored		Senile asthenia.
Leah Cropsie	Jan. 17	1864	100				Virginia		Colored		Dropsy.
Isaac Daniels	June 28	1864	109				Bedford, N. Y.		White		Senile asthenia.
Ann Jackson	July 10	1864	100				S. Island, N.Y.		Colored		Senile asthenia.
Rachel Stafford	July 13	1864	102	6	21		New Jersey		White		Senile asthenia.
Isabella Cook	Sept. 7	1864	100				Virginia		Colored		Senile asthenia.
Rose Gilligan	Dec. 14	1864	103				Ireland		White		Senile asthenia.
Mrs. D. McKinney	Jan. 7	1865	100				New Jersey		Colored		Cancer.
Johanna Waters	Feb. 4	1865	104				Ireland		White		Senile asthenia.
Frances Davis	March 13	1865	100				New York		Colored		Senile asthenia.
Minerva Ellis	June 4	1865	105				Jamaica, W. I.		Colored		Strang'd hernia.
Absalom Thornton	Aug. 9	1865	105	3	29		Ireland		White		Senile asthenia.
Thomas Golden	Aug. 18	1865	104				Ireland		White		Senile asthenia.
Thomas McAnnally	Aug. 21	1865	101				Ireland		White		Senile asthenia.
Patrick Noonan	Oct. 6	1865	100	5			Ireland		White		Senile asthenia.
James Quinn	Nov. 30	1865	100	10	18		Ireland		White		Senile asthenia.
Mary McMahon	Jan. 13	1866	104				New York	Life	White		Senile asthenia.
William Daily	May 4	1866	106				Ireland		White		Senile asthenia.
Mary Ann Bastine	May 15	1866	118				New York	Life	Colored		Senile asthenia.
Mary Griffin	July 17	1866	100				Ireland		White		Senile asthenia.
Bridget Noonan	Aug. 1	1866	100				Ireland		White		Senile asthenia.
Margaret Farrel	Sept. 12	1866	100				Ireland		White		Senile asthenia.
Phyllis Bees	Dec. 7	1866	105				New York		White		Senile asthenia.
Christina Renfort	Dec. 18	1866	105			Single	France	35 years	White	Domestic	Senile asthenia.
Rebecca Ward	Feb. 10	1867	100			Widow	Scotland	67 years	White		Senile asthenia.
Margaret Harty	Jan. 6	1867	100				Ireland	17 years	White		Senile asthenia.
Emilie C. Lorenz	March 25	1867	103			Married	Germany	18 years	White		do. and convulsions.
Judy Green	May 13	1867	109			Widow	New York		Colored	Cook	Senile asthenia.
Margaret Terry	June 12	1868	100			Widow	Ireland	13 years	White		Senile asthenia.
Maria M. Pessinger	Feb. 29	1868	100	6	11	Widow	United States		White		Senile asthenia.
Ann Mary Brown	July 3	1868	103			Widow	United States		Colored		Tumor of breast.
Honora Hanlon	April 26	1868	108			Widow	Ireland	28 years	White		Senile asthenia.
Mary Collins	May 7	1869	100			Widow	Ireland	19 years	White		Senile asthenia.
Florence McCarty	Dec. 19	1869	100				Ireland	8 years	White		Senile asthenia.
Francis McLellan	Sept. 29	1869	100			Widower	Ireland		White	Laborer	Senile asthenia.
Hester Cropper	March 24	1869	102			Widow	Maryland		Colored		Senile asthenia.
Margaret Hutchins	Sept. 24	1869	102			Widow	New Jersey		Colored	Cook	Apoplexy.
Elizabeth Murray	May 24	1869	103			Widow	At sea	40 years	Colored	Cook	Inanition.
Phœbe Williams	July 29	1869	103			Widow	New York		Colored		Senile asthenia.
Sarah Conway	May 5	1870	100			Widow	Ireland	24 years	White		Senile asthenia.
Sophia Williams	April 10	1870	100				Virginia		White		Senile asthenia.
Johannah Sullivan	Nov. 10	1870	100	10		Widow	Ireland	40 years	White		Senile asthenia.
Lipman Kristeller	Nov. 19	1870	100	1	7	Married	Prussia	25 years	White		Bright's disease.
Mary Myers	Dec. 18	1870	100			Widowed	Ireland		White		Senile asthenia.
Daniel Collins	Nov. 20	1870	101	3		Widowed	Ireland	26 years	White	Laborer	Senile asthenia.
Anne Ryan	Jan. 3	1870	102			Widowed	Ireland	50 years	White		Senile asthenia.
Kate Eagan	Sept. 11	1870	102			Widowed	Ireland	17 years	White		Senile asthenia.
Henry O'Flaherty	April 41	1870	103			Widowed	Ireland	23 years	White	Tailor	Senile asthenia.
Ellen Baird	Feb. 28	1871	101		14	Widowed	Ireland	35 years	White		Apoplexy.
Felix Boylan	March 12	1871	108	10	12	Widowed	Ireland	24 years	White		Senile asthenia.
Bridget Campbell	March 29	1871	100			Widowed	Ireland	15 years	White		Senile asthenia.
Cecelia Dixon	Jan. 23	1871	106			Married	West Indies	50 years	Colored		Phthisis pulmon.
James Daley	April 16	1871	100			Widowed	Ireland	22 years	White		Apoplexy.
Ann Flanagan	June 2	1871	100			Widowed	Ireland		White		Acute dysentery.
Bridget Carroll	Nov. 6	1871	106			Widowed	Ireland	7 years	White		Senile asthenia.
Julia Glynn	Nov. 28	1871	102			Widowed	Ireland	30 years	White		Senile asthenia.
Denis Haverty	Aug. 8	1871	103			Widowed	Ireland	20 years	White		Senile asthenia.
Sarah Slane	April 8	1871	103			Single	Ireland	60 years	White		Paralysis.
Margaret Morgan	Dec. 21	1871	105			Widowed	Ireland	6 years	White		Senile asthenia.
Ellen Moran	Dec. 29	1871	100			Widowed	Ireland	23 years	White		Senile asthenia.
Ann Leahy	May 20	1871	100			Widowed	Ireland	20 years	White		Pneumonia.
Daniel Sullivan	Jan. 4	1872	103			Married	Ireland	22 years	White		Ulcer of leg.
Mary Richmond	Feb. 18	1872	106			Widow	Ireland	25 years	White		Senile asthenia.
Mathew Lyon	March 8	1872	103			Widow	Ireland	56 years	White	Merchant	Epistaxis.
Phœbe Scott	April 29	1872	100			Widow	Africa	35 years	Colored	Nurse	Senile asthenia.
Ellen Brown	July 22	1872	100			Widow	Ireland	25 years	White		Disease of the heart.
Ellen Burke	Oct. 1	1872	103			Widow	Ireland	27 years	White		Senile asthenia.
Alice Riley	Oct. 7	1872	103			Widow	Ireland	8 years	White		Senile asthenia.
Rose Rourke	Oct. 23	1872	100			Widow	Ireland	27 years	White		Diarrhœa.
Nancy Lent	Nov. 17	1872	100	4	14	Widow	United States	13 years	Colored	Laundress	Hemiplegia.
Catherine Cahill	Dec. 26	1872	105				Ireland	20 years	White		Senile asthenia.
Mary McGrath	March 14	1873	100			Widow	Ireland	3 years	White		Senile asthenia.
Mary Monaghan	March 22	1873	102			Widow	Ireland	25 years	White		Senile asthenia.
Mary Tobin	April 1	1873	100			Married	Ireland	33 years	White	Housework	Dementia.
Thomas Craig	April 26	1873	102			Married	Ireland	40 years	White		Senile asthenia.
Alexander Scott	Nov. 23	1873	100			Widow	Delaware	28 years	Colored		Senile asthenia.
Mary Nixon	Aug. 26	1873	108			Widow	Ireland	25 years	White	Domestic	Softening of brain.
Patrick White	July 25	1873	102			Widowed	Ireland	19 years	White	Farmer	Senile asthenia.
James Reilly	Jan. 28	1874	106			Widow	Ireland	32 years	White		Senile asthenia.
William Louis	Feb. 4	1874	106	2	10	Married	France	26 years	White	Merchant	Pneumonia.
Margaret Cloonan, or Cronan	March 17	1874	103			Widow	Ireland	25 years	White		Chronic bronchitis.
Catharine Callahan	April 6	1874	104			Widow	Ireland	45 years	White		Pneumonia.
Mary Bliss	July 30	1874	108			Widow	Ireland	9 years	White		Senile asthenia.
Molly Sheridan	Sept. 6	1874	100			Widow	Ireland	46 years	White		Diarrhœa.
Ellen Lyons	Aug. 31	1874	112			Widow	Ireland	42 years	White		Senile asthenia.
Jacob Kissam	Oct. 17	1874	133			Widowed	New York		Colored	Laborer	Paralysis.

Thomas Craig, born in the County of Leitrim, Ireland, in 1771, came to the United States twenty-nine years previous to his death. His occupation in Ireland was that of a wheelwright and carpenter, and in this country he became a porter. He was twice married, but had no children. About a year previous to his death he was injured by falling from a car, and was more or less childish from that time until he expired, at over 100 years of age. His wife is still alive, and is aged eighty-three years.

Hannah Ruland, *née* Wilson, born Aug. 29, 1774, at Oyster Bay, Long Island, of Scotch parents, died in this city, October 26, 1873. She was married at the age of sixteen years, and was the mother of ten children. Her mother was married at the age of thirteen years and six months, and gave birth to sixteen children, eight girls and eight boys, all of them distinguished for remarkable longevity and robust constitutions. The youngest child was over fifty years old when the first death occurred in the family, and one of the male children nearly reached his one hundredth year. Mrs. Ruland performed her household duties with punctuality, and her longevity was attributed in a great degree to certain habits to which she rigidly adhered during lifetime—one of them being that of retiring to bed at sunset and rising with the sun. She always insisted on having eight or nine hours' sleep, and at regular hours; partook of plain and substantial food, with tea and coffee. She never wore corsets, or indulged in alcoholic liquors, and was robust and muscular. Her height was 5 feet 4½ inches.

Christopher Rush, colored, born in Craven County, North Carolina, in 1777, died in this city of senile asthenia July 16, 1873. He was brought to this city a slave in 1798, and gained his freedom about the year 1812. He joined the African M. E. Church in 1803, and was licensed to preach in 1815, ordained in 1822, and elected Bishop of the church in 1828. He lost his eyesight in 1859, and in 1868 became subject to fits at intervals of from one week to two months, which greatly impaired his memory, and continued until his death. Frugality in his earlier years enabled him to save enough money to make him independent, so that he lived comfortably in his old age. He was a hearty eater, very fond of coffee, of which he drank a great deal, and was an inveterate tobacco smoker. He was naturally robust and healthy, and drank no liquor stronger than cider.

Alexander Scott, colored, born in Delaware in 1775, died in this city of senile asthenia at the age of 100 years, at the Colored Home, to which he had been admitted in October, 1871. His father's death was caused by the rupture of a blood-vessel, and his mother died of old age.

John McGibney, born in Ireland in 1776, died in this city, Jan. 11, 1873, of pleurisy. He came to this country in 1866, and was employed as a laborer, working occasionally until a few weeks before his death. He was of temperate habits, and during his lifetime his diet consisted of the humblest fare. He was muscular and of medium stature, and enjoyed excellent health until his last illness.

5

Reprinted from *New Orleans Med Surg. J.* **16**:417–424 (1859)

LONGEVITY

Chaillé

" Can the limits of human life be extended ?   This is the question propounded by a celebrated professor of chemistry in a memoir presented
to the Academy of Sciences : ' upon the causes of old age, and senile
death.' This chemist is M. Ed. Robin. He believes human life may
be prolonged, and courageous in this opinion, seeks for rational

means to arrive at his conclusion. He will seek a long time still, says the reader. Such is our opinion, and, no doubt, M. Robin's, who, waiting further developments, furnishes us matters of interest on this topic.

"Living beings may be compared to furnaces, always kindled; life exists only in a state of combustion; but the combustion which occurs in our bodies, like that which takes place in our chimnies, leaves a residue, a detritus, ashes. This detritus, which is always accumulating, is, according to M. Robin, the principal cause of old age and senile death.

"Food, whatever may be its nature, whether vegetable or animal, liquid or solid, is charged with mineral matters which are left in different parts of the organism by the process of combustion. At first, these serve for nutrition; but when the bones are all consolidated they continue to flow into the system, and then incrust and mineralize different parts of the mechanism.

"The manner in which mineralization causes old age in man is clearly pointed out: on the one hand, ossification of the cartilages of the sternum, greater rigidity of the posterior ligaments of the ribs cause the respiration to become slower and slower, limits its extent, and finally render it altogether diaphragmatic: on the other, ossification of the vessels and their valves, diminution of the calibre of the arteries, obliteration of the capillaries, reduction of their number, and enlargment of the pulmonary cells, render the circulation more and more difficult, and diminish the respiratory surface.

"The air coming in less close contact with the blood does not so well aërate it, this liquid therefore becomes of a deeper color, engorges the venous system, as in asphyxia; and experiments upon the quantity of carbonic acid exhaled, upon animal temperature, upon the passage of certain elements of the blood in the urine, do not permit us to doubt, that beginning with a certain age, a combustion gradually less abundant takes place.

"As the combustion and heat diminish, so do the electricity and nervous fluid, therefore, sensibility and contractility are lessened, motion and the general activity decrease; enfeebled by all these causes, the nervous action contributes in its turn to diminish the combustion, and . . . . . all the world knows the result of this.

"By force of such arguments, which have some good in them, M. Robin hopes to prove, that it is easy to retard old age, and death in a large number of animals, by abating the phenomena of slow combustion.

" In consequence he proposes to institute three series of experiments upon animals whose lives are of short duration. One class will be fed upon those aliments which contain the smallest proportion of mineral matters of an incrusting nature ; another upon food entirely deprived of these matters by appropriate dissolvents, and the last upon ordinary food ; but with it is to be administered, beginning with a certain age, lactic acid, which has incontestably the power of dissolving mineral matters, and would appear to be sufficient to dissolve, during life, those which have been already deposited in the organism.

" If it be demanded, what we think of the subject which M. Robin has chosen for his researches, we would reply that we highly approve them, and encourage the author to persevere. We well know what will be said : Paracelsus ! Van Helmout ! etc. But names, whether good or bad, have but little weight with us ; and, for approving the researches of M. Robin, which are connected with one of those beliefs the most generally and deeply felt by humanity, which, in our opinion, would alone justify them, we have another reason still, or a principle which we may reduce to the following formula : *Every quality which appears to be an exception in a species, indicates a new rule, to which this species may be subjected.*

" Applying this principle to the present subject, we say, there are macrobites or centenarians in the human species ; then macrobie is compatible with the human organization, and since it exists, its cause may be determined. Now, to possess a knowledge of the cause, is to be master of the effect ; and that which has heretofore been the exception, may become the rule.

" The long life of the patriarchs provokes a smile. But in times less distant from our own, facts may be found which are but little more credible, and which cannot be disputed. It may gratify our readers to cite some of these facts :

" Ponce Lepage died in 1760, in the Duchy of Luxemburg, at the age of 121 years ; a short time before his death he cultivated his field, and made excursions on foot of six or seven leagues. Eleanor Spicer, died in Virginia, in 1763, aged 121 years. All her senses were perfect at the time of her death. Madame Barnet, died in Charleston in 1820, aged 123 years. She recalled perfectly events which had occurred a century before. Grandez died in Languedoc, aged 126 years. He was a journeyman goldsmith, and was in the habit of working still, ten or twelve days before his death. The Englishman John Newell died in 1761, at the age of 127 years, in the full enjoyment of reason. Another Englishman, John Bayles, a sheep-seller, died in 1706, aged 130 years. During the last years of his life he drove his flocks of sheep to the neighboring markets. Margaret Lawler, English, died in 1739, aged 135 years. A few days before her death she walked some three or four miles and returned home the same day. Joseph Barn, a negro, died in Jamaica in 1808, aged 140 years. A few days before he was in the habit of walking four miles. Polotiman, a surgeon in Lorraine, died in 1825, at the age of 140 years. The day before his death he operated upon a cancer with much dexterity. Thomas Parr died in London in 1635, at the age of 152 years. Until he was 130 years old he engaged freely in all the labors of a farmer, and even threshed his wheat.

" Obst, a village woman of Silesia, died in 1825, aged 155 years. She had labored in the field the evening before her death. Joseph Surrington, a Norwegian, died in 1797, aged 160 years. He preserved to the last his reason and his senses. John Bowin, born in the Bannat of Tameswar, died in 1740, aged 172 years. Peter Zortan, a countryman of the preceding, died in 1724, aged 185 years.

" If the life of these extraordinary beings be examined, it will be found very difficult to determine the causes of their longevity ; the privilege which they enjoyed appears to have been compatible with every mode of living. For instance, Annibal Camoux, who died when 121 years, and who figures in one of Horace Vernet's paintings, drank much wine, and lived upon the coarsest food ; so also the surgeon Polotiman, never passed a day without being intoxicated ; the peasant woman, Obst, who died at the age of 155, drank ordinarily two tumblerfuls of brandy daily. [At a recent meeting of the Detroit Historical Society, it was stated that a French resident of that city died a few years since at the age of 116 years, during 104 of which he never drew a sober breath.—ED.] From such examples it might be concluded that drunkeness gave one a lease for a long life.

" But on the other hand, Eleanor Spicer, who lived to her 121st year, never drank spirituous liquor ; Grandez, who died at 126 years, never drank wine ; John Effingham, who died at the age of 144 years, knew liquor only by sight. In addition to this contrast, here are some facts through which it is difficult to see clearly: Denis Guignard, who died at 123 years, dwelt in a cavern dug in sandy stone ; Draha-kemberg, who died in his 146th year, had been captured by Corsairs, and endured for fifteen years all the hardships of a cruel captivity ; Jean Lafitte, who died at the age of 136 years, had contracted from early youth the habit of bathing two or three times a week, and pre-served this habit to the end of his life ; Jean Causeur, who died aged 146 years, lived chiefly on milk food *(laitage)*; Jean d'Outrego, who died at 146 lived upon Turkey wheat and cabbage ; Thomas Parr, who died aged 152 years and 9 months, fared all his life upon bread, old cheese, milk, whey and table-beer ; and, in conclusion, Peter Zortan, who died at 185 years of age, lived solely upon vegetables.

" All of this is sufficiently contradictory, nor is it easy to deduce from these facts, rules for a regimen proper to produce macrobie ; so that it is not here that it is necessary to seek for them. The know-ledge afforded by these facts is sufficiently precious without demand-ing more from them ; like all exceptions to natural laws, they furnish us with a revelation. By proving to us that human life may be pro-longed far beyond its ordinary limits, they invite us to researches, which, in their absence, would not have been thought of, except to reject at once the idea of them. It is now left to us to discover the causes, and to conquer the means to obtain the result. This research does not appear to us a matter of indifference ; and if, in order to enjoy longevity, it is sufficient to subject oneself to a regimen of lactic acid, we would willingly submit to it.

"If it were true, that the art of greatly increasing the duration of human life, was accessible to us, we could only applaud the contrast of future longevity, with the brevity of existence in the past. How-ever short the life of our fathers, it sufficed for them to sow an am-ple harvest of sorrows ; and however long may be the lives of our sons, or ourselves, it will not suffice to exhaust the noble pleasures which the remunerating future holds in reserve for good and honest men."

Dr. Legrand remarks upon the above : " So let it be, say we ; and we have only to add that Harvey has left us some curious details in regard to Thomas Parr, whose autopsy he made. He was married at 120 years, and at 130 he was summoned before the House of Com-mons for a misdemeanor. Harvey is said to have been an eye witness to a coïtion successfully accomplished by Thomas Parr, at 140 years of age. One is not a great anatomist without being possessed by the demon of curiosity !"—[Translated from *L'Union Médicale.*]

In the "Curiosities of Medical Experience" it is stated that "Henry Jenkins lived to 169, and we have on record the case of a negress, aged 175. The Hungarian family of John Rovin were remarkable for their longevity : the father lived to 172, the wife to 164 ; they had been married 142 years, and their youngest child was 115 ; and such was the influence of habit and filial affection, that this *child* was treated with all the severity of paternal rigidity, and did not dare to act without his *papa's* and *mama's* permission."

To these might be added a number of reliable cases who lived more than 150 years, and some to 180. We will mention only three of the most recent: Marie Prion died in 1838, aged 158 years. A Polish peasant died in 1834, aged 188 years ; and about ten years since, Madelon, a negress and a native of Louisiana, died at Pass Christian, Mississippi, who had seen her century and a half. Her daughter and grandson, living at that time, had reached a very old age; and Madelon is reported not only to have recovered the sight, which she had lost, but to have been blessed with a third set of masticators.

These instances of modern longevity suffice to prove that, in this respect, at least, mankind is not retrograding. The oldest of the biblical patriarchs did not surpass them. Abraham attained but 175 years, and his son Isaac only 180.

As to ancient Methuselah and the balance of the antediluvians, it is supposed, for good reasons, that their years were estimated by our seasons, and should consequently be divided by four. However, in non-medical works are recorded many cases of persons who lived two, three, and even more than four centuries ; but, once trusting ourselves to these, we find such records vastly eclipsed by the equally reliable case of the Wandering Jew, who was *actually seen* by various parties some 600 years ago, and is thought by some credulous individuals to be still engaged in those peregrinations which he has so industriously prosecuted for the last 1800 years and more !

Dr. B. Dowler, in his researches upon the vital statistics of New Orleans, found in the African Cemetery that there was one centenarian in every fifty interments selected at random, which gives a proportion thousands of times higher than is recorded of any other race, or in any other part of the world.

[Although these enumerations (here alluded to by my friend and editorial associate, Dr. Chaillé,) were made at random, they were all taken from *monumental inscriptions*, and may virtually (without on my part intending it) have the *numerical effect of selection, if, as is probable, the ratio of monumental inscriptions be less for infants and young persons than for the adult and the aged class.*—B. DOWLER.]

There are various sources of error which might render these selections at random unreliable as a true indication of the ratio of centenarians to the total mortality ; still there is no doubt that among the natives of Louisiana and our Gulf shore, there is to be found a larger proportionate number of persons who have passed their hundredth year, than in other parts of the United States or in Europe. The official statistics of the deaths in New Orleans for the past three and a half years, give us sixteen centenarians, which is one in less than nineteen hundred of all the deaths. If from this calculation the yellow fever deaths be excluded, as they should be (since these are among our unacclimated strangers), the proportion would amount to one in less than fourteen hundred. In either case the ratio is far more favorable than is afforded by any European statistics.

The United States census for the decade ending with the year 1850 equally proves how favorable our Southern climate is to longevity, the number of centenarians being vastly greater, in proportion to the population, in the Southern than in the Northern States, and this holds true whether in reference to the black or white race, the slaves or freemen. In no States is the proportion of centenarians so large as in Texas and Louisiana.

The learned physiologist, M. Flourens, has written an interesting work on "Human Longevity." He concludes that the normal duration of man's life is one hundred years, and fortifies this conclusion by researches in comparative anatomy and physiology. He states that the duration of life, in mammalia at least, is proportionate to the duration of growth ; the duration of growth to that of gestation, and the duration of gestation to the height. The larger the animal, the longer the gestation, etc. Buffon and other naturalists, as far back as Aristotle, have asserted that there was a fixed ratio between the duration of life and that of growth ; but M. Flourens claims to have discovered the certain sign that marks the term of growth, which is the union of the bones with their epiphyses, after which the animal necessarily ceases to grow.

He finds in all animals which he has subjected to his observation and investigations, that the duration of their lives is five times that of their growth. For instance, the union of the bones with their epiphyses (*i. e.* the term of growth) occurs, in the camel at 8 years, and this animal lives about 40 years ; in the horse at 5 years, and this animal lives about 25 years ; in the ox at 4 years, and this ani. mal lives about 20 years ; in the lion at 4 years, and this animal lives about 20 years ; in the dog at 2 years, and this animal lives about 10 years ; in the cat at 1½ years, and this animal lives about 8 years. From these and many similar examples he concludes, that, since in man the union of the bones with their epiphyses is effected at 20 years of age, the normal duration of his life must be 100 years.

We may conclude this paper, which, perhaps, is more curious than instructive, with the following quotation from Flourens : " Just as the duration of growth, multiplied a certain number of times, say five times, gives the ordinary duration of life, so does this ordinary duration, multiplied a certain number of times, say twice, give the extreme duration. A first century of ordinary life, and almost a second century, half a century (at least) of extraordinary life, is then the prospect science holds out to man." We leave it for those who love it, more than the undersigned to say, Amen!

6

Reprinted from *New Orleans J. Medicine* **23**(1):96–104 (1870)

PHYSIOLOGY AND CHEMISTRY OF OLD AGE

S. P. Cutler, M. D.

Holly Springs, Miss.

THAT slow but sure and gradual process that sweeps and under-mines all animated nature, may be regarded as a normal or physiological, not pathological or diseased action in a strict sense.

There is probably a probationary stage in man and animal, or a period of greater or lesser duration in different individuals, when decay and reproduction exactly balance each other, which marks a given period in each individuality, before which time the reproductive, after which decay predominates.

It is right here a question, whether the rapidity of develop-ment or growth in anywise governs the process of future decay, or is in any way coincident with physiological decline? We have good reason to believe that after the close of this stationary stage, that the organism gradually becomes mineralized, or, as it were, fossilized, by the cells becoming clogged with unoxidisible matter; in consequence, lowering cell activity and lessening vital heat and force or energy, and in proportion the *vis vitae.*

There is a gradual filling up of cells with life antagonistics, gradually crowding life out of the least vital first, then the more vital, until ultimately, by this stealthy encroachment, life is driven out by displacement. The above statements may be strikingly illustrated by the fact that the meat of old animals is less nutritious, unless made suddenly fat from a lean condition. The meat of all young animals is more juicy than that of old. Young and tender, old and tough, is a very old adage.

Why will not a given amount of carbon and hydrogen as ternary food taken into the organism of old age produce the same amount of physical force or energy as in youth or middle age, digestion being equal in both cases? If the same amount of food be equally digested in both cases, then absorbed into the circulation and carried into the tissues and cells, and then oxidized in the same time, the same amount of physical force would be developed in each case.

We may admit that the same amount of carbon and hydrogen is taken in a give time in each and digested, still, this does not prove the fact that this food is oxidized in the same ratio after entering the tissues in both cases; admitting that the same amount of oxygen enters the organism in both cases, does not prove the fact that this oxygen is all consumed in both cases equally, as a portion may pass out in the one case un-oxidized, in the other, not in the form of debris, as also might a certain portion of the food pass out after undergoing normal digestion, as debris.

The food entering the tissues is not proof that it all entered the cells where the greatest amount of oxidation takes place. If then, a portion of the ingested food enters the portals of the tissues without entering into the sanctum sanctorum or inner chambers of the tissues, it may pass out again unchanged by the reversal of the forces that carried it in, that is, by a change of its polarity and becoming dead, instead of living matter, so far as its relations to the organism at the time is concerned. It might be asked why the same amount of ingested food is not permitted to enter the cells in both cases?

The only answer I can give at present, is that the cells themselves are already partially filled with unoxidizable materials or mineralized matter; thereby mechanically excluding a portion of the nutritive elements. Under such circumstances, this additional quantity of food, more than can be consumed, must act as a clog, obstruct and weaken the animal forces; as a certain amount of force is required to carry in and out this useless load which can be of no service whatever; on the contrary, an injury, having a tendency to produce plethora, gout, and other diseases.

It might be asked, why the cells become clogged with mineralized matter as age advances? Could we give the answer, the mystery of old age, if not life itself, would be solved.

It is extremely difficult to find access to cell structures so as to recognize changes taking place during life, even if such a thing were possible, their size being so small, it would be perhaps an impossibility to distinguish any actual difference in the character of cell contents. This could be determined by chemical analysis.

There are certain tissues that may be made the basis of comparison at different stages of life, that may serve to throw much light on this recondite subject. I allude to the hard tissues or bones; the most accessible being the dental structures, as they can be readily procured, even from the living subject, at all ages.

We find these organs when first ruptured, with a larger hollow or canal, having a greater per cent. of cartilage or dentine, than in middle life, and more in middle than in old age. Whether there is actually a probationary or stand-still stage in these and other hard structures, is not yet settled; the probability is, that there is a slow, but constant change steadily going on.

There certainly must be a period or culminating stage when the fullest perfection and most favorable balance of destructive and reproductive elements is attained This particular period might possibly be ascertained or approximated, and when these organs have remained healthy, might furnish an index to all other tissues of the body. After this period has been reached by these organs, there commences, and steadily progresses, a change in the anatomical constituents, which progresses pari-passu; no doubt with similar changes throughout the entire organism, until as before stated, life is entirely crowded out.

Death by old age, that slow but stealthy and certain process of crowding out of life from the organism, by filling up the cells with non vital, mineral elements, thereby not allowing room, if I may so express it, for life to continue its ceaseless roll. If this hypothesis be correct, we are gradually driven out of our earthly taberanacle by an enemy that never raises his siege. Some may, and do, hold out longer than others, though it is only question of time. It may be infered that nature or the organism gradually succumbs to antagonistic forces, acting both from within and without. When organic, or what are called chemico-vital forces, first counteract each other, physiology is sustained intact, and any deviation from these counterpoises converts physiology into pathology.

38

These counterbalances may be inferred to be decay and reproduction, oxidation and waste on the one hand and nutrition or
reproduction on the other.   Oxidation in the cells makes room
for nutrition, otherwise no such thing could take place.   Hypo
and hyper nutrition and other causes may influence these conditions to a certain extent.

Why this condition from the highest endowments of organic
life should be gradually undermined and destroyed by antagonistic forces so as to entirely break up the organization, has not
yet been discovered or revealed any farther than the supposition
that each architypal, primordial cell may have received its im-
press of limitation from the Creator subject to limited modifications from certain modifying circumstances.

The greater the amount of normal oxidation taking place in the
organism, the greater the amount of vital force of such organism.
Energy of nutrition just neutralizing such oxidation, the resultant
being *a tertium quid,* called life force or energy.   It is in other
words, the oxidising and breaking up of organic elements of the
organism, and the conversion of it into organic elements that
developes life force—life being motion, and oxidation being the
cause of such motion, the bent spring, the falling weight, the
dynamical battery.   To return to the hard tissues.   The teeth,
like bones, continue to ossify inwards from childhood to old age,
until in extreme cases all life ceases and the tooth becomes dead
from occlusion of pulp canal and tubuli, with great preponderance, of earthly salts over animal elements, and becomes friable
and brittle.   All other bones may be supposed to be in a similar
condition, more ossified, less vital, more brittle and friable, the
consequence would be a cooling of these tissues to such an extent
as to seriously chill the sarcode and fluids, and ultimately causing death, from cooling down below a certain life-sustaining
point.

As the organs cool, vital energy ebbs pari passu, unless sustained by artificial stimulants, such as alcohol and certain others,
a portion of which passes the rounds of the circulation unchanged
and by its direct agency on the blood and vessels, additional
vigor is imparted so long as under its influence.   Some of the
alcohol may be burned as combustible food, also favoring oxidation in the cells generally, so long as under its influence.

Life itself could not be prolonged to any considerable extent by any such artificial means, but their proper use would be of service, in fact, would be essential in old age, as excitors of vital forces.

As the food of old persons varies but little from that of youth, there must be an excess of unappropriated lime salts retained in the organism an indefinite time—which, the osseous system failing to appropriate, seems to clog the system by finding its way into the cells, more especially cartilage and all similar tissue cells first, but subsequently into more vital structures, shutting out oxidation or all activity as well as mechanically obstructing life, energy, or force.

After a given amount of arrestation of cell activity, life itself sinks below the life-sustaining point by both cooling and mechanically obstructing as in cases of calcification of the valves of the heart and other important structures.

The question here arises, is there any known or unknown means of arresting this mineralization of tissues, especially in the bones of advancing age, as other tissues *a priori* calcify only after the hard tissues fail to make farther use of the lime salts taken with food in the form of normal nutrition.

Other tissues harden in a given ratio, which may vary in different individuals, and in the same individual under different circumstances.

Can there be any means devised that will retard this mineralising process in any way; possibly there can. It is evident that if lime-water is used for drink and food, known to contain a large per cent. of this salt, that there are at least more favorable opportunities afforded favoring this process. I might here make two suggestions: First, to use food and water known to be the most free from phosphates. Secondly, To make use of food containing a large per cent. of vegetable acids, such as fruits, also vegetables in their green or fresh state, and vinegar largely, during meals. Eggs and milk are known to contain all the minerals in excess of almost all other kinds of food ; butter may be used freely, also fat meats, both forming combustible food chiefly. Sugar, lemons, oranges. apples, cherries, plums, peaches, currants, and many other fruits and berries, are good. The rinds or peelings of fruit should always be discarded in advancing age, as they contain the chief minerals. In young subjects this order should be reversed, as they need an excess of minerals up to the time of full development and growth.

All acids containing hydrogen, as most vegetables do, decompose phosphates and carbonates, forming soluble salts, which could not be deposited permanently in the cells, either of bones or other tissues.

Any free lime salts floating in the system, or even in the cells, may be decomposed and more salts formed and washed out of the organism. Not only this, but even the bones themselves may be made to give up any surplus portion of lime in this way in old age, so as to render them less dense and friable, and more susceptible of nutrition, and old age even put farther off indefinitely.

The object of vegetable acids, as diet, would be to establish an acid diathesis, similar to the disease called rickets in children, which depends on such a diathesis that removes lime from the bones, and in some cases, in very young children, prevents even the deposit of lime in certain bones and portions of bones. Mellitis osseum in adults, especially females, after puberty, and pregnant women, necessarily depends on a morbid acid diathesis, unlike the former disease. I do not propose to carry the acid to such an extent as to develope a diseased condition of the bones or any part of the organism, only to use sufficient to prevent a too rapid accumulation of lime in the system. Normal waste of bones can take place from no other cause, save that of acid action, dissolving out the lime salts, while oxygen alone removes the gelatine or cartilage, similar to any other soft or fleshy tissue. Any vegetable acid containing hydrogen, as above stated, will decompose both phosphate and carbonate of lime, either in or out of the organism, if sufficiently concentrated.

I do not propose medication as a prophylactic or preventive of old age, but only suggest proper dietetic regulations, in order to prevent premature old age. This much I believe to be possible.

Bone decay or waste depends on a double or dual process, namely, that of acid removing lime, and oxygen removing the osteine, similar to any tissue which gives place to nutrition, which

41

can follow after waste only. In this respect bone nutrition is unlike any other. The exhalation of all other tissues is the work of oxygen only. Decay and reproduction, old tissues disintegrated and new protoplasm added is the order of life, death and regeneration; die that we may live. Without death, there can be no life, so said Bichat, who first propounded this great fundamental truth.

All decay is chemical action, acting both in harmony and in opposition to vital action, and both essential to vital existence; both acting in concerted antagonisms. All chemical action depends on molecular physics, and all life manifestations are based on molecular polarity or dynamics similar to that of chemical. Again, the food of children should contain an excess of lime salts, also that of pregnant females. The food of advancing age should contain the smallest possible amount of lime salt, and the largest amount of vegetable acids. Females who have borne the most children, are frequently the longest lived, gestation imparting additional vital energy for the time being, by setting up new energies in her system; at the same time, drawing heavily on the lime salts of the food for the new growth or development of osseous structures. At the same time, there is generally set up in the enciente female, an acid diathesis, which acts heavily on the bones, this is made apparent by dental decay during this period. The above facts go to sustain my hyphothesis or theory.

Excess of food or overeating, even of the proper kind, is injurious in advancing age; serving to over-distend the cells, causing undue deposits of minerals, which clog the system and check vital energy, and to a greater extent and more permanently in the bones than in the sarcode.

All the tissues in old age become less oxidizable and less vital, even the fat in the cells, owing to loss of water and excess of carbon. Gray hairs show and wrinkled skin indicate less of vital energy; in fact the whole system becomes yellow and less fair in advancing age.

In short, the system becomes mineralized and carbonized and mummyfied. The bone cells first become clogged and cooled, causing a heavy dragging sensation as if the bones were becoming heavy and cold. This is actually the case, the earth in the bones increases, consequently, they become less vital and nutritious. Fragilia Osseum Senilis the result.

How to remedy the loss of water in the soft tissues and excess of carbon, is not so easily determined. One fact is observable, as people grow old they drink less water, also sleep less, the tissues become dryer and less juicy. A very old truism, young and tender, old and tough.

The most of old animals are tougher, dryer and less nutritious, unless the they are rapidly fattened from the lean state, as before stated.

Carbonaceous matters and minerals predominate in old persons. The predominance of carbon may depend on evaporation of water or its elements in advanced age.

Wood of any kind, when kept dry, loses elements of water, and continues to do so for centuries, turns yellow and becomes brittle The same may be said of all organic substances, either in the living or dead state. These are significant facts.

Mineralizing of cell contents and carbonizing of cell walls or structures, seems to be the only constitutional causes of decay, and old age. Some may die of old age, ten, twenty or more years sooner than others. Some may live to be one hundred and fifty or more years, and even then not die of old age.

As I have already stated in a published article on physiology, all heat and vital force depends exclusively on oxidation, but the probable mode of such oxidation and per cent. of different oxidizable elements of the various proximate and elementary principles, do not at present concern us.

All life forces may be regarded as the sum or aggregate of all the forces of the different elements that enter into organisms as pre-existent, only acting in new directions and under different circumstances, the new endowments being the result of new combinations not found to exist outside of organic life. In new endowments of matter only, are new directions of forces exalted or lifted up.

Finally, who shall say, what is really the outside limits of life under different circumstances? Who shall gainsay that man's organism may not be so retained in its youthful condition as to furnish boys and girls at one hundred years, by scientific classification of food for the human family?

From recent researches of Darwin, Spencer and others, what may we not hope for, if the human family can but receive a share of the scientific labors of such men in relation to longevity as set forth in the above article?

Removal to warmer climates in advancing age, where more light and heat are absorbed, may add to the years, other things being equal. In a recent article on food by Leibeg, no distinction is made, nor is any reference made to the opinions of many of the eminent authors in relation to longevity.

7

Reprinted from *L'Union Médicale* 13(5):65–71 (1859)

PEUT-ON RECULER LES BORNES DE LA VIE HUMAINE?

M. F. Legrand

Dans le numéro du 4 décembre dernier, nous prenions l'engagement d'entretenir bientôt les lecteurs de l'UNION MÉDICALE du troisième volume des *Essais scientifiques* (1) que publie M. Victor Meunier, le savant et spirituel rédacteur en chef de l'*Ami des sciences*. Nous prenions aussi l'engagement, à la même date, de présenter quelques réflexions sur la manière de comprendre le rôle de la presse scientifique et la fonction qu'elle est appelée à remplir.

Nous ne tiendrons aujourd'hui qu'une partie de nos promesses; l'espace dont nous disposons ne nous permettant pas de les tenir toutes. Nos lecteurs n'y perdront rien; ce n'est qu'une prorogation.

Le troisième volume que nous avons sous les yeux, et qui est dédié à M. Ferd. de Lesseps, porte, en sous-titre : *Simples feuilletons*. C'est la réimpression de quelques-uns des articles si remarquables et si avidement lus que M. Victor Meunier fit paraître dans la *Presse,* alors qu'il était chargé, dans ce journal, de ce qui concernait les sciences. Nous en extrayons le chapitre qu'on va lire; il nous semble n'avoir rien perdu de son actualité, ou mieux, de son intérêt.

« Peut-on reculer les bornes de la vie humaine? C'est un professeur de chimie, renommé pour ses méthodes d'enseignement, qui pose cette question dans un mémoire présenté à l'Académie des sciences, et intitulé : *Sur les causes de la vieillesse et de la mort sénile.* Ce chimiste est M. Edouard Robin. Il croit que la vie humaine peut, en effet, être prolongée; et comme il a le courage de son opinion, il cherche les moyens rationnels d'arriver à ce résultat. — Il cherchera longtemps encore, dites-vous, lecteur. — C'est notre opinion; c'est aussi, sans doute, celle de M. Robin, qui, en attendant un plus fort versement, nous apporte un intéressant à-compte. Au reste, à supposer qu'il y ait dans une telle recherche un excès d'audace, nous ne voyons pas de mal, pour notre part, à ce qu'on commette des excès en ce genre, cela fait contre-poids.

..... Les êtres vivants peuvent être comparés à des fourneaux toujours allumés : la vie n'existe qu'à la condition de la combustion; mais la combustion qui s'opère en nous, comme celle qui a lieu dans nos cheminées, laisse un résidu, un détritus, des cendres. Ce détritus, qui toujours s'accumule, voilà, suivant M. Robin, la cause principale de la vieillesse et de la mort sénile.

L'aliment, quelle que soit sa nature, végétal ou animal, liquide ou solide, est chargé de matières minérales que la combustion lui fait abandonner dans les différentes parties de l'organisme; elles servent d'abord à la nutrition et c'est seulement quand le squelette est consolidé, que, continuant d'affluer, elles incrustent et minéralisent les pièces du mécanisme.

La manière dont la minéralisation détermine la vieillesse chez l'homme paraît nettement indiquée : d'une part, l'ossification des cartilages du sternum, la rigidité plus grande des ligaments postérieurs des côtes déterminent une respiration de plus en plus lente, de moins en moins étendue, et qui finit par être entièrement diaphragmatique; d'autre part, l'ossification des vaisseaux et de leurs valvules, la diminution du calibre des artères, l'oblitération des capillaires, la diminution de leur nombre, l'agrandissement des cellules pulmonaires, rendent la circulation de plus en plus difficile et diminuent la surface respiratoire.

L'air se mettant de moins en moins en contact avec le sang, ce liquide devient moins artérialisé, il se fonce en couleur, il engorge le système veineux comme dans l'état d'asphyxie, et les expériences sur la quantité d'acide carbonique exhalé, sur la température animale, sur le passage de certains éléments du sang dans les urines, ne permettent pas de douter qu'il se produit, à partir d'un certain âge, une combustion graduellement moins abondante.

Avec la combustion et la chaleur, l'électricité et le fluide nerveux diminuent, partant, la sensibilité et la contractilité deviennent moindres, les mouvements se ralentissent, l'activité générale décroît : affaiblie par toutes ces causes, l'action nerveuse contribue à son tour à la diminution de la combustion, et... tout le monde sait comment cela finit.

Fort de ce raisonnement, qui a du bon,

(1) Paris, 1858. Au bureau de l'*Ami des sciences,* rue Cassette, 9. In-12.

M. Robin espère prouver qu'il est facile de retarder la vieillesse et la mort d'un grand nombre d'animaux, et cela en ralentissant les phénomènes de combustion lente.

En conséquence, il se propose d'instituer trois séries d'expériences portant sur des êtres dont la vie a peu de durée.

Les uns seront nourris avec ceux des aliments qui contiennent le moins de matières minérales incrustantes.

Les autres avec des aliments plus ou moins privés de ces matières au moyen de dissolvants appropriés.

Les derniers, enfin, avec des aliments ordinaires, mais à la condition d'administrer, à partir d'un certain âge, de l'acide lactique, qui a incontestablement la propriété de dissoudre les matières minérales et paraît propre à dissoudre, pendant la vie, celles qui se sont déjà déposées dans l'organisme.

Si l'on nous demande ce que nous pensons du sujet des recherches dont M. Éd. Robin a fait choix..., nous répondrons que nous l'approuvons fort, et que nous engageons l'auteur à persévérer.

Nous savons bien ce qu'on dira : Paracelse ! Van Helmont ! etc. Mais d'abord les noms, ni en bien ni en mal, ne nous en imposent guère ; d'ailleurs, ceux-là sont de très grands esprits ; et puis, nous éprouvons une forte répugnance pour ces jugements tout faits qui circulent dans le public, comme la monnaie de billon, et que chacun porte de confiance et sans nouvel examen sur ces grandes doctrines qui, des profondeurs du passé, brillent encore à nos yeux comme des éclairs et des volcans en ignition.....

... Mais, pour approuver les recherches auxquelles se livre M. Robin, et qui se rattachent à l'une des croyances les plus générales et les plus vivaces de l'humanité, ce qui, selon nous, les justifie, nous avons une raison encore, un principe que nous formulons ainsi :

Toute qualité qui apparaît exceptionnellement en une espèce, est l'indice d'une règle nouvelle à laquelle cette espèce peut être soumise.

Appliquant ce principe au sujet dont il s'agit, nous disons :

Il y a des macrobites ou centenaires dans l'espèce humaine : donc la macrobie est compatible avec l'organisation humaine. La conséquence n'est point forcée. Mais, remarquez-le, dès que la macrobie se produit, sa cause peut être déterminée. Or, posséder une cause, c'est être maître de l'effet ; et ce qui, jusqu'ici, est l'exception, peut devenir la règle.

S'il vivait, Hippolyte Royer-Collard ne me démentirait pas.

La longue existence des patriarches provoque le sourire. Mais, dans des temps beaucoup moins éloignés de nous, on trouve des faits qui ne sont guère plus vraisemblables et qu'on ne peut contester. Nous croyons ne pas déplaire au lecteur en en citant quelques-uns :

Ponce Lepage, mort en 1760, dans le duché de Luxembourg, à l'âge de 121 ans ; peu de temps avant il cultivait son champ et faisait à pied des trajets de six à sept lieues.

Éléonore Spicer, morte dans la Virginie, en 1763, à l'âge de 121 ans. Elle conserva l'usage de ses sens jusqu'au dernier moment.

La dame Barnet, morte à Charleston, en 1820, à l'âge de 123 ans. Elle se rappelait parfaitement les événements arrivés un siècle auparavant.

Grandez, mort en Languedoc, en 1754, à l'âge de 126 ans. Il était compagnon orfèvre, et travaillait encore dix à douze jours avant sa mort.

L'Anglais Jean Neuwel, mort en 1761, à l'âge de 127 ans, dans toute la plénitude de sa raison.

Un autre Anglais, Jean Bayles, marchand de moutons, mort en 1706, à l'âge de 130 ans. Pendant les dernières années de sa vie, il conduisait les troupeaux de moutons aux marchés de son voisinage.

Marguerite Lawler, Anglaise, morte en 1739, à 135 ans. Peu de jours avant, elle allait à pied à une distance de trois à quatre milles et revenait chez elle le même jour.

Joseph Barn, nègre, mort à la Jamaïque, en 1808, à 140 ans. Peu de jours auparavant, il faisait des courses de quatre milles.

Pololiman, chirurgien en Lorraine, mort en 1825, à l'âge de 140 ans. La veille de sa mort, il pratiqua l'opération d'un cancer avec beaucoup de dextérité.

Thomas Parr, mort à Londres, à l'âge de 152 ans, en 1635. Jusqu'à l'âge de 130 ans, il put se livrer à tous les travaux du cultivateur et même battre le blé.

Obst, villageoise en Silésie, morte en 1825, à l'âge de 155 ans. Elle avait travaillé aux champs le veille de sa mort.

Joseph Surrington, Norwégien, mort en 1797, à 160 ans. Il conserva jusqu'au dernier moment, sa raison et ses sens.

Jean Bowin, né dans le bannat de Temeswar, mort en 1740, à l'âge de 172 ans.

Pierre Zortan, compatriote du précédent, mort en 1724, à 185 ans.

Si l'on compulsait la vie de ces êtres extraordinaires, on reconnaîtrait qu'il est bien difficile de déterminer les causes de leur longévité ;

le privilége dont ils étaient doués paraît compatible avec tous les genres de vie.

Je relève quelques exemples :

Annibal Camoux, mort à 121 ans et qui figure dans un tableau d'Horace Vernet, buvait beaucoup de vin et vivait d'aliments très grossiers; de même le chirurgien Pololiman, dont il a été question ci-dessus, n'a jamais passé un jour sans s'enivrer; la paysanne Obst, morte à 155 ans, buvait ordinairement deux verres d'eau-de-vie dans sa journée. En se pressant un peu trop de conclure, on pourrait donc ériger l'ivrognerie en brevet de longue vie.

Mais voici Éléonore Spicer, morte à 121 ans, qui n'a jamais bu de liqueur spiritueuse ; Grandez, mort à 126 ans, n'avait jamais bu de vin ; Jean Effingham, mort à l'âge de 144 ans, ne connaissait les liqueurs que de vue. En outre de ce contraste, voici des faits dans lesquels il n'est pas aisé de voir clair :

Denis Guignard, mort à 123 ans, habitait une caverne creusée dans le tuf; Drahakemberg, mort à 146 ans, avait été pris par les corsaires et avait supporté, pendant quinze ans, toutes les souffrances d'une dure captivité ; Jean Laffitte, mort à 136 ans, avait pris, dès sa première jeunesse, l'habitude de se baigner deux ou trois fois par semaine et l'avait conservée jusqu'à la fin de sa vie ; Jean Causeur, mort à 137 ans, faisait grand usage de laitage ; Jean d'Outregro, mort à 146 ans, se nourrissait de blé de Turquie et de choux ; Thomas Parr, mort à 152 ans et 9 mois, se nourrit toute sa vie de pain, de vieux fromage, de lait, de petit lait et de petite bière; enfin, Pierre Zortan, mort à 185 ans, vivait uniquement de légumes.

Tout cela est assez contradictoire, et je ne pense pas qu'on en puisse aisément déduire les règles d'un régime propre à produire la macrobie ; aussi n'est-ce point là ce qu'il faut y cher-cher. L'enseignement que ces faits portent en eux est assez précieux pour que nous ne leur demandions rien de plus; comme toutes les exceptions naturelles, c'est une révélation qu'ils apportent. En nous prouvant que la vie humaine peut être prolongée bien au delà de ses limites ordinaires, ils nous invitent à une recherche dont, en leur absence, l'idée n'eût pu se présenter à notre esprit sans que nous la rejettassions aussitôt. A nous maintenant de découvrir des causes et de conquérir les moyens.

La recherche ne nous semble point indifférente, et si, pour vivre jusqu'au dénouement de l'action actuellement engagée sur ce globe, il suffisait de se mettre au régime de l'acide lactique, nous nous y mettrions volontiers.

S'il était vrai que l'art d'accroître dans de grandes proportions la durée de la vie humaine nous fût accessible, nous ne pourrions qu'applaudir au contraste de la longévité future avec la brièveté de l'existence dans le passé. Si courte que fût la vie de nos pères, elle leur suffisait pour faire une ample moisson de douleurs; si longue que puisse être la vie de nos fils ou la nôtre, dans nos existences futures, elle ne suffira pas à épuiser les nobles délices que l'avenir rémunérateur tient en réserve pour les hommes de bonne volonté. »

Ainsi soit-il, dirons-nous; et nous n'ajouterons que deux mots : c'est, d'abord, que les lignes qui précèdent ont été publiées, pour la première fois, en février 1853; et, ensuite, qu'Harvey nous a laissé de curieux détails sur Thomas Parr, dont il fit l'autopsie. Il s'était marié à 120 ans; à 130, il fut cité devant la Chambre des communes pour attentat aux mœurs. Harvey dit avoir été témoin oculaire du coït accompli par Thomas Parr à 140 ans. On n'est pas un grand anatomiste sans être possédé du démon de la curiosité.

47

8

Reprinted from *J. Anthropol. Inst. Great Britain and Ireland* 2:69–78 (1872–1873)

The COMPARATIVE LONGEVITY *of* ANIMALS *of* DIFFERENT SPECIES, *and of* MAN; *and the Probable Causes which mainly conduce to promote this Difference.* By GEORGE HARRIS, F.S.A., Vice-President of the Anthropological Institute.

HISTORY, both sacred and profane, attributes to mankind who lived in the early ages of the world, a longevity very far exceeding what we have experience of in our day. To some extent this difference may possibly be accounted for by the different modes in which eras of time were calculated. Possibly also the planetary system by whose revolutions periods of life were reckoned, may have undergone certain changes during that space of time. Easton, however, appears to give entire credit to the literal interpretation of the statement as to the longevity recorded of the patriarchs, and accounts for the limitation of the period of life since their time by remarking that "the productions of the earth were then of a different nature. The surface of the globe was in the first ages of the world less solid and compact. The period of man's existence may have gradually diminished in proportion as the surface of the earth acquired more solidity by the constant action of gravity."*

Dr. Whewell, the late able and learned Master of Trinity, accounted for the longevity of the patriarchs by the fact that Adam and Eve had eaten of the tree of life, and that its virtue was transmitted through several successive generations, till at last it became dissipated and lost, and man was reduced to a miserable tithe of his first possession.†

Lord Bacon, referring to the general period of the life of man,

---

* "Human Longevity", Introd., p. xxvii.
† "Life; its Nature, Varieties, and Phenomena". By Leo. H. Grindon. P. 114.

asserts that "man's age doth exceed the age of all other living creatures."[*]

In the early records of our own country accounts are preserved of people living to a much greater age than they now do. Among the ancient Britons people commonly lived to the age of one hundred and twenty years. There are isolated instances in modern times of men living much beyond this age.

An able and well-written article on the general subject of longevity is contained in the *Edinburgh Review* for January 1857, which is attributed to Sir Henry Holland. It, however, throws some doubt on the reality of the great age asserted to have been attained by Jenkins and the Countess of Desmond,—one hundred and sixty-nine and one hundred and forty-eight years respectively; but confirms the account given of the longevity of Thomas Parr, and refers to the dissection of his body by the celebrated Harvey, who concluded from its appearance that he might have lived much longer but for the surfeit of food and changes in his habits which followed his removal to London, and to the kitchen of the palace.

Extraordinary and perhaps extravagant notions were entertained by the ancients as to the longevity of certain animals. According to a passage in Hesiod, referred to by Sir Thomas Browne,[†] ninety-six is the period of the life of a man, while that of a deer extends to above three thousand, and that of a crow to considerably beyond that period. But naturalists also of high repute and great credit, modern as well as ancient, afford us extraordinary accounts of the longevity attained by certain animals. Smellie, in his " Philosophy of Natural History," alludes to the great longevity of certain animals. Elephants live beyond two hundred years.[‡] " In proportion to the size of their bodies, birds live longer than either men or quadrupeds. Swans have been said to live three hundred years."[§] A goose is said to live beyond one hundred years,[||] as do also ravens.[¶] " Gesner gives an instance of a carp in Germany which he knew to be one hundred years old. Buffon informs us that he had seen carps of one hundred and fifty years of age, and he mentions one which he supposed to be two hundred years old."[**] Pike have been known to live to two hundred and sixty-seven years.[††] The tortoise is said to have attained one hundred and seventy-five years,[‡‡] and the falcon one hundred and sixty-two years."[§§] A Greenland whale, we are told, will live from three hundred to four hundred years.[||||] Parrots and several other ani-

---

[*] " History of Life and Death".   [†] " Vulgar Errors".
[‡] P. 283.   § P. 512. || Ibid.
[¶] Ibid.   ** Smellie, p. 514.   †† Gesner, quoted by Yarrell.
‡‡ Grindon on Life.   §§ Hufeland, " Art of Prolonging Life".
|||| Grindon on Life.

mals, including some reptiles, are also said to afford extraordinary instances of longevity; while certain other animals, not apparently differing essentially in their nature and constitution from those to which I have referred, are as remarkable for the brief space to which their lives are ordinarily limited. Some trees are supposed capable of attaining an extraordinary age. The oak will live for fifteen hundred years, and the yew for three thousand two hundred.*

The opinions which have been entertained by different writers who have examined minutely into the subject, as to the principal causes of longevity both in animals and men, are deserving of attention, although no satisfactory conclusion has as yet been arrived at, and they differ essentially from one another in their theories on this topic. The famous Roger Bacon wrote a treatise entitled "The Cure of Old Age."† But the wonderful genius who six hundred years ago predicted travelling by carriages and by boats propelled by machinery, and navigating through the air, and to whom the inventions of printing and the telescope were also known, failed to produce any recipe for attaining long life beyond a few ordinary maxims regarding health. Paracelsus boasted that he could make a man live four hundred years or more if he might bring him up from his infancy, and diet him as he chose.‡ And Burton tells us in his "Anatomy of Melancholy" that some physicians hold that there is no certain period of man's life, but it may still by temperance and physic be prolonged.§ Lord Bacon, in his "History of Life and Death," discusses the causes of longevity, and he attributes the varieties in this respect to variations in the density of the vital spirits, and other causes affecting those spirits, and lays down the following maxims of prolonging life : " Alimentation from without, at least some other way than by the stomach, is most profitable to long life, if it can be done," canon xxiii ; " Curing of diseases is effected by temporary medicines, but lengthening of life requireth observation of diet," canon xxx.

In his " Natural History"|| Lord Bacon also states that "It conduceth unto long life, and to the more placid motion of the spirits, which thereby do less prey and consume the juice of the body; either that man's actions be free and voluntary, that nothing be done *invita Minerva*, but *secundum genium* ; or, on the other side, that the actions of men be full of regulation and commands within themselves, for then the victory and performing of the command giveth a good disposition to the spirits, especially if there be a proceeding from degree to degree, for then the sense of

* Grindon on Life.
† " De Retardandis Senectutis Accidentibus".   Oxford, 1590.
‡ " Lib. de Vitâ Longâ."   § Part i, sect. 2.
|| P. 292, " Experiment solitary touching prolongation of life".

the victory is the greater. An example of the former of these is in a country life; and of.the latter in monks and philosophers, and such as do continually enjoy themselves."

Sir John Sinclair, in his "Code of Health and Longevity," vol. ii, gives a catalogue of one thousand four hundred and twenty "foreign publications on the subject of health and diet." In the "Appendix," vol. ii, to the above work are "rules by which a person will be enabled to prolong life to the latest period." Rule 10 advises people to refrain from dinner once a week.

Mr. Herbert Spencer* attributes the apparent absence of inherent decay in many trees, in fish, and in some reptiles, to their exceedingly small expenditure; trees and plants generally exhibiting no personal expenditure at all; whilst fish and certain cold-blooded reptiles show very little indeed.

The period occupied in the growth of an animal has sometimes been adopted as the test to what that of its life will extend. But this has been found to vary extensively in the case of different animals. Bodily strength, vigour, and health also fail to afford any certain indication as to the period to which life will reach, as the strongest and healthiest not unfrequently die early, while the frail and sickly turn out to be long-lived. Climate is said to occasion but little difference as to the period to which the lives of persons extend, although there is some difference of opinion in this respect, and certain climes appear to be peculiarly favourable to longevity. At one period Italy seems to have been remarkable in this respect. Cornwall, too, has been noted for longevity. Air and diet have always been supposed to exercise an important influence on longevity. Certain writers have attributed the longevity of the ante-diluvians to their sobriety and the simplicity of their manners, to their abstaining from eating flesh, and to the excellence of the fruits and herbs of those days, also to the purity of the air in those times.† But while some men who lived temperately, and even abstemiously, have lived to a great age, others who followed the very opposite course have been equally long-lived.‡ In general, however, notwithstanding a few exceptions, it appears to be generally admitted that "temperance, a placid and cheerful disposition, moderate exercise, and proper exertions of mind contribute in no uncommon degree to the prolongation of life."§

Some pursuits are also obviously much more favourable to longevity than are certain others. The clergy are proverbially long-lived; and, strange to say, the lawyers, too, frequently ex-

* "Principles of Biology".
† Rees's "Cycl." Art., Longevity.
‡ Smellie, p. 505.   § Ibid.

hibit great tenacity with regard to life, as they do with regard to other matters also. According to averages taken by Dr. Caldwell, the lives of twenty mathematicians extended to seventy-five years, while those of twenty poets extended to only fifty-seven years.*

The quality of the air is thought by some to cause the chief difference in longevity.† It has indeed been proved by statistical returns that fresh air is one of the main conducives to it. In the case of wild winged birds, who partake of it to the utmost possible extent, this is probably one of the principal causes of their being so long-lived. And wild animals in general have the full benefit of it, and in its purest state. According to Easton, "fresh air is more immediately necessary to life than food."‡ He asserts also that "there is a vivifying principle contained in the atmosphere."§ In general there are more old men in high than in low countries.‖ And yet in thickly-populated cities which are placed in a low situation some extraordinary instances of longevity may occasionally be observed.

Artificial food, both as regards meat and drink, may be supposed to be far less favourable to longevity than that which is in a natural state. Indeed, according to certain statements, the people of this highly-civilised age and country live mainly upon poison! Civilisation, however, may be presumed to be in many respects favourable to longevity, but that civilisation should be untainted by luxury. It should be such a state of civilisation as will provide against want, and afford regular exercise both to the mental and physical powers, but without leading mankind to indulge in those excesses of various kinds to which men in society are so frequently addicted.

Domestication appears to have a corresponding effect upon animals with what luxury has upon mankind. Lord Bacon tells us in his "History of Life and Death" that "in tame creatures their degenerate life corrupteth them; in wild creatures their exposing to all weathers also intercepteth them". But besides their exposure to the weather, wild animals are ever exposed to attacks from each other. But while tame animals are protected from many of these casualties, few domesticated animals are long-lived. The habits into which they are forced are contrary to nature. They take but little exercise. They feed on artificial diet, and their instincts become blunted. It is accordingly among wild animals that the extraordinary instances of longevity alluded to are afforded. Mr. Lankester, however, tells us that animals in

---

* Combe's "Principles of Physiology", p. 366; Caldwell on "Physical Education", pp. 84, 86.   † Smellie, p. 510.
‡ "Human Longevity", Introd., p. xxi.   § Ibid.
‖ Smellie, p. 510.

a domesticated state, which are supplied with food and protected from the attacks of other animals, may live much longer than in a state of nature.* But this proves nothing as regards their natural longevity. They are less liable to die from want or violence, which are mainly destructive in the case of wild animals, but their natural term of life is considerably abridged. In the case of wild animals there is, of course, much greater difficulty in ascertaining the precise period to which their lives are extended than in the case of those that are domesticated. This, however, may in many instances be successfully accomplished. Singular it is that in localities where wild animals abound we so seldom meet with instances of old and decrepit animals, and still less with the remains of animals that have died of old age. Among our domestic animals, instances of decrepitude from old age are very common, notwithstanding the alacrity with which they are killed off before they get too old to serve for domestic use. This apparent longevity of certain wild animals affords some support to the statements of the ancients as to the extraordinary longevity of certain animals, and also of the patriarchs, whose longevity has been accounted for by their living in a state of nature, as is the case with wild animals, feeding only on diet which is pure, simple, and unadulterated. On the other hand, savages, who certainly have certain advantages in this respect over civilised people, do not have their lives prolonged beyond the ordinary term. But then it should be borne in mind that savages, where they live in large hordes, have generally adopted some artificial habits which are at variance with nature and inimical to longevity; besides which, as is the case with the natives of New Zealand, they have often a difficulty in procuring sufficient and good food, and live in unwholesome dwellings, all which renders their case very different from that of the patriarchs.

Nevertheless, it cannot be doubted that if some particular animals do really enjoy a longevity far beyond the rest of their species, as to which there are assertions apparently well authenticated, there must necessarily be some special cause existing, either in their constitution or their mode of life, which occasions such longevity. And if this affects one animal, it will affect another; and if life may be prolonged in one case to a period far beyond its natural extent by the application of certain causes, it may be by a corresponding application in another case. If the life of a beast, or a bird, or a fish, may be extended to ten times its natural length by special agencies, is there any reason to suppose that the life of man is not subject to the same influences?

* "Comparative Longevity in Man and Animals".

The late Dr. Monro went so far as to maintain, in his anatomical lectures, that " as far as he could observe the human body, as a machine, was perfect; that it bore within itself no marks by which we could possibly predicate its decay ; that it was apparently calculated to go on for ever; and that we learned only by experience that it would not do so".*

Is it altogether irrational to suppose that some principle analogous to that of vaccination, or to that supposed to be contained in the very tree of life itself, may at some distant period in the progress of science be brought to light by which the animal frame may be revigorated and rescued from decay, and so fitted to endure, I will not presume to say for ever, but to an age corresponding with that to which we are told that both the patriarch and many animals have attained ? Not improbably, indeed, there may be numerous natural medicines to which the instincts of wild animals spontaneously direct them, such as certain plants and springs, resort to which may have the effect at once of producing those particular results, and those alterations in their system, which capacitate it to endure for a long period. We see proof of this to a certain extent in certain cases, and it may reasonably be inferred that it exists to an extent considerably beyond our experience. If our science served us as efficiently as their instinct does them, we possibly might make corresponding discoveries with corresponding results. Possibly the patriarchs did possess this knowledge. Among certain savage tribes of men, whose instinctive powers are largely developed, while those of the reason are but little cultivated, a remarkable sagacity as to the medicinal properties of some natural productions has been occasionally exhibited.

In order to determine the points now at issue, we must inquire and ascertain as far as possible what is the real principle on which the comparative duration of life in every animated frame depends, and which appears to me to be as follows. In every such frame, commencing with the very germ itself, there is implanted a principle of growth or composition, by the operation of which, aided by nutrition and accretion, the frame goes on increasing and enlarging, rapidly at first, but gradually more slowly, and very languidly in old age. On the other hand, there is another principle contemporaneous with this, that of waste, or decay, or decomposition, which operates at first very slowly, but gradually increases in rapidity and strength, being very speedy and powerful in old age. The operation of these two principles is best and most clearly exhibited in the case of vegetable frames. But in those of animals and also of man it may be clearly perceived. So long as the growth in question exceeds

* Appendix to Combe on " The Constitution of Man", p. 434.

or keeps pace with decay, life is maintained; but whenever the progress of decay, or decomposition, exceeds that of growth, the frame declines, and death speedily ensues.   Certain causes tend to promote the action of one of these principles, and certain causes tend to promote that of the other.   Some of these causes are very powerful and obvious, and act in a direct manner. Others appear to be but feeble, and are scarcely perceptible, and act only indirectly.   For instance, intemperance, incontinence, and irregularity of life, as also excessive toil, unwholesome food, and bad air, are directly calculated to hinder growth and promote decay.   On the other hand, the opposite of these causes are as directly calculated to promote growth and retard decay.

The very essence of certain diseases is in reality but the triumph of decay, or waste, or decomposition, over growth or renovation; and therefore, if the complaint in question be of long continuance, it necessarily terminates in the dissolution of the frame, and in death.   We see this more particularly and clearly evinced in the case of the disease termed consumption. People in reality die of old age, not when they have lived so many years, but when they are worn out—by the progress of waste and decay outstripping that of growth and renovation. As many, therefore, die of old age, from being worn out, at eighteen as at eighty.

It may, I think, be assumed that the real and only scientific test as to the capacity of any particular individual animal frame to last for a greater or less period of time, turns on the constitution of such frame, whether as regards its material texture, its temperament, its organisation, or its fluids, more especially the blood.   Different animal frames no doubt differ extensively one from another in this respect.   For instance, women are said to live longer than men, because " the bones, the cartilages, the muscles, as well as every other part of the body, are softer and less solid than those of men".[*]   But if animated beings of the same species differ one from another as regards their adaptation for longevity owing to a difference in their constitution, we may suppose that animated beings of a different species will differ far more extensively from the same cause.   Thus fishes, we are told, " live during several centuries, because their bones and cartilages seldom acquire the density of those of other animals".[†]

Comparative longevity, therefore, depends mainly on natural constitution.   Nevertheless, inasmuch as whatever be the natural constitution, there are certain causes which will tend to abridge longevity, such as incontinence, intemperance, unwholesome diet,

[*] Smellie's " Philosophy of Nat. Hist.", p. 509; Barr's Buffon, pp. 3, 4, 100.
[†] Smellie, p. 509.

and adopting many artificial habits; are there not also certain causes which in a corresponding manner, whatever be the natural constitution of the individual, will tend to increase longevity? To determine this point, we must decide the question how far artificial appliances are able to alter to any great extent those qualities of the frame already alluded to, on which longevity is supposed mainly to depend. In fact, the real and sole essential question at issue is this. Can any measure be adopted which will have the effect to any important extent of checking waste or expenditure, on the one hand, and of increasing growth or reproduction, on the other? . This is a subject open to experiment in many ways of a most interesting kind. Certain waters, for instance, are said to have an effect upon the cartilages in the way stated; and it is to causes of this kind that the patriarchal longevity has been by some writers attributed. Probably their most powerful and direct effect is seen in the difference they appear to occasion in the duration of the life of animals that are domesticated and those that are wild.

Mr. Easton well observes that " the more a man follows nature, and is obedient to her laws, the longer he will live; and that the further he deviates from these, the shorter will be his existence".*

The question then arises, what are we to do in order completely and fully to follow nature, especially in our present highly-civilised, not to say luxurious, state of society, when so much that is entirely contrary to nature is peremptorily imposed upon us? Mr. Easton particularly recommends plenty of exercise, plain food, and fresh air. The two latter are, however, in many cases difficult to obtain.

The German writer, Hufeland, in his " Art of Prolonging the Life of Man," which is to a great extent based on Lord Bacon's work, already referred to, has arrived at certain conclusions as to the causes of the duration of life, which he considers to be dependent on the quantity of vital force contained in the body, and the promotion of the influences which contribute to decrease or diminish that force. He does not, however, even attempt to suggest any mode of producing or accelerating these influences, beyond stating that " a body which has the most perfect means of regeneration, both internal and external, will endure a longer time than one not provided with these means"; which is simply saying that a frame which is fitted to last a long time will last longer than one not so fitted, but without attempting to tell what we are to do to make the frame so last.

No doubt with our present limited scientific knowledge it appears far easier to shorten life than to prolong it. But if causes operate alike and with equal force in each direction, it must be

* " Human Longevity", Introd., p. xi.

solely owing to our ignorance of the mode of rightly using these appliances that such is the case.   We have proof positive, indeed, of the fact that "increased attention to the organic laws has greatly reduced the rate of mortality in Europe, and it cannot be supposed that further improvement is impracticable".[*]   Con-. siderable changes have accordingly taken place in the average duration of life in England during the last hundred years.   At the early part of this period it was twenty-eight years.   According to more recent tables it was thirty-two years ; and it has been calculated that it may fairly be expected to extend to forty years.[†]   From the tables of the average duration of life in Geneva during the last two hundred and sixty years, it appears that while from 1560 to 1600 the average was only eighteen years, from 1815 to 1826 it was nearly thirty-nine years.[‡]

Nevertheless, admitting all this, I must beg to suggest that it is clearly erroneous to contend that the increased average in the duration of human life affords any actual proof of increased longevity.   All that it proves is, not that men are longer-lived than they used to be, but that owing to increased attention to sanitary laws, they are less frequently cut off by diseases resulting from the neglect of sanitary precautions.   It is very possible, indeed, for mortality in a particular district to be very great, owing to the neglect of sanitary laws, and yet in the same district for remarkable instances of longevity to be found.

The entire question, therefore, resolves itself into the following simple points, the satisfactory solution of which will decide the whole matter at issue : 1. Are the statements which have been made to us by historians and naturalists as to the extraordinary longevity of the patriarchs, and other early inhabitants of the earth, as also of animals of a certain species, both in ancient and modern times, entitled to our credit ? 2. Are the causes which have been assigned as occasioning the extraordinary longevity in question, such as may be reasonably supposed to have been productive of it ? 3. Are these causes controllable in any way, and is it possible by any resort to artificial appliances extensively to increase or diminish longevity in the case of either man or animals ?

----

* Combe's "Principles of Physiology", p. 387.
† Combe, "On the Constitution of Man", p. 234.
‡ Appendix to Combe "On the Constitution of Man", p. 434.

9

Reprinted from *J. Nat. Assn. Promot. Soc. Sci.* 498–504 (1857)

ON THE EVIDENCE OF THE PROLONGATION OF LIFE DURING THE EIGHTEENTH CENTURY

Southwood Smith

WE possess a record which demonstrates the fact that a very remarkable increase in the duration of life took place in this country in the course of the eighteenth century. This record relates, it is true, only to a particular class, and that in some degree a select one; but slight consideration will show that selection in this instance cannot count for much, and that the inference is inevitable that a similar prolongation of life has occurred in the population generally.

In the year 1693, and again in the year 1790, the interval being exactly a century short of three years, a loan was raised for the service of the State; the first by King William and Mary, the second by Mr. Pitt. This loan was effected by the method of Tontine.* The

---

* Objections have been taken to these Tontines as a standard of comparison :—
  1. That they are select lives.
  2. That the numbers are too small.
  3. That there is a discrepancy between the death-rates of the two sexes.
It is replied—
  1. The selection is the same for both Tontines.
  2. The smallness of the number is to all intents and purposes compensated by the accuracy and completeness of each individual fact. No actuary would make such an objection. Mark the data on which he relies in other instances. The well-known Carlisle Tables are founded on the deaths recorded in the parish registers of that town during the eight years which succeeded the extinction of the first Tontine (1779). The real ages of the deaths so stated can hardly be deemed authentic in any case. Omitting those under the age of 5, the deaths were :— males, 464; females, 564; total at all ages above 4, 1028   In the Tontine the deaths of the males are 594; females, 408; total, 1002. But here the ages are vouched on oath at admission, and the age at death is known by the cessation of the annuity. The law of mortality is simply the relation between the living and the dead at each age. Now, to compare the dead with the living at each age, we must have the correct number of the living as well as of the dead at each such age. To do this at Carlisle, Dr. Heysham went round, in 1780, and asked at each house the ages of the inmates. He did the same in 1787. In this first census there were—males, 2817; females, 3482. In the second—males, 3864; females, 4813. Does any one believe that these people would state their exact age of their own free will to oblige Dr. Heysham ? There are some hundreds of life assurance and annuity institutions whose recorded deaths are very much fewer than those of either of the above observations, and yet they have the means of knowing at what rate their mortality advances. But voluntary statements of age are never to be relied on, whether in a single town or among a whole nation.
  3. As to the discrepancy between the death-rates of the two sexes, Mr. Finlaison was the first to discover not only a diminishing rate of mortality with regard to the female, but also to show that this apparent discrepancy in the mortality of the sexes is a natural law, and that at all times, and under all circumstances, there is, after the age of ten, a discrepancy steadily increasing with advancing age in favour of the female. It has been said, that if the Tontine results are true there must have been, at the periods referred to, circumstances *unknown* to the present age, which made *that large difference* between the death-rates of the sexes. On the contrary, those circumstances are well-known to the present age. At that stage of civilization the male was pre-eminently exposed to causes which shorten life, from which the female was comparatively exempt. One of the most obvious was the

---

term Tontine is derived from the name of the originator of this scheme of life annuity, the principle of which is this: The person who advances 100*l*. is at liberty to name any life he pleases, during the existence of which he draws a certain annuity. The shares of the dead nominees are distributed among the living ones, and consequently the value of the annuity continually increases until the last survivor gets the whole income.

In this case there is obviously the strongest inducement that the shareholder should carefully select from among the youngest infants within his reach the very healthiest he can find. Practically, however, this power of selection is, as has just been stated, restricted within narrow limits. The shareholder cannot draw his annuity without proof of the existence of his nominee at the time; and he cannot easily keep sight of a child grown up and sent out into the world, unless it be his own or that of a relative.

Nevertheless, it is still true that the nominees of a Tontine are collectively a select class. They are the children of such wealthy persons as are able to lend money to the State. In the expectation of life they have clearly some advantages over their contemporaries, especially over the large class of the labouring poor.

When, however, we compare the fate of the nominees of one Tontine with that of the nominees of another (and the peculiar value of the record in question is that it gives us the means of making such a comparison), it is evident that the circumstances of the parties in each Tontine are precisely the same. A comparison of the experience of two Tontines gives us, then, the exact measure of the effect produced on the duration of life by such changes in the social condition of these people as may have occurred in the interval between the respective Tontines.

The Tontine of 1690 (3) consisted of 408 females and 594 males; that of 1790, of 3974 females and 4197 males. These are not large numbers, but the age of each individual, on nomination, was verified on oath, and the Government would take care to ascertain the period of death in each case, because then the annuity ceases; and actuaries

---

necessity imposed upon the male, by the exigencies and habits of the time, of seeking a position in life often in maritime and colonial adventures, and in the army and navy. But, besides all this, of the males who remained at home it is too true that in very many cases they spent their days in quarrels, brawls, and fights- their nights in gorging highly stimulating food, and in drinking to excess intoxicating liquors whenever they could compass the means of doing either, or both. In those days it was hardly deemed reputable for any man to go to bed sober who had the means of going to bed in a state of intoxication. So general was this mode of living, that it made England a bye-word for gluttony and intemperance among all the nations of the world. Dr. Caius, one of the founders of the London College of Physicians, coupling Germany and the Netherlands in this common reproach, says:—'These three nations destroy more meats and drynkes without all order, convenient time, reason and necessitie, than all other nations under the son, to the great annoyance of their bodies and wittes.' Now, this mode of living shortened life—1, by powerfully predisposing to disease; 2, by giving to all diseases either a highly inflammatory or a highly putrescent character; and 3, by producing directly positive organic disease in the main organs of the nutritive system, and in the excretories of that system.

are agreed that a small number of facts, complete in themselves, afford a reliable basis for reasoning and induction.

It must be further borne in mind that the Tontine of 1790, known as Mr. Pitt's Great Tontine, is not yet extinct. Far from it; for on the 1st of January, 1851, there remained alive 1312 females out of the original 3974; and 977 males out of the original 4197. They were alive at all ages from a little above 60 and upwards; so that the difference between the mortality of the nominees of 1690 and that which (as is about to be shown) has already occurred to those of 1790, is not so great as it will ultimately prove to be.

On the data afforded by these Tontines, Mr. Finlaison, the Government calculator, has worked out in a very elaborate manner the means of making a comparison between them. His paper is full of interest. It displays the ground on which we may safely rest our faith in one of the most cheering promises of modern civilization. The following are among some of the more important results.

That a prolongation of life took place in the interval between the seventeenth and eighteenth centuries is proved by this observation in two ways,—first, by the difference in the death-rate at the two periods; and, secondly, by the actual addition of an ascertained number of years to the life of each individual at the latter period.

The differences between the death-rates are shown in the following way. The arithmetical conclusions deducible from a careful examination of every one of the facts given in on oath as they originally stood on the record, are so presented that every man may verify them for himself; but in order to obtain a clearer perception of the relation of the numbers to each other which are thus worked out, it seemed desirable to survey them by a measure common to them all. For this purpose, it is supposed that ten thousand persons passed through each and every interval of age in the two Tontines, instead of the various numbers set forth according to the actual facts.

On this assumption, the comparative numbers of the dead stand as follows:—

Take first the female sex under the age of 28. If 10,000 deaths under that age had taken place in the Tontine of 1690, there would have died in the Tontine of 1790 only 6416.

With reference to the male sex under 28, for every 10,000 who would have died in the Tontine of 1690, there would have died in the Tontine of 1790 only 5772.

The results are worked out for the more advanced periods of life, including all ages up to 84; but for the sake of brevity I omit the details on this occasion.

On the other hand, in order to show the positive increase in the duration of life, tables have been constructed showing the comparative expectation of life in years and weeks, under each Tontine, for both sexes at every age from 90 to 4.*

---

* See Lectures on Epidemics considered with relation to Climate and Civilization, by Dr. Southwood Smith, p. 42, Appendix No. vii.

I pass on to consider the difference in the expectation of life in another point of view. Suppose it to be expressed in years and decimal fractions of a year; the facts will then stand thus:—

In the period commencing 1690, the expectations of life of a man at the age of 30 would have been 26·665; in 1790 it would have been 33·775 years. These results have been worked out for all ages, but, of course, I can only here give examples.

There is, however, still another mode of measuring the sum added to the amount of life during the eighteenth century. On a minute examination of the facts, it will be found that if to the sum of existence actually obtained by the nominees of the Tontine of 1690 we add one-fourth part of that sum, the product will express very nearly the sum actually enjoyed by the nominees of the Tontine of 1790; that is to say, a portion nearly equivalent to one-fourth of the total period of existence was added to human life in the progress of that century. Take, for example, the total existence obtained by eight persons— that is, four of each sex—at the ages of 80, 75, 70, and 65, in the Tontine of 1690. The total sum obtained was 56·935 years. Add to this sum one-fourth part of it. That will make 14·234 years. The increased sum altogether is 71·169 years. But eight persons at the same ages in the Tontine of 1790 got 68·496 years; that is, there was added to the whole term of their existence just one quarter short of 2·637 years.

In like manner, eight persons between the ages of 60, 55, 50, and 45, in the Tontine of 1790, obtain an addition to their existence of one-fourth short of three years and a fraction; but with respect to these short-comings, it must be borne in mind that many of these nominees are still living, and that before they attain the maximum of existence they will probably exceed the gain of one-fourth; as it is certain, with reference to the earlier ages, that they have already actually obtained some small excess beyond it.

Now, an increase in the length of life of a population is an expression and a measure of the sum of comfort experienced from the whole collective circumstances that make up national prosperity. In other words, it is an expression and a measure of the degree in which the individuals composing a nation have enjoyed a due supply of certain physical agents, on which our Creator has made human life dependent. These agents may be comprised under air, light, food, and warmth. What we call progress in civilization is improvement in the means of securing regularly and unfailingly, in abundance and purity, those physical agents to the bulk of the population. The accomplishment of this object is the main cause of all the activity and energy by which the state of civilization is characterized. Agriculture, architecture, commerce, manufactures, science, and art, have for their first object the supply of these first necessities of existence, by the creation, collection, and distribution of them, in the form, quantity, and quality best fitted for healthful and enjoyable life. Intellectual and moral qualities, indeed, on which we are apt to fix our attention almost exclusively, as distinguishing a high state of civilization, necessarily and rapidly follow the production and diffusion of the physical, nay, are generated and developed by the labour and training indispensable for turning the physical to use; but the existence in any high degree of the intellectual and moral must be preceded by a liberal possession and enjoyment of the physical.

It is a matter of familiar history that in this country the spirit of improvement which had been awakened in the two preceding centuries, exerted itself with extraordinary activity during the whole of the eighteenth century. Already forests had been cleared, marshes and swamps had been drained, and from the more settled government of the country, cities and towns, being no longer fortresses, had extended beyond the walls of their fortifications. But precisely at this period special attention also began to be paid to the well ordering, cleansing, and paving of towns. The narrow streets were widened, great numbers of houses were entirely taken down and rebuilt, slate being substituted for thatch and brick for timber, while the manufacture of glass was so much increased that glass windows, even in the poorer houses, became common. The general result was to render the houses more substantial and commodious, and the rooms larger, higher, lighter, warmer, and better ventilated. Agriculture took a surprising start, multiplying a hundredfold the production of fresh vegetable food, and increasing, perhaps, in a still more remarkable degree, the amount of fresh animal food, by the extension of the comparatively new art of collecting, storing, and preserving fodder for cattle in winter. The increased and successful activity of manufactures gave improved and cheap clothing to the people—clothing not only conducive to health through warmth, but almost equally so through cleanliness, for the articles of clothing now began to be composed of such tissues and textures as favour and compel frequent washing. At the same time disease in general assumed a milder form, and epidemics in particular became less frequent and far less formidable in their character.

The combined operation of these causes goes far to account for so wonderful a change in the sanitary condition of the country as must have taken place before any considerable portion of the community could have obtained a lengthened life, equivalent to a fourth of its whole term.

It is true these sanitary changes were effected without any knowledge of their sanitary nature or tendency, but they were not the less sanitary in their operation because that operation was undesigned and uncontemplated, nor because the changes in question were the pure result of the force of the onward current of civilization.

It was a notion universally received by antiquity, and not altogether repudiated in modern times, that luxury shortens life. Even now there are persons who look back with regret on the good old times—that is, the times when the greater part of England that was not forest was swamp or morass; when the dwellings were hovels without chimneys, without windows of glass, and without any kind of furniture in the modern sense of that term; when the king's chambers were furnished with straw, and that not superstitiously clean; when the personal clothing was scanty, coarse, and filthy; when the food was alike coarse and scanty, and the supply even of that most uncertain; when dearth and famine sometimes occurred every five years, and often every ten; and when the recurrence of pestilence in some fearful shape or other, in the language of Sydenham, was as regular as the return of the swallow in spring.

If the advancing civilization of the eighteenth century was accompanied by such a prolongation of life as we have seen was gained, what has been gained in the half century that followed—in the time in which we ourselves live? We cannot tell, because we have no record of definite facts to inform us. We know, indeed, that every sanitary agency that could have been in operation in the eighteenth century has acquired greater energy in the nineteenth; that several powerful sanitary influences have been superadded, and that the main conditions on which life and health depend have recently experienced an expansion and improvement to which no former age presents a parallel. We know, moreover, that Tables of Insurance constructed in the middle of the last century on the then value of life, and according to which the Public Life Annuities in this country were sold down to the year 1830, were at last peremptorily abolished by the Government, because they were proving ruinous to the revenue, and causing the loss of many millions to the country. So far the facts are positive and satisfactory; but we want more particular and definite information. We want to be able to say, 'In the first ten years of this century we gained so much; in the next ten years so much; in the next so much,' and so on. Why should we not adopt some means of procuring this information? If there be no better mode of obtaining it, why should not Government institute another Tontine, to which there seems to be no objection in principle, and which is rather a popular mode of raising a loan? No doubt the Registrar-General will tell us much in time. But he is slow, and he is pressed down by a fearful burthen. He has to bear the weight of the populous masses that form the base of the pyramid of society—masses which the wave of civilization has not yet touched, or touched only to injure—masses which still live in a state essentially the same as that which existed in the middle ages, and in which we still see the like conditions producing inexorably the like results, those results being summed up in this astounding fact, that this portion of the people actually, at this present moment, lose one-half of the term of existence which is enjoyed by their contemporaries who live in healthy localities and in healthy homes.

It will be the duty and the noble aim of this Association to remove (for it is removable) this crying disgrace to our country—to bring this unhappy class of the people within the pale of civilization. Until this is done the columns of the Registrar-General can give no fair representation of the results of sanitary improvement. But in the meantime I do think it is an object which the Association should not neglect (for it will help the progress of sanitary reform), to devise some larger means of showing how, step by step, life lengthens with the advance of civilization, as it is solely that advancement which enhances the value of life as a boon.

The conclusion, from the facts which have been stated, is one of the most encouraging the mind can conceive. From the evidence which has been adduced, it is clear that no sanitary improvement, whether designed or undesigned, can be effected without improving the physical, and, through that, the intellectual and moral condition of the people. The value of the proof of this afforded by the record to which I have called attention, which, as far as I know, is the only one of the kind we possess, it is difficult to over-estimate. But if so much has been done without plan or purpose, what may not be effected now, when, as I have just said, all the influences which have a sanitary operation are in tenfold force; when men's minds are steadily and anxiously directed to the subject; when the evils are known; when the remedies also, to a great extent, are known, and when the Public Health is rapidly assuming its place as a science ? Surely, under these circumstances, we may hope that the term of life of the very lowest class in the community, instead of being cut short by one-half as it is at present, will at least be protracted to the full extent of that enjoyed by the nominees of 1790. How far the term of life to the classes above may be extended we do not know. It is clear, however, that to the prolongation of that term it is not easy, it is not possible, as yet to set a limit.

PART III

THE BROWN-SÉQUARD REPORTS AND REACTIONS: REPLACEMENT THERAPY IN NINETEENTH CENTURY GERIATRICS

Editor's Comments
on Papers 10 Through 15

The "father of endocrinology" is almost as well known as a gerontologist because of his graphic descriptions of the reinvigoration (he said it was not rejuvenation) of old men by testicular extracts. In his classic communication of June 1, 1889 to the French Society of Biology, on "Effects of subcutaneous injections of guinea pig and dog testicular extracts in man," he draws an analogy between the person castrated in infancy or adolescence and old men. Eunuchs are notably weak both mentally and physically according to Brown-Séquard, who said that abstinence from coitus or masturbation deprives the body of some principle which energizes the nervous and probably also the muscular system. To him, weakness of elderly males was traceable to failure of gonadal function. The four papers and two comments (Papers 10–15) are translated by me and also reproduced in their original language. They represent a unit essential to get the entire research presentation and worldwide response. An English language paper by Dr. Brown-Séquard is reproduced as Paper 1 in C. S. Carter (ed.), *Hormones and Sexual Behavior*, Benchmark Papers in Animal Behavior, vol. 1.

Although endocrinologists have questioned that any androgenically active principle could have been present in the aqueous extracts injected, gerontologist are impressed with Brown-Séquard's descriptions of the ability to reverse complaints of the elderly. His tenacity and ability to give excitingly vivid descriptions of his experiments have stimulated many others to seek ways to alleviate some of the distress occurring during the later years of life. One is impressed with his methodological approach in performing these experiments upon himself.

Regarding the question of active principles in the fluids injected, this writer believes that because hardly any water was added in his early experiments, some active androgen complexed to protein may have been injected. (Admittedly this procedure would not give a highly potent androgen preparation.) Additionally, histamine and other biogenic amines, either present in the materials injected or endogenously released due to the foreign macromolecules injected, I believe accounted for some of the reported effects, as is inferred also in the papers. But even if, as some believe, Brown-Séquard had completely deluded himself in these experiments, the president of the French Biological Society was an effective advocate of geriatric therapy.

Reprinted from *C. R. Seances Soc. Biol.*, Ser 9. **1**:415–419 (1889)

DES EFFETS PRODUITS CHEZ L'HOMME PAR DES INJECTIONS SOUS-CUTANÉES D'UN LIQUIDE RETIRÉ DES TESTICULES FRAIS DE COBAYE ET DE CHIEN

C. E. Brown-Séquard

On sait que la castration faite dans l'enfance ou dans l'adolescence, chez l'homme, est suivie de modifications profondes de l'individu au physique et au moral. On sait, en particulier à cet égard, que les eunuques vrais sont remarquables par leur faiblesse et leur défaut d'activité physique et intellectuelle. On sait aussi que des défectuosités analogues s'observent chez les hommes qui abusent du coït ou de la masturbation. Ces faits, avec nombre d'autres, montrent clairement que les testicules fournissent au sang, soit par résorption de certaines parties du sperme, soit autrement, des principes qui donnent de l'énergie au système nerveux et probablement aussi aux muscles. J'ai toujours cru que la faiblesse des vieillards est *en partie* due à l'amoindrissement des fonctions des testicules. En 1869, dans mon cours à la Faculté de médecine, m'occupant des influences que les glandes peuvent exercer sur les centres nerveux, j'ai émis l'idée que, s'il était possible d'injecter sans danger du sperme dans les veines des vieillards du sexe masculin, on pourrait obtenir chez eux des manifestations de rajeunissement, à l'égard à la fois du travail intellectuel et des puissances physiques de l'organisme. Guidé par cette idée, j'ai fait en 1875, à Nahant, près de Boston (États-Unis), un grand nombre d'expériences, parmi lesquelles une douzaine sur de vieux chiens sur lesquels j'ai essayé vainement, excepté une fois, de greffer de jeunes cobayes entiers ou des parties de cobaye. Le succès que j'ai obtenu dans un seul cas avait donné tout ce que je pouvais espérer d'expériences de cette espèce, c'est-à-dire une confirmation des vues auxquelles j'avais été rationnellement conduit; mais les procédés expérimentaux étaient tels que tout essai de ce genre sur l'homme était impossible.

Depuis quelques années, j'ai conçu un autre mode de recherches; mais je n'ai pu commencer à en faire l'essai qu'il y a cinq ou six mois. Des expériences faites à cette époque sur de vieux lapins, ayant bien démontré, d'une part, l'innocuité du procédé et, d'une autre, l'importance de son emploi, je me suis décidé à faire sur moi-même des recherches qui me paraissaient devoir être, à tous égards, bien plus décisives que celles faites sur des animaux.

I. *Exposé du procédé expérimental employé.* — Ce procédé consiste en injections sous-cutanées d'un liquide obtenu par le broiement de testicules de chien ou de cobaye, avec l'addition d'un peu d'eau (de 2 à 3 centimètres cubes par testicule). Ce liquide provenait de trois sources : du sang des veines testiculaires, liées avant l'extirpation de la glande, du tissu propre des testicules et du sperme contenu dans ces organes et dans leurs canaux excréteurs. Il est bon d'ajouter qu'une fois j'ai mêlé au testicule d'un cobaye une portion des substances semi-fluides contenues dans les vésicules séminales. Le liquide recueilli n'a été employé qu'après filtration tantôt à travers un filtre en papier, tantôt à travers le filtre Pasteur.

Les injections, au nombre de huit jusqu'aujourd'hui (1er juin), ont été faites les 15, 16, 17, 24, 29 et 30 mai dernier. La quantité moyenne de liquide par injection a été d'un centimètre cube environ, c'est-à-dire le cinquième ou le quart de ce qui était fourni par un testicule après addition d'eau. Les trois premières injections ont été faites avec du liquide obtenu d'un testicule de chien de deux à trois ans, extrêmement vigoureux ; les autres avec du liquide provenant des testicules de plusieurs cobayes très jeunes ou adultes. Il me semble certain que le liquide testiculaire du chien a été plus efficace que celui fourni par les cobayes, bien que le maximum des effets favorables ait été atteint le lendemain de l'emploi du liquide provenant des testicules d'un très jeune cobaye.

Avant de faire ces essais sur moi-même, j'avais, — je n'ai guère besoin de le dire, — tout lieu de croire à l'innocuité du liquide que j'allais employer. En effet, en outre des expériences dont j'ai parlé, M. d'Arsonval avait fait, à ma prière, une vingtaine d'injections sous-cutanées de liquide testiculaire, chez un très vieux chien, qui n'a jamais paru en souffrir d'une manière quelconque. Mais, quoi qu'il en soit à l'égard des expériences sur des animaux, j'ai reconnu, dès après le premier essai que j'ai fait sur ma personne, que, si l'injection du liquide dont je m'occupe est sans danger à beaucoup d'égards, elle peut, au moins, donner lieu à des troubles locaux et à des douleurs d'une extrême intensité. Au moment de l'injection, la douleur est légère et ne diffère guère de celle qu'occasionne, le plus souvent, l'emploi de l'atropine, de la strychnine ou de la morphine en injections sous-cutanées. Cette douleur cesse, en général, au bout de quelques minutes ou d'un quart d'heure au plus, mais elle revient bientôt et son intensité croît rapidement. Son degré maximum, acquis au bout d'une ou deux heures, persiste de cinq à douze heures ou même plus. C'est une sensation semblable à celle que donnerait une plaie assez étendue, avec un sentiment quelquefois très vif de cuisson. Dans une zone

69

de peau qui est quadruple de celle qui recouvre le liquide injecté, on constate, avant l'absorption de celui-ci, un peu de gonflement et une rougeur diffuse, érythémateuse, avec des stries d'angioleucite. Après une diminution très considérable, la douleur peut persister assez longtemps. Une des parties injectées est encore un peu douloureuse aujourd'hui (1er juin), sept jours après l'injection (1).

Deux injections ont été faites au bras gauche; les autres aux membres inférieurs. La douleur a été bien moins vive au bras qu'aux jambes et à la cuisse.

II. *Des effets produits par les injections sous-cutanées de liquide testiculaire.* — J'ai soixante-douze ans, depuis le 8 avril dernier. Ma vigueur générale, qui a été considérable, a diminué notablement et graduellement durant les dix ou douze dernières années. Avant les expériences dont je m'occupe, il me fallait m'asseoir après une demi-heure de travail debout, au laboratoire. Après trois ou quatre heures et même quelquefois après deux heures seulement de travail expérimental, au laboratoire, bien que je m'y tinsse assis, j'en sortais épuisé. En rentrant chez moi, en voiture, vers six heures du soir, après quelques heures ainsi passées au laboratoire, j'étais, depuis nombre d'années, tellement fatigué qu'il me fallait me mettre au lit presque aussitôt après un repas pris hâtivement. Quelquefois, l'épuisement était tel que, malgré le besoin de sommeil et une somnolence qui m'empêchait même de lire des journaux, je ne pouvais m'endormir qu'après plusieurs heures.

Aujourd'hui et depuis le second jour et surtout le troisième après la première injection, tout cela a changé et j'ai regagné au moins toute la force que je possédais il y a nombre d'années. Le travail expérimental, au laboratoire, me fatigue fort peu maintenant. J'ai pu, au grand étonnement de mes assistants, y rester debout pendant des heures entières, sans ressentir le besoin de m'asseoir. Il y a quelques jours, après trois heures et un quart de travail expérimental debout, j'ai pu, contrairement à mes habitudes depuis plus de vingt ans, travailler à la rédaction d'un mémoire, pendant plus d'une heure et demie, après le dîner. Tous mes amis savent quel changement immense cela implique chez moi (2).

Je puis aussi maintenant sans difficulté, et même sans y penser, monter

_____

(1) Le mardi, 4 juin, j'ai pu dire, dans un manuscrit remis à la *Gazette hebdomadaire de médecine* (numéro du 7 juin, p. 363), que deux parties, ayant reçu des injections, sont encore un peu douloureuses, dix jours pour l'une, cinq jours pour l'autre après l'injection.

(2) Mes amis savent que, depuis un très grand nombre d'années, le travail après le dîner m'était impossible et que j'avais l'habitude de me coucher vers sept heures et demie ou huit heures du soir, et de me mettre au travail le matin, entre trois et quatre heures.

et descendre des escaliers presque en courant, ce que j'avais toujours fait jusqu'à l'âge de soixante ans. Au dynamomètre, je constate une augmentation incontestable de la force des membres. A l'avant-bras, en particulier, je trouve que la moyenne des essais postérieurs aux deux premières injections est supérieure de 6 à 7 kilogrammes à la moyenne antérieure aux injections.

J'ai pris comparativement, avant et après la première injection, la mesure du jet de l'urine, quant à la longueur du chemin qu'il parcourait pour atteindre la cuvette d'un water-closet, et j'ai trouvé que la moyenne de cette longueur, pendant les dix jours qui ont précédé l'injection, était inférieure d'au moins un quart à ce qu'elle est devenue depuis les deux premières injections. Ces expériences comparatives ont été faites après un repas qui a toujours consisté en aliments et en boisson de même quantité et de même espèce.

On sait combien les vieillards souffrent de la faiblesse des contractions du rectum. L'expulsion des matières fécales était devenue chez moi, depuis une dizaine d'années, extrèmement laborieuse et elle était même presque impossible, sans l'emploi de purgatifs ou de moyens artificiels. Je faisais usage régulièrement de laxatifs, moins contre la constipation, qui n'était que rarement très considérable, que pour augmenter l'action motrice des parois intestinales. Dans les quinze jours qui ont suivi jusqu'ici la première injection, un changement radical est survenu dans l'acte réflexe de la défécation : d'une part, j'ai eu bien moins besoin de laxatifs et, d'une autre part, l'expulsion des matières fécales, même grosses et assez dures, a pu se faire sans assistance mécanique et sans lavement. Ce retour à l'état normal d'il y a nombre d'années est, avec le fait de la puissance de me tenir debout pendant plus de trois heures, sans fatigue notable et sans avoir le besoin de m'asseoir, ce qui prouve le mieux l'amélioration de l'état de ma moelle épinière.

J'ajoute que le travail intellectuel m'est devenu plus facile qu'il n'a été depuis plusieurs années et que j'ai regagné, à cet égard, tout ce que j'avais perdu. Je puis dire aussi que d'autres forces qui n'étaient pas perdues, mais qui étaient diminuées, se sont notablement améliorées.

J'espère que d'autres physiologistes, d'un âge avancé, répéteront ces expériences et montreront si les effets que j'ai obtenus sur moi-même dépendent ou non de mon idiosyncrasie personnelle. Quant à la question de savoir si c'est à une sorte d'auto-suggestion, sans hypnotisation, qu'il faille attribuer entièrement les changements si considérables qui se sont produits dans mon organisme, je ne veux pas l'examiner aujourd'hui. L'ouvrage si intéressant du Dr Hack Tuke (1) est plein de faits montrant que la plupart des changements que j'ai observés chez moi, après les

(1) *Illustrations of the influence of the mind upon the body.* Second edition. London, 1884. 2 vol. Cet ouvrage, traduit en français, a été publié à Paris.

injections que je me suis faites, peuvent être opérés par la seule influence d'une idée sur l'organisme humain. Je ne veux pas nier qu'en partie, au moins, ce soit de cette manière que ces changements ont eu lieu ; mais, comme ils sont survenus après l'introduction dans l'organisme de substances capables de les produire, il faut bien admettre que les injections ont tout au moins contribué à leur donner origine.

10

EFFECTS IN MAN OF SUBCUTANEOUS INJECTIONS OF FRESHLY PREPARED LIQUID FROM GUINEA PIG AND DOG TESTES

C. E. Brown-Séquard

This article was translated expressly for this Benchmark volume by Geraldine M. Emerson, University of Alabama in Birmingham, from "Des effets produits chez l'homme par des injections sous-cutanées d'un liquide retiré des testicules frais de cobaye et de chien," C. R. Seances Soc. Biol., Ser. 9, 1:415–419 (1889)

It is known that castration either during infancy or adolescence of man causes profound modifications of the individual both physically and morally. It is known, in that particular regard, that true eunochs are remarkable in their feebleness and their deficit in physical and intellectual activity. It is well known that analogous defects are observed in men who abuse coitus or masturbate. These along with numerous other facts, clearly show that the testicles furnish to the blood, be it reabsorption of some substance in semen, be it otherwise, principles which give energy to the nervous system and probably also to the muscles. I have always believed that the weakness of old men is partly due to decreasing function of the testicles. In 1869, in my course at the Faculty of Medicine, I was concerned with the influences that glands can exert on neural centers. I had expressed the idea that if it were possible to inject semen without danger into the veins of old males, their rejuvenation should be possible both in intellectual work and physical effectiveness. Pursuing that idea, in 1875 at Nahant near Boston (USA) I performed a large number of experiments, among them a dozen on old dogs on whom I tried unsuccessfully, except in one case, to graft whole young guinea pigs or their parts. Success in that one case was all that I had allowed myself to hope to obtain from that type of experiment; that is to say, a confirmation of the prospects whichI had rationally predicted, but the experimental procedures had been such as to preclude any trial of that kind on man.

Several years ago, I conceived another type of research, but I was unable to do anything on them until 5 or 6 months ago. Experiments done then on old rabbits, demonstrating on the one hand the innocuousness of the procedure, and, on the other, the importance of its use, made me decide to perform upon myself studies which appeared to me ought to be, in every respect, more decisive than those on the experimental animals.

I.   Experimental procedure.   The procedure consists of subcutaneous injections of a liquid obtained by crushing dog or guinea pig testes, with the addition of a little water (2-3 cc/tesicle). The liquid comes from 3 sources: blood of the testicular veins, tied before extirpation of the gland; testicular tissue proper; and the semen contained in these organs and their excretory canals. It should be added that at one time I had mixed with guinea pig testicle a portion of the semifluid substances contained in the seminal vesicles. The liquid was used only after filtration sometimes through filter paper and sometimes through a Pasteur filter.

The injections (eight as of today, the first of June) were made the immediately past May 15, 16, 17, 24, 29 and 30. The average volume of each injection was approximately 1cc—that is to say, 1/5 or 1/4 the volume furnished by a testicle after water is added. The first 3 injections were with liquid from 2-3 year old dog testes (extremely vigorous dogs); the remaining injections were from many very young or adult guinea pig testes. I believe strongly that the injections from the dogs are more effective than those from the guinea pigs, although the greatest benefits were attained on the day after an injection containing material from a very young guinea pig.

Before undertaking these trials on myself, I scarcely need to say, I had taken every precaution to insure the innocuousness of the liquid I was going to use. In fact, besides the experiments I have spoken of, M. d'Arsonoval had done, at my request, about 20 subcutaneous injections of testicular fluid into a very old dog, who never showed any deleterious effect at all. But, however it might be on experimental animals, I recognized after the first trial on myself that if the injection of the liquid with which I had occupied myself is without danger in many regards, it can, at least, give rise to extreme pain and local soreness. At the time of the injection the pain is slight and hardly differs from that on occasion of using atropine, strychnine or morphine in subcutaneous injections. The pain subsides generally at the end of a few minutes to a little more than a quarter of an hour, but returns soon with rapid increase in intensity. Its maximum, reached in 1 or 2 hours, persists 5 to 12 hours or even more. It resembles a rather extended wound, with a sometimes rather great feeling of burning. In one area of skin, 4 times as big as that receiving the injection, one can see, before absorption a little swelling, a diffuse redness, erythematous, with stria of white cells. After a considerable diminution, the pain can persist for a very long time. One injected site is still somewhat painful today (first of June) seven days after the injection.[1]

---

[1]Tuesday, June 4th, I could state in a manuscript appearing in the GAZETTE HEBDOMADAIRE DE MÉDICINE (number of 7 June, p. 363), that the two sites having received the injections, are still a little painful, 10 days for one, 5 days for the other after the injection.

II. Effects of the subcutaneous injections of testicular sap.

I was 72 years old on last April 8. My general vigor, which had been considerable, has greatly and gradually diminished during the past 10-12 years. While performing experiments, it became necessary for me to be seated after 1/2 hour of work on foot in the laboratory. After 3-4 hours and even sometimes after only 2 hours of experimental work in the lab, although I had remained seated, I was worn out. On returning home, by carriage, toward 6 P.M., after spending several hours as stated in the laboratory, for a number of years I had had such fatigue that it was necessary for me to go to bed almost immediately after an early meal. On many occasions my weakness was so great that in spite of the need to sleep and a drowsiness which kept me from reading the journals, I could only fall asleep after several hours.

Today and since the second day--and especially the third--following my first injection all that has changed and I have at least regained the strength I had a number of years ago. My laboratory work causes very little fatigue now. I am able, to the amazement of my assistants, to remain standing whole hours without feeling the need to sit down. There were several days when after 3 1/2 hours of standing doing experimental work, I was able, contrary to my habits of 20 years, to do editing of an article for an hour and a half after dinner. All of my friends have noted this remarkable change in me.[2]

I can now without difficulty, even without thinking of it, ascend and descend stairs almost on a run, something I had always done until the age of 60. On the dynamometer, I have unquestionably increased the force of all my members. In the forearms especially, I have an average of 6-7 kilograms greater than the average prior to the first two injections.

I have made comparative measurements, before and after the first injection of the length of the path of the urine jet in reaching the toilet bowl, and I have found that for the ten days prior to injection it was about 1/4 less on the average than it became after the first two injections. These comparative experiments have been made after a meal always including the same nutrients, beverage of the same quantity and even of the same kind.

It is well known that the aged suffer from weakness of rectal contractions. Expulsion of fecal materials had become for about 10 years in me, extremely laborious and had been nearly impossible without use of purgatives or artificial means. I used laxatives regularly, less against constipation, which was only rarely considerable, but to stimulate the

---

[2]My friends know that, for a large number of years, work after dinner has been impossible for me and that I had habitually retired at 7:30 or 8:00 in the evening and that I was only able to get to work at 3 or 4:00 A.M.

motor activity of the intestinal wall. During the fifteen days following the first injection, a radical change has occurred in the reflex act of defecation: on the one side, I have had much less need of laxative and on the other, expulsion of fecal materials, even large and hard, has been possible without mechanical or lavage assistance. This return to a state normal a number of years ago is with the ability to remain standing for more than 3 hours without notable fatigue and without having to sit down, that which best proves the amelioration of my listless spinal state.

I add only that intellectual work has become much easier for me than it had been for a large number of years and that I have regained, in that regard, all that I had lost. I can add that those other powers which had not been lost but only diminished are now notably ameliorated.

I hope that other older physiologists will repeat these experiments and demonstrate whether or not these effects in me depend only on my idiosyncrasy. As to the question of determining if it is a sort of auto-suggestion, without hyponosis, to which one can attribute entirely the the considerable changes which have occurred in my body, I do not wish to examine these questions today. The interesting work of Dr. Hack Tuke[1] is full of facts showing that the majority of the changes which I have observed in myself, after the injections, can be brought about solely by suggestion in the human organism. I wish not to deny that a part at least have occurred in that manner, but since they follow the introduction into the organism of a substance capable of producing them, it must be granted that the injections have at least contributed to their origin.

---

[1]ILLUSTRATION OF THE INFLUENCE OF THE MIND UPON THE BODY. 2nd Ed. London, 1885, 2 vol. A French translation has been published in Paris.

11

Reprinted from *C. R. Seances Soc. Biol.*, Ser. 9, **1**:419 (1889)

REMARQUES AU SUJET DE LA COMMUNICATION DE M. BROWN-SÉQUARD

Dumontpallier

Certes, les résultats constatés par M. Brown-Séquard à la suite d'injections sous-cutanées d'un liquide spécial qui tiendrait en suspension des éléments spermatiques offrent un très grand intérêt, et, si les mêmes résultats, dans les mêmes conditions expérimentales, sont constatés de nouveau par d'autres expérimentateurs sur les mammifères et sur l'homme, notre savant Président aura ajouté une découverte très importante aux découvertes considérables que lui doivent la médecine et la physiologie.

Mais, tout en admettant que la plus grande part des résultats obtenus par M. Brown-Séquard soit due à la nature spéciale du liquide injecté sous la peau, qu'il me soit permis de mentionner que les injections sous-cutanées d'éther sulfurique et des irritations traumatiques m'ont permis de rappeler à la vie des malades dont l'existence était gravement menacée, et que la survie a été de sept jours dans une observation et de plusieurs années dans une seconde observation, bien que dans l'un et l'autre cas les lésions organiques existantes dussent fatalement avoir pour conséquence, prochaine ou éloignée, la mort. — M. Brown-Séquard, mieux que personne, sait que les irritations périphériques vulgaires, plus ou moins répétées, irritations non inflammatoires, dans un grand nombre d'expériences physiologiques ou thérapeutiques, déterminent souvent des phénomènes dynamogéniques qui se traduisent par le réveil plus ou moins durable des principales fonctions. — En conséquence, une certaine part des résultats dans les expériences de M. Brown-Séquard ne pourrait-elle pas être rapportée à l'irritation du système nerveux périphérique ? — Quoi qu'il en soit de la valeur de ces remarques, elles ne sauraient diminuer en rien l'importance des expériences de notre savant Président.

11

REMARKS ON THE COMMUNICATION OF M. BROWN-SÉQUARD

Dumontpallier

This article was translated expressly for this Benchmark volume by Geraldine M. Emerson, University of Alabama in Birmingham, from "Remarques au sujet de la communication de M. Brown-Séquard," C. R. Seances Soc. Biol., Ser. 9, 1:419 (1889)

Certainly the effects following subcutaneous injections of a special fluid having the spermatic (testicular) elements in suspension is extremely interesting and if these same results, under the same experimental conditions, are established anew by other experimenters on mammals and on man, our knowledgeable President will have added a discovery of tremendous significance to his already considerable findings in medicine and physiology.

Granting that the majority of the effects obtained by Brown-Sequard are due to the special nature of the liquid injected under the skin, permit me to mention that subcutaneous injection of sulfuric ether and traumatic pain have enabled me to recall to life invalids whose survival was gravely in doubt and that one survived 7 days and another several years. Although in both cases the existing organic lesions must end, although after an extension, in death.--M. Brown-Sequard better than anyone, knows that common peripheral irritations, more or less repeated, non-inflammatory irritations in many physiological and therapeutic experiences often show dynamic effects manifesting themselves by some degree of return of major (physiological) functions. --Therefore, is it not entirely possible that some of the results in M. Brown-Sequard's experiments are due to stimulation of the peripheral nervous system?-- Whatever be the value of these remarks, they should not diminish a whit the importance of the experiments of our learned President.

12

Reprinted from *C. R. Seances Soc. Biol.*, Ser. 9, **1**:420–422 (1889)

SECOND NOTE SUR LES EFFETS PRODUITS CHEZ L'HOMME PAR DES INJECTIONS SOUS-CUTANÉES D'UN LIQUIDE RETIRÉ DES TESTICULES FRAIS DE COBAYE ET DE CHIEN

C. E. Brown-Séquard

I. — Non seulement il n'y a pas à s'étonner que l'introduction dans le sang de principes provenant de testicules de jeunes animaux soit suivie d'une augmentation de vigueur, mais encore on devait s'attendre à obtenir ce résultat. En effet, tout montre que la puissance de la moelle épinière et aussi, mais à un moindre degré, celle du cerveau, a, chez l'homme adulte ou vieux, des fluctuations liées à l'activité fonctionnelle des testicules. Aux faits que j'ai mentionnés, à cet égard, dans la séance du 1er juin (voyez ci-dessus, p. 417), je crois devoir ajouter que les particularités suivantes ont été observées un très grand nombre de fois, pendant plusieurs années, chez deux individus âgés de quarante-cinq à cinquante ans. Sur mon conseil, chaque fois qu'ils avaient à exécuter un grand travail physique ou intellectuel, ils se mettaient dans un état de vive excitation sexuelle, en évitant cependant toute éjaculation spermatique. Les glandes testiculaires acquéraient alors temporairement une grande activité fonctionnelle, qui était bientôt suivie de l'augmentation désirée dans la puissance des centres nerveux.

II. — Depuis ma première communication, je ne me suis fait que deux injections de liquide testiculaire provenant d'un cobaye adulte très vigoureux. Les effets locaux ont été les mêmes que ceux que j'ai déjà signalés. C'est le mardi 4 juin qu'elles ont été faites. Aujourd'hui, onze jours après ces dernières injections, j'ai encore tous les bons effets obtenus depuis les premières. L'inflammation et les douleurs causées par toutes les injections a disparu depuis près d'une semaine. Il faut donc admettre que l'augmentation de puissance des centres nerveux peut durer très longtemps après la cessation des irritations locales causées par les injections. Je ne puis pas croire que la dynamogénie produite ne disparaîtra pas dans un temps assez court. Je me propose d'attendre que cette disparition ait eu lieu pour faire de nouveaux essais.

III. — Il est évident que la douleur et l'inflammation locale, dont j'ai souffert après chaque injection, pourraient être diminuées d'une manière très notable par l'emploi d'un liquide plus étendu d'eau et aussi par l'injection d'un demi-centimètre cube seulement au lieu du double. C'est ce que je me propose de faire lorsque je reviendrai à l'introduction sous la peau du liquide testiculaire. Mais avant de faire ces nouveaux essais, j'aurai à employer un autre procédé, bien qu'il me paraisse devoir être inefficace. Je veux parler de l'injection du liquide testiculaire dans l'intestin. Il est probable que je pourrai introduire dans la cavité rectale un liquide beaucoup moins irritant à cause de la quantité d'eau que je pourrai lui adjoindre. Les effets irritatifs locaux seront ainsi très notablement diminués, sinon annulés. Mais j'ai tout lieu de craindre que les principes du liquide testiculaire, qui augmentent la puissance des centres nerveux, soient modifiés par les sucs intestinaux et que les choses se passent alors comme dans l'estomac, où le travail digestif change si complètement les substances organiques qui se trouvent dans nos aliments. Je crains bien que nous soyons forcés de laisser de côté tout espoir de faire entrer dans le sang les principes actifs du liquide testiculaire, si nous n'employons pas le procédé des injections sous-cutanées.

IV. — Je n'ai pas besoin de dire que les effets produits chez moi par les injections de liquide testiculaire ne dépendent pas de changements organiques, mais de modifications nutritives ou d'effets purement dynamiques. C'est la moelle épinière surtout qui est influencée, dans toute sa longueur assurément, mais d'après toutes les apparences, un peu plus là où se trouvent les origines des nerfs des organes génitaux, de la vessie et du rectum.

V. — En répétant fréquemment et avec persévérance pendant des mois entiers des injections de liquide testiculaire, arriverai-je à changer organiquement l'état des muscles, des nerfs et des centres nerveux? Je ne possède pas de faits capables de conduire à une solution *à priori* de cette question. J'ai toujours craint et je crains encore que le travail nutritif qui produit les changements organiques que l'on sait exister depuis l'état primitif embryonnaire jusqu'à la mort par vieillesse, ne soit absolument fatal et irréversible. Mais, de même que nous voyons des muscles ayant eu, par maladie, des altérations organiques considérables, regagner quelquefois leur état normal, de même les changements organiques plus ou moins profonds qui dépendent de la vieillesse pourraient aussi disparaître, permettant ainsi à ces tissus de revenir à un état organique semblable à celui de l'âge adulte. Cela est certainement possible et il importe assurément, surtout en présence des résultats que mes expériences ont déjà donnés, de chercher à résoudre cette grande question. J'ajoute que, tout en craignant un échec, il y a lieu au moins d'espérer que les injections de liquide testiculaire arrêteraient ou diminueraient la vitesse des transformations dans la structure des tissus, liées au progrès de l'âge.

VI. — J'ai toujours professé que les glandes à conduits excréteurs ont, comme les glandes sanguines, la fonction de modifier le sang par une sorte de travail sécrétoire intérieur. Pour le rein, par exemple, alors qu'une inflammation ou d'autres maladies organiques l'ont atteint, je crois, comme je le disais dans mon cours à l'École de médecine, en 1869, que les phénomènes urémiques, si variables, qui se produisent alors, peuvent dépendre, en outre de l'élimination en quantité insuffisante de certains principes qui doivent sortir du sang, de trois facteurs, qui sont : — 1° L'absence ou l'insuffisance d'une modification chimique du sang, qui s'opère à l'état normal et qui est analogue à celle exercée sur le sang par la rate, la grande thyroïde, etc. (1) ; 2° l'existence de modifications chimiques morbides du sang, donnant à ce liquide une puissance délétère ; 3° des influences morbides, exercées par les nerfs du rein irrités, sur les centres nerveux et sur nombre d'autres organes, par action réflexe. Les testicules malades, ainsi que je l'ai observé dans des cas d'orchite ou d'autres affections de ces organes, peuvent, comme les reins, donner lieu à des phénomènes morbides dépendant de causes analogues à celles de l'urémie. Pour aujourd'hui, je n'ai à m'occuper que d'un ou de deux de ces différents points. Quand j'emploie le liquide testiculaire dans mes injections sous-cutanées, le principe actif provient-il du sperme ou de principes chimiques dépendant de modifications exercées sur le sang par le tissu glandulaire, ou d'autres principes existant dans ce tissu lui-même? Je me propose d'étudier à part (et toujours sur moi-même) l'action du sperme employé seul, celle du sang des veinules testiculaires, et enfin celle du tissu du testicule après en avoir retiré autant que possible le sperme et le sang. Il y a non seulement à chercher ce qui produit les effets d'invigoration que j'ai signalés, mais aussi ce qui produit le travail inflammatoire si pénible que toute injection de liquide testiculaire a causé chez moi jusqu'à présent.

VII.— Il est évident, *à priori*, que si les injections de liquide testiculaire réussissent, comme je l'ai constaté sur moi-même, à augmenter l'énergie des centres nerveux, chez l'homme, un succès semblable serait obtenu chez la femme, affaiblie par la vieillesse, si on lui faisait des injections des substances retirées, par écrasement, d'ovaires frais d'animaux jeunes, avec l'addition d'un peu d'eau. Je n'ai pas encore fait d'expériences sur les animaux à cet égard, et je n'engage aucune personne du sexe féminin à faire d'essais sur son propre corps avant de s'être assuré que le liquide retiré de l'ovaire peut être injecté impunément chez des femelles de chien, de lapin ou de cobaye. Je me propose de faire ces jours-ci des expériences de ce genre (2).

(1) J'ai trouvé dans ces dernières années que les capillaires de toutes les glandes sont des lieux de formation de globules sanguins.

(2) Au moment où je corrige cette épreuve, je puis dire que j'ai fait cette expérience et qu'elle ne semble pas avoir produit un mauvais effet quelconque.

12

SECOND NOTE ON THE EFFECTS PRODUCED IN MAN BY SUBCUTANEOUS INJECTIONS OF A LIQUID OBTAINED FROM FRESH GUINEA PIG AND DOG TESTICLES

C. E. Brown-Séquard

This article was translated expressly for this Benchmark volume by Geraldine M. Emerson, University of Alabama in Birmingham, from "Seconde note sur les effets produits chez l'homme par des injections sous-cutanées d'un liquide retiré des testicules frais de cobaye et de chien," C. R. Seances Soc. Biol., Ser. 9, 1:420–422 (1889)

I.   Not only should it not surprise one that the introduction in the blood of basic substances of the testicles of young animals should be followed by an increase in vigor, but also one should expect to obtain this result. In fact, everything indicates the strength which the spinal cord and also, more than minimally, the brain has in an adult or elderly man , depends on changes connected to the functional activity of the testicles.   To the facts which I mentioned in that regard during the session of June 1 (see p. 417), I believe I should add that the following particulars have been observed very often during many years, in two persons aged 45 to 50 years.   On my advice, each time they were going to perform some great physical or intellectual work, they have gotten themselves into a state of lively sexual excitement, while avoiding any spermatic ejaculation.   The testes then acquired temporarily a great functional activity, that was soon followed by the desired increase in functioning of the central nervous system.

II.   After my first report, I gave myself only two injections of the testicular fluid obtained from a very vigorous adult guinea pig.   The local effects were the same as those I have already described. It was Tuesday June 4 when I took them.   Today, 11 days after these last injections I still have all the good effects obtained after the first ones.   The inflammation and the pain caused by all the injections disappeared after nearly a week. It must be admitted that the increase in strength of the nerve centers can last quite a while after the cessation of the local irritants caused by the injections. I cannot believe the energy produced will disappear during a relative short time. I plan to wait until that disappearance takes place before making new experiments.

III. It is evident that the local pain and inflammation from which I suffered after each injection would be lessened very noticeably by using a liquid more diluted with water, and also by the injection of only 1/2 cc instead of twice that. I propose to do that when I resume subcutaneous injections of testicular liquid. However, before I make these new experiments, I will have to use another method, even if I think it must be ineffectual. I mean the injection of the liquid into the intestine. It is probable that I could introduce into the rectal cavity a much less irritrating liquid because of the amount of water I could add to it. Thus the local irritating effects will be rather notably diminished, if not negated. But I have every reason to believe that the extract of testicular liquid which increases the power of the nervous centers, might be modified by the intestinal secretions, and that things might happen there as in the stomach, where the work of digestion so completely alters the organic substance found in our food. I really believe we will be forced to discard all hope of getting the active elements into the blood if we don't use the subcutaneous procedure.

IV. I don't need to say that the effects produced in me by the injection did not depend on organic changes, but on modifications in nutrition or on purely dynamic effects. It is above all the spinal cord that is affected, certainly in all its length, but to all appearances, a little more where the nerves to the genital organs originate, and those to the bladder and rectum.

V. Repeating and perservering for months with the injections, will I succeed in changing organically the state of the muscles, the nerves, and the nerve centers? I have no facts leading to an a _priori_ solution to that question. I have always believed, and I still believe that the _nutritional work_ which produces the organic changes known to exist from the primitive embryo until death by aging are not absolutely fatal and irreversible. However, just as we see muscles having become, by illness, considerably altered, regain their normal condition sometimes, so the more or less serious organic changes consequent to age could also disappear, thus letting these tissues revert to an organic state similar to that of adulthood. This is certainly possible, and it indicates surely, especially in the results of my experiments. A search to resolve this big question. I add that, while fearing setback, there is reason to hope that these injections would stop or diminish the speed of structural changes in tissue connected with aging.

VI. I have always claimed that the glands with exterior ducts have, like the "blood glands" the function of modifying the blood by a sort of internal secretion. In the kidney, for example, when an inflammation or other organic malady has attacked it, I believe, as I was saying in my course at the medical school, in 1869, that the urine specimens, so variable, which are produced then, can depend, besides the elimination in insufficient quantity of certain elements that should come from the blood, on three factors, which are.

—1. The absence or insufficiency of a chemical modification of blood, which is operative in the normal state and which is analogous to that effected on the blood by the thyroid gland, etc.[1]; 2. the existence of pathological chemical changes of blood, causing deleterious effects; 3. pathological influences, caused by the nerves of the irritated kidney on the nervous centers and on a number of other organs, by reflex action. Damaged testicles, such as I have observed in the case of orchitis or other maladies of these organs, can, as in the kidneys, give rise to morbid symptoms due to causes analogous to those of uremia. Today, I need only mention one or two of these points. When I use this liquid in my injections, does the active principle come from the sperm or from chemical substances caused by changes made on blood by glandular tissue, or from other substances existing in the tissue itself? I plan to study separately, (and always on myself) the action of sperm used alone, that of blood from veins of the testes, and finally that of tissue, free as far as possible from semen and blood. It is not only necessary to seek what produces the effects of invigoration which I have noticed, but also what produces the painful inflammatory trouble which every injection has caused me up to now.

VII. First, it is evident that if the injections succeed, as I have proved on myself, in increasing the energy of the nervous centers in males, a similar success would be obtained in females, weakened by age, if one gave injections of substances derived, by crushing, or fresh ovaries from young animals, with the addition of a little water. I have not yet done experiments with animals in this regard, and I have not found a person of the feminine sex to try it on herself without being assûred that the liquid can be injected safely into female dogs, rabbits, or guinea pigs. I plan to do such experiments soon.[2]

---

[1] I have found recently that the capillaries of all the glands are the site of secretions to the blood.

[2] As I correct this proof, I can say that I have made this experiment, and there seem to be no ill effects whatever.

13

Reprinted from *C. R. Seances Soc. Biol.*, Ser. 9, **1**:429–430 (1889)

CORRESPONDANCE IMPRIMÉE. REMARQUES DE M. BROWN-SÉQUARD A L'EGARD DE LA RÉCLAMATION DE M. CONAN

C. E. Brown-Séquard

Le Dr Conan, auteur d'un traité d'homo-homœopathie, écrit au Président pour revendiquer la priorité au sujet de l'emploi que M. Brown-Séquard a fait récemment d'un liquide retiré de testicules de cobaye et de chien.

M. Conan dit que, dans ce traité, il a établi une méthode générale de traitement, consistant à donner à l'homme, ayant un organe malade, des parties du même organe prises sur un mouton. Ainsi, à la page 172 de cet ouvrage, il donne une liste de médicaments à employer mêlés avec des morceaux de rein, de vessie, de verge et de testicule dans les cas de maladie des organes génito-urinaires.

REMARQUES DE M. BROWN-SÉQUARD A L'ÉGARD DE LA RÉCLAMATION
DE M. CONAN.

Je ne crois pas avoir besoin de donner beaucoup de raisons pour montrer que je n'ai en rien essayé de faire ce que M. Conan croit avoir fait, et que, conséquemment, sa revendication porte à faux.

En premier lieu, M. Conan ne s'est occupé que de modes de traitement de maladies. Mes communications à la Société n'ont eu pour objet aucune maladie, et je n'ai eu en vue que les changements causés chez l'homme par la vieillesse et les effets produits par les injections sous-cutanées d'un certain liquide chez un vieillard en bonne santé, à part du

85

rhumatisme et du mérycisme. Il va sans dire que M. Conan, ne s'occupant que de thérapeutique, n'a pas signalé la production des effets physiologiques si remarquables que j'ai fait connaître. De plus, il a fait usage de tout autre chose que ce qui peut être actif dans le testicule, comme le montre sa manière de traiter les différentes parties de l'organisme des moutons qu'il emploie comme médicaments. Il détruit toutes les propriétés organiques de ces parties avant de s'en servir. En effet, *pendant six jours il les soumet à la dessiccation dans une étuve chauffée à* 70° !! Après cela, personne ne trouvera que ce que j'ai fait ressemble en quoi que ce soit à ce qu'a fait le médecin homœopathe auquel je réponds.

M. le Dr GIMBERT (de Cannes) fait hommage à la Société d'un exemplaire de son mémoire sur un *système spécial d'injection hypodermique de certains médicaments irritants ou caustiques.*

13

PRINTED CORRESPONDENCE AND COMMENTS

C. E. Brown-Séquard

This article was translated expressly for this Benchmark volume by Geraldine M. Emerson, University of Alabama in Birmingham, from "Correspondance imprimée. Remarques de M. Brown-Séquard a l'egard de la réclamation de M. Conan," C. R. Seances Soc. Biol., Ser. 9, 1:429–430 (1889)

Dr. Conan, author of a treatise on homologous homeopathy, wrote to the president (Brown-Sequard) to demand <u>priority</u> in the use which M. Brown-Sequard recently made of a liquid derived from the testicles of dogs and guinea pigs.

M. Conan said that, in his teatise, he had established a general method of treatment, consisting of giving to a man with a damaged organ, parts of the same organ taken from a sheep. Thus, on page 173 of that work, he gives a list of medicaments to use mixed with bits of kidney, bladder, penis, and testicle in the case of malady of the genito-urinary organs.

<u>Remarks of M. Brown-Séquard in regard to the claim of Dr. Conan:</u>
I don't believe I need give many reasons to show that I did not try to do at all what M. Conan believes he has done, and that, consequently, his demand is in error.

In the first place, M. Conan is occupied only with methods of treating illnesses. My communications to the Society have had the object not illness; I have had in mind only the changes caused in man by age and the effects produced by subcutaneous injections of a certain liquid in an old man of good health [aside from rheumatism and merycisme (chewing of regurgitated food)]. It goes without saying that M. Conan was occupied only with therapeutic results, and did not report the production of physiological effects as remarkable as I have made known. Moreover, he has made use of many other things than those which can be active in the testicle, as is shown by his manner of treating the different organs of the sheep that he used as medicines. He destroyed all the organic properties of these parts before using them. In fact, for six days he subjected them to desiccation in a stove at 70°!! After that, no one will find that what I did resembles in any way that which the homeopathic doctor did.

Dr. Gimbert (from Cannes) presents the Society with a complimentary copy of his memoir on a <u>special sytem of hypodermic injection of certain irritating or caustic substances.</u>

14

Reprinted from *C. R. Seances Soc. Biol.*, Ser. 9, **1**:430–431 (1889)

TROISIÈME NOTE SUR LES EFFETS DES INJECTIONS SOUS-CUTANEES DE LIQUIDE TESTICULAIRE

C. E. Brown-Séquard

I. — Depuis le 4 de ce mois (il y a seize jours) je ne me suis pas fait d'injection. Les bons effets que j'ai signalés dans mes deux précédentes communications continuent, *sans diminution marquée*, ce qui montre bien qu'ils n'ont pas été produits, comme l'a cru un des membres de la Société, par des irritations de la peau, celles-ci ayant cessé complètement depuis au moins une dizaine de jours, les dernières injections n'en ayant pas causé de durables. J'ai lieu de croire, cependant, que l'influence exercée sur la moelle dorso-lombaire va diminuer, car le jet de l'urine est un peu moins énergique et il me semble aussi que la défécation n'a pas la même vigueur. Par contre, certains bons effets paraissent indiquer un peu plus de force. J'ai pu, en particulier, travailler à la rédaction de mémoires, pendant trois heures après mon dîner, ce que je n'avais pu faire depuis plus de douze ou quinze ans.

II. — Ce ne sont pas seulement les effets d'une diminution ou d'une cessation de l'influence du testicule qui démontrent combien cette influence est considérable; ce sont aussi les effets d'une augmentation considérable de cette influence, lorsque le sperme s'accumule dans l'organe qui le sécrète. Dans le premier cas, il y a anémie spermatique; dans le second, il y a pléthore. Les gens trop continents sont sous l'influence d'une excitation générale, quelquefois très considérable. De même qu'il suffit d'un temps très court pour que cet état d'excitation disparaisse (après un seul coït quelquefois), de même il peut suffire d'une nuit sans pollution et malgré une insomnie absolue, pour qu'un individu ayant des pertes séminales nocturnes constate que sa force diminuée lui est revenue (1). Ces faits montrent que les testicules, en outre de leur rôle dans la génération, ont une fonction dynamogénique de la plus haute importance chez l'homme. La faiblesse, chez les vieillards, dépend de deux causes : des changements organiques et l'absence de la stimulation exercée sur les centres nerveux par des testicules actifs. Je dois le répéter : l'idée qui m'a conduit dans mes expériences est que les injections que j'ai faites remplaceraient l'inefficacité de testicules peu actifs ou inactifs. J'ai tout lieu de croire que, si d'autres personnes réussissent chez elles-mêmes à obtenir les résultats favorables que j'observe sur moi, on trouverait un palliatif considérable contre les mauvais effets des pertes séminales par des injections de liqueur testiculaire des mammifères.

III. — Il est incontestable que les physiologistes et les médecins, qui voudraient répéter mes expériences sur eux-mêmes, pourraient se mettre à l'abri de la douleur en employant simultanément, avec le liquide testiculaire, de la cocaïne. Je crois qu'on éviterait le travail inflammatoire de la peau si, au lieu d'une injection d'une quantité trop considérable, comme celle que j'ai employée, on divisait celle-ci de façon à en injecter en un point le dixième seulement et en se faisant, dans une même journée, dix injections au lieu d'une, avec l'addition d'un peu d'eau distillée.

14

THIRD NOTE ON EFFECTS OF INJECTING
TESTICULAR LIQUID

C. E. Brown-Séquard

This article was translated expressly for this Benchmark volume by Geraldine M. Emerson, University of Alabama in Birmingham, from "Troisième note sur les effets des injections sous-cutanées de liquide testiculaire," C. R. Seances Soc. Biol., Ser. 9, 1:430–431 (1889)

I.   Since the 4th of this month (16 days ago) I have had no injection. The good effects which I reported in my two previous papers continues, without marked diminution, which probably shows that they were not produced, as one member of the society believed, by irritation of the skin (those having ceased completely after about 12 days); the last injections not having caused such lasting irritation. I have grounds to believe, however, that the influence on the dorso-lumbar part of the spine is going to diminish, because the jet or urine is a little weaker, and it seems to me also that defecation is less vigorous. On the other hand, certain good effects appear to show a little more strength. I have been able, particularly, to work on the writing or editing of papers for 3 hours after dinner, which I had not been able to do for more than 12 or 15 years.

II.   It is not only the effects of a decrease or cessation of the influence of the testicle which show how great this influence is; there are also the effects of a considerable increase in this influence, when semen accumulates in the organ which secretes it. In the first case, there is a lack of semen; in the second, too much. Very continent people are under the influence of a general excitation, sometimes quite considerable. Just as this state of excitation can disappear in a very short time (sometimes after a single act of coitus), so one night without "pollution," and in spite of complete insomnia, can enable an individual who has had nocturnal seminal emission to claim that his lessening of strength has reversed itself.[1]

---

[1]See Lallemand, Des pertes séminales involontaires. Paris 1836, Vol. 1, page 451.

These facts show that the testicles, besides their role of generation, have a dynamic function of greatest importance in man. Weakness in the old comes from two causes: organic changes and the absence of the stimulation exercised on the nervous system by active testicles. I must repeat: the idea which led me to my experiments is that the injections I made would replace the ineffectiveness of testicles that were inactive or only slightly active. I have every reason to believe that, if others will succeed in obtaining on themselves the favorable results I observed, one would find considerable help against the bad effects of seminal deterioration by injection of testicular liquor from mammals.

III. It is incontrovertible that physicians and physiologists who would like to repeat my experiments on themselves, could avoid pain by using cocaine simultaneously with the testicular liquid. I believe one could avoid inflammation of the skin, if instead of injecting a rather considerable quantity, as I did, one could divide dosage so that one could inject 1/10 of it at one place and make 10 injections in one day, instead of only one, and that with the addition of a little distilled water.

Reprinted from *Arch. Physiolog. Norm. Pathol.* **1**(5):739–746 (1889)

DU ROLE PHYSIOLOGIQUE ET THÉRAPEUTIQUE D'UN SUC EXTRAIT DE TESTICULES D'ANIMAUX D'APRÈS NOMBRE DE FAITS OBSERVÉS CHEZ L'HOMME

C. E. Brown-Séquard

Depuis que les expériences que j'ai faites sur moi-même ont été publiées, la presse politique des deux mondes en a parlé sans les connaître et a malheureusement fait naître chez des milliers d'individus affaiblis par l'âge, les abus de puissance sexuelle ou les maladies, des espérances absurdes qui ont dû être promptement déçues. Aux États-Unis surtout, et souvent sans connaître ce que j'avais fait, ni les règles les plus élémentaires à l'égard d'injections sous-cutanées de matières animales, plusieurs médecins ou plutôt des médicastres et des charlatans ont exploité les désirs ardents d'un grand nombre d'individus et leur ont fait courir les plus grands risques, s'ils n'ont pas fait pis.

Je voudrais pouvoir dire quels ont été les résultats des milliers d'essais d'injection de suc testiculaire qui ont été faits en Amérique et ailleurs. Malheureusement, les principaux éléments d'une appréciation sérieuse manquent presque complètement, surtout parce que je ne connais les faits de la plupart des médecins des États-Unis que par des articles de reporters dans les journaux politiques. J'indiquerai tout à l'heure les travaux publiés par un certain nombre de médecins ; mais il importe pour pouvoir les comparer à ceux d'autres

observateurs que je fasse connaître ce qui ressort des expériences que j'ai faites sur moi-même et qui sont rapportées
dans un autre mémoire (ci-dessus, p. 651).

L'idée qui m'a conduit dans ces expériences a été que la
faiblesse des vieillards dépend, en partie, de la diminution
d'activité des glandes spermatiques. J'ai cru et je crois
encore que les faits que j'ai rapportés donnent la preuve que
la vigueur des centres nerveux et d'autres parties de l'organisme est liée avec la puissance sécrétoire des testicules.
Cela étant admis, il était tout naturel de penser qu'en donnant au sang d'un vieillard, par injections sous-cutanées, un
liquide extrait des testicules d'animaux jeunes et vigoureux,
on arriverait à suppléer à l'insuffisance de sécrétion spermatique existant chez lui. Il y avait aussi lieu de croire
que, en outre de cette influence spéciale, le liquide injecté
augmenterait aussi l'activité de sécrétion des testicules.

Il semble, d'après des faits rapportés par des médecins
sérieux, que cet effet spécial a été obtenu chez des vieillards
aussi bien que chez des hommes encore jeunes et épuisés
par des excès vénériens.

Quelques personnes ont pensé que toute l'action de certains
éléments du liquide injecté consistait en une stimulation des
centres nerveux ou d'autres parties. En vérité, il faudrait ou-
blier complètement les plus simples notions sur l'action des
agents physiques, des médicaments et des poisons sur l'organisme animal pour accepter une opinion semblable. En effet,
nous savons que deux espèces d'effets peuvent être produits
par ces agents ou substances : l'un consistant en une stimulation suivie d'une mise en jeu de la partie irritée, l'autre consistant en une augmentation ou en une diminution de puissance d'action. Dans tous les changements que j'ai signalés comme ayant eu lieu chez moi, il n'y a eu de *mise
en jeu* d'aucune puissance et, de plus, ces changements
ont duré des semaines entières (et il y en a un qui dure
encore aujourd'hui plus de trois mois et demi après la dernière injection : c'est l'amélioration de la défécation), ce qui
suffit pour démontrer absolument que la stimulation n'est pas
la cause de ces changements. Il est clair que ce qui a eu lieu

est une augmentation de puissance d'action. Ce qui reste à décider, c'est de savoir si c'est une véritable dynamogénie, c'est-à-dire un pur changement dynamique qui a eu lieu.

Quelques-uns des effets sont si prompts à se montrer qu'il semble très probable que, pour eux au moins, c'est là ce qui se produit ; mais d'autres effets sont assez lents, et il paraît certain que c'est à la suite d'un travail nutritif amélioré, c'est-à-dire d'un changement organique, que la force s'augmente dans certaines parties. Le liquide extrait des glandes sexuelles mâles agirait donc probablement en produisant dans quelques parties une pure dynamogénie, et dans d'autres en activant la nutrition. On montre une grande ignorance en soutenant que chez les vieillards un retour vers un état organique meilleur et ressemblant à celui d'un âge antérieur est impossible, puisque des changements organiques dus à une amélioration de la nutrition sont possibles à tous les âges [1].

Je ne veux pas aujourd'hui discuter la question de savoir quelles sont les substances contenues dans le liquide injecté,

[1] Des critiques de mes idées ont dit que les faits bien connus de dégénération et de dénutrition séniles opposeraient des obstacles insurmontables à toute amélioration réelle de fonction dans les centres nerveux et dans les appareils moteurs et sensitifs. L'étude de l'excellent ouvrage de Charcot sur la vieillesse (*Leçons sur les maladies des vieillards*. Paris 1868) et de nombre d'autres ouvrages montre que rien ne caractérise d'une manière absolue ou constamment la sénilité. Les vaisseaux sanguins s'altèrent (athérome, anévrysme, etc.) ; mais si c'était la vieillesse qui produisait ces altérations elles se montreraient avec beaucoup moins de variétés et sinon au même âge, au moins simultanément avec d'autres changements séniles. Or il n'en est pas ainsi : les altérations vasculaires varient d'espèce, qu'elles se montrent soit seules, soit associées, tantôt avec une espèce d'altération, tantôt avec d'autres espèces. Qu'un âge avancé soit favorable au développement de ces changements organiques, ce n'est pas douteux ; mais qu'ils soient des phénomènes apparaissant fatalement comme ceux que nous savons dépendre des âges, cela n'est évidemment pas exact, et ces altérations sont des manifestations morbides des maladies de tissus, appartenant surtout à un âge avancé.

Si les dégénérations, si les altérations séniles sont des maladies, un jour viendra où l'on pourra les guérir. Je n'ai jusqu'à présent aucun fait à mentionner qui montre que les injections de liquide testiculaire pourraient produire un changement organique favorable soit pour empêcher, soit pour retarder, et surtout pour faire disparaître ces changements morbides. Mais ce n'est pas là ce que j'ai essayé de montrer. Du reste, la question n'est certainement pas de savoir si ces injections rajeunissent (ce que je crois être impossible, ainsi que je l'ai déclaré), la question est de savoir si l'on acquiert les forces d'un âge moins avancé, et ceci me paraît certain.

auxquelles sont dus les effets des injections. Des expériences extrêmement nombreuses devront être faites pour obtenir la solution de cette question. Tout ce que je puis dire, c'est que les animalcules spermatiques, qui ont un rôle physiologique tout spécial, ne participent en rien à l'influence dynamogénique du liquide employé dans mes expériences, puisque ces particules solides ne passent pas à travers le filtre Pasteur, ce dont M. Hénocque s'est positivement assuré. Je dois dire que je connais, pour l'avoir étudié avec soin, un cas extrêmement remarquable et décisif qui démontre que les animalcules spermatiques ne sont pas la partie du liquide sécrété par les testicules qui donnent à l'homme les diverses activités physiques, morales et intellectuelles qui manquent chez les eunuques. En effet, chez un officier remarquable par sa force et ses autres qualités morales et physiques, et aussi par sa puissance sexuelle et la quantité de sperme qu'il produit, les spermatozoïdes manquent dans cette sécrétion. Le professeur Cornil s'en est assuré depuis longtemps déjà, et M. Hénocque et moi dans ces derniers temps.

Du reste, il était probable *a priori* que les spermatozoïdes **ne** participent pas à l'action dynamogénique de mes injections, puisque nous savons qu'ils ne peuvent pas être absorbés, et que c'est la partie liquide du sperme qui, étant résorbée, est l'agent vivificateur des individus jeunes ou adultes, qui ont des testicules actifs.

Tout ce que j'avais voulu obtenir par les publications que j'ai faites jusqu'ici était que des médecins ou des physiologistes âgés fissent sur eux-mêmes des expériences semblables aux miennes. Autant que je le sache, deux seulement, à Paris, ont fait quelques expériences, dont le résultat général a été favorable. J'en parlerai tout à l'heure. Malheureusement, les effets produits n'ont pas été rigoureusement étudiés. Dans les meilleures observations publiées jusqu'ici (celles du Dr Variot, de Paris; du Dr Villeneuve, de Marseille, et du Dr Loomis, de New-York), les individus soumis aux injections ne l'ont été que pendant un certain temps. On s'est assuré que certains bons effets ont été produits et, après une ou deux semaines, les opérés ont été laissés de côté.

Il y a deux côtés à l'égard des influences exercées par le liquide extrait des testicules, dont l'un consiste purement et simplement dans l'étude des effets physiologiques qu'il produit, et l'autre dans la recherche des effets thérapeutiques. Personne n'a encore, à ma connaissance, fait séparément ou parallèlement l'étude de ces deux espèces de manifestations. On aurait dû rechercher sur des vieillards en bonne santé quels sont les effets produits : cela n'a malheureusement pas été fait. On s'est surtout occupé de guérir des malades, et l'on a obtenu les échecs que l'on méritait d'avoir et des succès qui, à part quelques cas, ne sont pas suffisamment établis.

Le Dr Variot a le mérite d'avoir été le premier à étudier sur plusieurs vieillards l'action du suc retiré des testicules, dans le but de s'assurer si ce que j'ai trouvé sur moi-même se montrerait sur d'autres personnes. Je ne puis ici que mentionner très brièvement ce qu'il a constaté.

Obs. I. — Homme, 54 ans, atteint d'anémie et de diarrhée persistante. On fait deux injections de liquide testiculaire. Le soir, sensation de bien-être inaccoutumé, qui dure le lendemain. Il a, dit-il, la tête plus libre, les membres plus souples, et plus de force. L'œil est beaucoup plus vif; il peut marcher sans fatigue, etc. La puissance sexuelle disparue revient.

Obs. II. — Homme, 56 ans, ne pouvait guère rester debout ni marcher pendant quelques instants sans être obligé de s'asseoir. Après les injections, il gagne en force considérablement, devient gai, plein d'entrain, etc. Appétit très augmenté.

Obs. III. — Homme, 68 ans, quitte peu son lit. Le lendemain des deux premières injections, il se promène avec plaisir, se sent plus fort. Appétit extrêmement augmenté. Érection matinale intense ; il n'en avait plus eu depuis deux mois. Défécation devenue possible sans lavement.

Depuis que M. Variot a publié ces trois cas (*Comptes rendus de la Soc. de biol.*, 5 juillet 1889, p. 451), il a employé les injections de suc extrait de testicules de lapin ou de cobaye sur nombre d'autres malades. Il ne m'est pas possible de donner une analyse de tous ces cas, dont quelques-uns ont été négatifs. Je n'en mentionnerai que quatre ou cinq.

Un des cas ayant le plus d'importance parmi ceux du Dr Variot est celui d'un médecin de 60 ans, qui, après un traitement à Vichy, était excessivement faible et se sentait épuisé. Il a, d'après son dire, gagné considérablement en activité cérébrale et en force à l'égard de la puissance musculaire et du pouvoir sexuel. Il n'a eu que quatre injections, faites deux par jour. C'était en août dernier. Il m'écrit, à la date du 6 octobre, que les bons effets ont continué, bien qu'il n'ait pas fait de nouvelles injections.

Dans un autre cas, il s'agit d'un médecin de Paris de 35 ans, atteint d'impuissance sexuelle et de faiblesse très notable. Après six injections (deux par jour), augmentation de force (50 au lieu de 40 au dynamomètre) et possibilité de relations sexuelles.

Chez un vieillard de 81 ans et demi, sans infirmité marquée, il n'y a pas eu d'effet notable des injections jusqu'après quelques semaines, ou il a écrit au Dr Variot que « les injections ont complètement réussi chez lui, et surtout les deux dernières. Je sens, dit-il, une grande augmentation de force sous tous les rapports, et comme si j'avais 20 ou 25 ans de moins ».

Dans une expérience de contrôle, le Dr Variot a fait deux injections avec de l'eau teintée de sang, et a constaté que le patient, âgé de 58 ans, atteint de diarrhée et de bronchite, n'a éprouvé aucun bon effet. Sans qu'il fût prévenu d'un changement de liquide, la liqueur retirée d'un testicule d'animal fut injectée, et, dès le lendemain, cet homme a affirmé qu'il était beaucoup mieux, qu'il avait le cerveau plus libre, et qu'il éprouvait un bien-être inaccoutumé. Les érections ont reparu quinze jours après l'injection dernière. Il dit avoir été remis sur pied par cette injection, dont les bons effets ont persisté plus d'un mois et demi.

Un travail très intéressant a été publié par un des plus distingués médecins de New-York, le Dr H. P. Loomis (*The Medical Record*, Aug. 24, 1889, p. 206) rapportant des faits d'injection du liquide retiré de testicules de mouton. Malheureusement, ces injections, comme celles des autres médecins qui ont répété mes expériences, ont été faites presque exclusivement sur des malades. Les cas favorables ont été ceux de vieillards âgés de 56 ans, de 62 ans et de 77 ans (c'est le plus remarquable de tous). Sept autres malades n'ont pas eu de bons effets ou ont vu leur maladie s'aggraver (ceci a eu lieu dans un cas de rhumatisme et un cas d'ataxie locomotrice) [1].

---

[1] Je connais cinq cas d'ataxie locomotrice, en outre de celui du Dr Loomis, ou les injections de suc testiculaire ont été employées. Le mal ne s'est aggravé chez aucun, mais deux malades n'ont eu aucun changement de leur état ; deux ont eu une amélioration légère, et le cinquième a obtenu une amélioration des plus considérables.

Je ne dirai qu'un mot d'un mémoire d'un médecin bien connu, le Dr W. A. Hammond (*The N. Y. Medical Journal*, Aug. 31, 1889, p. 232). Ce travail contient neuf observations qui toutes, à part une où l'injection avait été faite sur une femme, montrent des effets extrêmement favorables, non seulement contre la faiblesse, mais contre diverses maladies et surtout certaines affections du cœur.

Un autre médecin américain, le Dr Brainerd, de Cleveland (Ohio), jusqu'au 15 août dernier, avait employé les injections sur vingt-cinq personnes, dont cinq femmes. La plupart de ces individus étaient des malades, et des effets extrêmement favorables ont été obtenus chez presque tous. Le liquide employé était retiré de testicules de mouton, comme dans les cas des Drs Loomis et Hammond.

J'ai reçu du Dr Dehoux, de Paris, et du Dr Grigorescu, de Bucharest, deux faits partiellement favorables.

Je n'ai plus à parler que des recherches du Dr Villeneuve, qui ont paru dans le *Marseille médical* (30 août 1888, p. 458), et qui sont très intéressantes à plusieurs égards. Il s'est servi de testicules de chien, de cobaye ou de lapin. Chez des malades atteints d'affections plus ou moins graves, il n'y a eu aucun effet favorable après deux injections. Au contraire, chez d'autres et même chez un blessé âgé de 90 ans, il y en a eu de très nets, surtout chez un homme de 50 ans, dont le cas a été très bien étudié, et qui a obtenu une augmentation très considérable à tous égards, et en particulier en ce qui concerne son activité cérébrale (p. 465)[1].

Les faits que j'ai signalés et nombre d'autres encore ne permettent plus de supposer que ce que j'ai observé sur moi ait dépendu, en partie ou entièrement, d'une idiosyncrasie spéciale ou d'une auto-suggestion.

Malgré l'insuffisance de détails dans toutes les observations publiées jusqu'ici, malgré nombre de critiques que l'on a incontestablement le droit d'adresser à la plupart d'entre elles, il en ressort néanmoins, et d'une manière évidente, que le suc

---

[1] M. Villeneuve a employé un liquide extrait d'ovaires de cobaye sur une femme privée de ses ovaires, et il en a obtenu des effets extrêmement remarquables (p. 466).

testiculaire employé a produit sur les centres nerveux tous les effets dynamogéniques que j'ai observés sur moi-même, et d'autres encore, quelques-uns dans certains cas, le reste dans d'autres cas. La recherche des effets produits a été si incomplète dans la plupart des cas que rien n'a été observé, tantôt à l'égard de certains d'entre eux, tantôt à l'égard de certains autres. Rien ne montre qu'ils n'existaient pas, mais, je le répète, chacun des effets signalés par moi a été observé un très grand nombre de fois. D'autres phénomènes de dynamogénie ont été aussi trouvés chez des malades, et surtout dans des cas de faiblesse de l'action du cœur.

Il n'est donc pas douteux que les injections sous-cutanées du suc dilué, extrait de testicules d'animaux vivants ou venant de mourir, possèdent sur les centres nerveux une puissance dynamogénique considérable, au moins chez un grand nombre d'individus. Il n'est pas douteux aussi que ces injections soient sans danger lorsqu'elles sont faites avec toutes les précautions que les médecins instruits savent être essentielles lorsqu'on introduit sous la peau des matières animales [1].

---

[1] Jusqu'ici les médecins américains ont employé presque uniquement les testicules de mouton. En Europe, on a fait usage du chien, du cobaye ou du lapin. J'ai recommandé les testicules d'un veau agé pour les cas où, au lieu d'agir sur l'homme. on voudrait donner de la vigueur à des chevaux ou à d'autres grands animaux. Autant que je le sache, l'espece d'animal n'a pas une très grande importance. Ce qui est essentiel, c'est que l'animal soit jeune, vigoureux et sain, que les testicules employés proviennent d'un individu encore vivant ou venant d'être tué, et enfin qu'on fasse l'injection une ou deux heures, ou à peine plus, après la mort de l'animal ou après l'extirpation du testicule sur un individu encore vivant. J'ai donné les règles suivantes : le testicule employé doit être pesé ; on l'écrase ensuite avec deux ou trois fois son poids d'eau; puis, avant de le jeter sur le filtre, avec le liquide obtenu, on y ajoute huit fois son poids d'eau. Après filtration, on fait l'injection du dixième de la quantité recueillie à une jambe ou un bras, et une ou deux autres injections semblables ailleurs. Ces injections doivent être répétées tous les deux jours pendant deux ou trois semaines. Il faudra ensuite y revenir tous les deux, trois ou quatre mois. S'il se produit un érythème très douloureux, il faut diluer davantage la liqueur employée.

15

THE PHYSIOLOGICAL AND THERAPEUTIC ROLE OF ANIMAL TESTICULAR EXTRACT BASED ON SEVERAL EXPERIMENTS IN MAN

C. E. Brown-Séquard

This article was translated expressly for this Benchmark volume by Geraldine M. Emerson, University of Alabama in Birmingham, from "Du role physiologique et thérapeutique d'un suc extrait de testicules d'animaux d'après nombre de faits observés chez l'homme," Arch. Physiolog. Norm. Pathol. **1**(5):739–746 (1889)

Subsequent to the publication of my experiments on myself, the political press of two worlds have reported it without understanding and unfortunately has given rise by thousands of old weak persons to abuse, misuse, or overindulgence of their sexual ability or false hope of cure of their illnesses which can only be decried.

In the U.S. especially, and often without exact knowledge of my experiments, without the most rudimentary consideration of rules regarding subcutaneous injections of animal materials, many clinicians but more often quacks and charlatans, have exploited the deep desire of a large number of individuals and have exposed them to the greatest risks at the least, if they have not done worse.

I would like to be able to talk about the results of thousands of trial injections of testicular extracts in America and elsewhere. Unfortunately, the principal elements of a serious appraisal are lacking almost completely expecially since I do not know the facts concerning most U.S. doctors but only the reports appearing in political newspapers. Each time, I will indicate published work, but it is necessary to compare with these other observers whom I make known and who use my experiments on myself which have been reported in another memoir (p. 651). My thought in these experiments was that the weakness of the old men is partly due to decreased activity of the "glandes spermatiques". I have believed and I do believe still that these experiments which I reported prove that the vigor of the central nervous system and other parts of the organism is connected with the effective secretory ability of the testicles. That being admitted, it is only natural to think that in giving to the blood of the old man, by subcutaneous injections, a liquid extract of young and vigorous animal testicles, there is the supposition of supplementing the deficit from his inadequate spermatic secretion (GME--ie the concept of replacement therapy is introduced). There was also reason to believe that this exogenous injection may effect an increased activity in the recipient's testes.

It seems, from results of dedicated doctors, that this special effect has been obtained in old men as well as in still young men exhausted by venereal excess.

Several persons have thought that all the action of particular elements of the liquid injected consisted in stimulating the CNS or other parts. Truthfully, it would be necessary to forget the simplest ideas on actions of physical agents, medicinals and poisons, on the animal organism in order to accept such as opinion. Actually, we know of two kinds of effects which can be produced by these agents or substances: one is stimulation followed by a taking over by the irritated part (stimulated part); the other consists of augmentation or by diminution of the force of action (function). In all the changes I have reported to take place in me, there has not been any putting into play of any effectiveness and, moreover, these changes have lasted an entire week. There is still one of them in effect today, more than 3 1/2 months after the last injection (amelioration of defecation). This suffices absolutely to show that stimulation cannot be the cause of these changes. It is clear that it was the cause of an augmentation of force of action. That which remains to be settled; is to know if it is a veritable dynamo -that is to say a purely dynamic change which has taken place.

Several of the effects are so immediate as to make it seem probable that for them at least they are a consequence (of the treatment); the other effects are slow enough that it seems probable they result from a nutritive improvement an organic effect of the treatment on certain parts (of the organism). The liquid extract of the male sex glands show most probably in producing in several parts a pure dynamogenesis and in others an activation of nutrition. They show great ignorance who maintain that it is impossible in old men to reverse their organic state so that they resemble that of an earlier age, especially since the organic changes resulting in bettering nutriture is possible at all ages.[1]

Today I do not wish to discuss the question of what substances are in the injected liquid, but rather the effects of the injections. Many experiments must yet be done to answer that question. All that I can say, is that the spermatic molecules have a special physiological role not sharing at all in dynamogenic influence of the liquid employed in my experiments, since the solid particulates did not pass through the Pasteur filter, of which I have been assured by M. Henocque. I must say that I know, for I have studied with care, an extremely remarkable and decisive case which shows that the animacules spermatiques are not the portion of the liquid secreted by the testicles which gives to man his various activities physical, moral and intellectual, which are absent in eunochs. Indeed, in an officer, outstanding in strength and other moral and physical qualities; and also by his sexual power and quantity of semen he produced, the spermatozoa are deficient in that secretion. Professor Cornil long ago assured himself of the foregoing and M. Henocque and I in recent times.

Of the rest, it would be probable, a-priori that the spermatazoa do not participate in the dynamogenic action of my injections, since we know that they cannot be absorbed and it is the liquid part of semen which, being reabsorbed, is the active agent of both young and adult individuals, who have active testes.

---

[1]Critics of my ideas have said that it is well known that senile degeneration and wasting present insurmountable obstacles, especially return of neural center function both in the sensory and the motor apparatus. A study of the excellent work of Charcot on Aging (Studies of Diseases of Old Men, Paris, 1838) and a number of other works show that nothing about senility is constant nor absolutely characterized. The blood vessels are altered (atheroma, aneurysm, etc.); but if the state of age produced these alterations it would show up with much less variability and if not less at the same age at least with relationship to other changes of aging. Now it is not that alone: the vascular alterations take various forms: either they are seen alone; or they are associated with some other kind of alteration. Advanced age favors organic changes, no one challenges that, but if these be fatal changes which are known to depend upon age, that is not exact evidence, but these are morbid manifestations of disease of tissues which do appear predominantly at an advanced age.

IF THE DEGENERATIONS, IF THE SENILE ALTERATIONS ARE DISEASES, A DAY WILL COME WHEN IT WILL BE POSSIBLE TO CURE THEM. (emphasis belongs to GME) Up to the present I know of no work which shows that the aqueous testicular injections would be able to cause favorable organic changes either for impeachment or retardation and ESPECIALLY TO REVERSE morbid changes (emphasis GME). But that is not what I'm trying to prove. Of the rest, the question is certainly not whether the injections rejuvenate (that I believe to be impossible, just as I have previously said) the question is to know if one can approximate the strength of a younger person, and to me THAT APPEARS CERTAIN.

What I have hoped to achieve by these publications of my research to date is that doctors or older physiologists carry out on themselves experiments analogous to mine. Especially so since I know of only two in Paris who have done such experiments, with generally favorable results. I'll speak of them shortly. Unfortunately, the results have not been rigorously studied. In the best observations published to date (those of Dr. Variot of Paris, Dr. Villeneuve of Marseille and Dr. Loomis of New York) the individuals injected were only for a short or restricted period of time. They were sure that some good effects had been produced and after one or two weeks, the work had been dropped. There are two sides when considering the influences of testicular extract: one is purely and simply the physiological effects produced; the other is the therapeutic effects. No one has yet, as far as I know, made separately or concomitantly, observations on these two kinds of effects. One ought to investigate old men in good health--the effects of such injections on them; that unfortunately has not been done. We have been primarily preoccupied with curing the sick and have obtained from these setbacks which one is likely to have, and successes, which except in some cases, have not been established sufficiently.

Dr. Variot, noteworthy for having been the first to study in several old men the action of the sap drawn from the testicles for the purpose of assuring himself if what I have found in myself will be shown in other persons. I can here but briefly mention his findings:

Case 1. 51 year old man, anemic, with persistent diarrhea. 2 injections of testicular extract given. That evening he has unaccustomed feeling of well-being lasting until the next day. According to him, his head was clearer, members more supple, and he was much stronger; his eyes were much brighter; he could walk without fatigue, etc. Sexual power, which had disappeared, returned.

Case 2. 56 year old man, was barely able to stand erect and walk for several moments without being obliged to sit down. After the injections he gained considerable strength, became bright and full of life, etc. Appetite was stimulated.

Case 3. 68 year old man who seldom left his bed. The day after his first two injections he walked with pleasure and felt stronger. His appetite was much improved. Hard erections every morning, an occurrence he had not had for two months. Defecation without enema became possible.

Following publication of these three cases (C. rend. de la Soc. de biol., 5 July, 1889, p 451) M. Variot has used injections of rabbit or guinea pig testicular fluid on a number of other patients. He told me it was not possible to give an analysis of all these cases, but several have been negative. I will mention only 4 or 5. The most important case of Dr. Variot is a 60 year old physician, who after a treatment at Vichy had been extremely feeble and felt worn out. He has, according to his statement, gained considerably in cerebral activity, muscular strength and sexual power. He had had only 4 injections, 2 per day. That was last August. On 6 October he wrote me that the benefits have continued, so much that no more injections have been given.

In another case, a 35 year old Paris physician, succumbed to sexual impotency and extreme weakness. After six injections (2/day) augmentation of strength (50 instead of 40 on the dynamometer) and possibly sexual relations.

In a 81.5 year old man having no obvious weakness, no notable effect was seen until several weeks of injections had been given, when he wrote to Dr. Variot the injections have completely rehabilitated him and especially the last two. I note, said he, a great augmentation of strength under all conditions as if I were 20 or 25 years younger.

In a control experiment, Dr. Variot gave two inections of blood tinted water and reported that the 58 year old patient suffering from diarrhea and bronchitis had no improvement. Without the patients knowledge he then substituted injection of animal testicular fluid and the next day the man said he was much better; that he had a freer head and an unaccustomed feeling of well being. Erections appeared 5 hours after the last injection. He was said to have been put back on his feet and the good effects lasted more than 1.5 months.

A very interesting study has been published by one of the most famous doctors in New York. Dr. H. P. Loomis (The Medical Record, Aug. 24, 1889, p.206) reported the effects of injection of liquid made from sheep testicles. Unfortunately, these injections, like those of other doctors who have repeated my experiments, have been done almost exclusively in the ailing. The favorable cases have been those of of old men of 56, 62, and 77 years (the most remarkable of all, 7 other cases did not have the good effects or had their illness aggravated-this occurred in a case of rheumatism and one of locomotor ataxia--).[1]

I will say only a word about the report of the well known Dr. W. A. Hammond (New York Medical Journal, August 31, 1889, p232). There are 9 observations which all aside from one injection in a female, showed quite favorable effects, not only for weakness but also against diverse illnesses and especially certain heart problems.

Another American doctor, Dr. Brainerd of Cleveland (Ohio) until last August fifteenth, had used the injections on 25 persons, five of whom were female. The majority of them were sick, and extremely favorable effects were observed in almost all. Sheep testicular fluid, as was true in Drs. Loomis and Hammonds' experiments, was used by Dr. Brainerd.

---

[1] I know five cases of locomotor ataxia, besides those of Dr. Loomis, in which testicular extract has been used. The illness was not aggravated in any, but two had no change in their status; two had their condition slightly ameliorated and the fifth had a more considerable amelioration.

I have received from Dr. Dehoux of Paris and Dr. Grigorescu of Bucharest two particularly favorable reports. I will briefly mention the research of Dr. Villenuve, which has appeared in Marseille Medical (Aug. 30, 1888, p458) which has several interesting aspects. He used dog, guinea pig and rabbit testicles. In patients having more or less grave illnesses he saw no improvement in their conditions after two injections. On the other hand, in others including even an injured man of the age of 90 years, thre were very definite good effects, especially in a 50 year old man, whose case had been very well studied, who was improved in all respects, most notably in cerebration (465).[1]

From the works I have cited and numerous others no longer permit me to suppose that the effects I observed in myself, depended partly or entirely on one special idiosyncrasy or an auto-suggestion.

In spite of a paucity of details in all the publications to date; in spite of some critics who undeniably have the right to address the question, for the most part among themselves, it is nevertheless evident and very clearly so that the testicular fluid used has produced on the central nervous system all the dynamic effects that I have observed on myself and others also in some of the cases. (Here is just repetition of the foregoing).

There is no doubt that subcutaneous injections of the diluted essence, testicular extract of living animals or those just dead have a considerable dynamic effect on the nervous centers, at least in a large number of individuals. It is also true that these injections can be given without danger when done according to all the precautions medically known to be essential when injecting under the skin animal materials.[1]

---

[1]M. Vielleneuve had used guinea pig ovary extract on a female without ovaries and extremely remarkable improvement resulted (p. 466).

[1]Heretofore, the American doctors have used almost uniquely mouton (sheep) testicles. In Europe, dog, guinea pig and rabbit have been used. I have recommended testicles of matured calf when one wants to give to man the vigor of horses or other large animals. However the species of animal is not so important. What is essential is that the animal be young, vigorous and healthy and that the testes are removed from a still living or just slaughtered animal and finally that the injection is made within two hours or a little more after removal from the animal. My procedure is as follows:

The testicle is weighed; then mashed and two or three times its weight of water added; then, separating the particles by filtration, to the filtration are added eight times its weight in water. After filtration, injections of a tenth of the quantity recovered is made in a leg or arm, and one or two other injections at other suitable sites. These injections should be repeated every two days for two or three weeks. It may be necessary following them to reinstitute in two, three or four months. If an extreme erythema is produced one should dilute the liquid employed.

Part IV

CLINICAL APPROACHES IN GERIATRICS IN THE TWENTIETH CENTURY

Editor's Comments
on Papers 16, 17, and 18

16   LEAKE
Russian and Iron Curtain Proposals for Geriatric Therapy

17   KANT and STERNE
Evaluation of Chronically Ill Patients Treated for One Year with Procaine

18   SMIGEL et al.
H-3 (Procaine hydrochloride) Therapy in Aging Institution-alized Patients: An Interim Report

In introducing this section, the philosophy is set by a quote from Dr. Lewis Thomas (1974):

> Disease is, fundamentally, unnatural. It is not, in my view, a normal or natural part of the human condition for aging human beings to become paralyzed and idiotic for long years before they finally die, any more than it is for young people to develop acute leukemia.

SPECIFIC THERAPEUTIC MEASURES—PROCAINE, NOVOCAINE, GEROVITAL, GEROVITAL H–3

Twenty-five years ago, Dr. Anna Aslan of the C. I. Parhon Geriatric Clinic near Bucharest, Romania published glowing accounts of rejuvenation after use of her special novocaine containing preparation. Since then the Romanian government has been reporting the excellent results throughout the world with invitations to vacation at this "rejuvenation mecca." Such tourist vacations advertised in the United States stress institution of prevention starting during late young adulthood (40 years of age) rather than waiting until one is a candidate for rejuvenation. We have been unable in any reasonable period of time to secure the copyright owner's permission to reproduce articles requested and must refer the reader to the original publications (Aslan, 1957, 1958, 1962). Many "anecdotal" or "testimonial" accounts of patient treatment are given by Dr. Aslan but the publications do not contain results of rigorously controlled experiments such as we scientists expect to see. Dr. Aslan's reports of rejuvenation fire the imagination. Younger inexperienced individuals cannot but be enthusiastic about a fountain of youth in a capsule, tablet or syringe!

Although unacceptable to the United States Food and Drug Administration and therefore unavailable here, these novocaine containing preparations variously known as Gerovital, Gerovital H-3 or the newer Aslavital are available throughout Europe. I am indebted to Dr. Ludwig Kornel of Rush-Presbyterian-St. Luke's Medical Center, Chicago, Illinois, U. S. A., for furnishing me with drug inserts from several packages of these novocaine containing preparations which in Dr. Kornel's words "are very popular in Europe." In comparing inserts from preparations sold in Switzerland "Geriatric Pharmaton," Germany "K. H. 3," and the original Gerovital, one finds little constancy except for the novocaine. This makes it impossible to compare results from one formulation with another. Gerovital has *four* ingredients, the amount of each is given in the brochure. The amount of *each* of the *twenty-eight* ingredients in Geriatric Pharmaton is given. No amount for any one of the *seven* ingredients in K. H. 3 is revealed. In this connection it is well to recall that early in this work Dr. Aslan indicated that "failures" by others using her novocaine method probably resulted because the investigator did not use the exact formulation of her Gerovital preparation. From an inspection of the marketed products, however, it would appear that there is much permissible latitude in their formulation. From the pharmacologist's standpoint delineation of the efficacious principle or principles from such mixtures is exceedingly difficult. It is unfortunate that people so seek rejuvenation or prevention of aging that they purchase and consume "age retardant" preparations indiscriminantly.

A thoughtful evaluation of the original Aslan publications was made in the 1950s by Dr. Chauncey D. Leake (Paper 16) who suggested that Aslan's Gerovital H-3 deserved well-controlled experimental animal and clinical trials in the United States to determine the feasibility of its use here. Reports of two clinical trials appear in Papers 17 and 18. Even twenty-five years later the majority scientific viewpoint here is that novocaine preparations are without physiological benefit to the patient.

There is currently some use of measures which alter the levels of *biogenic amines* in the geriatric patient. (It has been suggested that this partially explains any procaine effect.) Interest is directed toward the physiologic effects of the biogenic amines in the older person (see Finch, 1973, and Robinson, 1975).

16

Reprinted from *Geriatrics* **14**(10):670–673 (1959)

RUSSIAN AND IRON CURTAIN PROPOSALS
FOR GERIATRIC THERAPY

Chauncey D. Leake

■ Several letters have recently been received from readers of *Geriatrics* regarding news releases and other publicity about procaine therapy in geriatric patients, as developed by Professor Anna Aslan of the C. I. Parhon Institute of Geriatrics, Bucharest, Rumania. The recent publicity given to the visit of the Archbishop of Canterbury to this institution has aroused further publicity. It might be helpful to attempt to review some of this material, and such an attempt is offered herewith.

Background Studies

For a quarter of a century there have been many efforts on the part of Russian and related clinical workers to develop effective products for promoting healing, delaying the process of aging, and extending life span. During World War II, there was extensive publicity among the Allies on the work of A. A. Bogomoletz on "Anti-Reticular Cytotoxic Serum" (ACS). The early reports emphasized the role of ACS as a stimulator of the reticuloendothelial system. There were reports describing its value in promoting wound healing and fracture repair, and speculations on its possible use in the treatment of premature aging. In the December 1943 issue of the *American Review of Soviet Medicine*, there were published three articles on ACS, describing its general action, its methods of preparation, and its clinical application in frostbite and battle injuries.

This work was derived from the early use in 1900 of tissue antisera by E. Metchnikoff who was the teacher of Bogomoletz. These early studies came to little because there was no method for estimating the serum potency. It was Bogomoletz's observation that the reticuloendothelial system in old people remains in a healthy condition, as indicated by their resistance to disease and to degenerative tissue changes, that suggested the antireticular cytotoxic serum.

In general it may be said that clinical and experimental studies from Russia partially confirmed Bogomoletz's ideas. The observations of Bogomoletz and his colleagues have also been partially confirmed in this country. These confirmations extend to experimental studies in tissue culture and to clinical studies in the repair of fractures and in the management of certain infections. On the other hand, there is no clear evidence that ACS is particularly useful in the treatment of premature aging or in extending the life span or delaying the onset of degenerative conditions in old age.

A careful critical evaluation of antireticular cytotoxic serum (ACS) was made by Thomas S. Gardner and David M. Speaker (*Texas Rep. Biol. Med.* 9: 448-490, 1951). This careful review includes 160 references on the subject from contributors in various parts of the world. It is pointed out that: "The action of ACS, both cytotoxic for large doses and stimulating for small doses, have been verified by tissue culture techniques. The stimulatory effects in wound and fracture healing have been verified. The relief of pain in human cancer . . . (has) been demonstrated. The suppression of rickettsia in animals has been verified." On the other hand, ACS has been shown to have little value in treating arthritis, and there is no verification of its antiaging claims.

Professor C. I. Parhon began studying geriatrics before World War I. At first he experimented with pineal gland extracts, but these came to nothing. He indicated that there are metabolic variations with aging that involve protein, lipid, and water metabolism. His studies on the metabolic mechanisms in aging led to the establishment of an Institute of Geriatrics. This was founded in Bucharest in 1951 and named in honor of Professor Parhon.

Careful metabolic studies have been made on a relatively large group of institutionalized aged people in this institute. Systematic treatment has been undertaken with various tissue and gland extracts and with various vitamins. At this same time a smaller number of patients were started on treatment with procaine solutions.

Dr. Anna Aslan, who is a member of the C. I. Parhon Institute of Geriatrics in Bucharest, has described the background of her interest in the use of procaine solutions in treating the aging process (*Therapiewoche* 7: 14-22, 1956). Doctor Aslan's clinical experience with Professor D. Danielopolu had convinced her of the value of procaine therapy by intra-arterial injections in embolic conditions, and then in arthritis, and in arthrosis with a tendency to ankylosis.

It is her opinion that the vasodilatory and local anesthetic effects of procaine may reduce the inflammation and pain in arthritic joints. It was her opinion that the same factors may operate in connection with trophic ulcers.

Experimental studies in animals on experimental arthritis confirmed her clinical impressions, and she noted further that the treated animals showed a general trophic action with improvement in the hair, the appetite, and the general activity of the experimental organisms. Again in some of her clinical studies on older persons, she noted general improvement in memory and various aspects of vitality, including increased muscle tone. This led her to investigate effects of prolonged and periodic procaine treatment in old people.

Clinical Reports

A number of clinical reports on procaine therapy in old age have been published in *Die Therapiewoche*. This is an East German journal, and not readily available. Translations have been made by Consultants Bureau, Inc. of New York City. The articles are:

ANNA ASLAN: A new method for the prophylaxis and treatment of aging with Novocain— eutrophic and rejuvenating effects. Therapiewoche 7: 14-22, 1956.

C. I. PARHON: Prevention and treatment of diseases of the aged. Therapiewoche 8: 1-3, 1957.

C. DAVID: Biochemical and physiological criteria of aging and the effect of treatment thereon, used as indices on rehabilitation. Therapiewoche 8: 4-9, 1957.

ANNA ASLAN: Recent experiences on the rejuvenating Action of Novocain (H₃), together with experimental, clinical, and statistical findings. Therapiewoche 8: 10-19, 1957.

ANNA ASLAN and C. DAVID: Results of Novocain treatment in dysmetabolic arthropathies. Therapiewoche 8: 19-23, 1957.

M. BURGER and F. H. SCHULTZ: Significance of biomorphosis for the aging process, disease, and rejuvenation. Therapiewoche 8: 24-28, 1957.

C. KOHLER and F. MANPEL: First experiences with Novocain treatment of old people. Therapie woche 8: 28-30, 1957.

A. I. IAROSHEVSKI: Effect of intravenous injections of Novocain on the blood system: changes in the composition in the blood resulting from repeated injections of Novocain. Bull. Exper. Biol. Med. USSR 5: 50-53, 1958.

A. I. IAROSHEVSKI: Changes in composition of the blood after single injection of Novocain. Bull. Exper. Biol. Med. USSR 8: 36-41, 1958.

I. F. UDALOV: Effective procaine on tolerance of white rats to high altitudes. Bull. Exper. Biol. Med. USSR 8: 71-72, 1958.

There are other Soviet publications on the trophic action of procaine. When I was in Leningrad and Moscow in 1956, I discussed the trophic action of procaine with several experimental workers in the physiology research laboratories in these cities. However, I was not impressed at the time that there was anything very significant in these studies except that intramuscular injections of procaine seemed to have some benefit in experimental arthritis and perhaps in certain experimental stress conditions.

It is difficult to evaluate satisfactorily the reports of Professor Anna Aslan and her colleagues. The general conclusions are that intramuscular injections of 5 ml. of a 2 per cent procaine hydrochloride solution (pH 4.2-5) three times weekly for a series of 12 injections, followed by a ten-day rest, and repetition of the injections, result in significant trophic improvement in old age. There are claims for renewed production of endocrines, with regression of signs of senility of the skin, with stimulation of new hair growth, with improved cardiovascular reaction and better muscle power, with a higher production of granulocytes and globulin content, and with general eutrophic action. These effects are considered to be due in part to the hydrolysis of procaine with the formation of para-aminobenzoic acid, which has a general eutrophic vitamin action.

David made rather detailed studies of various biochemical and physiological criteria of aging, indicating that regression in these various factors associated with aging tends to reverse following procaine treatment. Aslan offers several photographs and other objective evidence indicating improvement in aging people following procaine treatment. Aslan's statistical study deals with 1,142 cases of older people in whom it is claimed that procaine therapy has resulted in general trophic improvement. She claims that procaine may exert the vitaminlike action by its gradual transformation into para-aminobenzoic acid and folic acid and designates this effect of procaine by the symbol "H_3". She refers to many other publications on procaine as a eutrophic agent, but the publications are not readily available.

In 100 old people afflicted with degenerative arthropathies, Aslan and David report 60 per cent improvement, with no undesirable effects, using as controls patients treated with ACTH and cortisone. In some 75 patients, Kohler and Manpel report improvement in 46 under procaine therapy, with no change in 29. They find remarkable improvement in arteriosclerotic and arthritic conditions. They doubt that there is any significant effect on the aging process and deplore the thought that this form of therapy involves any sort of "rejuvenation."

In experimental studies in animals Iaroshevski reports an increase in hemoglobin and in the number of red blood cells following once a week injections of 5 ml. of 1 per cent Novocain solution. This study, on 30 rabbits, revealed no change in the rate of blood formation. Following a single injection of 5 ml. of 1 per cent Novocain in rabbits, an increase in leukocytes was noted. Udalov notes that p-aminobenzoic acid, a metabolic product of procaine, increases the survival of rats where oxygen concentration is reduced in inspired air. P-aminobenzoic acid apparently increases body resistance to oxygen lack.

Procaine hydrochloride is rapidly split in the body. It breaks down to para-aminobenzoic acid and diethyl-amino-ethanol. Practically all of the para-aminobenzoic acid formed appears in the urine within twenty-four hours, combined with glycine and glucuronic acid. About a third of the diethyl-amino-ethanol that is formed also appears in the urine within a day, and the balance seems to be destroyed in the body. Procaine hydrochloride injections are very safe to be used because of the speedy breakdown of the drug. Indeed intravenous infusion in man at the rate of 2 grams of procaine per one hundred minutes does not lead to a plasma level exceeding 0.2 mg. per liter. Under these conditions, the concentration of para-aminobenzoic acid may rise to 10 mg. per liter, and the concentration of diethyl-amino-ethanol to 3 mg. per liter.

P-aminobenzoic acid is necessary for the normal metabolism of living cells, and tends to maintain growth equilibrium in cells. It is the blocking of the action of para-aminobenzoic acid by the sulfonamides that results in the antibacterial action of the sulfonamides. This was beautifully demonstrated in a classic study by D. D. Woods (*Brit. J. Exper. Path.* 21: 74-90, 1940). Diethyl-amino-ethanol is a mild local anesthetic agent, reducing pain due to congestion in tissues with which it may come in contact. It has a depressant action on cardiac muscle and relieves spasm of smooth muscle. It has rather remarkable anti-allergic effects. While it does not seem to have any generally beneficial trophic action on cells in the promotion of growth, it nevertheless does have a beneficial effect in reducing allergic tendencies and thus in maintaining more satisfactory cellular activity.

Procaine hydrochloride infusions in humans for control of tachycardia was popular a few years ago. The action, however, is fleeting due to the rapid destruction of procaine in the body. In order to get around this situation, procaine-amide solutions are used. Procaine-amide does not split up in the body readily, so that its effects are more prolonged. Infusions of this drug are used to control cardiac arrhythmias, but no particular eutrophic effects have been reported in Western medical literature.

In general, it would seem that the reports by Anna Aslan and her associates are interesting enough for further exploration. It would be hoped that she and her associates would publish more detailed case histories, together with a more complete statistical survey of the large number of cases which they must have accumulated by now. It would seem that careful and direct experimental studies on small animals should tell readily whether or not repeated procaine hydrochloride injections intramuscularly can delay the aging process, prolong life, and generally interfere with degenerative processes associated with aging. It might be wise for results of studies of this sort to be well publicized before extensive premature clinical use of procaine hydrochloride in slowing the aging process. On the other hand, the safety of the drug indicates that cautious and well controlled clinical studies might yield results that would tell definitely whether or not any further use of the drug for these purposes is justified.

CHAUNCEY D. LEAKE
The Ohio State University, Columbus

17

Reprinted from *J. Am. Geriatrics Soc.* **10**(5):408–412 (1962)

EVALUATION OF CHRONICALLY ILL PATIENTS TREATED FOR ONE YEAR WITH PROCAINE

SAMUEL KANT, M.D.* AND DAVID M. STERNE, Ph.D.†

Veterans Administration Hospital, Vancouver, Washington

Recent interest in the care of the aged has stimulated a wealth of research directed toward diagnosis and treatment of specific diseases that by their nature are prone to attack the elderly. Medical centers abroad have reported that Novocaine (procaine hydrochloride)[1] therapy can cure many degenerative diseases and delay the signs of aging. Sweeping claims have been made in Roumanian and German publications for studies from the clinics of Aslan (1), Parhon (2), and Köhler and Mampel (3). Of particular interest were the reports of improvement of mental activity, subjective well-being, cardiovascular conditions and arthritis, and of favorable changes in blood chemistry and other laboratory findings. The control of these clinical studies is open to question, and the claims appear to conflict with accepted physiologic principles. Further investigation appeared desirable (4, 5).

The 100-bed long-term service for chronically ill patients at the Vancouver VA Hospital offered an appropriate setting for conducting a year-long, controlled study. The population of patients is relatively static and is representative of the group of aging male veterans.

Certain difficulties in the study were recognized from the outset. It was necessary to make extensive use of laboratory and clinical measurements that are subject to considerable day-to-day variation. Although it was desirable to continue the procaine treatment for a full year in order to evaluate its long-term effect, this prolonged period increased the likelihood of any changes being confounded with the continuing degenerative impact of an additional year of age. On the other hand, a basis for control data lay in the fact that all the subjects were well known to the staff and had been treated with standard maintenance medication, adapted individually, for a considerable period of time before this study was started. Complications, when they arose, had been treated by conventional established methods.

SUBJECTS AND PROCEDURE

According to the procedure suggested in the original papers (1–3), 5 ml. of a 2 per cent solution of procaine[1] (pH 4.2–5.0) was injected intramuscularly three times per week for a period of four weeks, followed by a pause of ten days. This schedule was continued for a full year. Prior to the initiation of treatment, all subjects were tested for sensitivity by the intracutaneous method; all were

---

* Chief of the Long-Term, Chronically Ill Service.
† Clinical Psychologist.
[1] In this paper the terms procaine, procaine hydrochloride and Novocaine are used interchangeably.

found non-reactive. No adverse reactions were observed throughout the year of the study.

Subjects

The following criteria were employed in the selection of patients:

1. Each understood the purpose and nature of the study.

2. Each gave free consent, and assurance of his willingness to undergo all necessary investigative procedures.

3. Though chronically ill, early death was not anticipated.

4. None had acute complications when the study was started.

5. Continuous medical care was required, justifying hospitalization throughout the year.

On this basis, we selected 20 subjects who were fairly typical of the patients treated on this service. All were males, and they ranged in age from 60 to 93 years, with a mean of 76 years. In each case there were multiple diagnoses. The most common disorders were arteriosclerotic heart disease, peripheral arteriosclerosis obliterans, residuals of cerebrovascular accidents, peptic ulcer, osteoarthritis, emphysema, visual and auditory impairment, and intellectual deterioration.

Method

A double-blind design was employed. Ten patients were drawn at random for the study sample; the remaining 10 were used as controls.

It was necessary to replace one 89-year-old subject immediately after four weeks of treatment, when coronary thrombosis developed, followed by death. The replacement underwent the standard testing procedures and his status, whether experimental or control, also remained unknown until the study was concluded. Although several other medical complications occurred in the patients during the course of the study, the schedule of injections was maintained.

The test subjects were given sterile pyrogen-free 2 per cent procaine hydrochloride[2] in 0.9 per cent benzyl alcohol solution at pH 4.4. The control subjects were given a sterile solution of physiologic sodium chloride. Division of the subjects into test and control groups was made only by the hospital Chief Pharmacist; the data were recorded in a single sealed copy turned over to the hospital Chief of Staff. The group identifications were not divulged to anyone until after completion of the final evaluation. Aside from these injections no changes were made in the general treatment routine.

Evaluative techniques

The following laboratory tests were made prior to the study, six months after its initiation, and again when the year was completed: Routine urinalysis, including albumin, sugar and microscopic examination; red blood cell count, hematocrit and hemoglobin concentration; white blood cell and differential count; erythrocyte sedimentation rate; levels of blood urea nitrogen, uric acid, serum cholesterol, total protein (including albumin/globulin ratio), and urea clearance.

The same schedule was followed for electrocardiograms, blood pressure readings and resting pulse rates. At the same intervals, the attending medical and nursing staff discussed the current status and any behavioral changes noted with each subject. This procedure also included presentation of each subject to the evaluating group, without taking into account the laboratory or test findings. The group then classified the patients into 4 categories: improved, slightly improved, unchanged, or worse. At the conclusion of the entire study, the results of this evaluation were combined with the laboratory and test data to provide a representation of over-all change.

---

[2] Procaine hydrochloride was supplied by Don Hall Laboratories, Portland, Oregon.

TABLE 1

	Year 1959	Year 1960	Difference	Significance level
Differential blood count:				
basophils (%)	.25	1.1	+.85	<.01
abnormal (%)	1.15	0.2	−.95	<.05
Serum cholesterol level (mg./100 ml.)	230.75	204.25	−26.5	<.001
Serum uric acid (mg./100 ml.)	3.48	2.26	−1.22	<.01
Blood urea nitrogen (mg./100 ml.)	22.15	18.15	−4.00	<.001
Serum total protein (gm./100 ml.)	7.55	6.62	−.93	<.05
Serum albumin (gm./100 ml.)	4.83	4.48	−.35	<.01
Urea clearance (ml./min.)	19.59	12.68	−6.91	<.02
Oscillometric index (Collens): below knee, left	5.29	4.65	−.64	<.01

The following measures were employed at the beginning of the project and after one year: Chest roentgenograms, including cardiac size, aortic knob calcification, presence of cardiac failure, the transverse diameter of the heart, and the TD ratio; skin turgor and hair color; texture of the brachial and radial arteries; oscillometric studies of the lower extremities; estimation of pulmonary ventilation; and psychometric determinations of manual dexterity, memory and general intellectual functioning.[3]

After each four-week series of injections, the patients were interviewed individually and asked to describe any immediate reaction to the injections and to indicate whether or not they had noted any changes in general well-being.

RESULTS

When all the data gathered in 1960 were compared with those obtained a year earlier, none of the changes noted in the procaine-treated group differed significantly from those noted in the control group. Five of the treated subjects usually reported immediate reactions to the injections, such as dizziness, light-headedness, and hot flashes lasting ten to fifteen minutes. Similar effects were reported consistently by 1 control subject; the difference between the groups approached the .05 level of significance. There was no evidence of any appreciable correlation between clinical and behavioral changes. On the assumption, there-

[3] The tests included a measure of manual dexterity derived from the Minnesota Rate of Manipulation Turning Test, the number of designs correctly reproduced on the Benton Visual Retention Test, the number of errors made on the reproduction of the Benton designs, the scaled scores obtained on the Digit Span subtest of the Wechsler Adult Intelligence Scale (WAIS), the number of digits forward which could be immediately recalled by subjects, the number of digits which could be immediately recalled when subjects were asked to repeat these in reverse order, the scaled score made on the WAIS Vocabulary subtest, the scaled score made on the WAIS Block Design subtest, the scaled score made on the WAIS Picture Arrangement subtest, and a composite measure of intellectual functioning (IQ) drawn from the 4 WAIS subtests used (6). Although every effort was made to use the same tests for all of the subjects, factors such as pronounced visual impairment and extreme manual incoordination made it impossible to do so with a small number of the patients. In these few cases, other reasonably equivalent techniques were substituted.

fore that, apart from the immediate reaction, the treated and control patients did not differ in the response to procaine, their data were combined. Statistically significant changes that occurred during the year of study are presented in Table 1.

DISCUSSION

Our investigation provided no confirmation of the favorable response of older people to treatment with Novocaine, as reported by Aslan and others. In addition to consistently negative laboratory and psychometric findings, our classification of patients into 4 categories representing the over-all response to treatment showed no difference between the test group and the control group. When the patients were re-classified according to whether or not they had improved during the year, it was found that there were equal numbers of test subjects and control subjects in each category. No significant difference could be discerned between the subjective reports of improvement made by the test subjects as compared to those made by the controls. Only 4 of the patients treated with procaine consistently reported improvement, as compared to 7 of those treated with physiologic saline solution. The only response to the experimental variable which approached significance in differentiating the 2 groups of subjects was the immediate reaction to the injections—an effect readily explained on the basis of temporary vasodilation.

The minimal changes noted in the differential blood cell count, the level of serum total protein, the AG ratio, and oscillometric readings for the whole group of 20 subjects do not appear to have clinical significance. The lowered serum cholesterol and uric acid levels can be explained by the diet, which was carefully planned and systematically followed; it contained about 2400 calories per day, with a restricted fat intake. The reduction in the concentration of blood urea nitrogen was probably due to the generally favorable living conditions and routine treatment procedures. However, this finding was inconsistent with the slight decrease in urea clearance, already considerably below normal limits at the beginning of the study. This decrease was most likely due to progressive arteriosclerosis of the kidneys.

An interesting and not totally unexpected finding was that half the patients were quite enthusiastic about the improvement, which they attributed to the injections—despite the fact that only 4 of the enthusiastic 10 had received procaine. One suspects that psychologic factors such as the desire to improve, the response to increased professional attention, and the impact of reading articles about "wonder drugs" in the lay press, were just as effective as procaine in producing subjective feelings of benefit. Such factors conceivably may account for certain of the favorable claims made elsewhere for this treatment.

SUMMARY

In a one-year double-blind study, procaine hydrochloride was administered intramuscularly to 10 long-term, chronically ill, hospitalized male veterans; 10

control patients received injections of physiologic saline. No significant differences were found between the two groups of subjects, as determined by extensive laboratory and psychometric measurements.

The results of this study do not confirm the beneficial effects claimed for this treatment by others.

REFERENCES

1. Aslan, A.: A new method for the prophylaxis and treatment of aging with novocain-H_3— Eutrophic and rejuvenating effects, *Therapiewoche* **7**: 14 (Oct.) 1956.
2. Parhon, C. I.: Prevention and treatment of diseases of the aged—Views concerning the treatment of old age, *Therapiewoche* **8**: 1 (Oct.) 1957.
3. Köhler, U., and Mampel, F.: First experiences with novocain treatment of old people, *Therapiewoche* **8**: 28 (Oct.) 1957.
4. Smigel, J. O.; Piller, J.; Murphy, C.; Lowe, C., and Gibson, J.: H-3 (procaine hydrochloride) therapy in aging institutionalized patients, *J. Am. Geriatrics Soc.* **8**: 785 (Oct.) 1960.
5. Leake, C. D.: Russian and Iron Curtain proposals for geriatric therapy, *Geriatrics* **14**: 670 (Oct.) 1959.
6. Doppelt, J. E.: Estimating the full scale score on the Wechsler adult intelligence scale from scores on four subtests, *J. Consult. Psychol.* **20**: 63 (Feb.) 1956.

18

Reprinted from *J. Am. Geriatrics Soc.* **8**(10):785–794 (1960)

H-3 (PROCAINE HYDROCHLORIDE) THERAPY IN AGING INSTITUTIONALIZED PATIENTS: AN INTERIM REPORT*

JOSEPH O. SMIGEL, M.D.†, JACOB PILLER, M.D.‡, CHARLES MURPHY, M.D.‡, CARL LOWE, M.D.‡ AND JOHN GIBSON, R.N., R.P.T.§

Pinehaven Nursing Home & Sanitarium, Inc., Pinewald, New Jersey

It is important to call attention to some of the background for this study. Suddenly the Western World has been made aware of claims for a new approach to longevity and for relief from the effects of many chronic ailments. From the Parhon Institute of Geriatrics in Roumania come reports by Dr. Anna Aslan (1) on the use of H-3, a compound apparently identical with procaine hydrochloride. The Roumanian Government and the governments and clinics in other satellite countries make it a point to let no possible chance escape to obtain publicity for H-3. As a result, popular lay magazines in the United States and Canada publicize the "miracles" of H-3. The symbol itself is a potent panacea—mysterious, alluring and newsworthy. Claims of a second youth have poured forth, until either denial or confirmation has been deemed imperative.

Editorials in medical journals point out the need for double-blind studies in order to eliminate the distortion due to psychologic reactions and thus furnish a true evaluation. A noted medical editor has stressed that we are "only young once." The editor is quite right; nevertheless, the remark begs the question. The primary question is: does H-3 have therapeutic value? A secondary question is: does it allay symptoms to such an extent as to make one feel young again? The answers are of importance.

Ponce de Leon did not really fail to find the Fountain of Youth; he simply did not recognize it as the subterranean stream by which the average span of youthfulness has now been extended by more than thirty years. That it will stop at the present juncture is hardly probable, though it may be some time before we reach an era like that of Methuselah.

According to Dr. Aslan, rejuvenation is not the major value of H-3, but rather its curative properties in a variety of disorders. This is a moot question. British medical workers are at odds about the value of H-3. Since miracles have been claimed by Dr. Aslan's followers and protagonists, and since we are skeptical of panaceas and man-made miracles, we at Pinehaven decided to explore this field with a double-blind study. This method safeguards against psychologic errors, and was not used by the East European group. Our study of procaine (H-3) was undertaken despite the fact that, procaine therapy was previously rated as a failure in this field.

* Presented at the Annual Convention of the National Geriatrics Society, Miami, Florida, May 12, 1960.

† Medical Director.

‡ Associate Resident Physician.

§ Physical Therapy Director.

Some thirty years ago it was noted that when procaine hydrochloride was used as a pain killer, it had some therapeutic value in arthritis, nervous disorders and certain other conditions. Along with many another American physician, the author tried it for a while, with fear and trepidation. However, the dosage used was too small (1 to 2 ml.), it was administered for too short a time, and there was no knowledge of the rationale. Medicine in those days was more empiric.

Dr. Aslan states that H-3 exerts its action by means of the para-aminobenzoic effect, the vitamin prototype effect, and an effect on the central and sympathetic nervous systems. Whether or not this be so, past failures with procaine therapy should not be allowed to stand in the way of a thorough investigation. In view of the almost hysterical propaganda, great care should be taken to avoid the error of fitting the facts to the theory rather than adapting the theory to the facts. We attempted to conduct such a study.

MATERIAL

Since the material would have to be the same as that used by Dr. Aslan, we wrote to her and were told that our pharmaceutical houses produce a compound identical with H-3. Procaine hydrochloride (Novocain®)[1] in 2 per cent solution, pH 3–5, is H-3. A buffer is used, but only for the purpose of preserving the desired balance between alkalinity and acidity of the injectable material; it is not an active therapeutic agent. Later in our work we used Gerocaine (Kirk) instead of procaine, because claims were being made that it was more closely allied to Dr. Aslan's H-3. However, we found no difference in effect, and standard procaine is much cheaper. For the controls, we used physiologic solution of sodium chloride or buffered sterile water.

METHODS AND PATIENTS

The procaine solutions were allotted two separate numbers, and the control solutions two other numbers. This multiple numbering was used in order to make the possibility of distinguishing procaine more difficult for the staff.

All patients were tested twice for allergy to procaine before receiving it. The initial test was made by injecting 0.5 ml. of solution either intradermally or subcutaneously; if no reaction was noted within twenty-four hours, a second injection (2 ml.) was given intramuscularly. If there was still no reaction, only then was treatment begun.

Treatment consisted of injecting 5 ml. of solution intramuscularly three times a week for four weeks, followed by a ten-day interval with no treatment, after which the next series of twelve injections was started. Thus far, 4 courses have been administered.

Sixty geriatric patients were chosen for the study from a group with arthritis, nervous disorders and senile mental disturbances (Tables 1 and 2) who had received little or no benefit with previous treatments; 30 were given procaine solution and 30 were given control solutions. The odd-numbered patients received procaine and the even-numbered received the control material.

The design of the double-blind study involved taking a sample from the patients in the control group who remained unaffected, and another sample from those in the procaine group who might receive benefit, and then switching the treatment. The intent was to see if those whose mental or physical health was not influenced by the control solutions would be affected by the procaine solutions, and whether those receiving procaine would become worse when it was omitted.

---

[1] In this paper we use the terms procaine (procaine hydrochloride), Novocain and H-3 interchangeably.

Later, when Kirk's Gerocaine was obtained, the subsequent 5 odd-numbered patients from the master list were given Gerocaine in order to compare the effects with those of procaine.

Among 65 patients tested for sensitivity, 2 had allergic reactions, in contrast to the claims of the Roumanians and Russians that the frequency is less than 1 in 1000. Any subject who showed a reaction was removed from the sample and the next alternate was put in his place. This was the only type of substitution allowed, except for that involving Gerocaine.

Late in the second course and during all of the third course, a respiratory epidemic swept Ocean County, New Jersey, felling both old and young. In some of the old people a fulminating type of pneumonia developed which sometimes caused death within twenty-four hours; in other cases, after apparent recovery, death occurred ten or twelve days later from either a cerebral or a coronary embolus. Thirty-two patients died in this period from all causes; 8 of these had terminal cancer and were omitted from the percentages of all deaths. The other deaths were as follows:

Patients receiving procaine therapy . . . . 1 death (3.3 per cent)
Patients receiving control solutions . . . . 3 deaths (12.0 per cent)
General institutional population . . . . 24 deaths (10.6 per cent)

In our locality the epidemic was thought to be Asiatic influenza. We did not concur in this diagnosis, since almost all of our staff and over 90 per cent of our patients had received the combined influenza vaccine a few months previously. The State Health Laboratory was called in. They took specimens of sputum and throat smears, both at Pinehaven and at the nearby Lakehurst Naval Air Base. These materials were injected into monkey kidney tissue and into eggs. The report for Pinehaven was that the cultures produced "no evidence of virus after three weeks." The causative agent was not determined. Whatever the cause, the disease was sometimes fatal and in many other cases constituted a setback which we were unable to evaluate.

RESULTS

During the first course, marked euphoria was noted in the patients receiving the water solution as well as in those receiving the procaine solution. However, there was no objective evidence of physical improvement in either group.

During the second course, only a few of the subjects receiving the control solutions manifested improvement, whereas those receiving procaine gradually projected the feeling of well-being into physical improvement that could be observed and recorded.

When the respiratory epidemic struck, there was a reversal which took nearly two weeks to overcome. The injections were continued in all except the patients who had pneumonia. Even in these cases no more than one or two injections were omitted during the height of the fever and respiratory embarrassment, and they were made up later at the end of the series before the pause interval.

The changes were slow in appearing. They were subtle rather than dramatic, and affected certain symptoms and signs entirely apart from those we had tentatively chosen as criteria. For example, one of the patients had hemiplegia and osteoarthritis which caused deformity but not total ankylosis. He wsa totally incontinent, had an extremely nasty disposition, and was such a personality problem that in no domicile had he responded either to the carrot or the stick. By the administrator's request, he had eventually been removed from every nursing home and hospital in which he had been a patient. He had been with us for four years and had been vile to the doctors, nurses and fellow-patients—

cursing, swearing and foul-mouthed at the drop of a pin. Somehow, he was persuaded to take procaine solution. During the third course, his mood changed. He became docile and cooperative, and it is now difficult for his fellow-patients to even needle him into a vile or nasty response. This alteration in mood has continued, and is most gratifying. So far, however, it is only that and nothing more. The arthritis has not responded to procaine therapy, nor has there been any change in the incontinence and hemiplegia.

During the third and fourth courses the changes that occurred were only slight, but they were increasingly observable and took place in more of the patients.

There have been no cures, but small improvements are acceptable gains in the development of individual personality. In these severely afflicted and otherwise unresponsive patients, any amelioration is a distinct benefit if it even slows progression of the disease or halts deterioration.

Two of the control group of subjects showed early slight improvement with respect to incontinence—an effect we had hoped to observe in the procaine group, but which failed to appear.

In the procaine group, slight improvement of various symptoms was widely distributed, and occurred even in an occasional case of brain syndrome. These manifestations were: 1) alteration in the gait associated with cerebrovascular disease (Critchley), 2) improvement in mood, 3) increased mobility, 4) decreased rigidity, and 5) the onset of a sense of well-being.

The medical staff did not notice any dramatic changes such as are produced by analeptics, tranquilizers and cerebral stimulants, or by physical therapy and measures to overcome decubitus ulcers induced by incontinence.

In any institution, the grapevine works with startling and spontaneous dispatch to bring total coverage of news about improvement or the contrary. Even when a patient has been bedridden for years and is unknown to 90 per cent of the other patients, any alteration such as sitting up in bed is at once noted and magnified.

As professional people, neither the doctors nor the nurses could accept such slight changes as dramatic. Nevertheless, some fair short-term results were observed, especially in view of the fact that they occurred in patients who had received no benefit or had regressed during previous treatment. The following are some representative case abstracts:

Case 1. On admission, this 60-year-old woman had arthritis with marked deformities. She had been treated with a variety of agents including gold therapy and massive doses of cortisone. During cortisone therapy, moon-face and camel hump had developed but the arthritic deformities and immobile joints had remained unchanged. She was allergic to aspirin and to aspirin products. She could tolerate the pain most of the time, but on occasion had to take opiates for relief.

After admission to Pinehaven, she was treated with prednisolone (Meticortelone) and later with triamcinolone (Aristocort); each drug afforded slight relief of pain and there were no side-effects, except for a high serum sodium level. This finding led to temporary discontinuation of the medication. She also received physical therapy, which has been continued to date. After treatment with procaine, she was able to manipulate her wheelchair by herself, whereas she could not do so before procaine therapy. She could feed herself by flexion of the elbow, which remained the least affected joint.

During the second course of procaine, slight freedom of motion developed in both shoulders and slight improvement of motion in the knuckles and wrists. The deforming nodes and distortion of the joints were unaltered, but during both active and passive motion the improvement was such that the patient began to paint in recreational therapy classes. She can now raise her arms to about the shoulder level.

After the second course of procaine, her disposition improved, in association with freedom from pain and the hope engendered by the increased mobility of the joints.

She was one of the patients affected by the epidemic of respiratory disease.

Case 2. This 72-year-old woman was admitted in 1953 with left hemiplegia and myocarditis with decompensation. According to the doctor who referred her, she was "unable to care for self, unable to walk, must be lifted, is incontinent with Foley's catheter and has massive decubiti." The incontinence and edema cleared up in the course of a year. Then progress stopped. For five years, pain in the joints continued and her condition was static.

This patient, too, was affected by the epidemic of respiratory disease. In the previous month she had begun to experience beneficial effects from procaine therapy. She was generally improved; the pain disappeared except for slight recurrence at less and less frequent intervals; swelling of the hands disappeared; and she was able to move her shoulders although she could not lift her arms.

Case 3. Eight years ago this 76-year-old woman was admitted with right-sided hemiplegia and cardiovascular-renal disease. Motion of the right temporomaxillary joint was inhibited, and there was marked pain in the articulation of the right jaw associated with occasional moderate swelling of the right side of the face. Edema of the ankles was also present. Her voice seldom rose above a whisper and it was difficult to understand her speech. Though entirely bedridden, she was a cheerful, pleasant person.

During the second course of procaine therapy her voice became stronger and her speech more understandable. She could enter into conversation with her roommates. The swelling and pain in her face subsided. After many years in bed, she began to sit up and eventually could be out of bed two or three hours a day.

Case 4. This 50-year-old woman with advanced multiple sclerosis was paralyzed in both legs and the left arm. Though she was usually of a cheerful disposition, she fought any attempted improvement as useless. For years she had been entirely bedridden.

With procaine therapy, improvement began at the end of the second course and became progressively more marked. She could be transferred from her bed into a wheel chair daily, and was able to take part in the social life of the institution. She finally accepted physical therapy, which until then she had refused.

This patient also was affected by the epidemic of respiratory disease.

Indices of improvement

At the end of the fourth course, 29 of 30 patients originally in the procaine group were still receiving injections, but only 21 of those in the control group were receiving injections. Although no patient in the procaine group refused treatment, 6 in the control group thought it was useless. On this basis, one might be tempted to read significance into the results from the viewpoint of mental health.

TABLE 1

Clinical Data on Patients Treated with Procaine

Procaine Patient No.	Age & Sex		Diagnosis	Opinion Regarding Progress			Score for Agreement of Opinions	
				Patient	Nurses	Regular physicians	On progress	On lack of progress
1	67	M	Arthritis	+	+	+	3	
2	76	M	Peripheral vascular disease	+	+	+	3	
3	69	F	Conversion hysteria; lymphadenoma	*	+	*	1	2
4	74	M	Cerebrovascular accident; fracture of femur	*	*	*		3
5	49	F	Multiple sclerosis	+	+	+	3	
6	52	M	Parkinson's disease	+	+	+	3	
7	72	F	Cerebral arteriosclerosis; chronic brain syndrome; anxiety neurosis	*	+	+	2	1 (patient.)
8	78	F	Cerebral arteriosclerosis	+	*	+	2	1 (nurse)
9	85	M	Cerebral arteriosclerosis	+	+	+	3	
10	60	F	Arthritis	+	+	+	3	
11	49	F	Multiple sclerosis	+	+	+	3	
12	64	F	Psoriasis	*	*	*		3
13	76	F	Right hemiplegia	+	+	+	3	
14	89	F	Senility	+	+	*	2	1 (doctor)
15	87	M	Heart block	+	+	+	3	
16	76	M	Cerebral arteriosclerosis	+	+	+	3	
17	68	M	Senility	*	+	+	2	1 (patient.)
18	60	M	Multiple sclerosis	+	+	*	2	1 (doctor)
19	86	M	Cerebral arteriosclerosis	+	+	*	2	1 (doctor)
20	93	M	Arteriosclerotic heart disease; ulcers of stomach	+	+	+	3	
21	56	M	Cerebral arteriosclerosis; cerebrovascular accident	+	+	*	2	1 (doctor)
22	69	M	Cerebral arteriosclerosis; chronic brain syndrome	+	+	*	2	1 (doctor)
23	50	M	Parkinson's disease, post-encephalitic	+	+	+	3	
24	35	M	Syringomyelia	+	+	+	3	
25	90	F	Senility; cerebral arteriosclerosis	*	*	*		3
26	94	F	Arthritis; senility; cerebrovascular accident	+	+	+	3	
27	72	F	Cerebral arteriosclerosis; left hemiplegia	+	+	+	3	
28	61	F	Malignant hypertension	—	—	—		3†
29	98	F	Senility; chronic brain syndrome (complicated by abscess of neck, now resolved)	+	*	+	2	1 (nurse)

* No progress or became worse.

† Patient worse.

Twenty-four patients (aside from the terminal cancer patients) died in the institution during this period. The percentage of deaths among the controls approximated that in the institution at large, whereas the percentage of deaths among the procaine patients was only one-third as great. Whether this disparity will persist remains to be seen.

As may be noted in Table 1, among 29 patients receiving procaine, 25 (83.3

TABLE 2

Clinical Data on Control Patients

Control Patient No.	Age† & Sex		Diagnosis	Opinion Regarding Progress			Score for Agreement of Opinions	
				Patient	Nurses	Regular Physicians	On progress	On lack of progress
1	71	M	Arthritis	*	*	*		3
2	50	M	Multiple sclerosis	*	*		1 (doctor)	2
3	95	F	Senility; blind; cerebro-vascular disease	*	*	*		3
4	80	M	CVA; chronic brain syndrome	*	*	+	1 (doctor)	2
5	63	M	Hemiplegia	+	+	+	3	
6	86	F	Parkinson's disease	*	*	*		3
7	58	M	Hemiplegia	+	*	*	1 (patient)	2
8	78	F	Senility; cerebral arterio-sclerosis	*	*	*		3
9	84	M	Cerebral arterio-sclerosis	+	+	*	2	1 (doctor)
10	84	M	Senility; cerebral arterio-sclerosis	*	+	*	1 (nurse)	2
11	90	M	Senility; prostatic enlargement	*	*	*		3
12	90	F	Senility; chronic brain syndrome	*	*	*		3
13	53	M	Parkinson's disease	*	*	+	1 (nurse)	2
14	86	F	Cerebral arterio-sclerosis	*	*	*		3
15	85	F	Chronic brain syndrome	*	*	*		3
16	72	M	Chronic brain syndrome	*	—	*		3
17	85	F	Left hemiplegia; general arteriosclerosis	*	*	*		3
18	83	F	Arteriosclerotic heart disease	+	*	+	2	1 (nurse)
19	80	F	Ulcers of stomach	+	+	*	2	1 (doctor)
20	77	F	Cerebral arteriosclerosis; myocarditis	*	*	*		3
21	80	M	Cerebral arteriosclerosis	*	*	*		3

† The average age of the original 30 patients was 77.1 years. Those who refused to continue treatment were mostly the younger group without cerebral irritation.

Three patients died. Six refused to continue treatment because they were not receiving any benefit.

* No progress or became worse.

per cent) showed improvement of some kind, even though slight. In many instances this improvement was progressive. Eventually, in a fair number, there was evidence of restorative values.

Table 2 shows the data for the control group of 21 patients. Nine (30 per cent) experienced improvement of some kind. One manifested marked and rapid restoration of faculties.

The scores for agreement concerning improvement are shown in Tables 1 and 2. One credit (plus sign) each was allowed for the opinion of the patient, the charge nurse, and the regular physician. Thus 3 credits in the "agreement on

TABLE 3

Laboratory Data on Patients Receiving 4 Courses of Procaine Therapy

Patient No.	Leukocyte Count (per cu. mm.)		Serum Cholesterol (mg./100 ml.)		Serum Calcium (mg./100 ml.)	
	At beginning	At end of 4th course	At beginning	At end of 4th course	At beginning	At end of 4th course
1	7800	+9000	250	−200	20.0	−11.6
2	12000	−10200	170	−125	11.6	−10.0
3	7800	+8400	340	−160	14.8	−14.4
4	7600	+8000	200	−125	13.6	−8.4
5	7400	+7800	200	−160	11.6	11.6
6	9100	+10500	220	−205	19.6	−12.0
7	9900	−8000	100	+230	20.0	+24.0
8	9500	−8000	100	+180	13.6	+25.6
9	7900	+8200	200	−150	13.6	13.6
10	8400	+11900	170	−110	13.6	−11.6
11	9100	+11100	140	+225	8.4	+16.4
12	7000	+9800	140	+230	10.0	+13.6
13	7300	+9000	200	−125	14.8	+20.0
14	6500	+9200	170	−70	11.6	+16.8
15	7800	+8000	185	−100	14.0	−11.6
16	6300	+9600	100	100	10.0	+11.6
17	7000	+8400	200	−125	12.8	+15.6
18	8000	−7900	170	−85	12.0	+13.6
19	8700	−8600	250	−125	10.0	+20.0
20	8900	−8500	150	−140	14.8	+20.0
21	7800	+8700	150	−100	13.2	+13.6
22	7500	+8250	125	−85	14.0	−6.0
23	6700	+12800	200	−80	11.6	−8.8
24	8700	+15000	200	−90	17.6	+18.8
25	6000	+6500	250	−100	8.0	+10.0
26	7200	+9400	100	+200	14.8	+18.0
27	5400	+7900	140	−130	12.4	+19.2
28	8000	+13000	190	−100	8.8	+14.8
29	7200	+7800 (+23)*	230	−140 (−23)†	11.6	−8.4 (+17)*
Averages	7806	8600	177	138	13.2	16.6

* Number of patients showing an increase.
† Number of patients showing a decrease.

progress" column indicates marked improvement; 2, moderate improvement; and 1, slight improvement. The scores were as follows:

Control group: 1 marked, 3 moderate, and 5 slight.

Procaine group: 15 marked, 9 moderate, and 1 slight.

Early benefit from procaine therapy consisted of a sense of well-being, a more normal mental attitude toward self and others, greater muscular power, and improved texture of the skin. Sphincter control was not significantly altered. As the number of courses increased, so did the number of patients showing improvement—in contrast to the control group.

A pattern slowly emerged of disorders in which procaine had early therapeutic effects; namely, arthritis, senile parkinsonism, cerebral arteriosclerosis with or without chronic brain syndrome, cerebral palsy (regarding muscle control), and multiple sclerosis.

Laboratory data (Tables 3 and 4)

In the early stages of procaine therapy there was no change in liver function (blood tests) or in the serum sodium and potassium levels.

TABLE 4

Laboratory Data on Patients Receiving 4 Courses of Control Treatment

Patient No.	Leukocyte Count (per cu. mm.)		Serum Cholesterol (mg./100 ml.)		Serum Calcium (mg./100 ml.)	
	At beginning	At end of 4th course	At beginning	At end of 4th course	At beginning	At end of 4th course
1	6200	+7000	170	+175	3.6	+8.4
2	6800	+7500	110	+150	11.6	+13.6
3	7500	−7000	200	−140	18.8	−12.4
4	8200	8200	175	−170	14.4	+14.8
5	8000	−6800	150	+220	12.2	+17.2
6	7000	+7800	180	+190	11.6	11.6
7	8100	−8000	280	−260	14.8	+17.2
8	7300	+7800	200	+220	13.6	−11.6
9	8400	−8000	140	140	17.6	−17.2
10	7200	+8600	165	−150	14.6	+15.6
11	8000	−6400	170	+180	14.4	+17.2
12	7500	+9000	230	−205	16.4	−14.8
13	6900	+7200	185	+210	13.6	+23.2
14	8500	−8200	140	140	10.6	−8.0
15	8000	−6900	200	+230	17.2	−15.2
16	7500	+7900	150	−120	17.6	−11.6
17	7000	+7600	100	+305	15.2	−11.6
18	7200	+9800	200	−180	12.4	+16.4
19	7400	−7100	160	+250	14.0	14.0
20	6900	+8900	170	+250	11.6	+24.8
21	6200	+11500 (+12)*	170	−110 (−8)†	6.0	+15.6 (+11)*
Averages	7420	7960	173	188	13.46	+14.6

* Number of patients showing an increase.

† Number of patients showing a decrease.

There was a decrease in the blood cholesterol level in 23 of the patients in the procaine group. Dr. Aslan, on the other hand, found an increase in cholesterol concentration. The difference may be due to the higher initial level caused by the high fat content of the American diet.

Serum calcium concentration increased in 17 of the patients in the procaine group. A rise was also observed in some of the patients in the control group.

There was an increase in the leukocyte count, with no alteration in the differential count, in 23 of the patients in the procaine group. This, too, is not in accord with Dr. Aslan's findings of a decrease in the leukocyte count.

SUMMARY AND CONCLUSIONS

So far, we have found no evidence to substantiate Dr. Aslan's claims that procaine (H-3) therapy reduces the biologic age below the chronologic age. Neither have we noticed increased libido in the patients studied.

There were no side-effects in our series of patients, who were all pre-tested with procaine.

Enough potential worth has been revealed, however, to justify continuation of the study, using procaine as adjunctive treatment.

Despite the fair results obtained in a group of previously unresponsive patients, no long-term conclusions can be drawn on the basis of such a short period of study. It will take at least a year before any realistic evaluation can be made.

Meanwhile procaine may safely be given in addition to other treatment in pre-tested patients afflicted with nervous disorders or senile mental disturbances, with the expectation that some of them will experience improvement of mood and personality traits. After patients with chronic brain syndrome have been followed for longer periods, perhaps a pattern of benefit may emerge, as noted already in some patients with arthritis and certain chronic nervous disorders.

REFERENCE

ASLAN, A.: A new method for the prophylaxis and treatment of aging with novocain—Eutrophic and rejuvenating effects, *Die Therapiewoche* 7: 14, 1956.

Editor's note added in proof:

Exercising its option, which is open to each of these fifty United States, to permit use and sale of any alleged therapeutic agent so long as it is not entered into interstate commerce (at which point U. S. Food and Drug Administration approval is required) Nevada approved use of Gerovital as reported in *The Wall Street Journal*, Thursday, June 2, 1977, p. 38.

Editor's Comments
on Papers 19 Through 23

SPECIFIC THERAPEUTIC MEASURES—HORMONAL REGIMENS

In 1950 Korenchevsky (1950) remarked that it was most improbable that complete rejuvenation of the senile organism would be possible since that meant immortality. He reported that hormonal replacement had both beneficial and deleterious effects on senility. There has been and continues to be controversy concerning treatment of gonadal failure of the female during her fifth to sixth decade. One persistent proponent of hormonal replacement is Dr. Robert A. Wilson (Paper 19), who shows that the weight of evidence favors estrogen-progestin replacement in the female:

> Estrogen does not induce cancer. The evidence presented indicates that estrogen and progesterone are prophylactic to breast and genital cancer to an unknown degree. It is urgent that this process be intensively investigated. It would seem advisable to keep women endocrine rich and, consequently, cancer poor throughout their lives. A consequence of this would be the elimination of the menopause. A major problem is that of reeducation.

A study of forty elderly males who, if not improved, were no worse because of combined androgen and estrogen therapy given by Dr. Harris is reported in Paper 20.

As for other hormones, Dr. Gregory Pincus' group (Romanoff et al., 1961) reported that in eight elderly men, 65–73 years of age, the excretion rate of the major urinary metabolites of cortisol was unaltered from that of eight young men, if expressed on the basis of creatinine excretion. However, absolute values were 75 percent those of the young group. Dr. Pincus suggested that probably there was no age diminution in the adrenal cortex *but that cortisol release was appropriate to the muscle mass of the individual.*·

There is a "third sex as comprising all individuals in the 60-year range" because of differential gonadal hypofunction with respect to the other endocrine glands, according to Dr. W. H. Masters. In Paper 21, Dr. Masters advocates use of a 20 androgen to 1 estrogen regimen in replacement of the lost gonadal function, stating the no other hormonal replacement is required since hypofunction of the other endocrine glands is not an aging accompaniment. To him, "there is not the slightest evidence to suggest, nor has any claim been made, that steroid replacement increases longevity by even a single day. However, adequate well controlled sex-steroid replacement can provide significant physical and mental stimulation or support."

In Papers 22 and 23, Dr. McGavack, having described treatment procedures, stated, "Finally, the physician is charged with the responsibility of bringing health and happiness to his patients. Prolonging life without alleviating some of its undesirable aspects scarcely is worthy of his best efforts. To live better is more important than to live longer."

19

Copyright © 1962 by the American Medical Association
Reprinted from J. Am. Medical Association 182(4):327–331 (1962)

The Roles of Estrogen and Progesterone in Breast and Genital Cancer

Robert A. Wilson, M.D., Brooklyn, N.Y.

The incidence of mammary and genital cancer was investigated in a group of 304 women whose ages ranged from 40 to 70 years (average 50.8) and who were treated with exogenous estrogens for periods up to 27 years (average 7.8). The breasts were thus exposed to estrogen for 2,387 patient-years. The genital exposure was only 1,852 patient-years because 86 patients underwent total hysterectomy and oophorectomy. The author estimates that 18 cases of cancer, either mammary or genital, were to be expected in the group; instead, no cases occurred. On this basis, it is urged that estrogens and progestins be studied more intensively for possible prophylactic effects against mammary and genital cancer.

THERE is no convincing proof that estrogen has ever induced cancer in the human being. Nevertheless, there is a widespread feeling that in some obscure way estrogen is carcinogenic in breast and endometrial cancer, despite the large amount of clinical evidence to the contrary in the literature. Even authorities in this field consider it a moot question, yet certain contradictions are apparent when, for example, the doctor who considers estrogen a carcinogen does not hesitate to use it for the amelioration of advanced cancer of the breast or of the prostate gland.

"Cancer inducing" and "cancer promoting" are often confused. In view of the improvement in vitality and cellular metabolism brought about by additional estrogen, a preexisting neoplasm, in the breast, for example, will share in the estrogen benefits with the rest of the body. Any resulting augmented growth, however, is a far cry from causing cancer. A physician interested in the use of estrogen and progesterone should examine some of the available evidence. The report of the symposium on *Biological Activities of Steroids in Relation to Cancer,* is recommended.

It is advisable to consider endogenous and exogenous estrogen separately; an attempt will also be made to fit progesterone (or the new progestogens) into the picture.

Endogenous Estrogen

Prolonged unopposed stimulation by endogenous estrogen has been postulated to produce changes in the endometrium of postmenopausal women. These changes range from simple hyperplasia and endometrial polyps, through cystic and adenomatous hyperplasia, to carcinoma.[1-5] This claim, including the association of hyperplasia and carcinoma in the same patient at the same time, has been studied by observers[5-8] with various results and interpretations. Retrospective studies of patients who have endometrial carcinoma in which diagnoses of previous biopsies or curettages have also given varying results and interpretations[4,5] are reviewed.

However, Greene and Brewer,[9] proceeding differently and using prospective or future studies in which early changes are followed to a final diagnosis of carcinoma, found no significant correlation with estrogen. This has been confirmed by Emge.[10]

Endometrial cancer can develop in a woman who has no ovaries. In 8 of 130 unselected castrated women, Cianfrani[11] found cancer an average of 10.6 years after removal of their ovaries. In the literature he found further such instances. Many cases occur years after the menopause, when vaginal smears indicate an extremely low, or absent, estrogen effect.

McBride[12] studied the ovaries, tubes, uninvolved endometrium, cervix, and vagina of women with carcinoma of the corpus. He was unable to demonstrate any difference in degree of estrogen stimulation in these cases and in a similar control group.

Chun et al.,[13] who used the criteria for detection of estrogen stimulation of the tubal and cervical epithelium described by Papanicolaou, Traut, and Marchetti,[14] examined the tubes of 37 postmenopausal women who had endometrial carcinoma and also the tubes of 47 normal postmenopausal women. They also examined the cervices of 34 of the former and compared them with 36 of the latter. No significant differences were found in these 2 groups, either in the cervices or in the tubes, in respect to evidence of estrogenic stimulation.

From the Department of Obstetrics and Gynecology of the Methodist Hospital of Brooklyn.

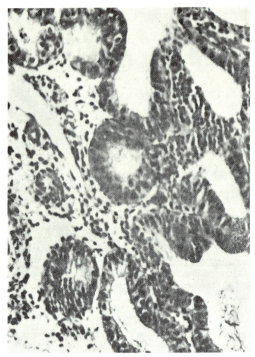

Fig. 1.—Endometrial tissue diagnosed by competent pathologist as adenocarcinoma of endometrium, Grade 1, focal. (Three others did not consider it to be malignant.) During last 2 years patient had received conjugated estrogens 1.25 mg. almost daily and alpha-estradiol benzoate 1.66 mg. intramuscularly every 2 weeks (× 300).

Ovarian stromal hyperplasia has been indicated as supplying a source of endogenous estrogen that produces endometrial cancer. Smith, Johnson, and Hertig[15] found this entity present in 87% of 180 patients who had endometrial cancer. Novak and Mohler[16] reported similar findings. This was further strengthened by the work of Sommers and Meissner[17] and others.[18, 19] This appears incriminating until we realize that, as Chun and colleagues state, "in none of these reports was it demonstrated that ovarian stromal hyperplasia actually did produce estrogen." It was simply assumed that it did. Actually, it has never been proved that such hyperplastic ovaries secrete estrogen.[13] Recently, in an attempt to settle the question, Roddick and Greene,[20] used fresh surgical specimens as controls. They found no significant difference in the ovarian stroma of patients who did or did not have endometrial malignancy.

Feminizing mesenchymomas such as granulosa and theca-cell tumors, the glamour tumors of the gynecologist, are not common. It is principally from the theca-cells that estrogen is derived. They are believed by some to have an injurious effect on the endometrium.[21]

Hertig[22] has shown that 81% of active mesenchymomas are accompanied by an abnormal endometrium. However, almost 4 years previously Emge[23] had stressed the pitfalls of interpreting the degree of estrogenic activity in an ovarian tumor on the basis of endometrial patterns alone. Reporting on 753 feminizing mesenchymomas collected from 30 clinics, he did not find adenomatous hyperplasia to be a common accompaniment. He found only 25 coexisting endometrial carcinomas, an incidence of 3.3%. Other low figures have been published.[24, 25]

Approaching the problem from studies primarily devoted to endometrial carcinoma, Emge[26] found only 7 feminizing tumors associated with 1,990 cases of this disease. Randall and Goddard[24] reported only 5 mesenchymomas in 531 endometrial malignancies, an incidence of 0.9%, which is normal for women past 50. Such data emphasizes the probable insignificance of ovarian-tumor estrogen in the genesis of endometrial carcinoma.

Dockerty and co-workers[27] have stated that about 20% of women under 40 in whom carcinoma of the uterine fundus developed gave clinical evidence of the Stein-Leventhal syndrome. Stein[28, 29] feels strongly that an etiological relationship between polycystic ovaries and carcinoma of the endometrium is lacking. He found the endometrium to be predominantly in the early midproliferative phase. Ingersoll[30] reported on 19 preoperative biopsies; 17 revealed proliferative activity, 1 was atrophic, and 1 was hyperplastic. Available data show that there is no elevation of estrogen in this syndrome.[31, 32]

About 15,000 cases of endometrial carcinoma occur annually in the United States, usually in obese, hypertensive, sterile, diabetic women (with hirsutism) a few years past the menopause. It has been shown that some responsible investigators have tended to attribute endometrial carcinoma to the excessive production or to the administration of estrogen. Starting in 1950, Sherman and Woolf[33] studied the ovaries of more than 300 postmenopausal women who had endometrial carcinoma. They found that in 80% of their first 133 cases, and in all subsequent ones, such ovaries contained large clusters of Leydig cells. These cells are also known as hilar, hilus, and sympathecoteopic cells. If not identical with, they are very similar to the Leydig cells of the testes. Less than 6% of the control ovaries showed such cells. However, 52 control patients who had postmenopausal hyperplasia had an incidence of 23%. This relationship—endometrial cancer, 100%, hyperplasia, 23%, and normal endometrium, 5.88% of hilar cells—is striking.

Pituitary luteinizing hormone (LH) stimulates these Leydig cells to produce male hormone, or an abnormal hormone, either of which is called a sexagen. The urine of controls and of those with endometrial carcinoma was tested for the presence of LH and all patients with this malignancy were found to excrete excessive amounts. In every case, the LH levels became normal after removal of the ovaries. Both authors theorize, on the basis of their findings and those of others, that women in whom endometrial carcinoma develops are destined to do so because they are born with abnormal Leydig cells. The cells are suppressed during the reproductive years by regular monthly production of estrogen and LH inhibiting progesterone. At the menopause, with its failure of progesterone production, LH rises to excessive amounts and stimulates the Leydig cells. The Leydig cells grow and produce prodigious amounts of a sexagen which is not able to suppress further LH production. Presumably the sexagen alone, or in conjunction with excess LH, adversely affects the endometrium. They also showed that if a progestin was given to these patients, LH production promptly dropped off. This led them to consider the possibility that a synthetic progestin might prevent endometrial carcinoma.

Additional evidence of the inhibiting properties of estrogen or progesterone, or both, on cancer cells, endometrial hyperplasia, and endometrial cancer has appeared recently. Pincus[34] obtained 412 Papanicolaou smears from women who were taking an estrogen-progestin combination for ovulation control. He compared the smears with 11,664 such tests made by Lee and colleagues[35] in 1956 (this nontreated group contained a good proportion of older women and so is not strictly comparable). The proportion of normal vaginal smears was much higher in the treated group; the occurrence of cancer was much lower (no malignant cancers, 1 carcinoma in situ of the cervix, probably antedating treatment). Pincus states: "In any event, no suggestion of carcinogenic effect is evident and the implication of cancer inhibition calls for further study."

Huggins[36] induced mammary cancer in all of 550 female rats of the Sprague-Dawley strain within 50 days by a single feeding of 20 mg. of a polynuclear hydrocarbon (7, 12-dimethylbenz (a) anthracene). When the affected rats were fed daily doses of 10 mg. of estradiol and 4 mg. of progesterone for 30 days, the carcinoma was extinguished in every case and did not recur.

Bimes and collaborators[37] markedly inhibited active cultures of malignant cells of the He La strains by adding 20 gammas of either estradiol or testosterone per cubic centimeter of culture medium.

Alvizouri[38] injected female rabbits with a mixture of progesterone plus 1 mg. of beta-estradiol daily for 40 days. He was able to protect the animals against hyperplasia with 35 mg. of progesterone. When 50 mg. was injected the endometrium showed marked regressive changes.

Kistner[39] reported that certain progestogens may cause cystic and adenomatous hyperplasia to re-

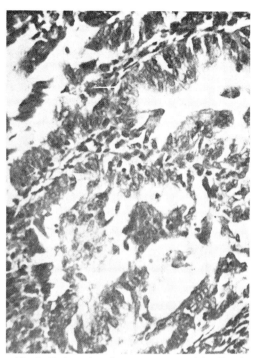

Fig. 2.—Endometrium from uterus removed for fibroids. Bleeding necessitated administration of 250 mg. of methyltestosterone daily for several days 3 weeks preoperatively. Three days before operation 50 mg. was given intramuscularly. In addition, patient received 20 mg. of medroxyprogesterone acetate daily for 12 days before surgery. Diagnosis was: endometrium: focal in situ adenocarcinoma, and diffuse decidual reaction with focal hemorrhages ($\times$ 300).

gress. He included 2 cases of carcinoma in situ but does not know if they were converted into secretory glands or removed by the curette.

Varga and Henriksen[40] reported encouraging results in the treatment of 13 cases of endometrial carcinoma by one of the newer high-potency progestins. In all instances there was a reduction in the size of the uterus, less bleeding, and a clearing of malodorous necrotic discharge. On pathology evaluation, 5 showed tumor alterations which they called secretory or acanthomatous conversion and in 1 case no residual tumor could be found. There is also the recent report of Kelley and Baker[41] that shows that moderate doses of progestational agents may induce prolonged symptomatic improvement and objective regression of carcinoma of the endometrium. It is evident from the preceding 7 reports, none antedating 1959, that a new field of research, particularly clinical, has been opened.

Exogenous Estrogen

Continuous exogenous estrogen therapy over a period of years has been implicated as a cause of fundal cancer. Novak[42] reported such a case after

12 years of continuous estrogen. Another has been reported by Fremont-Smith and co-workers.[43] Gusberg and Hall[44] reported 23 such cases, gathered from the material at Sloan Hospital for Women over the past 20 years. Among the sources of estrogen mentioned are: estradiol, estrogen, hormone pills, and hormone injections. Apparently urinary estrogen excretion determinations were not made. Vaginal estimates are not mentioned. Without one or the other of these, such cases, however interesting to the doctor concerned, have little scientific value.

It is remarkable that so few cases are reported. By coincidence or by the laws of chance we should expect many more reports as the rate of production of estrogenic substances shows the use of estrogen by millions of women. In 1954, Larson,[45] after extensive investigations, concluded that no correlation exists between estrogen and endometrial cancer. He dismissed the theory as mythical.

A mistaken diagnosis of endometrial adenocarcinoma is made with considerable frequency. The best pathologists differ in their interpretations (Fig. 1). Novak and Villa Santa[46] have written of this problem, pointing out that there is no sharp line of demarcation between the appearance of certain proliferative forms of hyperplasia and early adenocarcinoma. They mention the many sections referred from other clinics erroneously interpreted as adenocarcinoma in situ and treated by irradiation or hysterectomy, or both. A number of these showed typical cystic hyperplasia and not a few showed normal progestational changes. The growing use of progestogens and of other steroids increases the risk of a mistake in diagnosis, therefore the pathologist should always be informed of such medication (Fig. 2).

Geschickter and Hartman[47] administered massive doses of estrogens to rhesus monkeys for periods up to 7 years. Some received as much as 1,000,000 rat units per year. There was not 1 instance of carcinogenic change in any organ. The close relationship of the monkey to man is important, for it makes these experiments particularly valid in evaluating the possible dangers of estrogens in humans. Zondek[48] reported that enormous doses of natural estrogens failed to produce new growths in rats and in a large number of human subjects. Newman[49] reported the results of 40,000 vaginal smears. She stated that, of the patients found to have breast or pelvic cancer on initial examination, "not one had been having estrogen therapy." No case of carcinoma was diagnosed in 206 patients treated by large doses of estrogen over a 5½-year period by Geist, Walter, and Salmon.[50]

Mustacchi and Gordan[51] reported 120 postmenopausal women treated cyclically with estrogen for a total of 601 patient-years. No cancer was observed, although 5 to 6 malignancies were to be anticipated. Wallach and Henneman[52] reported a study

of 292 patients who had menopausal symptoms and osteoporosis. It is part of their review of records of women treated with estrogens during the past 25 years. Each received estrogen therapy for 1 or more years (the mean was 5.1 years per patient), a total of 1,480 patient years. In the 25 years, carcinoma of the breast was not detected in any patient during estrogen therapy. Only 1 genital cancer, a cervical carcinoma in situ, was detected in the last 10 years of this study, despite increased use of cervical cytological techniques.

Statistics from our own study are reported (Tables 1 and 2). Each patient was examined, including a vaginal smear, every 6 to 8 months. The smear report served to regulate estrogen intake as well as to indicate any atypical findings. All were asked to promptly report untoward symptoms or unplanned bleeding and all were trained in the self-examination of the breasts. Conjugated estrogens equine (Premarin) was the principal source of estrogen

Table 1.—Ages and Duration of Treatment of 304 Women Treated by Administration of Estrogen According to Vaginal Smear

Age	Cases, No.	%
40-49*	115	37.8
50-59	132	43.4
60-69	50	16.4
70-79†	7	2.4
	Average age 50.8 years	
Years of Treatment		
1- 5‡	137	45.1
6-10	81	26.7
11-15	42	13.8
16-20	25	8.2
20 plus§	19	6.2
	Average duration of treatment 7.8 years	

* Youngest patient (40 years).
† Oldest patient (73 years).
‡ Shortest period of treatment (14 months).
§ Longest period of treatment (27 years).

Table 2.—Incidence of Breast and Genital Cancer in 304 Women Exposed to High Medium to High Dosage of Exogenous Estrogen as Indicated by the Vaginal Smear

Type	Patient-Years of Exposure	Cases, No.
Breast cancer	2,387	0
Genital cancer	1,852*	0
Anticipated cancers (breast and genital)	2,387	18†

*Exposure of adnexa, uterus, and cervix was reduced because of 86 total hysterectomies with bilateral-oophorectomy performed before or during treatment.
†Based on the cancer incidence expectancy studies of Mustacchi and Gordan.[51]

because it was tolerated without side effects by almost all patients. Stilbene derivatives were not used. With a few exceptions, the exogenous opposing progestogen administered in 83 cases was medroxyprogesterone acetate (Provera). There were no breast or genital cancers during 2,387 woman-years of treatment. There were 2 deaths from unrelated causes.

From time to time a postmenopausal patient of ours, who is taking unopposed estrogen, bleeds unexpectedly or irregularly. Whenever bleeding is not cyclic or according to plan, hospitalization is usually advised as we do not feel that endometrial biopsies performed in the office or clinic are adequate. Simple hyperplasia is the usual finding.

Prolonged, uninterrupted, unopposed estrogen will not necessarily produce excessive stimulation of the ductal system of the breasts (ropy breasts) or troublesome endometrial hyperplasia as are shown in the following brief case reports.

Summary Report of Cases

CASE 1.—Female, aged 63, given alpha-estradiol benzoate, 1.66 mg. every week intramuscularly from 1941 to 1960 (19 years), no problems.

CASE 2.—Female, aged 62, given conjugated estrogens, 1.25 mg. daily, since 1947 (14 years), no difficulties.

CASE 3.—Female, aged 59, given conjugated estrogens, 1.25 mg. daily, and alpha-estradiol benzoate 1.66 mg. intramuscularly monthly, continuously since 1940 (20-plus years), no complications.

Proliferation goes so far and no further. An unknown factor, or factors, appears to be needed to produce more advanced or atypical findings. One can only speculate on the number of women with asymptomatic hyperplasia.

Comment

The incidence of cancer of all sites in women shows a constant increase with age, while at the same time the production of estrogen steadily declines. McAllister et al.[53] recently determined urinary estrogens after endocrine ablation. With the method of Brown (*Biochem J* 60:185, 1955) estriol, estrone, and estradiol-17-B were determined in a group of women with inoperable or metastatic breast cancer before and after oophorectomy, adrenalectomy, or radio-active implantation of the pituitary. Response to these forms of therapy was accepted only when there was objective evidence of regression of tumor deposits. The mean estrogen levels in those patients whose cancers regressed did not differ significantly from those in whom no improvement occurred. Therefore, the regression may not be related to estrogen but due to other reasons.

If estrogen were carcinogenic, malignancy of the breast would be frequently encountered in pregnancy because the estrogen level rises to great heights, especially in the later months. Malignancy of the breast is very rare in pregnancy and lactation, only 3 per 10,000 pregnancies.[54] Even in the few reported cases, the tumor may well have antedated the pregnancy.

In 1960, Berkow[55] wrote an inspiring biography of Dr. Ludwig Augustus Emge. In it is stated Dr. Emge's position in regard to estrogen and cancer. Emge feels that estrogen's position is entirely secondary; that it is merely the fertilizer which enhances the growth already under way; that tissue proliferation induced only by estrogen stimulation in the absence of a receptive constitution and yet unknown exciting factor, is self-limited.

Our attitude toward breast and genital cancer is that it is a complex drama of subtle relationships among the pituitary, adrenals, and gonads, with metabolic and herediary factors prominent and a viral or other unknown causative agent lurking in the background. Estrogen and progesterone are but 2 of many actors in the tragedy.

Conclusions

Estrogen does not induce cancer. The evidence presented indicates that estrogen and progesterone are prophylactic to breast and genital cancer to an unknown degree. It is urgent that this process be intensively investigated. It would seem advisable to keep women endocrine rich and, consequently, cancer poor throughout their lives. A consequence of this would be the elimination of the menopause. A major problem is that of reeducation.

90 Eighth Ave., Brooklyn 15, N.Y.

This study was aided by a grant from the Lindridge Research Fund of the Methodist Hospital, Brooklyn, N.Y.

Generic and Trade Names of Drugs

Estrogenic Substances, Conjugated—*Amnestrogen, Conestron, Estrifol, Premarin.*

Progesterone—*Corlutone, Corpomone, Lipo-Lutin, Lutromone, Progesterone, Progestin, Proluton.*

Piperazine Estrone Sulfate—*Sulestrex Piperazine.*

Medroxyprogesterone Acetate—*Provera.*

Estradiol—*Dimenformon, Estradiol, Lip-Oid, Progynon.*

References

1. Gusberg, S. B.: Precursors of Corpus Carcinoma; Estrogens and Adenomatous Hyperplasia, *Amer J Obstet Gynec* 54:905-927 (Dec.) 1947.

2. Meissner, W. A.; Sommers, S. C.; and Sherman, G.: Endometrial Hyperplasia, Endometrial Carcinoma, and Endometriosis Produced Experimentally by Estrogen, *Cancer* 10:500-509 (May-June) 1957.

3. Novak, E., and Rutledge, F.: Atypical Endometrial Hyperplasia Simulating Adenocarcinoma, *Amer J Obstet Gynec* 55:46-63 (Jan.) 1948.

4. Speert, H.: Premalignant Phase of Endometrial Carcinoma, *Cancer* 5:927-944 (Sept.) 1952.

5. Hertig, A. T., and Sommers, S. C.: Genesis of Endometrial Carcinoma; Study of Prior Biopsies, *Cancer* 2:946-956 (Nov.) 1949.

6. Bamforth, J.: Carcinoma of Body of Uterus and Its Relationship to Endometrial Hyperplasia; Histological Study, *J Obstet Gynec Brit Emp* 63:415-419 (June) 1956.

7. Jones, H. O., and Brewer, J. I.: Study of Ovaries and Endometrium of Patients with Fundal Carcinomas, *Amer J Obstet Gynec* 42:207-217 (Aug.) 1941.

8. Roddick, J. W., Jr., and Greene, R. R.: Relation of Nonmalignant Postmenopausal Endometrial Changes to Ovarian Morphology, *Amer J Obstet Gynec* 75:235-239 (Feb.) 1958.

9. Greene, R. R., and Brewer, J. I.: Relation of Sex Hormones to Tumors of Female Reproductive System, *Amer J Roentgenol* 45:426-445 (Mar.) 1941.

10. Emge, L. A.: Geriatric Aspects of Primary Endometrial Cancer, *J Amer Geriat Soc* 2:553-565 (Sept.) 1954.

(Additional references are available from the author on request.)

20

Reprinted from *J. Am. Geriatrics Soc.* 6(4):297–305 (1958)

EFFECTS OF ORAL SEX HORMONES AND RESERPINE IN ELDERLY MEN

RAYMOND HARRIS, M.D.*

The Ann Lee Home and St. Peter's Hospital, Albany, N. Y.

Sex hormones control important metabolic functions and regulate secondary sex characteristics. With aging, the decline of gonadal activity in both sexes results in deficiencies of androgen and estrogen which normally play a vital role in the growth, development and maintenance of genital organs and many other body tissues. Attempts to modify the apparently inevitable changes of senescence have led to numerous studies in which hormonal replacement therapy has been used in an effort to retard the aging process physiologically. Careful investigations by Kountz (1), Masters (2), and others have demonstrated that the administration of combined estrogen and androgen can result not only in symptomatic improvement in the well-being of senior citizens but also in revascularization of tissue. Nevertheless, the value of sex hormone therapy in the aging post-climacteric individual has not yet been satisfactorily appraised, and opponents of this form of treatment can marshal considerable contrary evidence.

After reviewing previous studies we could not help questioning whether the results in the male justify its use, especially since most of the studies were with women in whom the results are easier to assess.

In this study we sought to determine whether oral sex hormones would improve the well-being of the geriatric male; and if so, whether the employed combination of hormones was given in suitable dosage. The problem of dosage is important since, as Masters (3) points out, "The most serious roadblock to successful long-term steroid replacement is the problem of conversion of the well-defined intramuscular dosage into a correct orally absorbed ratio." We also decided to study the effect of adding reserpine therapy to the combined sex hormone regimen, because our previous work showed that reserpine can be of benefit to the elderly patient (4, 5).

METHODS

Forty fairly well-matched male residents of the Ann Lee Home were selected. Their ages ranged from 59 to 87 years. All were ambulatory. Twenty-three of the 40 patients had known heart failure or other cardiac disease. Many had arthritis, pulmonary disease and other chronic conditions frequently found in the aged. All medications given prior to the study were continued unchanged. A complete physical examination, x-ray examination of the chest, spine and femur (for detection of abnormal bone conditions or osteoporosis), a complete blood count, urinalysis, a twelve-lead electrocardiogram and determination of the serum cholesterol level were performed: 1) three weeks after the start of the study, 2) during placebo therapy, 3) four to six weeks after test medications were started,

* Assistant Medical Director.

and 4) at the end of the study. Serum protein levels were determined by chemical and paper electrophoretic methods.[1] Psychologic tests[2], including the Albany Behavioral Rating Scale (6) and a modified Fergus Falls Rating Scale, were performed on each patient at these times. These results will be reported later.

All patients received a placebo initially. After three weeks of placebo therapy, they were divided at random into 8 groups and then, arbitrarily according to their grouping, were given Linguets[3] from bottles labelled A, A$_2$, B, B$_2$, C, C$_2$, D or D$_2$. All Linguets were identical in appearance and taste. Originally they were to be administered sublingually, but in order to assure complete ingestion in all patients, the oral route was finally chosen. Two Linguets were given daily, Monday through Friday. All patients received the same number of tablets from the same person.

Each group received the same medication until the completion of the study. The shortest period of observation was seven months, and the longest nine months. Neither the investigator nor the nurse giving the medication knew the contents of the Linguets. As a further check, the author did not know which Linguets each patient received until each patient's data had been completely evaluated and tabulated at the end of the study.

When the code was broken, it was learned that 4 patients (Group C) continued to receive placebo tablets, 5 (Group B) received reserpine and placebo tablets, 19 (Groups B$_2$, C$_2$, D, and D$_2$) received Femandren tablets, and 12 (Groups A and A$_2$) received Femandren and reserpine tablets. The average age of the patients in each group was 74 years, except for those in the placebo group whose average age was 77. The only other apparent initial difference was that Group C (placebo) and Group B (reserpine and placebo) patients had fewer cardiac problems.

RESULTS

General clinical condition

As judged by strength, vigor, vitality, general well-being and activity, an obvious overall improvement in clinical condition occurred in most patients. There was improvement in 75 per cent of the reserpine-Femandren-group, in 72 per cent of the Femandren group, in 60 per cent of the reserpine-placebo group, and in 25 per cent of the placebo group. Since only 4 patients were receiving placebo, the improvement rating of 25 per cent is probably high (Tables 1, 2, 3 and 4).

---

[1] Analyses performed by Philip Luther, M.D., Bender Laboratory, Albany, N.Y.

[2] Devised by Leo Shatin, Ph.D., Chief Psychologist, V. A. Hospital, Albany, N. Y.

[3] Supplied through the courtesy of Ciba Pharmaceutical Products, Inc.

A, A$_2$ = 0.02 mg. of ethinyl estradiol combined with 5 mg. of methyltestosterone (Femandren), plus 0.2 mg. of reserpine (Serpasil).

B = 0.2 mg. of reserpine (Serpasil) plus placebo.

C = Placebo.

B$_2$, C$_2$, D, D$_2$ = 0.02 mg. of ethinyl estradiol combined with 5 mg. of methyltestosterone (Femandren).

137

Weight

Appetite and weight gain (5 pounds or more) were definitely better in the reserpine-Femandren patients than in the Femandren patients (Tables 1 and 2) and much better in both groups than in the placebo group. Anything less than

TABLE 1

Reserpine and Femandren (Groups A and A₂)

No. of patients—12. Av. age—74 yrs. (range, 65–85)

Prior Cardiac History		Appetite		Weight Change (5 or more pounds)			Prostate Size	Breast Size	Strength & General Well-Being	
Yes	Cardiac failure	No.	%	During study	%	Post-study			No.	%
7	4									
Increase...................		7	58.3	5	41.7	1	3	3	9	75
No change..................		5	41.7	4	33.3	1	8	9	3	25
Decrease...................				3	25.0	8	1			

Laboratory Studies	Change Greater Than				Osteoporosis, If Present
	1 m. RBC	1 Gm. Hg	10% of Total Proteins	10% of Cholesterol	
Increase................	2	8	1	4	
No change..............	8	1	10	2	4
Decrease...............	2	3	1	6	3

TABLE 2

Femandren (Groups B₂*, C₂, D and D₂)

No. of patients—18. Av. age—74 yrs. (range, 62–87)

Prior Cardiac History		Appetite		Weight Change (5 or more pounds)			Prostate Size	Breast Size	Strength & General Well-Being	
Yes	Cardiac failure	No.	%	During study	%	Post-study			No.	%
11	5									
Increase...................		8	44.4	3	16.7		4	4	13	72.2
No change..................		8	44.4	12	66.6	8	12	14	3	16.7
Decrease...................		2	11.2	3	16.7	6	2		2	11.1

Laboratory Studies	Change Greater Than				Osteoporosis If Present
	1 m. RBC	1 Gm. Hg	10% of Total Proteins	10% of Cholesterol	
Increase................	4	12	2	3	
No change..............	14	6	14	10	13
Decrease...............			2	5	1

* One patient died from pneumonia before the final evaluation and is not included in the results. His appetite, weight and hemoglobin level had undergone significant improvement.

TABLE 3
Reserpine and Placebo (Group B)
No. of patients—5.   Av. age—74 yrs. (range, 59–85)

Prior Cardiac History		Appetite		Weight Change (5 or more pounds)			Prostate Size	Breast Size	Strength & General Well-Being	
Yes	Cardiac failure	No.	%	During study	%	Post-study			No.	%
2	0									
Increase		2	40	1	20	2		2	3	60
No change		2	40	2	40	2	5	3	2	40
Decrease		1	20	2	40					

Laboratory Studies	Change Greater Than				Osteoporosis If Present
	1 m. RBC	1 Gm. Hg	10% of Total Proteins	10% of Cholesterol	
Increase	1	2	1	2	
No change	4	2	4	2	2
Decrease		1		1	1

TABLE 4
Placebo (Group C)
No. of patients—4.   Av. age—77 yrs. (range, 69–87)

Prior Cardiac History		Appetite		Weight Change (5 or more pounds)			Prostate Size	Breast Size	Strength & General Well-Being	
Yes	Cardiac failure	No.	%	During study	%	Post-study			No.	%
1	0									
Increase		1	25	1	25	1	1		1	25
No change		3	75	2	50	1	3	4	3	75
Decrease				1	25	1				

Laboratory Studies	Change Greater Than				Osteoporosis If Present
	1 m. RBC	1 Gm. Hg.	10% of Total Proteins	10% of Cholesterol	
Increase		2	2	1	
No change	4	1	2	3	3
Decrease		1			

a 5-pound weight change was considered to be no change. After the medications were stopped, the weight was followed for several months in some patients. Eight of 10 patients who had been receiving reserpine-Femandren lost weight; only 1 continued to gain weight. Six of 14 patients taking Femandren lost weight; in 8 there was no change. No patient in the reserpine-placebo group, and 1 patient in the placebo group lost weight following cessation of therapy.

139

Laboratory findings

The increase in hemoglobin (1 gram per 100 ml. or more) in the reserpine-Femandren and Femandren groups was the only notable laboratory change. No supplementary hematinic drug was given at any time. Total cholesterol (Bloor method) levels varied too greatly to have any meaning.

Cardiovascular system

Since sex hormones and especially androgens possess electrolyte and water-retaining properties, they should be administered cautiously to cardiac patients. We were particularly interested in the effects of these medications on the cardio-vascular status of the men in our series.

Seven of the 12 patients in the reserpine-Femandren group had heart disease. Four of the 7 had previously had congestive heart failure. No patient in this group showed cardiac deterioration or congestive heart failure during therapy. An 80-year-old man with arteriosclerotic cardiovascular disease and auricular fibrillation had edema of his legs during the control period. After treatment he felt stronger, ate better and became more active, and the peripheral edema disappeared. A second patient with arteriosclerotic heart disease, a greatly enlarged heart and pulmonary emphysema felt much better during therapy and showed no evidence of failure. Two months after the Linguets were discontinued, his appetite waned and he became weaker. During the hormonal period his weight rose from 130 to 133½ pounds. Two months after the hormones were stopped, his weight had dropped to 121½ pounds. A third patient in this group, an 83-year-old man who had previously had heart failure, improved remarkably. In the control period he weighed 121½ pounds. During the year of treatment with reserpine-Femandren he gained 10 pounds, displayed increased energy and vitality, and worked more. He actually looked younger than he had at the beginning of treatment. His hemoglobin level rose from 13 grams to 14.4 grams per 100 ml. The weight gain initiated by hormones and reserpine continued, so that he weighed 143 pounds five months after the end of drug therapy. In this group, there was 1 patient in whom an acute cardiac posterior-wall infarction developed five months after beginning therapy; recovery was uneventful and complete.

Twelve of 19 patients receiving Femandren had heart disease. Five of the 12 had congestive heart failure during the control period and required digitalis, diuretics and other cardiovascular medications. Only 1 of these 5 patients, a 64-year-old man with chronic congestive heart failure, became worse during Femandren therapy; he improved only slightly after it was discontinued. In a 75-year-old man, right and left heart failure and edema developed two months after Femandren was started. During the following eight months the heart failure improved while he was taking Femandren. An 87-year-old man had a slight increase in edema of the legs during Femandren therapy but otherwise experienced definite improvement in vitality and vigor. Moderate prostatic hypertrophy developed. The resultant interference with urinary flow may have contributed to the edema of the legs by increasing salt retention. In an 82-year-old patient, the electrocardiographic pattern became normal during therapy, whereas it had indicated left heart strain initially.

Two of the 9 patients in the reserpine-placebo group had previously had heart disease—in 1 it was heart failure. In no person in this group did heart failure develop during the study.

In all groups no significant changes in blood pressure or pulse were observed.

With the doses used, combined hormonal therapy caused no significant deterioration of the cardiovascular system. On the contrary, the improved mental and physical well-being of the patient as reflected by better nutritional status and higher serum protein and hemoglobin levels, indirectly improved the condition of the heart. Patients performed their duties with less physical strain and effort. An improved cardiovascular status was indicated by their improved ability to walk and work. There was no evidence of a direct specific effect on the myocardium. Significant edema or increased salt retention was no serious problem.

Osteoporosis

Since changes in bone density are difficult to interpret, the radiologist[4] read the x-ray films rather conservatively. He compared the three sets of films without knowing the nature of the study or the medications received. Nevertheless, in 3 of 7 patients with osteoporosis in the reserpine-Femandren group and in 1 of 14 in the Femandren group, there was a decrease in osteoporosis during therapy. In 1 of 3 men with osteoporosis in the reserpine-placebo group, there was slight improvement. In none of 3 patients with osteoporosis in the placebo group was there a decrease in the amount during therapy.

DISCUSSION

In evaluating these results, we recognize that we cannot "make a silk purse out of a sow's ear." We cannot expect any medication to reverse completely in all instances the long continued malfunctioning of tissues and organs which chronic disease has frequently damaged irreversibly. The patient cannot be put into any better physical or functional shape than his aging cardiovascular system will allow, despite the stimulating action of the sex hormones on the anabolism of protein and osseous tissue. It is to be expected that some patients will respond, whereas others will continue to deteriorate because of factors unassociated with the decline in gonadal activity and decreased sex hormones.

Overall results

The difference in well-being between the Femandren and the reserpine-Femandren groups was negligible. However, when the effect on weight and appetite is also considered, the reserpine-Femandren group received more benefit. Masters (3) noted that "roughly 75 per cent of the individuals involved have shown significant improvement in either clinical or mental well-being or both." Our results are similar, and indicate that oral administration of combined sex

---

[4] We are indebted to Dr. Donald Baxter, Radiologist, Albany Hospital, for the roentgenologic comparisons.

hormones can be as effective as parenteral administration. That the 25 per cent improvement listed for the small placebo group is too high is indicated by the observation that when all 40 patients were receiving placebo therapy, little improvement in weight, strength or well-being occurred. Furthermore, the fact that some patients in the Femandren and reserpine-Femandren groups voluntarily requested reinstitution of the medication after the study was ended indicates they believed it to be beneficial. No patient in the reserpine and placebo groups made this request.

Weight gain

Weight gain is a well known side-effect of reserpine, which probably accounts for the greater improvement in appetite and weight in the reserpine-Femandren patients. The rapid weight loss, both in this group and in the Femandren group, within two months following cessation of therapy indicates that these drugs accounted for the gain in weight and its maintenance. The anabolic properties of the sex steroids are important in the maintenance of body weight. That the weight gain was not simply water logging is indicated by the fact that (with rare exceptions) no edema developed in these patients.

Osteoporosis

The amount of improvement in osteoporosis noted by x-ray examination was significant. In such a comparatively short period of time, x-ray changes cannot be 'expected to be dramatic. Weinberg (7) feels that "The x-ray picture is not a useful criterion, as it may be years, if ever, before such improvement is evident."

Prostatic size and gynecomastia

As far as the effects on the prostate and the breast were concerned, the patients could be divided into three categories: 1) those in whom gynecomastia developed, 2) those in whom the prostate increased in size, and 3) those unaffected by therapy. From these data it might be inferred that the patients in the first category received too much estrogen and the patients in the second category did not receive enough. However, since methyltestosterone alone has produced gynecomastia (8), such an interpretation is open to question.

Dosage

The change from parenteral hormonal therapy to the more practical and desirable oral medication was a problem.

The patients treated with hormones received 2 Femandren Linguets orally five days weekly. Thus the weekly dose of ethinyl estradiol was 0.2 mg. and that of methyltestosterone was 50 mg. Since the percentage of improvement in patients receiving this amount was similar to that in patients receiving parenteral therapy, it would seem that Femandren is a satisfactory oral equivalent. However, since this study concerned only males, it cannot be concluded that this dosage is necessarily the answer for all older patients. Because oral or even sublingual absorption is unlikely to be exactly the same in all persons, additional amounts of estrogen or androgen may be indicated. This fact is further demonstrated by the fact that in a few patients the prostate increased in size, whereas in others slight gynecomastia developed. In no instance were these changes severe enough to require discontinuation of medication.

Clinically there was no evidence of prostatic carcinoma in any of the patients receiving hormones. Provided a proper pretreatment examination and adequate follow-up of the patient are performed, there seems to be little likelihood of the precipitation of cancer by the use of hormones. Since the death rate from cancer of the breast and genital organs is no greater now (1950) than it was before crystalline estrin was discovered and used (1929), it would appear that the fear of cancer from its use is greatly exaggerated (9). Lesser *et al.* (10) conducted a careful gross and microscopic study on 100 patients and concluded that ". . . there was no evidence that testosterone propionate in the dosage used had initiated carcinoma or activated latent carcinoma of the prostate gland."

Reserpine

Our previous study (5) showed that the tranquilizing properties of reserpine were very valuable in helping some elderly patients to become adapted. We reached similar conclusions in the present study. We feel, however, that reserpine administration should be on an individual basis.

SUMMARY AND CONCLUSIONS

1. The results are reported of a double blind study concerning the effects of an orally administered androgen-estrogen combination (Femandren) with or without reserpine in a group of 40 elderly male residents of the Ann Lee Home.

2. Seventy-two per cent of the men receiving Femandren improved in strength and well-being. Seventy-five per cent of the men receiving reserpine-Femandren improved similarly. The addition of reserpine enhanced the weight gain but did not materially add to the general well-being.

3. The percentage of improvement in this study (75 per cent) is the same as that reported in studies in which the hormones were given parenterally. Apparently, oral administration of hormones can be as satisfactory as parenteral administration.

4. For the majority of patients the dosage employed was satisfactory. In a few there was some increase in the size of the prostate, and in a few others slight gynecomastia developed.

5. There was x-ray evidence of a decrease in osteoporosis in a small number of patients receiving combined sex hormones.

6. Combination androgen and estrogen replacement therapy by the oral route will improve the general well-being and weight in a significant proportion of elderly patients. The addition of reserpine may augment the gain in weight.

REFERENCES

1. KOUNTZ, W. B.: Revitalization of tissues and nutrition in older individuals, *Ann. Int. Med.* **35**: 1055 (Nov.) 1951.
2. MASTERS, W. H.: Rationale of sex steroid replacement in the "neuter gender," *J. Am. Geriatrics Soc.* **3**: 389 (June) 1955.

3. MASTERS, W. H.: Endocrine therapy in the aging individual, *Obst. & Gynec.* **8:** 61 (July) 1950.
4. HARRIS, R.: Clinical use of reserpine (Serpasil) in geriatrics, *Ann. New York Acad. Sc.* **59:** 95 (Apr.) 1954.
5. HARRIS, R.: Reserpine therapy in hypertension, *J. Am. Geriatrics Soc.* **4:** 269 (March) 1956.
6. SHATIN, L., AND FREED, E. X.: A behavioral rating scale for mental patients, *J. Mental Sc.* **101:** 644 (July) 1955.
7. WEINBERG, M.: Osteoporosis: diagnosis and treatment, *J. Am. Geriatrics Soc.* **4:** 429 (May) 1956.
8. McCULLAGH, E. P., AND ROSSMILLER, H. R.: Methyl testosterone I. Androgenic effects and the production of gynecomastia and oligospermia, *J. Clin. Endocrinol.* **1:** 496 (June) 1941.
9. SHELTON, E. K.: The use of estrogen after the menopause, *J. Am. Geriatrics Soc.* **2:** 627 (Oct.) 1954.
10. LESSER, M. A.; VOSE, S. N., AND DIXEY, G. M.: Effect of testosterone propionate on the prostate gland of patients over 45, *J. Clin. Endocrinol. & Metab.* **15:** 297 (March) 1955.

21

Reprinted from *Obst. Gynec.* 8(1):61–67 (1956)

Endocrine Therapy in the Aging Individual

WILLIAM H. MASTERS, M.D.

ONE OF THE MOST controversial subjects in medicine today is that of sex-steroid replacement in the aging individual. The controversy not only rages within the membership of those trained in gynecology but also is of major moment to the overlapping disciplines of gerontology and endocrinology. It should be noted at the outset that the controversy exists not only over the question of whether sex-steroid replacement is indicated by the aging process but also as to the manner or type of replacement to be used when a considered indication arises. Certainly the burden of proof rests with the proponents of replacement technics. Clinical proof ultimately must be effectively related not only to the efficacy of replacement technics but also to the innocuousness of such supportive procedures.

I am completely convinced that a third sex exists and is rapidly multiplying in our society today. The basic components of this third sex or "neuter gender" are presently considered to consist of former males and females who have reached the age of approximately sixty years. Such age conformity is of course only loosely adhered to by the new-gender members. There are obviously many women who have joined the "neuter gender" age group before their fiftieth birth-

day. Equally obviously, there are a significant number of males who could not be considered candidates for the third sex even after their seventieth birthday. It is fair to generalize that the female will be a third-sex candidate roughly fifteen years ahead of the male. At present the components of the "neuter gender" must be delineated by clinical observation. Perhaps in time satisfactory laboratory evaluation will be available.

If the existence of a third sex is acknowledged, the remainder of the concept of "puberty to grave" sex-steroid support is easily explained. The entire purpose of the long-range replacement technics is an attempt to develop a happier, better adjusted, and more useful member of the "neuter gender" as he or she lives out the ever-increasing life span. There is not the slightest evidence to suggest, nor has any claim been made, that steroid replacement increases longevity by even a single day. However, adequate, well-controlled sex-steroid replacement can provide significant physical and mental stimulation or support.

ENDOCRINE CONTROL OF PHYSIOLOGIC FUNCTION

One of the real keys to the aging process is the humoral control of our basic physiologic functions. The entire process of organ growth, function, and retrogression is fundamentally stimulated or controlled by the glands of internal secretion. In succession, the pituitary, adrenals, thyroid, pancreas, and gonads are responsible for individual

Presented at the Fourth Annual Meeting of the American Academy of Obstetrics and Gynecology, December, 1955, Chicago, Ill.

From the Department of Obstetrics and Gynecology, Washington University School of Medicine, St. Louis, Mo.

phases of growth and function of the various organ systems. It is therefore of vital concern to consider the function potential of the entire humoral system during the degenerative or aging phases of the human body, as both male and female components approach the neuter phase of life.

Reserve Potential of Organs

Within the last two years it has become increasingly apparent that the gonads are the Achilles heel of the endocrine system in its continual battle against the aging processes. The apparent functional failure of the gonads would appear to be the result of an inherent lack of organ-function reserve, when the gonads are compared to the other glands of internal secretion.

Work described by Albert supports the results of investigation in our own laboratory[11] in the contention that there is marked organ-function reserve for the pituitary gland, even in the 75-year age group. Starr showed that there is effective thyroid gland function in the aging individual. Gallagher and Tyler are in complete accord as to the organ-function potential of the adrenal glands of the aged individual. The effective secretory activity of the pancreas in the aged individual was established as early as 1940 by Meyer and Necheles. Thus we are faced with the obvious factor of a functional involution of the gonads alone among the endocrine glands as the individual approaches the neuter age group. Obviously the rate of involution varies from individual to individual and, in essence, must be a direct reflection of a reduced organ-function potential for the gonad involved.

Gonadal Failure

Some suggestive evidence for the early failure of gonadal function is found during mature adult life. It has long been noted clinically that both ovaries and testes are easily influenced into dysfunction during the reproductive years. The gonads are infi-nitely sensitive to the influence of other elements of the endocrine chain. In addition, any general body dysfunction or chronic infectious process may easily interfere with adequate ovarian or testicular hormone production. Thus, it is relatively apparent that the short-lived activity of the gonads represents the complete effort of the individual reproductive gland. Once failure of function sets in, involution is relatively rapid. The short-lived clinical burst of full gonadal activity exhausts not only the normal functioning process but also whatever organ function reserve the individual gonad possesses.

The short life expectancy of the gonads when compared to the other glands of internal secretion has been a well-discussed clinical phenomenon for years. Not only do gonadal influences develop later than other humoral forces, but it is now apparent that endocrine glandular involution is first demonstrated by the failing reproductive powers of the gonads. It is unfortunately true that not only do the reproductive powers of the gonads fail but also, shortly thereafter, the steroid-producing capacity of the gonads is markedly reduced, until the residual production is essentially insignificant from a clinical point of view. These parallel involutions of gonadal effort are the major buttress upon which the third-sex definition is based. If, for instance, only the reproductive prowess of the gonads were slackened as the fiftieth or sixtieth birthday approaches, while the basic sex steroid productivity is maintained, there would be no delineation of the third sex or "neuter gender." Certainly in this situation steroid replacement technics would have little or no clinical value.

PROBLEMS IN STEROID REPLACEMENT

If one accepts the plausibility of sex-steroid replacement for the aged individual, many basically unsolved problems remain to confront the investigator—technics of replacement; individual types or combinations of steroid replacement; and the proper time to initiate, and length of time to maintain, steroid replacement. The fundamental investigative approach to this problem has been to devise steroid-replacement technics that would be adequate for long-range support of the former female and then to transpose these technics directly to the aged former male for similar clinical trial and evaluation.

Vaginal Bleeding

The major concern of sex-steroid replacement in the aging female is, of course, the probability of inciting vaginal bleeding. Estrogen, progesterone, and testosterone are given in the following various stimulative combinations:

1. Cyclic estrogen exhibition and withdrawal at regular intervals to shed the endometrium.
2. Constant estrogen influence with cyclic progesterone exhibition and withdrawal to shed the endometrium.
3. Constant estrogen influence with cyclic testosterone exhibition and withdrawal to shed the endometrium.
4. Constant estrogen influence and testosterone opposition to such a degree that hyperplasia is avoided and shedding of the endometrium unnecessary.

The first three technics necessitate the distress of vaginal bleeding at certain stated intervals in order to avoid the development of endometrial hyperplasia with subsequent estrogen breakthrough bleeding, unfortunate long-continued vaginal spotting, or even hemorrhage.

There is a great deal to be said for any technic that will fundamentally avoid vaginal bleeding and yet accomplish the basic results desired from steroid replacement. Thus it was decided that the fourth technic—using a combination of estrogen and testosterone, which taken individually would satisfy the basic patient concerns of steroid replacement and taken in combination could avoid vaginal bleeding during maintained therapy

stages—would in theory be the most effective type of replacement. This is the essence of, and the rationale behind, the long-continued efforts to combine estrogen and testosterone as a clinically effective weapon.

TESTOSTERONE-ESTROGEN COMBINATION

The 20:1 absorbed ratio of testosterone over estrogen, milligram for milligram, has proved to be the combination of choice over a period of years. Original research components of this 20:1 ratio were testosterone propionate and estradiol benzoate, which, administered in a twice-weekly dosage of 1 mg. of estradiol benzoate and 20 mg. of testosterone propionate intramuscularly, will achieve the desired clinical effects of steroid replacement. In major support of this particular absorbed ratio of the two sex steroids is the fact that vaginal bleeding will not occur. The exception to this last statement, however, is the situation in which one uses the 20:1 ratio to alleviate symptoms in an individual who has a large or recently stimulated uterus. Within 4–6 weeks of the time the medication is initiated, a minimal amount of spotting may occur, which will not last more than 2–4 weeks. If the medication is continued at the present suggested levels, the spotting will stop, and there should be no future recurrence. The physiologic inability of the endometrium to break through and bleed in a 20:1 absorbed ratio of testosterone over estrogen is demonstrated in Figs. 1 through 3.

An interesting clinical note may well be injected here. When endometrial biopsies were first obtained in the elderly female subjects of this experiment, the uterus had already been well stimulated by previous estrogen substitution. Endometrial biopsy was thus relatively easy to obtain because the uterus was normal functional size and the mature uterine-cervical ratio had been returned through long-continued estrogen substitution. The uterus was noted to shrink in size and a 1:1 ratio of corpus to cervix was established at 3–4 months of therapy interval. The cervical canal rapidly became more tenuous. After approximately 6 months of therapy, it was no longer possible to obtain routine endometrial biopsies, due to the return of the corpus to a senile state. Any further routine biopsy procedures would have necessitated actual hospitalization and anesthesia. In addition, from the fourth month of therapy, the tissue obtained by routine biopsy was markedly decreased in amount. The usual senile 1:2 ratio of corpus

female patients who have been treated with this technic.

Depression of Hirsutism

Brief mention should be made of other theoretical indications for the combined steroid type of replacement therapy. The problem of hirsutism in individuals whose steroid replacement is confined purely to the testosterone-type compounds has been well established. It has become apparent over the last few years that not only is the estrogenic

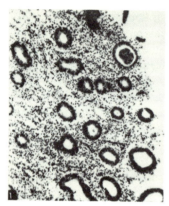  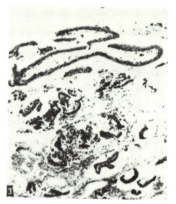

Fig. 1. Biopsy taken after 4 weeks of 20:1 testosterone-estrogen therapy, showing essentially unstimulated stroma and glands. (× 58)

Fig. 2. Biopsy taken after 13½ weeks of 20:1 therapy. Note fibrosis of stroma, paucity of glands. Those glands present show minimal secretory activity. (× 58)

Fig. 3. Biopsy taken after 6 months of estrogen-androgen therapy. Stroma and glands senile in stature. Minimal tissue return despite severe biopsy effort. (× 58)

to cervix was established, and the cervix was quite firm and very difficult to dilate.

Basic Effect

The basic effect on the human uterus of the 20:1 ratio of testosterone over estrogen is now well established. The normal-sized uterus shrinks to senile stature. The endometrium becomes very thin and scanty in amount, and has a completely unstimulated appearance microscopically. Thus it is not at all difficult to understand why endometrial breakthrough bleeding has not occurred on this maintained dosage after the first 4–6 weeks of therapy in the many scores of

influence toward breakthrough bleeding opposed by the testosterone component of the combined therapy, but also that estrogen depresses the tendency toward hirsutism as expressed by the testosterone component alone. There has been no evidence of progressive hirsutism in the female, even though three times the presently considered effective clinical dosage of intramuscular medication has been maintained for as long as 6 months.

Foci of Activity

One of the most intriguing of theoretical questions concerned with the use of the combined steroid therapy in aging is the exact focus of physiologic function for this steroid dosage. Kochakian has presented an exhaustive survey of the relation of androgens to nitrogen and phosphorus storage, energy metabolism, creatine-creatinine metabolism, and even the regulation of storage and excretion of various electrolytes. Loeser also extols the virtues of the male hormone as an anabolic agent, with particular reference to deficiency states even including the aging process. The site of function for the anabolic effects of testosterone has long been one of cloudy speculation. It is now fairly well established that the basic physiologic effect of estrogen is one of increasing cell permeability.[7] Thus, we can understand the interesting possibility of the added effect of estrogen influence to the protein-storage tendencies of testosterone. The constant estrogen influence on cell permeability may, in theory at least, increase the anabolic effectiveness of the concomitantly administered testosterone dosage.

Long-Range Results

Brief mention should be made of the results obtained with long-range steroid-replacement technics. The results of steroid stimulation on the target organs in the female have been widely published. Of particular interest to the investigators has been the marked increase in cellular activity in the media of the blood vessels leading to the stimulated organs.[9] Whether this is a direct action of steroid replacement or the result of work hypertrophy is, of course, open to speculation. Of more generalized interest and certainly of more fundamental import has been the general improvement of physical and psychologic components of individuals studied in the multiple replacement-technic experiments. These results, too, have been published in detail, not only in the fields of gerontology, but of psychiatry.[3, 4, 10] Although the target organs are particularly stimulated by the replacement technics, the entire individual is subject to this replacement influence.

It is most important to emphasize that the replacement technics are in no sense a panacea to the problems of the aging population. In terms of the multiple experiments conducted, roughly 75 per cent of the individuals involved have shown significant improvement in either clinical or mental well-being, or both. The remaining 25 per cent have shown little, if any, response to the supportive therapy technics. Once improvement has been attained, it is reasonable to expect continued demonstrable progress for roughly a year after the onset of therapy. At this time a therapy plateau is attained beyond which the individuals do not significantly progress. This is particularly true when one measures the components of psychologic testing such as memory for recent events, capacity for definitive thinking, etc. After the plateau has been reached, retrogressive changes then continue in the normally expected fashion. However, it is grossly apparent that the individual does obtain support from continued therapy. If therapy is removed during the long periods of evaluation, physical and psychologic involution becomes a marked and immediate trend, with physical and mental senility a consequence in a short time.

DISCUSSION

Many problems concerned with steroid replacement remain as yet unsolved or unproved. Such problems as (1) how to convert the presently considered effective intramuscular dosage of the combined therapy into its oral component, (2) when to initiate therapy, and (3) whether the symptoms of the climacteric may be successfully treated by the combined steroid technics—these are but a few of the unresolved questions immediately at hand. At present the most serious roadblock to successful long-term steroid replacement venture is the problem of the conversion of the well-defined intramuscular dosage into correct orally absorbed ratios. We are all well aware that there is marked variation in the individual estrogenic component in terms of its absorption rate from the gastrointestinal tract.

Dosage and Method of Administration

Table 1 demonstrates the marked variation in dosage necessary to obtain vaginal withdrawal bleeding by various estrogenic compounds. There is also great variation in

TABLE 1. QUANTITY OF VARIOUS ESTROGENS PER WEEK NECESSARY TO INDUCE WITHDRAWAL BLEEDING
Given for Three Weeks in Approximately 50 Per Cent of the Trials

	Mg. per week
Ethinyl estradiol orally	0.40
Estradiol orally	13.40
Estrone orally	31.50
Sodium estrone sulfate orally	17.50
Sodium estriol glucuronidate orally	42,000 oral units
Mixed estrogens orally	< 126,000 int. units
Stilbestrol orally	3.00
Mono-methoxystilbestrol orally	< 35.00
Dimethoxystilbestrol orally	> 14.00
Hexestrol	> 10.50

Used with the kind permission of Dr. Willard M. Allen.[2]

the absorption percentages associated with the direct mucosal absorption technics. If there is to be any long-range public health approach to steroid-replacement technics, the source of supply must be oral ingestion rather than parenteral injection. Such concerns as facility of therapy, cost of material, and convenience to the patient, demand oral ingestion technic as a primary source of steroid replacement. At recent count there were sixteen different orally ingested estrogen-androgen combinations marketed by a variety of drug houses throughout the country. Most of these products do not represent efforts at adequate clinical evaluation. Their long-continued usage will usually result in

either vaginal bleeding or excessive hirsutism in any female subjected to their influence. It is most important to point out by way of warning that the milligram-for-milligram ratio described on the bottle's label is in no sense the ultimate absorption ratio from the gastrointestinal tract. Many of the pharmaceutical companies are now at work on this particular problem. One can certainly expect effective evaluation and correction of the ultimate absorption ratio of their marketed product within, at most, the next year or two.

Time of Therapy Initiation

Finally, there is the completely unresolved problem of when to initiate replacement therapy. Original investigative procedures were directed toward reclamation of individual states of body and mind in early senility. As results were returned, it became appallingly obvious that therapy confined to the end of the line would be a gross theoretical mistake.

Present consideration is directed exclusively toward treating the climacteric syndrome in either the male or the female by the combined-steroid therapy technics. The "puberty to grave" steroid consideration is obviously a gross clinical experiment designed to avoid, in so far as possible, the crippling onset of senile physical and mental symptoms as a premature debilitating entity during the normal aging process. The results of such experiments now in operation will need at least another 10 years for adequate clinical evaluation.

SUMMARY

Steroid replacement technics in no sense represent a panacea for the problem of aging. There is no evidence of increased longevity for those patients under combined steroid influence. However, in the majority of treated patients there is significant physical and mental resurgence of power potential. The treated patients are in no sense insured against physical and mental disability occurring during treatment. Many patients have demonstrated conclusively that they are better adjusted and equipped to face the exigencies of the physiologic aging process, as well as infinitely better psychologically oriented, when treated as individual members of the third sex during the concluding years of their normal aging process.

REFERENCES

1. ALBERT, A. Arden House Conference on Hormones and the Aging Process. May, 1955.
2. ALLEN, W. M. The biological activity of various estrogens. *South. M. J. 37*:240, 1944.
3. CALDWELL, B. M. An evaluation of the psychologic effects of sex hormone administration in aged women: II. Results of therapy after eighteen months. *J. Gerontol. 9*:168, 1954.
4. CALDWELL, B. M., and WATSON, R. I. An evaluation of the psychologic effects of sex hormone administration in aged women: I. Results of therapy after six months. *J. Gerontol. 7*:228, 1952.
5. GALLAGHER, T. F. Technical advances in steroid measurement. Presented at the Annual Meeting of the American Geriatrics Society. San Francisco, Calif., June, 1954.
6. KOCHAKIAN, C. D. Protein anabolic effects of steroid hormones. *Vitamins & Hormones 4*: 255, 1946.
7. KORENCHEVSKY, V. Rejuvenative or eliminative and preventive treatment of senility, as suggested by experiments on rats. *Rev. méd. Liège 5*:687, 1950.
8. LOESER, A. A. Testosterone propionate, the anterior pituitary and hyperthyroidism. *Lancet 1*:1134, 1938.
9. MASTERS, W. H. Long range sex steroid replacement: Target organ regeneration. *J. Gerontol. 8*:33, 1953.
10. MASTERS, W. H., and GRODY, M. H. Estrogen-androgen substitution therapy in the aged female: II. Clinical response. *Obst. & Gynec. 2*:139, 1953.
11. MASTERS, W. H., and MAGALLON, D. T. Unpublished data.
12. MEYER, J., and NECHELES, H. The clinical significance of salivary, gastric and pancreatic secretion in the aged. *J.A.M.A. 115*:2050, 1940.
13. STARR, P. Thyroxine therapy in preventive geriatrics. *J. Am. Geriatrics Soc. 3*:217, 1955.
14. TYLER, F. H., et al. Adrenal-cortical capacity and the metabolism of cortisol in elderly patients. *J. Am. Geriatrics Soc. 3*:79, 1955.

22

Reprinted from *West Virginia Med. J.* 59(3):61–64 (1959)

The Aging Process in Daily Medical Practice*

Thomas Hodge McGavack, M. D.

Aging has been described as "the inherent process (es) whereby organisms exhibit a gradual change in their psychological, chemical and physiological properties after reproductive maturity." Aging is a complex interaction with positive as well as negative values. These and similar statements scarcely are compatible with any concept which makes of aging a passive degenerative condition in which the organism or its individual components simply "wear out." On the contrary, there arises from the above concept a recognition of aging as an active dynamic and vital state capable of alteration in several ways.

From the biological point of view certain changes with time are age-dependent while others are age-independent. For example, Strehler and Mildvan[1] recently analyzed data concerning some important functions in man and found that these decreased, after the age of 30 years, as an almost straight line function of increasing age at the rate of from 0.5 to 1.3 per cent per year. Here they placed such diverse physiologic factors as basal metabolism, vital capacity, maximal breathing capacity, glomerular filtration rate, standard cell water and nerve conduction velocity, all of which are said to be age-dependent. The gradual diminution of function is our challenge to search for effective control of degrading influences. Maintaining physical and mental vigor beyond the present threescore and ten years is well within our grasp but cannot be gained without effort.

Genetic and environmental factors are difficult to appraise, and often remain as unknowns to the physician charged with the care of the individual

*Presented before a Postgraduate Symposium on Management of the Older Veteran Patient at the VA Center in Martinsburg on April 25, 1962.
Submitted to the Publication Committee, August 18, 1962.

The Author

- Thomas Hodge McGavack, M. D., Associate Chief of Staff and Chief, Intermediate Service, VA Center, Martinsburg, W. Va.; Special Lecturer in Metabolic Diseases, George Washington University School of Medicine, Washington, D. C.

patient. He will do well, however, to recognize four aspects of aging with which he is confronted daily in the practice both of preventive and reparative geriatrics:

(1) Failure of integration
(2) Reversible nature of some facets of aging
(3) Organ specificity of aging
(4) Impact of organ aging on the organism as a whole

Failure of Integration

In the most complex of the mammalian species, man, we must deal not only with the immediate intracellular and extracellular environments but also with means of controlling these from a distance. Two major means of more rapid communication and control exist via nerve pathways and endocrine secretions, both of which are essential to the continuing integration of the complex processes carried on by the organism as a whole. Through day to day contact with aging men and women during the past 30 years, it becomes increasingly clear to me that failure, albeit minor, in integration of the activities of all parts of the body and mind is the first clinical manifestation of aging. This may be lowered tolerance for ordinary stimulants such as coffee, tobacco and alcohol. It may be increasing aberration in skilled movements such as reversely striking the keys of a typewriter, or so simple a thing as biting the lip in chewing food, or becoming dizzy on a sudden movement of the head, as when quickly stooping or standing. Realization that such things can occur should, to the keen physician, be sufficient indication to look for them. Their presence should forewarn him of greater danger and the direction of such danger.

Reversible Nature of Some Facets of Aging

To be forewarned by the little symptoms, just as in the vascular field the keen clinician takes heed of "little strokes," often will enable the physician to prevent further trouble, or even to correct the dysfunction already observed. Reconditioning of the older individual is indeed far from impossible.[2] Bortz[3] calls for an entire reappraisal of the physical and mental potentials of "mature older citizens in today's world." Many of the functions commonly looked upon as declining with years can be restored to a more useful level by educational redevelopment.[2, 4] Raab[5] emphasized the same point in his development of reconditioning centers for adults of all ages.

If we turn to the endocrine field (in which I have had most experience), we find many changes with age which are reversible. For example, it is now well known that estrogen can completely recornify the atrophic vaginal mucosa of the older woman. The same hormone favorably influences the reconversion of hyaline fibrous tissue of the older uterine musculature to a fibrillar cellular structure, with concomitant increase in interstitial cells, blood vessels, endometrial glands and their secretory capacity. Reciliation, revascularization and re-epithelization of the turbinated tissues of the nose of the older subject is readily accomplished through the local or systemic use of estrogen. The thin, atrophic epidermis of the older person can be thickened and made more pliable and elastic, even by the local application of ovarian hormone.[6, 7, 8] The atrophic thyroid gland of persons past middle life hypertrophies and increases its secretory activity to the level of that seen in younger individuals promptly following administration of thyrotropin.[9] Testosterone has been shown to increase the rate of growth of the beard of elderly individuals[10] and to improve their muscular strength, resistance to fatigue and fusion frequency of flicker.[11]

The ground substance of connective tissue increases with age in most locations, a change which can be partially reversed by the use of thyroid hormone.[12, 13]

These are a few illustrations of the reversibility of some of the changes commonly seen in aging. They represent changes in regulatory mechanisms. The desirability of altering the status of the older person by such measures must be determined in the individual case. In general, the tissues of the older subject are less amenable to the use of hormonal substances than those of the younger person, although this is not universally true.

Organ Specificity of Aging

Plant life abounds in illustrations of sharply defined aging and death of one organ while other organs and functions are retained and their status even enhanced. It is equally true, though not so patent, that in the highly complex human being, aging does not proceed equally in all parts of the body and in every organ. Moreover, some functions and some organs are well preserved despite their absolutely and relatively greater usage. For example, the heart muscle, operating at the rate of 70 beats per minute, will beat more than 100,000 times in 24 hours, more than 36,000,000 times in a single year and approximately 2,520,000,000 times in an average life span of 70 years. During that period it may show no functional sign of decompensation, whereas any other muscle subjected to the same stress would succumb within a relatively short time.

Even in a single tissue, changes commonly accompanying aging do not go on equally in the various parts of the body where such a tissue is found. For example, changes in collagen content commonly associated with aging connective tissue are more marked in the muscle of the leg of the older person than in the muscle of the abdomen.

The thymus, which has to do with establishing immunity, atrophies in late childhood, while other lymphoid tissues are well preserved.

Of the endocrine glands, earliest changes with aging are ascribed to the gonads. Next, alterations occur in the pituitary gland and in the thyroid. Quite late in life, the adrenals may be affected. These changes, far from being detrimental to the average individual, probably serve an important function in preserving the integrity of the entire organism. Many plants die promptly after flowering and fruiting; the entire strength of their whole being is utilized in the process of reproduction. In at least one species of insect, the bee, the male is destroyed in the act of copulation, which secures the survival of the hive. In the endocrine system of human beings, is it not logical that reproductive capacity is at least partially sacrificed in the interest of the preservation and maintenance of integration of the individual?

Impact of Organ Aging on the Organism as a Whole

An increase in collagen deposition is one factor in the decreasing elasticity of the skin in older animals. Loss of gonadal function around middle age and beyond always influences the activity of other members of the endocrine system, often to the detriment of their functional activity and sometimes without regard to the interests of the organism as a whole. For example, after spawning, salmon of the Pacific Northwest die as a result of pituitary-adrenal overactivity, apparently initiated by the intensity of the preceding gonadal activity.[14]

The major hormone concerned with the repair of tissue at all ages is growth hormone of the pituitary. Once adulthood is attained and growth has ceased, the secretory rate for this material is remarkably constant. Important also in the anabolism of protein are the androgenic and, to a lesser extent, the estrogenic steroids. In the male, loss of gonadal activity is accompanied by a rather dramatic decrease in androgen and in the female by a lesser change. The production of androgen and estrogen is continued by the adrenal cortex and, at least for a time, probably in amounts greater than those previously produced by that structure. If this were the only bodily change with aging, it is quite clear that the process could be completely reversed.

With waning gonadal function, the pituitary secretion of gonadotropin is temporarily increased, that of thyrotropin probably decreased and that of ACTH relatively unchanged. One endocrinologist has spoken of the adrenal as "the gonad of the aged." Certainly it is true that functions of the adrenal gland are better preserved in the aged than those of any of the other major endocrine structures.

Should decline in the function of the gonads initiate unfavorable changes in other glands or should these glands fail to respond normally to the usual changes in gonadal activity, the stage may be set for the devolpment of disease which, if not wholly endocrine in nature, may show at least an endocrine component. Among such diseases we must recognize hyperthyroidism, hypothyroidism, hypertension, diabetes (arteriosclerotic type and the Achard-Thiers snydrome), osteoporosis and perhaps other less well recognized conditions. The changes in the endocrines are not the only cause nor necessarily the chief cause of the diseases mentioned but their influence is not inconsiderable.

There is a close relation between thyroid and gonadal functions, so close indeed that overt disease discovered in one of the two glands may be expected (particularly in the female) to be associated sooner or later with conditions in the other gland which require vigorous treatment.

Routine use of endocrine preparations in older persons probably is unwise. If health is sound, however, it has been shown that mixtures of gonadal and thyroid therapy can retard and even reverse the onset of some of the changes of aging. In some cases in which these preparations are given, it may be necessary to administer adrenal hormones also, for optimal benefit. Androgenic therapy alone not only may not retard but actually hasten senescence and death. Estrogen alone may exert an over-all favorable influence on longevity in patients of either sex.

We have at our disposal, in the endocrine preparations, no gushing fountain of youth. Judiciously applied, however, they may add healthy, happy, useful years to life. Through their cautious, well planned use, the physician may prolong life; what is more important, he may thus impart a rich and meaningful purpose and spirit to a commonly drab and often fully resigned existence.

Finally, the physician is charged with the responsibility of bringing health and happiness to his patients. Prolonging life without alleviating some of its undesirable aspects scarcely is worthy of his best efforts. To live better is more important than to live longer.

References

1. Strehler, B. L. & Mildvan, A. S.: General Theory of Mortality and Aging, Sci. 132:14, 1960.
2. Raab, W.: Metabolic Protection and Reconditioning of the Heart Muscle Through Habitual Physical Exercise, Ann. Int. Med. 53:87, 1960.
3. Bortz, E. L.: Education, Aging and Meaningful Survival, J. Am. Geriat. Soc. 9:329, 1961.
4. Hettinger, T.: Histological and Chemical Changes in Skeletal Musculature Due to Muscle Training and Testosterone, Aerztl. Forsch. 13:570, 1959.
5. Raab, W.: Preventive Medical Mass Reconditioning Abroad—Why Not in USA? Ann. Int. Med. 54:1191, 1961.
6. Goldzieher, M. A.: Effects of Estrogens on Senile Skins, J. Gerontol. 1:196, 1946.
7. Goldzieher, J. W.: Direct Effect of Steroids on Senile Human Skin. A Preliminary Report, J.Gerontol. 4:104, 1949.
8. Chieffi, M.: Investigation of the Effects of Parenteral and Topical Administration of Steroids on the Elastic Properties of Senile Skin, J. Gerontol. 5:17, 1950.
9. McGavack, T. H. & Seegers, W.: Status of Thyroid Gland After Age 50, Metabolism 8:136, 1959.
10. Chieffi, M.: Effect of Testosterone Administration on the Beard Growth of Elderly Males, J. Gerontol. 4:200, 1949.
11. Simonson, E., Kearns, W. M. & Enzer, N.: Effect of Methyl Testosterone Treatment on Muscular Per-

formance and the Central Nervous System of Older Men, J. Clin. Endocrinol. 4:528, 1944.

12. Asboe-Hansen, G., in Tunbridge, R. E.: On the Structure and Functions of the Mast Cell, Connective Tissue Symposium, Springfield, Illinois, Charles C. Thomas & Company, 1957, pp. 12.

13. Iversen, K., in Asboe-Hansen, G.: Hormonal Influ-ence in Connective Tissue, Connective Tissue in Health and Disease, Copenhagen, Munksgaard, 1954, pp. 131.

14. Robertson, O. H. & Wexler, B. C.: Histological Changes in Organs and Tissues of Migrating and Spawning Pacific Salmon (Genus Oncorhynchus), Endocrinol. 66:222, 1960.

23

Reprinted from *Geriatrics* **18**:181–191 (1963)

Aging as seen by the endocrinologist

THOMAS HODGE MC GAVACK, M.D.
Associate chief of staff
Veterans Administration Center
MARTINSBURG, WEST VIRGINIA

Fixed in the minds of most of us is the concept that old age and death stalk hand in hand to find their victims. Montaigne once said, "Death is but an end to dying." Significantly, the participle "dying" in this statement becomes, at least in part, synonymous with aging.

Age and the passage of time are conventionally correlated; yet they have quite different connotations when applied to various types of living things. A flower ages and dies in a few days; man takes many years. Biologic systems are often said to evolve, mature, reproduce, and involute, but can these phases of activity be at any time sharply separated one from the other? Growth is usually looked upon as an evolutionary process ending in adulthood. However, were there no limiting factors to human growth, an infant, growing at the same rate as at birth, would be 8 times the size of the earth at the age of 21. Can the factors limiting such growth be rightfully called either wholly evolutional or involutional or indeed solely juvenescent or entirely senescent? Atherosclerosis, one of the so-called degenerative diseases, is present in the newborn infant. Are changes with increasing age early in life to be termed evolutionary and later involutionary, although ostensibly the result of identical metabolic processes? As one leader in the study of gerontology aptly put it, "pediatrics and geriatrics are closer than many realize."[1]

No biologic system has ever achieved immortality. From the individual cell, which may perpetuate itself by dividing every few minutes or hours, to the highly complex systems of cells integrated into a single living unit in mankind, perpetuation of the system has been maintained by more or less complex methods of reproduction. As has been well expressed by one student of aging, "a critical diagnostic feature of the living system is the capacity for self-renewal."[2] Many factors enter into the control of the life cycle of all biologic systems. Changes in any one or more of these may alter the

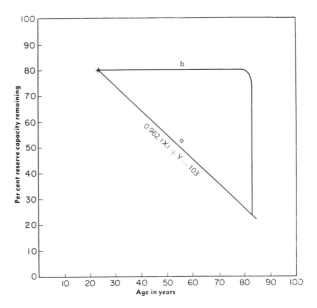

FIG. 1. *Curve a is theoretical equation, developed from the data compiled by Strehler and Mildvan,[3] indicating steady decline of body functions with increasing age. Curve b represents ideal, unimpaired maintenance of body functions until shortly before death and denotes a state which may be achieved through gerontologic study and geriatric therapy.*

system's capacity for self-renewal. Indeed, aging in its strictest sense must be looked upon as an inhibition of this capacity for self-renewal or self-duplication. The biologist has been more specific in his definition of aging, characterizing the term as "the inherent process(es) whereby organisms exhibit a gradual change in their physical, chemical or physiological properties after reproductive maturity."[3]

The above statements are incompatible with the concept that aging is a passive, degenerative process, in which the organism or its individual components simply "wear out." On the contrary, aging becomes a dynamic vital thing, capable of alteration in one, several, or many ways, if and when the proper influences are brought to bear. To the cellular chemist, the process(es) may be associated with alterations in the distribution[1] and behavior of ribonucleic acids (RNA)[5] or with the development of an increasing number of difficultly reversible crosslinkages of peptide moieties.[6] To the plant physiologist, senescence is an active series of events associated with flowering and fruiting and ending in death.[7] To the biologist, senescence presents age-dependent and age-independent characteristics.[3]

For both plant and mammal, the whole organism may age at an entirely different rate than do some of its parts. For instance, in the human being, aging of the thymus occurs rapidly during childhood with no well-known function ascribed to the organ beyond adolescence. While senescence of plants or parts of plants is closely related to reproduction, or, that is, to flowering and fruiting, these changes are less obvious in higher mammals, particularly in the human being. Indeed, some functions in man have been shown to decrease after the age of 30 years as an almost straight-line function of age,[8,9] such as basal metabolic rate, vital capacity, maximal breathing capacity, glomerular filtration rate, standard" cell water, nerve conduction velocity, and so forth, the actual rate of decline varying between 5 and 1.3 per cent per year (figure 1).[3]

Is aging of the endocrines a positive, active process, or a passive, degenerative "wearing out" of functional units, the speed of decline in which can be calculated along a curve similar to that illustrated in figure 1? For a long time, the latter concept has certainly predominated in the minds of physicians, who as a group have seemed to find little stimulation for studying aging or its problems or for attempting seriously any methods designed to alter processes connected with growing old. As far as the endocrine system is concerned, what are the facts?

Perhaps the active nature of the changes with aging, at least as far as the endocrine system is concerned, can best be appreciated by a brief summary of alterations with time in each of the commonly recognized structures. Whether these changes are in any way a cause rather than a result of aging is certainly not clear but that the process(es) is active rather than passive should be settled by thoughtful reflection upon the character of the variations observed.

The table illustrates the early decline which may take place in the function of some glandular structures and the influence of the secretions of endocrine glands upon each other. While the thymus may or may not be an endocrine gland, it is readily subject to endocrine influences and changes so strikingly in early life as to justify its inclusion. The parathyroid glands have not been included because their activity seems to be rather independent of other glandular structures. Their maximum size is attained in the young adult and does not change thereafter in men, while they become somewhat smaller in older women. Many other glandular influences are brought to bear upon calcium and phosphorus metabolism, probably without the mediation of the parathyroids

The thymus. In relation to body weight, the thymus is largest at birth, weighing approximately 12 gm. in the average infant. However, the maximum absolute weight of 35 to 40 gm. is achieved shortly before puberty, after which the gland rapidly shrinks and, in late life, may weigh as little as 6 gm. (see table) . That the thymus is an endocrine organ has been seriously questioned.[10] Identifiable, hormonally active materials have not been isolated from the glandular structure constituting the thymic body. Histologically and functionally, it may be best to consider it a part of the lymphatic system, as it behaves in response to other endocrine secretions in much the same way the lymph nodes and other lymphatic structures do. In any event, if aging is a regressive phenomenon, it is already at work in this structure at birth, with fat from the surrounding connective tissue replacing functioning cells.

Ascribed to the thymus is a very active role in the development of nonspecific immunity during the early weeks and months of life, a function which continues to be served in decreasing degree until the onset of puberty.

Thymic hypertrophy occurs when (1) thyroid function is high, (2) thyrotropin is administered or (3) adrenal or gonadal activity is lowered[11] (see table) . Conversely, at puberty, or following

Endocrine glandular changes with aging

Gland	Maximum size	Loss of function begins	Function influenced by other hormones Increased	Decreased
Thymus	Puberty	Puberty	Thyroid-stimulating hormone	Gonadal steroids
			Thyrotropin	11-oxy adrenosteroid
Pineal	Childhood	Puberty (?)		
Ovary	20-25	35-45	Follicle-stimulating hormone	Thyrotropin
			Luteinizing hormone Luteotropic hormone Thyrotropin	11-oxy adrenosteroid
Testis	20-25	35-40	Luteinizing hormone Thyrotropin	Thyrotropin
			Insulin	11-oxy adrenostreoid
Pituitary	20-25		Amount little influenced by other hormones	
Somatotropin		Unchanged		
Thyroid-stimu- lating hormone		Middle life		
Adrenocortocitropic hormone		Unchanged (?)	Influenced by each other and by level of gonadal, thyroidal, and adrenal activity	
Follicle-stimu- lating hormone		Postmenopausal in- crease; then decrease		
Luteotropic hormone		Postmenopausal loss		
Luteinizing hormone		Slow decrease (?)		

administration of gonadal or adrenal steroids, thymic atrophy ensues. Under normal conditions, the atrophy of the thymus at or shortly before puberty is associated with fatty replacement of glandular elements. Whatever function the gland ordinarily serves seems to have been accomplished by this time. Far from being a "wearing out" or passive "degenerative" process, this thymic atrophy appears to be the result of several very active positive changes in other endocrine structures. As long as any functional thymic elements remain, it is possible to see them hypertrophy, should hyperthyroidism or adrenal insufficiency occur. One can hardly speak of the degenerative changes of aging here.

The pineal body. "The pineal body is a small, high-powered metabolic unit."[12] What a change in our concepts of its function! Earlier it was recognized as a structure possibly related to melanophoric activity in many cold-blooded animals. However, in the human being, it seemed to possess no endocrine purpose and served mainly as a roentgenographic landmark following calcification at or about the time of puberty. In the past, calcification in this structure has been considered synonymous with cessation of function. Therefore, function was presumed to cease at or around the

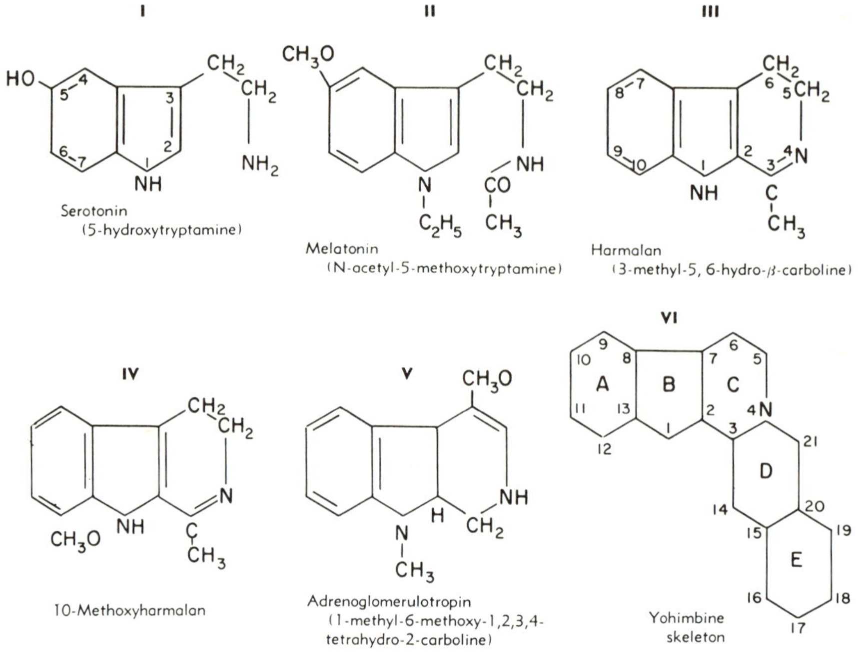

FIG. 2. *With the exception of chemicals IV and VI, these products are all secreted by the pineal body. Adrenoglomerulotropin (V) has been shown to be the tropic hormone of the adrenal which governs, at least in part, aldosterone secretion; 10-methoxyharmalan (IV) is an abnormal product probably produced in the pineal body but found in brain under abnormal metabolic conditions and causing psychic disturbances. It is thought that the action of yohimbine (VI) is closely related to the presence of the modified carboline ring.*

time of puberty (see table). More recently even the partially calcified gland has been found to be quite active, so that the time of diminution of function is not really known. In this instance, can the presence of calcium be looked upon as a sign of aging—as a hallmark of degeneration and disintegration? Or is it a sign of activity, appearing as a result of the high Ca $\times$ P product known to be present in the gland?[13]

This small body, with a wet weight of 100 to 200 mg. and an abundant blood supply, picks up both I^{131} and P^{32} faster than any part of the brain, and, on a per unit weight basis, accumulates iodine faster than any other structure in the body with the exception of the thyroid gland. Lerner[12] makes the comment that "It is possible that numerous oxidative reactions are occurring at greater rates on a unit weight basis in the pineal gland than in any other organs." Among the substances made and stored in the pineal are histamine, acetylcholine, norepinephrine, epinephrine, 5-methoxyindolacetic acid, 5-hydroxy-indolacetic acid, serotonin, and melatonin. Melatonin is the N-acetyl-5-methoxy derivative of tryptamine (3-[2-aminoethyl]indole). The close chemical relationships between some of these compounds are shown in figure 2. It can readily be seen that the methylation of norepinephrine to epinephrine or at least the presence of a higher percentage of the latter than the former in this gland is accompanied by a loss of most of the pressor effect with the development of central nervous system excitation and considerable enhancement of the hyperglycemic and metabolism-raising actions. Again, methylation and hydrogenation of the carboline ring give rise to 10-methoxyharmalan with the development of many neurologic symptoms, particularly a tendency to make errors in the carrying out of previously learned skilled movements. There is no proof that normal aging of the epiphysis is associated with the development of such errors in metabolism, but this possibility certainly exists and warrants further study.

Hormonally unique in the pineal is the formation of a substance called adrenoglomerulotropin, which stimulates the adrenal gland to secrete aldosterone without the intermediation of any other portions of the hypothalamus or the pituitary gland.[14] This material is a carboline derivative, closely related to harmalan and melatonin, chemically characterized as 1-methyl-6-methoxy-1,2,3,4-tetrahydro-2-carboline.

Aging as seen by the endocrinologist

Phosphorus pentoxide and several enzymes are necessary for the conversions and interconversions taking place in the pineal body. Among the enzymes present are 5-hydroxytryptophan decarboxylase and 5-hydroxy-indole-0-methyl transferase, the latter being an "almost unique product of the gland." As yet nothing is known about the activity of the pineal as a function of age, but partial calcification apparently does not interfere with the production of relatively large quantities of the substances mentioned.

The parathyroids. Regulation of calcium metabolism by the parathyroid glands is achieved, at least in major part, by an action upon 4 sites in the human being: gastrointestinal tract, bone, lactating mammary gland, and kidney. The primary factor governing the secretion of parathyroid hormone appears to be the level of serum calcium. No parathyrotrophic hormone has been found to exist in the anterior pituitary. However, growth hormone, insulin, adrenosteroids, and gonadal steroids all play accessory roles in regulating calcium and phosphorus metabolism throughout life. Both estrogen and androgen enhance osteoblastic activity and the formation of bony tissue. Beyond the reproductive period of life, this function is partially assumed by the androgen and estrogen formed within the adrenal cortex. However, the total excretion of these hormones is reduced to about one-third their earlier values, thus setting the stage for osteoporosis, a common disease in older individuals. It is probably true that continuous physical conditioning can partially offset this expected drain on body tissues.[15]

At this point, 2 things should be clear: (1) Aging in endocrine structures may begin in early extra-uterine or even in intra-uterine existence; and (2) more importantly, aging in these structures is an active rather than a passive process. We now turn to the glands in which functional alterations are commonly seen in middle or late middle life, that time of life conventionally associated with the beginnings of aging. Reference is made to the gonads, the thyroid, the

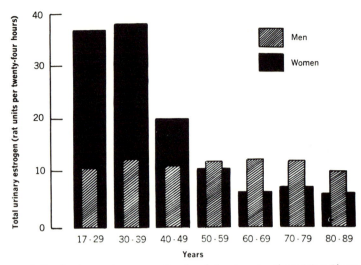

FIG. 3. *Total urinary estrogen excretion in relation to age and sex (after Pincus and associates[16, 17]). Although total urinary estrogen remains nearly the same throughout life in men, there is a changing proportion of estradiol, estrone, and estriol in both sexes.*

pituitary, and the adrenals, in which anatomic and physiologic changes occur as a function of time, somewhat in the order mentioned. While no part of the body and no bodily influence are without their effect upon these glands, their interlocking activities are as important to the changes of aging as are their individually specific functions. Both genetic and environmental influences predetermine the actual rate at which a given individual grows old. While the encoding upon the deoxyribonucleic acid (DNA) of the germ cell, once laid down, can probably not be altered, a knowledge of its nature may permit the altering of environmental influences in such fashion as to minimize adverse effects and further beneficial aspects of the individual inheritance. Studies of the gonadal and thyroidal function of more than 2,000 subjects during the past twenty-five years lead us to believe that much can be done to improve the lot of the oldster, although we probably cannot prolong his life. Endocrine changes from middle or late middle life onward can be best viewed with these facts and concepts in mind.

The gonads. The gonads reach their maximum size somewhere between the fifteenth and twentieth years of life and their maximal functional activity between 25 and 35 years of age.

In woman, there is a marked decrease in the urinary excretion of total estrogen from middle life onward—from an average of 38.2 rat units per twenty-four hours in early adulthood to 6.7 rat units per twenty-four hours at age 60 (figure 3). The early decline occurs in all 3 fractions, its magnitude being greatest for estriol and least for estrone, while from approximately 60 years onward the relatively constant value actually represents a further slight decrease in estradiol and estrone with an increase in estriol.[16, 17] There is little or no change in the figures for the male—11.7 rat units and 12.5 rat units per twenty-four hours for the corresponding ages mentioned for

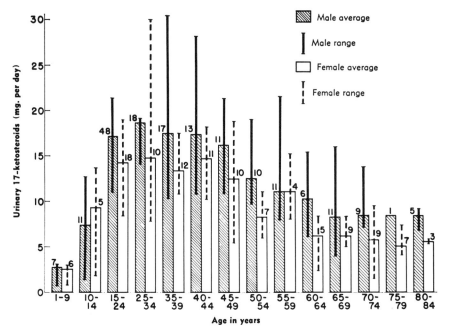

FIG. 4. *Values for total normal, neutral, urinary 17-ketosteroid excretion. Figures at top of column represent number of individuals from whom values were obtained by averaging daily analyses of three-day aliquots. Many subjects had more than 1 such three-day series, but this is not presented here.*

woman. However, this constant total figure for the male actually represents a steady slight decline for estrone and estradiol with a corresponding rise in estriol.[16,17] The symptoms of the female climacterium need no reiteration here and are promptly and completely relieved in 90 to 95 per cent of patients by the use of estrogen in moderate doses—0.01 to 0.02 mg. ethinyl estradiol daily orally or its equivalent in any other active estrogenic preparation. The waning function of the ovary at and beyond the menopause is presumed to initiate specific changes in the pituitary gland, such as an increase in follicle-stimulating hormone (FSH), a diminution in luteinizing hormone (LH), and a loss of luteotropic hormone (LTH). The increase in follicle-stimulating hormone is commonly thought of as a loss of a feedback mechanism by which estrogen normally controls the amount of follicle-stimulating hormone produced. The excessive amount of urinary gonadotropin excreted during this time has been looked upon by some investigators as an under-utilization by the ovary rather than an overproduction by the pituitary and by others as the reverse. If any one of these explanations is correct, is it not strange that similar events fail to occur in the male when gametogenesis decreases and testosterone production by the interstitial cells fails? Is it more likely that certain nervous centers in the thalamus and hypothalamus regulate all of the above changes and are only in part subject to restriction by ovarian and testicular secretions or activities?

In normal young men, we have found the mode of the twenty-four-hour output of urinary 17-ketosteroids to lie between 15 and 20 mg., while, after 65 years of age, it is between 6 and 10 mg. (figure 4). Values for women decrease to a lesser degree, since most of the percursors are synthesized by the adrenal cortex. In the young, the mode is found between 11 and 15 and in the old, between 5 and 9 mg. per twenty-four hours.

Qualitative as well as quantitative differences in urinary 17-ketosteroids between the young and the old are also of significance. Androsterone and ·etiocholanolone, cis- and transisomers, respectively, are the major urinary excretion products of testosterone. The androsterone-etiocholanolone ratio (A:E) in the normal young adult is approximately 2:3.[18] In the older individual this ratio is usually reversed, and at times, the fraction containing androsterone and its congeners all but disappears.[18,19] In this connection, it is interesting that etiocholanolone is capable of raising metabolism, while androsterone has no such effect.[18,20] Is this an attempted effort at compensation for the decreased energy production associated with a lowering of thyroid function?

The thyroid. Changes in the thyroid associated with aging include a lowering of basal metabolism, a decrease in the uptake of I^{131}, and a decrease in thyrotropin secretion and release.[21,22] There is no change in serum protein-bound iodine (PBI) or cholesterol. The thyroid is capable of influencing the production of neutral urinary 17-ketosteroid precursors. In hypothyroidism, total production by both the testis and the adrenal is very low, and the androsterone-etiocholanolone ratio in the urine also falls.[18] The lower total urinary values seen in the aged are associated with a decrease in the A:E ratio from a normal youthful figure of 40:60 to as low as 15:85 in the elderly.[19] In these changes it is evident that we have not just a loss in aging but an active alteration in the proportions of certain secreted materials. Such variants can scarcely be looked upon as part of a "simple degenerative process" but rather imply active positive forces at work.

The adrenals. With a lowering of thyroidal activity at any time in life, there is usually a decrease in the functioning of the adrenal cortex. However, the function of the latter is probably better maintained in late life than that of any of the other major glands of internal secretion. Romanoff and her associates[23] found a 30 per cent reduction in the secretion of 11-oxycorticoids between the ages of 25 and 70 years. West and his associates[24] noted similar changes. However, these decreases were shown to be directly proportional to the muscular mass, as measured by creatinine excretion. In other words, the loss of muscle mass with aging goes hand in hand with a diminution in the adrenal secretion of cortisol and its congeners. No studies have been made on the influence of physical conditioning of the older subject, but it seems likely that, were muscular mass thus increased, adrenal activity would be correspondingly enhanced. This point justifies study, particularly if we consider aging an active and not a passive process.

The pituitary. The characteristic histologic changes described

Some pathways of somatotropin in protein anabolism

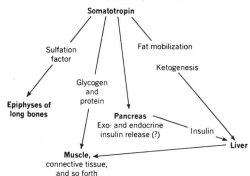

FIG. 5. *Although growth hormone in the pituitary is usually viewed as a factor promoting growth of long bones, it is obviously important in intermediary metabolism throughout life. Some of the relationships important in carbohydrate and fat metabolism are schematically indicated.*

in the pituitary of the aged human subject are not at all unlike those which are seen in the castrated individual. This may indicate that the pituitary shows outspoken effects of aging from the time of gonadal decline onward.

As far as hormonal secretions are concerned, growth hormone or somatotropin (STH) is present in as large quantities in the old as in the young. "Octogenarians have as much growth hormone (4 to 10 mg. per gland) as the rapidly growing child."[24] It seems that this hormone remains as the major material regulating protein replacement and repair throughout life. Not only its presence in maintained quantities in the pituitary but also the fact that a major portion of circulating somatotropin, even in the growing animal, can be found in the pancreas indicate its important role in anabolism. The accompanying chart (figure 5) illustrates both its direct and indirect effects upon the pancreas, the liver, and skeletal proteins. Insulin is synergistic to and necessary for the exhibition of its effects.

Thyrotropin secretion seems to decrease in middle or late middle life, apparently following the diminution in gonadal activity. Indeed, the thyroid remains responsive to exogenous thyrotropin long after clinical effects of aging are in evidence. Changes in the gonadotropins with age have already been discussed. There is little or no change with age in the production of adrenocorticotropin (ACTH) by the pituitary gland.

Aging and death are inevitable. We have no desire to prolong life, if such prolongation entails only added days and years of misery and suffering. On the other hand, for the first time in history man has within his grasp potent medications of many kinds, among the more important of which are specific hormones capable of retarding if not stopping some of the undesirable features of growing old.

It seems possible to employ our present knowledge in such fashion that the Mildvan-Strehler curve can be maintained at a more nearly horizontal level, eventually to drop abruptly when, like the one-horse shay, all the sustaining factors of life cease to function simultaneously.

A portion of the experimental work on which this paper is based was made possible by a grant from the Fretom Research Fund.

REFERENCES

1. STIEGLITZ, E. J.: Geriatric Medicine: The care of the Aging and Aged. Ed. 2. Philadelphia: W. B. Saunders Co., 1949.
2. COWDRY, E. V., and LANSING, A. I.: Problems of Aging, Biological and Medical Aspects. Ed. 3. Baltimore: Williams & Wilkins, 1952, p. 6.
3. STREHLER, B. L., and MILDVAN, A. S.: General theory of mortality and aging. Science 15:14, 1960.
4. WOHLGIEHN, R.: Untersuchungen über den zusammenhang zwischen Nukleinsauren und Erweissstoffwechsel in grünen Blattern. Flora 150:117, 1961.
5. OOTA, Y., and TAKATA, K.: Changes in microsomal ribonucleoproteins in the time course of the germination stage as revealed by electrophoresis. Physiol. Plantarum 12:518, 1959.
6. BJORKSTEN, J.: Aging: Present status of our chemical knowledge. J. Am. Geriatrics Soc. 10:125, 1962.
7. LEOPOLD, A. C.: Senescence in plant development. Science 134:1727, 1961.
8. FALZONE, J. A., JR., and SHOCK, N. W.: Physiological limitations and age. Pub. Health Rep. 71:1185, 1956.
9. SHOCK, N. W.: Age changes in some physiologic processes. Geriatrics 12:40, 1957.
10. BARD, P.: Medical Physiology. Ed. 10. St. Louis: C. V. Mosby Co., 1956, p. 883.
11. MCGAVACK, T. H.: The Thyroid. St. Louis: C. V. Mosby Co., 1951, p. 153.
12. LERNER, A. B.: The pineal. In Williams, R. H.: Textbook of Endocrinology. Ed. 3. Philadelphia: W. B. Saunders Co., 1962, p. 881.
13. BORELL, U., and ORSTROM, A.: Turnover of phosphate in pineal body compared with that in other parts of the brain. Biochem. J. 41:398, 1947.
14. FARRELL, G., MCISAAC, W. M.: Adrenoglomerulotropin. Arch. Biochem. 94:543, 1961.
15. MCLEAN, F. C., and URIST, M. R.: Bone: An Introduction to the Physiology of Skeletal Tissue. Chicago: Univ. of Chicago Press, 1955.
16. PINCUS, G., ROMANOFF, L. P., and CARLO, J.: Excretion of urinary steroids by men and women of various ages. J. Gerontol. 9:113, 1954.
17. PINCUS, G.: Aging and urinary steroid excretion. In Engle, E. T., and Pincus, G.: Hormones and the Aging Process. New York: Academic Press, 1956, p. 1.
18. GALLAGHER, T. F., HELLMAN, L., BRADLOW, H. L., ZUMOFF, B., and FUKUSHIMA, D. K.: The effects of thyroid hormones on the metabolism of steroids. Ann. New York Acad. Sc. 86:605, 1960.
19. MCGAVACK, T. H., PEARSON, S., and HAAR, H. O.: Steroid studies: Influence of anabolic steroids on chromatographic patterns of 17-ketosteroid excretion in hypogonadal and aged men. J. Am. Geriatrics Soc. 3:754, 1955.
20. KAPPAS, A., HELLMAN, L., FUKUSHIMA, D. K., and GALLAGHER, T. F.: Thermogenic effect and metabolic fate of etiocholanolone in man. J. Clin. Endocrinol. 18:1043, 1958.
21. MCGAVACK, T. H.: Status of the thyroid gland after age 50. Metabolism 8:136, 1959.
22. PITTMAN, J. A., JR.: The thyroid and aging. J. Am. Geriatrics Soc. 10:10, 1962.
23. ROMANOFF, L. P., MORRIS, C. W., WELCH, P., RODRIGUEZ, R. M., and PINCUS, G.: Metabolism of cortisol-4-C^{14} in young and elderly men. I. Secretion rate of cortisol and daily excretion of tetrahydrocortisol, allotetrahydrocortisol, tetrahydrocortisone and cortolone (20 alpha and 20 beta). J. Clin. Endocrinol. 21:1413, 1961.
24. DAUGHADAY, W. H.: The adenohypophysis. In Williams, R. H.: Textbook of Endocrinology. Ed. 3. Philadelphia: W. B. Saunders Co., 1962, p. 31.

Editor's Comments
on Papers 24 and 25

SPECIFIC THERAPEUTIC MEASURES—CARDIOVASCULAR PROBLEMS: TOTAL CARE

Paper 24 gives data on patient survival after cardiac arrest, showing that the elderly respond as well as younger patients do in this study by Bernard S. Linn and R. W. Yurt.

Insight into ways geriatrics is currently practiced in one retirement village setting is revealed by Dr. Eckstein in Paper 25.

24

Reprinted from *Brit. Med. J.* **2**:25–27 (1970)

Cardiac Arrest among Geriatric Patients*

BERNARD S. LINN,† M.D.

ROGER W. YURT,‡ B.S.

Summary: In a review of 292 hospital patients who had cardiac arrests over a period of two and a half years patients aged 60 and over were contrasted with those under 60, based on a 50-item clinical questionary completed at the time of the episode. Survival rates were identical (23%) in these two groups. On contrasting patients who survived with those who did not it was again found that age did not influence outcome. Patients with multiple arrests or without cardiographic evidence of ventricular standstill were much more likely to recover. Whether or not a doctor initiated therapy did not affect survival.

Introduction

Many reports concerning cardiac arrest have been published since Kouwenhoven, Jude, and Knickerbocker (1960) first described closed chest cardiac massage. Most of these studies have discussed results of resuscitation programmes in various hospitals. In view of the wealth of literature on the subject it is surprising that attention has not been specifically directed toward age as a factor in occurrence and outcome from cardiac arrest. The sole reference known to us concerning the relationship of age to outcome of resuscitation appeared in an article by Ayers and Doyle (1964) stating, "the ideal candidate for cardiac resuscitation is young and healthy."

This report focuses on age and cardiac arrest. Cardiac arrest means a sudden unexpected cessation of the normal heart beat, representing the most urgent type of medical emergency,

* Paper presented at the 8th International Congress of Gerontology Washington, D.C., August 1969.
† Associate Chief of Staff for Research and Education, Veterans Administration Hospital; Assistant Professor of Surgery, University of Miami School of Medicine, Miami, Florida.
‡ Research Assistant, University of Miami School of Medicine, Miami, Florida.

where there is no chance of saving the patient unless effective treatment is initiated within minutes. Recovery from cardiac arrest is defined as restoration and maintenance of a normal heart beat so that the patient either was discharged from hospital or had died from some other cause during the same admission.

To determine the effect of age on arrest three questions were asked. (1) Do arrests among geriatric patients differ from those occurring among younger patients? (2) If differences occur, are they related to the arrest itself—that is, to cause, treatment, survival, or technical problems? (3) If differences occur, are they related to characteristics of the patients such as diagnoses and on-going treatment regimens?

Method

From January 1967 to July 1969 292 men who had cardiac arrests requiring resuscitative efforts were studied. They were patients in a 1,000-bed general medical Veterans Administration Hospital. A 50-item questionary was completed by the charge physician and nurse immediately after each resuscitative procedure. Information was obtained concerning the patient, and the arrest, including such variables as age, cardiographic diagnosis, concomitant medical diagnoses, time and place of arrest, number of previous arrests, treatment, and technical problems encountered in managing the arrest. Data were punched on to I.B.M. cards and computer-analysed with multivariate statistical techniques. Patients were divided into two groups—those aged 60 and over and those under 60—to determine if the two age groups were significantly different. In a second analysis patients were also divided into two groups—those who survived and those who expired after the arrest. On the latter analysis age was entered as one of the items.

Results

Of the 292 patients studied, 130 were aged under 60 and 162 were 60 or older; 69 (23%) recovered from the arrest and 223 (77%) died. The characteristics of the total sample are considered first, then the factors related to age, and, finally, the factors related to recovery from arrest.

Total Sample

The average age of the patients was 60. A total of 330 arrests occurred in the 292 patients. Even though this averages slightly over one arrest per patient, the great bulk of the patients actually experienced only one arrest. As already mentioned, recovery occurred in 23% of the patients who sustained arrests. If, on the other hand, recovery rates are based on the arrests themselves, rather than on the ultimate outcome for each patient—as might be done, for example, in evaluating efficiency of resuscitative efforts—rates for recovery per resuscitation rise to 31%. As both types of figures are used rather loosely in the literature it is difficult to compare results from different series.

Age-related factors

A number of selected variables to compare the two age groups are listed in Table I. The difference between groups, based on all the variables used together, approached statistical significance but did not quite make the 0·05 level. It is

TABLE I.—*Comparison of Selected Variables in 292 Cardiac Arrest Patients According to Age*

Variables	Under age 60		60 and over		*t* Test
	Mean	S.D.	Mean	S.D.	
Related to arrest:					
Outcome-expired	0·77	0·42	0·77	0·43	0·08
No. of arrests per patient	1·17	0·55	1·14	0·51	0·54
Minutes till treatment	0·76	1·98	1·15	4·87	0·86
Occurring night shift	0·31	0·46	0·23	0·42	1·53
Month of year	6·34	6·01	6·28	6·12	0·36
Occurred on medical ward	0·65	0·50	0·70	0·46	0·71
Arrest diagnosed by physician	0·54	0·50	0·62	0·48	1·47
E.C.G. { Standstill	0·24	0·43	0·22	0·42	0·45
Fibrillation	0·23	0·42	0·28	0·45	0·91
Mechanical arrest	0·07	0·26	0·03	0·16	1·84
Treatment { Initiated by physician	0·60	0·50	0·66	0·48	1·06
No problems	0·56	0·50	0·53	0·50	0·46
Adrenaline	0·67	0·47	0·61	0·49	1·07
Bicarbonate	0·62	0·51	0·58	0·50	0·64
Associated diagnoses:					
Myocardial infarction	0·39	0·49	0·52	0·50	2·29*
Chronic cardiac	0·05	0·21	0·06	0·23	0·36
Haemorrhage	0·05	0·21	0·07	0·26	0·98
Neurological	0·03	0·17	0·00	0·00	2·26*
Liver disease	0·04	0·19	0·00	0·00	2·54*
Cancer	0·12	0·33	0·04	0·19	2·89†
Infection	0·05	0·21	0·01	0·11	1·76
Terminal	0·06	0·24	0·04	0·19	0·97
Postoperative	0·13	0·34	0·05	0·22	2·49*

*P <0·05 on univariate *t* test.
†P <0·01 on univariate *t* test.
Note: Multivariate difference between age group was P<0·06. Most items are scored 0 = no and 1 = yes, so that answers can also be read as percentages.

interesting that both age groups had almost identical rates of survival (23%). The number of arrests, minutes until resuscitation, place of arrest, and the persons diagnosing and treating the arrests were essentially the same. Further examination showed no difference between the age groups related to time of day the arrest occurred (the average being between 12 noon and 1 p.m. for each), to time of year (average around June to July), or to occurrence in the operating-room, recovery room, or surgical ward. As shown in Table I, most of the arrests occurred on medical wards. Furthermore, electrocardiographic findings were not different for the two age groups, with most showing ventricular standstill or fibrillation. Treatment was about the same for each age group, no more problems being encountered in the older than in the younger patients. In fact, the only significant differences between the age groups were in the associated diagnostic problems occurring within the two groups. At the 0·05 level more of the older patients had myocardial infarctions and more of the younger group had neurological problems, liver disease, and were postoperative patients. The only difference at the 0·01 level was the diagnosis of internal cancer in patients under 60.

Factors related to survival

The same variables as they related to survival and non-survival are shown in Table II. Age was analysed as an item but

TABLE II.—*Comparison of Selected Variables in 292 Cardiac Arrest Patients According to Survival*

Variables	Recovered		Died		*t* Test
	Mean	S.D.	Mean	S.D.	
Related to arrest:					
Age at time of arrest	60·60	15·00	61·24	12·61	0·35
No. of arrests per patient	1·41	0·86	1·07	0·32	4·82†
Minutes till treatment	0·83	3·79	1·03	3·89	0·38
Occurring night shift	0·28	0·45	0·26	0·44	0·25
Month of the year	6·68	8·68	6·13	4·93	0·66
Occurred on medical ward	0·65	0·48	0·69	0·46	0·60
Arrest diagnosed by physician	0·57	0·50	0·59	0·49	0·39
E.C.G. ⎰ Standstill	0·12	0·32	0·26	0·44	2·52*
Fibrillation	0·22	0·41	0·27	0·44	0·86
⎱ Mechanical arrest	0·03	0·17	0·05	0·22	0·71
Treatment ⎰ Initiated by physician	0·67	0·48	0·62	0·49	0·65
No problems	0·52	0·50	0·55	0·50	0·40
Adrenaline	0·43	0·50	0·70	0·46	4·03†
⎱ Bicarbonate	0·57	0·53	0·60	0·49	0·48
Associated diagnoses:					
Myocardial infarction	0·46	0·50	0·46	0·50	0·09
Chronic cardiac	0·10	0·30	0·04	0·19	2·17*
Haemorrhage	0·06	0·24	0·06	0·24	0·14
Neurological	0·01	0·12	0·01	0·12	0·06
Liver disease	0·00	0·00	0·02	0·15	1·25
Cancer	0·04	0·21	0·09	0·28	1·15
Infection	0·06	0·24	0·02	0·13	1·78
Terminal	0·04	0·21	0·05	0·22	0·20
Postoperative	0·03	0·17	0·10	0·31	1·93

*P <0·05 on univariate *t* test.
†P <0·01 on univariate *t* test.
Note: Multivariate difference between survival and non-survival was P < 0·0002.
   Most items are scored 0 = no and 1 = yes, so that answers can also be read as percentages.

showed no significant difference when patients who recovered from cardiac arrest were compared with those who did not. In this analysis overall group difference between survivors and non-survivors was highly significant at 0·0002. In studying individual item differences it was noted that one of the highly significant items was related to treatment with adrenaline, and that this treatment was predominantly used when resuscitative efforts were failing. To correct for any treatment-related factors another analysis was made, dropping all items related to treatment. Differences between survivors and non-survivors were still highly significant at 0·002.

The most important discriminant between the groups was the number of arrests per patient, with almost all of the multiple arrests occurring in patients who survived. Therefore a patient experiencing other than his first arrest was quite likely to survive the arrest itself. E.C.G. diagnosis of ventricular standstill was associated with failure to recover, whereas diagnosis of concomitant chronic cardiac condition related to survival. None of the items associated with time and place of arrest or with who diagnosed or first initiated treatment was significantly different.

Only those diagnoses that occurred frequently are included in Table II. All diagnosed cardiac conditions (accounting for slightly over 50% of the sample) are shown. The more common non-cardiac diagnoses listed accounted for an additional 34% of the sample. About 15% of the patients had a variety of other conditions associated with the arrest, such as pulmonary embolus, acute respiratory infection, chronic pulmonary disease, kidney disease, and iatrogenic causes, that are not shown in Table II as the numbers in these diagnostic categories were so small. Only three patients in the entire series had the diagnosis "arrest of completely unknown aetiology."

Discussion

With assistance from computers it is possible to analyse large amounts of data on many patients. Sometimes interesting and surprising findings are uncovered in research that at first may seem questionable from a clinical standpoint. Generally, as one shuttles back and forth from raw data to statistical results, conclusions are reached that are in harmony with clinical judgement. In this study there was no significant relationship between age and outcome in several hundred patients with cardiac arrest. This may seem strange, since age must of course ultimately bear some relation to death. The immediate effect of age, however, was not an important discriminant between groups who were successfully resuscitated and those who were not.

In spite of conclusively finding no correlation between age and outcome in hundreds of patients with cardiac arrest, the possibility of a preselected and perhaps biased sample must be considered. Even though patients were reviewed simply on the basis of whether or not they recovered from a given arrest, it should be remembered that we are not dealing with random assignment to groups as in an ideal experimental design. There are many opportunities for inherent and unrecognized bias to play a part in patient-selection and ultimate outcome. For example, the unspoken decision of the first individual on the scene of the arrest, or that of the physician who later takes charge of resuscitation, whether resuscitation is morally and ethically right for the given patient, can obviously affect who is selected or how vigorously resuscitation is pursued. These are unmeasurable factors and, by and large, uncontrollable in both the clinical and the investigational sense. They are mentioned in order that their potential role and effects are not forgotten.

Another significant finding that may be surprising is the fact that there was no difference in outcome whether or not resuscitation was initiated by a physician. This speaks well for the potential of efforts being developed in some communities to have non-medical teams of specially trained personnel available as the first team for resuscitative efforts.

In considering why certain morbidity might be associated with survival several explanations are possible. Patients who have had more than one arrest could form a unique subgroup in that, once identified as having had an arrest, they would probably be followed more carefully in terms of subsequent similar problems. In addition, the conditions underlying multiple arrests were more often amenable to resuscitative efforts. Finally, patients with chronic cardiac conditions had probably developed better collateral circulation than those whose arrest was the first indication of heart trouble, and this could account for their better outcome.

Conclusion

In a sample of 292 patients referred and treated for cardiac arrest age did not play a part in the immediate outcome. In fact, identical recovery rates occurred in groups of patients aged under 60 and those over 60. The only differences regarding age related to medical diagnoses or other associated conditions. Survival was actually linked to having more arrests, chronic cardiac conditions, or certain types of arrhythmias. It might therefore be surmised that recovery from cardiac arrest is related to inherent resistance of the patient and the severity of underlying morbidity rather than to age. This gives additional support to our general hypothesis that survival into geriatric age is an indication of physical toughness rather than frailty (Linn, Linn, and Gurel, 1969). So-called "old age" is therefore not itself a contraindication to cardiac resuscitation or, for that matter, to any other kind of therapy.

We wish to thank Mrs. Isabel Neves, clinical research assistant, for her help in the compilation of data and preparation of the manuscript and the Emergency Resuscitation Committee at this hospital.

REFERENCES

Ayers, W. R., and Doyle, J. T. (1964). *New York State Journal of Medicine*, **64**, 1929.
Kouwenhoven, W. B., Jude, J. R., and Knickerbocker, G. G. (1960). *Journal of the American Medical Association*, **173**, 1064.
Linn, B. S., Linn, M. W., and Gurel, L. (1969). *Gerontologia Clinica*, **11**, 362.

25

Reprinted from *Hospital Practice* 11:67–74 (1976)

Common Complaints of the Elderly

DAVID ECKSTEIN
Meadow Lakes Retirement Center

What happens when geriatric patients have unlimited access to sympathetic physicians? For one thing, they seldom come in without a good reason, though perhaps not the one they give. Common complaints should not be treated as trivia.

This discussion of common complaints of the elderly proceeds from what may be an uncommon set of circumstances: I am a primary practitioner in a retirement center that offers essentially unlimited access to ambulatory care. Neither cost nor distance sets up any barrier. Also, my practice is entirely geriatric. Many physicians have asked me what primary care is like in such a setting. Do the elderly tend to overutilize services and overwhelm the doctor? Is their pattern of complaints radically different from that of other patients?

My response to such questions is no, and this article will attempt to show why. In describing features of my practice and clientele, my objective is not to be encyclopedic about common complaints of the elderly but rather to suggest a philosophy and some of the strategies to which they give rise.

Despite the absence of tangible barriers, my patient population shows no appetite for extravagant physician use. By and large, patients have a good reason for seeing the physician, though the reason may not be the one the patient advances. But there are some *intangible* barriers they must overcome: patients tend to internalize pejorative stereotypes of old people, and they will avoid seeing the physician rather than risk being identified with those stereotypes. Their sensitivity in this area is hardly unusual. Similar reactions are seen in patients on Medicaid.

But the residents of the Meadow Lakes Retirement Center, Hightstown, N.J., are financially secure. They are educated, former business or professional people who have received good medical care all their lives. Medical and skilled nursing services for our 374 residents, who average 81 years of age, are prepaid in their housing contracts. Another full-time physician and I are their primary practitioners. Four surgeons, a urologist, two dermatologists, two ophthalmologists, two podiatrists, and a dentist conduct clinics at the center. We make referrals to specialists outside the center, too. Among our staff are a registered physiotherapist, a radiology technician, and the nurses and other personnel at our 90-bed nursing facility. We primary physicians have regular office hours and also make emergency calls to apartments and detached dwellings. All in all, the two of us handle about 3,000 patient visits per year.

Complaints referrable to the cardiovascular system account for 13% of our visits. The most common clinical diagnosis is arteriosclerotic heart disease. Ischemic or coronary artery disease underlies about half the congestive failure cases, which are predominantly of the low output kind. Auricular fibrillation and other arrhythmias are often found to be due to too much or too little digitalis, too much diuretic, or too little potassium replacement. Cerebral thrombosis, cerebral hemorrhage, aortic aneurysm, and peripheral vascular insufficiency are seen with some frequency, but the impact in our population is relatively mild. Transient ischemic episodes outnumber the foregoing conditions; they are frightening, frustrating, refractory to specific therapy, and usually prognostic of aggravations. For patients seeking relief of dyspnea, edema, orthopnea, weakness, and angina, we have found that rest is as important as

Dr. Eckstein is Medical Director of Meadow Lakes Retirement Center, Hightstown, New Jersey.

drug and dietary modalities. We tailor patients' activities to cardiac capacities by scheduling bedrest, identifying places where they should stop and wait en route to the centralized dining hall, and prescribing sedentary periods after meals and prior to exercise. Concurrent treatment of anemias and any other oxygen-restricting condition is of course essential, as is diet to maintain a low-normal weight.

Another 13% of visits involve muscles, tendons, joints, and bones. The figure understates the prevalence of these problems inasmuch as it refers only to patients with significant impairments. Most patients have some osteoarthritis; most accept it, if symptomatic, as a fact of long life. But it is upsetting to the person who enjoys the quarter-mile walk to and from the dining room.

In our women patients, osteoporosis frequently presents with pain from compression and overt fracture of dorsal and lumbar vertebrae. Minor falls, with a twisting motion, are disproportionate causes of femoral-neck damage. Sit-down injuries – pelvic fractures with poorly localized pain – are fairly common. In the seventh and eighth decades, men catch up statistically with women in frequency of osteoporosis. More often than with women, the fracture site in men is the femur, not the vertebrae. If the spine is involved, carcinoma of the prostate is considered before we accept a diagnosis of os-

teoporosis. In men and women with osteoporosis, Paget's disease must be considered.

Not too long ago, a femoral-neck fracture was virtually a ticket to the grave. We refer most patients for immediate surgery and count on having them returned to our skilled nursing facility in 10 days. The guiding word in postoperative therapy is "mobilization." Age is no deterrent if the circumstances are right. We recorded a successful operative result for our oldest resident, who had a femur fracture in her 100th year. She went on to celebrate her 101st birthday. This example does not mean we are complacent about femoral-neck repair. The preconditions for disaster linger on, in poor bone structure and proneness to accidental falls. It has been our experience that refracture produces total disability and accelerates the patient's general deterioration.

About 11% of office visits are for skin problems, generally of three kinds: 1) pruritus associated with dry skin; 2) senile actinic or seborrheic keratosis; 3) neoplasms, chiefly basal cell carcinoma. The keratotic lesions, which are almost never solitary, are excised if size, number, and locations indicate the need. Basal cell carcinomas often are spread among benign keratoses. Hence the importance of consultation with the dermatologist. The biopsies or excisions required for histologic confirmation are done in our clinic. We are less likely to see squamous cell car-

The 40-odd buildings of the retirement center are connected by enclosed walkways of which bridge seen at right in photo above is part. Residents thus can reach central complex (which includes dining hall and health center) on foot in any weather. Doctors' offices, clinic, and 90-bed skilled nursing facility are grouped in health center.

cinomas, which are of course more dangerous.

The chances of picking up dangerous lesions early are fairly good if they are prominent; concerned for their personal appearance, patients come in quickly to consult about blemishes on the face or hands. The most frequent complaint is itchy, dry, scaly skin; emollients and other compounds may be employed, but it is not easy to control a skin that has lost its lubricants. Pruritus can be set off by underclothes, detergents used in the wash, and even thiazides and other medications. Burns caused by improper use of heating pads are fairly frequent and heal with difficulty. We have found that it is important to provide instruction in the safe use of such devices.

About 8.5% of office visits are for urinary tract diseases. Our consulting urologist makes, or confirms most diagnoses and supervises treatment, utilizing measurement of residual urine, cystometry, and cystoscopy. Our investigation of urinary complaints is never casual; it includes microscopic examination of urinary sediment, urine culture, and antibiotic sensitivity tests. In men, obstructive uropathy secondary to prostatic hypertrophy is the single overriding concern. In women, the most frequent problems are incontinence and/or infection. Time and again, we are reminded that atrophic vaginitis must be considered and dealt with (often quite easily with topical estrogen creams), since symptomatic complaints will persist in the absence of adequate hormonal levels.

About 15% of the visits are prompted by annual screenings, which we have found well justified. Aside from overt skin lesions, the greatest yields are breast and colon diseases. For example, one series of screenings produced four cases of right colon carcinoma; two patients are alive without identifiable metastasis two years after surgery. We find two to four cases of breast carcinoma annually, and the survival rate with early identification and treatment appears excellent. Another 5% of the visits are represented by problems of vision and hearing, 5% by respiratory and 10% by gastrointestinal disturbances. The remaining are classified as miscellaneous.

This miscellaneous group includes overt emotional problems, mostly depressive. Chronic alcoholism in our population has about the same prevalence as in any other population of comparable age, background, and affluence. Many have no family; others have been abandoned. This can be disastrous when combined with social rejection and other stresses of group living. My full-time colleague and I do considerable counseling. We have that "luxury" in medical practice that most physicians lack – time to listen and

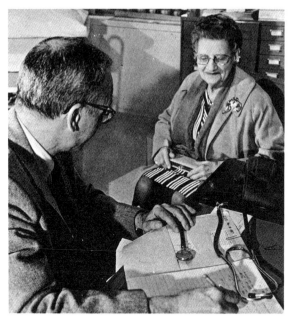

For ambulatory residents a visit to the doctor's office may be for an annual checkup (top), which all are urged to have, or a look at a sore throat (center). For the nursing facility patient (below) rounds may be as important for morale building as for medical problems.

Taking meals in central dining hall (top) gives opportunity for social contact; "breakfast club" for widowers and bachelors (lower photo) helps get day off to good start.

chat with patients. We believe that as a consequence our need to prescribe tranquilizers is minimal.

Depression, agitation, petulance, and aggression may signal serious underlying problems, especially organic senile dementia. This is truly our major problem. As the population's average age rises, the frequency and severity of senile dementia grow. Let me be quite clear: I refer to disorganized, disheveled, frequently slovenly individuals who only recently became that way; hardly a month or year before, they had been well oriented, neat, and capable of independence in activities of daily living (dressing, feeding, walking, etc.). More than half of our 90 nursing beds are occupied by residents unable to function on their own, most of whom have senile dementia.

As I suggested at the outset, when an elderly person comes to see us, the complaint must be taken seriously. Old people do not complain unnecessarily. Their complaints may not be a reasonable interpretation of what is wrong. It's up to the physician to find out. Most of the time, we find that the elderly underplay their symptoms and problems. When I say that the patient nearly always has a good reason for an office visit, I include loneliness as a good reason. The individual may need reassurance that somebody cares. One of the ways in which we convey that we care is to make certain all our residents are well aware that there is medical coverage on weekends. To dramatize my concern, when I first came to Meadow Lakes I would move up and down dining-room waiting lines on the weekend, asking for someone I knew would *not* be there. It was my way of saying: "I'm here if you need me."

During an office visit we encourage patients to talk about their families, vacations, or whatever interests them, so we can know them better. We emphasize touching. We never stand in a doorway and say hello to a bed patient. I instruct the staff to put skin on skin, even to take a pulse unnecessarily. This is our way of encouraging human relationships. One result is that it is easy to spot personality change and recognize the first signs of senile dementia.

There is an emotional price for this policy. It is not easy to watch one's patient-friends disintegrate, nor to be calm in dealing with a difficult person one might prefer to ignore. It is no surprise to me that physicians who are close to the elderly fear what they see, especially the impact of societal attitudes that view the elderly person as expendable, unimportant, or useless. These attitudes have a corrosive effect on the patient. As job, home, and other societal frames are removed, unless the physician is careful he can lose sight of the patient as an individual.

Elderly patients often conceal complaints out of fear of being identified as old and useless. They become apologetic about visiting the physician. "I hate to bother you," they say. The statement bothers *us* very much, because it means they tend to delay obtaining an office consultation that might save them many nights of worry. For example, a woman will suspect breast cancer but will rationalize avoiding the doctor because the lump is "only a little thing"; however, at night, alone, she worries. A man who has rectal bleeding and a 20-pound weight loss will conceal the problem in fear of putting a further strain on the family. Willing to die, the patient resists intervention. One woman delayed seeing us a year so that she would be beyond surgery for breast cancer. She had her wish and died uncomfortably. In my view, when a patient *stops* visiting the doctor, it may signal concealment bordering on martyrdom.

Sometimes the complaint is based on a surrogate symptom. It is up to the physician to probe for the real problem. The patient may tell the doctor, as he tells his wife, that the office visit is occasioned by a wart. Actually, he wants to be examined for chest pains. We are not deterred from exploring possible problems just because the apparent cause of the visit is trivial. We hold fireside conferences for groups of residents to emphasize that they should not trivialize

symptoms of potentially serious disease. Five minutes of consultation, we tell them, could prevent weeks of hospitalization. We urge them to articulate their worries, to ask questions about medical care, disease, and aging, to visit or telephone us about minor complaints, and to have an annual review of health status. We tell them that we must know about total drug intake, and we ask them to bring in the contents – often voluminous – of their medicine cabinets every six months; here we often find explanations of, or contributors to, their complaints. We talk about the potential adverse effects of cosmetics, deodorant sprays, and other grooming aids. We go over key points in nutrition, emphasizing how poor diet may be the underlying cause of certain symptoms.

The complaints I regard among the most serious concern mentation. Memory loss, confusion, and personality change are warnings of impending trouble, principally inability to cope with activities of daily living. These conditions may herald the beginning of the end of personal independence. Mental deterioration from cerebral arteriosclerosis or senile dementia progresses implacably, engulfing the individual finally in a dream world.

Some patients realize they are forgetting too many things. If they themselves do not request an office appointment, neighbors may urge them or may call them to our attention. It becomes important to us to

Transfer to the nursing facility is not solely for the bedfast. At left above, two health center staff members discuss food preferences with patients; at right, a corridor conference with physician during daily rounds.

know the kinds of social supports an individual may have; the individual who lacks neighbors and family may need closer medical supervision.

Complaints about worsening memory need not be calamitous; this may simply reflect lack of challenge, since memory can also go bad from disuse. In trying to discern the presence of true dementia, it is difficult to distinguish among memory loss, languor, and confusion. The search for a pattern of irrational behavior must be sophisticated, since confusion may not spread uniformly through all areas of activity or cognition. A woman may become well-nigh incompetent in most activities of daily living, but she will still know how to arrange her lipstick. A disheveled elderly woman, on the other hand, must be considered to be seriously ill. By contrast, men tend to become slovenly well in advance of serious mental deterioration, especially widowers who had depended heavily on their wives for self-maintenance. If the widower had already been a liberal user of alcohol, he is likely to begin drinking to excess. Since such individuals resist help, there will be considerable deterioration before the physician is alerted. At our center, we have organized a breakfast club of widowers and bachelors in an effort to build peer support.

With good social support, such as neighbors who render comfort and practical assistance, the need for institutionalization may be appreciably delayed. But sometimes neighbors and family have negative effects, which must not be overlooked. For example, we had a patient who was becoming paranoid and violent for no apparent physical reason. The problem turned out to be a domineering wife; it was she who needed counseling. In another instance, a man became depressed because the family exploited the physician's instruction against a dinner highball; it was part of a pattern of depreciating the man. The humiliation was especially profound because others at the dinner table imbibed freely.

In such situations, our experience has been that our own methods of counseling were as effective as referrals for psychiatric care. Finding that recovery from depression took no more time in our own hands, we restricted referrals to the most difficult cases. We learned that patients often simply need a chance to vent their feelings; they may have nobody other than the physician to talk to. At our center, fears of gossip and of being criticized restrain some patients from being intimate with their peers, and individuals with no family visitors depend on the doctor to listen. Our policy is to take the time to do so. In our view, in many instances depression and loneliness reflect an endemic social disease: the stereotyping of the elderly person as "senile" or "peculiar" when he or she acts individualistically.

Fatigue and insomnia, as well as depression, may

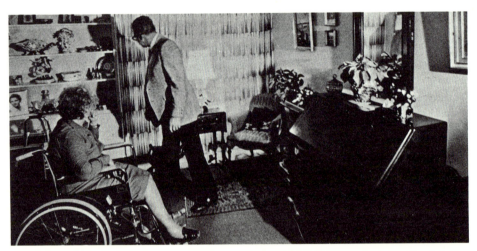

Residents furnish their own dwelling units and when time comes to enter nursing facility, it greatly eases the transi- *tion to take along as many as possible of their own possessions, as in the case of the woman seen above.*

reflect emotional tensions for which counseling provides a remedy. The complaints *can* be met by prescribing pills. But we do not prescribe until we have tried to identify and resolve the cause of tension. Fatigue may result from apprehension about health, love, disability, dependency, mental deterioration, and rapport with children. In our population of hard-driving achievers, the insecurities of the change in their lives may reinforce a habit of using sedatives and tranquilizers that cause fatigue – another reason for obtaining a thorough drug history.

This is not to say that we have a solution to offer for the functional disorders for which the elderly rely on drug palliation. Rather than sit in judgment, we yield to demands for minor drugs and injections, for example, vitamin B_{12}. If the injection or drug makes the patient feel better, we do not oppose it. It is well-nigh impossible, in our experience, to withdraw the elderly patient from such minor addictions.

Boredom or social withdrawal can also produce fatigue. Abandonment by family promotes withdrawal; it is a matter of embarrassment for the elderly person to be asked by peers why a son or daughter did not visit or why a vacation with one or the other lasted a few days instead of a few weeks. People who cannot cope with emotional crises or unpleasantness want to be left alone with their fatigue.

Fatigue, of course, may have other bases. We do not ascribe fatigue to an emotional cause until physical possibilities have been ruled out. Fatigue, shortness of breath, angina, and edema may originate in cardiac disease or anemia. Besides checking the heart, I routinely ask for a hemoglobin determination for the patient reporting chronic fatigue. In the event of rectal bleeding, my focus goes immediately to the colon and bowel. A surprisingly high number of cancers of the right and ascending colon have been found when this suspicion was followed up. In the man with skeletal pain, urinary difficulty, and bleeding, the seriousness of prostatic possibilities warrants an immediate referral to the urologist.

A patient in the midst of emotional upheaval will present with physical complaints based on genuine disability. Diverticulosis can flare up, complete with diarrhea and cramping. Similarly, existing cardiac disease can worsen because of tension, sleeplessness, and fatigue that are induced by emotional problems. An environmental change – such as change in nursing staff or absence of a friend or a change in residence – may destabilize an elderly person and produce agitation and confusion. Tranquilizers may aggravate the symptoms. (In our nursing facilities, where the staff is stable, we have found little need to tranquilize or restrain most patients.) Change must be viewed as the worst influence on a precariously stabilized or already unstable patient. The traumatic effects can be softened by minimizing environmental change. For example, if a patient must be removed from his apartment to our nursing facility, he is accompanied by a favorite chair, a treasured picture, familiar wardrobe, etc. And there is no medication to rival the support of friends, familiar figures among the nursing staff, and the physician with whom a successful rapport has been built.

The physician may never be sure where a common complaint may lead, of course. As I have pointed out, an emotional complaint may have a physical origin and vice versa. The possible interactions are innumerable and idiosyncratic. That is why I cannot overstress the value of the physician's knowing the patient as a personality rather than as a sequence of problems. The cue to probing for specific physical difficulties often comes from discerning behavioral change. Let me now give some consideration to a few of these difficulties.

Communicative disorders are among the most serious and widely experienced threats to the quality of life. They may present at first as behavioral problems. For example, the patient who develops paranoia may be growing deaf. He cannot make out what others are saying or laughing about and begins to think a conspiracy is afoot. Sometimes a hearing aid will help but sometimes it does not; because it funnels sounds unselectively, the aid may not help the patient focus on what he or she wants to hear. Failure to obtain anticipated results may exacerbate a patient's agitation. We routinely refer patients to a hospital-based audiologist for evaluation and discourage turning to commercial hearing-aid distributors (who have an obvious conflict of interest in making an evaluation and recommendation). Unfortunately, some patients will not accept a professional assessment when the prognosis is unpleasant.

Loss of vision, like loss of hearing, impedes activities our patients thrive on, such as reading, watching television, and writing, and brings out sensitivities to physical symptoms that otherwise might be ignored. The loss may prompt introspection and bitter complaining after the patient is told that little or nothing can be done. In general, patients tend to present earlier with visual than with hearing problems.

If they experience a sharp, severe pain and inflammation of the eye, patients waste no time in visiting us. Our community has been alerted to the possibility of glaucoma. Occasionally surgery can be done the same day a diagnosis is confirmed. Sometimes the surgeon finds the heartbreak of macular degeneration behind a cataract, and what should have been a successful operation becomes an unhappy occasion. By itself, macular degeneration provokes complaints of inability to focus and read, but there is no pain or discomfort, despite loss of central vision. We are frank to tell patients of the hopeless prognosis in order to deter them from a vain round of shopping for specialists and spectacles.

When musculoskeletal problems are combined with vision and hearing deficits, patients are enormously upset. They feel their world brutally contracting. By themselves, musculoskeletal problems are likely to be accepted. The most common complaints are: cervical or lumbosacral pain, difficulty in turning in bed, difficulty in bending to lace shoes, loss of arm strength and pain radiating down the arms, and occasional occipital headache (from cervical degeneration). Ordinarily the patient apologizes for seeing the doctor about these problems. They say they realize it's "old age." We refrain from saying to a complaining patient: "What do you expect at your age?" Nor do we ever categorize musculoskeletal disease by age; I have banished age from our medical charts. What we do attempt, with help of a rheumatology consultant, is to resolve a complaint, and we do not give up until we are certain nothing can be done. Elective surgical intervention and medical therapy have had encouraging results.

We and our patients must be on guard against falls, which can of course be devastating to the patient with fragile bone structure. We pay particular attention to symptoms of poor balance. Staggering, because of slower response by the vestibular mechanism, is a serious cause of accidents. The slower vestibular reaction tends to make the individual pitch or twist too far. Consequently, we try to train patients to compensate. They are advised to turn the whole body, not just the head alone, to sit for a while on the edge of a bed after arising, and to stand for a few seconds before walking away. We teach them to be careful after eating, explaining that the concentration of blood in the abdomen leaves the brain relatively anoxic. We assure worried patients that syncope by itself is not a premonitory sign of stroke. We urge them to report periods of weakness, confusion, or blackout, which in combination with headache, ocular changes, and carotid bruit suggest stroke.

Because muscle tone deteriorates, constipation is a frequent complaint. Patients may complain of constipation when they mean that they are not having the daily bowel movement they consider necessary. The expectation that bowels must move daily is erroneous, and this must be explained. However, even if the patient reports daily bowel movement, a complaint about discomfort in the lower bowel or rectum should be investigated. It is possible to have a bolus of impaction *and* a bypass stool or diarrhea.

Rectal discomfort seems to be well reported; patients apparently have little reluctance to mention problems arising from hemorrhoids and fissures. Even if these are not apparent, we routinely put a finger in the rectum and take a stool specimen to check for blood, a routine that should always be performed; this is especially important in a patient with poor vision, as a negative response to a question about stool color is meaningless from such a patient. (In contrast, patients are likely to report blood in the urine.)

How, then, to summarize our philosophy about the complaining elderly patient? Basically, we view common complaints not as trivia to be dismissed quickly but as opportunities to expand our rapport with patients. I would be the first to admit that our retirement center circumstances give us considerably more time to do this than the typical primary practitioner may have. But absent this advantage, good medical care of the elderly cannot be accomplished if the effort is not made.

Given the large burden of illnesses and disabilities the elderly endure, the relative paucity of their symptoms, their high threshhold of pain, and their keenness in distinguishing the important from the unimportant symptom, the complaints of the elderly are remarkably low-keyed and valid. They justify compassionate attention. It is a humbling experience to witness the great courage with which so many elderly people meet adversity. □

Selected Reading

Butler RN, Lewis MJ: Aging and Mental Health. The C.V. Mosby Company, St. Louis, 1973

Harris R: The Management of Geriatric Cardiac Disease. J.B. Lippincott Company, Philadelphia, 1970

Rodstein M, Savitsky E, Starkman R: Initial adjustment to a long-term care institution, medical and behavioral aspects. J Am Geriatr Soc 24:65, 1976

Eckstein D: Common symptoms and complaints of the elderly. J Am Geriatr Soc 21:440, 1973

Part V

RESEARCH IN GERONTOLOGY
(TWENTIETH CENTURY)

Editor's Comments
on Paper 26

26   EMERSON
A Brief Look At Aging

The United States Congress passed the Research on Aging Act, which was signed into law by President Richard M. Nixon on May 31, 1974. This act enabled the establishment of a new institute in the National Institutes of Health under our Department of Health, Education and Welfare. This NIA (National Institute on Aging) allows us all to admit now there are distinct health and welfare problems of our sexa-, septua-, and octa-genarians. Dr. Robert N. Butler became the first director of the NIA in the spring of 1976.

In spite of numerous popular reports of macrobiosis in the USSR, in the 1970 census the Soviet Union had apparently a somewhat younger population than the United States; those over fifty years of age represented approximately one-fifth of the Russian population; those over forty-five years of age in the United States represented about one-third of our population. Interestingly in 1970 the median age in the United States was 28.1 years, which was the lowest since the 1940 U.S. census. For a resume of research in the Soviet Union written by two members of the Institute of Gerontology, USSR Academy of Medical Sciences, the interested reader is referred to Chebotarev and Frolkis (1975).

An overview of aging research appears in Paper 26.

26

Reprinted from *Ala. J. Med. Sci.* **9**(4):424–427 (1972)

A Brief Look At Aging

*Geraldine M. Emerson**

Man ages—a very old observation. For centuries man has been interested in preventing or reversing it. For a much shorter time many speculations, hypotheses and theories concerning the nature or etiology of aging have arisen. In only the last 20 years or so has there been much research activity into the various biochemical, physiological and pathogical parameters associated with aging. This perhaps is a consequence of the fact that in this interval the number of persons over 65 years of age in the U. S. has increased. (65 years of age is an arbitrary figure. Some age must be used; perhaps 45 would be more meaningful). In 1950 the U. S. population was 151,326,000 whereas in 1970 it was 203,-185,000, an increase of 51,859,000 persons. In 1950 the 65 years of age and older group amounted to 12,295,000 (or 8.1%) and in 1970, 20,496,000 (or 10.1% of the population). (U. S. Department of Commerce 1971). Another timely topic is whether or not aging is a disease! The Assistant Secretary for Health and Scientific Affairs at the Department of Health, Education and Welfare was recently quoted (Biomedical News 1972) to be of the opinion that aging is not a disease. Be that as it may, there are many health problems associated with aging and many of the health dollars spent in the U. S. today are spent in health services for the elderly, the old, the senescent. There is no generally acceptable definition of these words. Webster's (1955) definitions of age "1. To become old. . . , 2. specif. a. To suffer with lapse of time a diminution of essential qualities or forces. . . . , 3. To become mellow or ripe. . ." with the further distinction made that AGED

implies extreme old age; OLD refers to one far advanced in years and ELDERLY means only having passed the prime of life; whereas SENILITY is "2. Med. A pathological excess of the decline characteristic of old age." My own operational definition of aging is the progressive inability of the organism to adjust to the various perturbations, to which all organisms are subjected, as a function of the years lived: or, aging consists of those processes occurring in an organism which render it less and less capable and finally incapable of further existence without outside support and which, in our present state of knowledge and ability, leads ultimately to the death of the organism. Now, that does not imply that lifespan and aging are synonymous for obviously they are not—a two year old dying from drowning did not die of aging any more than did a 50 year old who died from the same cause. Yet, for studies in experimental animals the lifespan criterion is as yet the only objective criterion available for measuring aging. This is an important point to consider however for if suddenly a whole city of people were to die, the lifespan for that population would be greatly decreased from prior generations and one might tend uncautiously to conclude that the event caused premature aging rather than premature death.

Perhaps because proteins are central to all aspects of living function, the currently emphasized theories of aging involve altered protein metabolism in one way or another.

Harrow (1946) suggested that there was decreased protein turnover rate. He postulated that the protein synthetic rate decreases with decreased hydrolytic rate, giving a longer half-life of the specific protein.

*Asst. Prof. of Biochemistry, Medical Center, U.A.B., Birmingham, Alabama 35294

Therefore, one would expect that a greater amount of the protein would be denatured leaving less functional protein present. An old observation that might be contributory to a decreased protein synthesis rate with age is that the intracellular amino acid concentration decreases with age so that it approaches the extracellular concentration eventually giving a 1/1 ratio. (Van Slyke and Meyer, 1913; Christensen, 1959; Christensen, et al., 1958).

H. M. Evans, et al. (1948) (also Li, et al. 1949) had shown that anterior pituitary growth hormone promotes growth; hypophysectomy in the rat is followed by a decreased cytoplasmic amino acid concentration. For all of these reasons, it appeared logical to us to administer growth hormone to old rats and follow the lifespan effects on them (Emerson and Emerson, 1955, 1961). Although there was no long-lasting effect, these old rats responded as well as the young adult rats treated at the same time and subjectively appeared younger for the period of time that they were responding to the growth hormone. Christensen (1959) also gave growth hormone to old rats and found increased amino acid uptake compared with the untreated controls.

Haining and Correll (1969) reported that the ratio of the synthetic rate to the degradative rate constant for the enzyme tryptophan pyrrolase in male Fischer 344 rat liver decreased from a value of 92 nmole kyneurenine formed/gram of liver in 1 month old rats; to 40, in 6 month; 33, in 12 month and 27, in 24 month old rats. However, their data did not reflect a systematic change in the parameters measured as a function of age. Methodology has been a barrier to accumulation of sufficient turnover data. At the moment there are insufficient data on insufficient organs and individual proteins to draw any conclusion about protein turnover and age.

H. J. Curtis (1963) proposed a somatic mutation theory which involves abnormal chromosomes. Altered DNA (mutated DNA due to free radicals, mainly) leads to production of altered proteins. H. J. Curtis, et al. (1966) indicated that the mutations would vary from cell to cell and therefore the altered proteins would also vary. Essentially however, the presence of the altered proteins would mean some altered cell function which eventually will lead to obvious senility and death.

Measurements of chromosomal aberrations have not correlated well with aging. One would predict that mutations would occur in the rapidly dividing cells such as bone marrow and gastrointestinal tract and that these mutated cells would be eliminated; consequently no altered protein would be present. It also appears that the more affected organs from the standpoint of aging are the ones which do not have rapid cell turnover (in fact, some are said to be irreversible post-mitotics, which they might well be). Nevertheless, there is evidence suggesting strongly that skeletal muscle is not invariably such an organ. (Emerson and Emerson, 1958). However, Burnet (1965) believes there is good reason to implicate somatic mutations in the basic causation of aging. Walford (1969) appears to support this view also with its profound consequences in the immune system.

One actively pursued theory at the moment is Orgel's (1963) hypothesis that aging is due to accumulated defective proteins specifically involved in nucleic acid metabolism. They are not the result of mutations but rather result from infidelity in the transcription-translation apparatus.

According to this theory there is reduced specificity of the protein synthetic machinery allowing error accumulation. If errors occurred specifically in the RNA polymerase complex, especially in post-mitotic cells, a positive feedback mechanism of error accumulation would lead to cellular chaos and death. Orgel then raises this very important point which would question his theory: "If any part of the aging process has to do with the accumulation of errors of polypeptide sequence, we need to know how it is that each new organism comes to have as clear a start as its parents . . . we have no reason to believe that the *enzymes* initially present in the egg have been subjected to a significantly reduced possibility of error." This objection has been largely ignored by others. A number of reports by Holliday (Harrison and Holliday, 1967; Holliday, 1969; Holliday and Tarrant, 1972) have purported to support Orgel's hypothesis fully.

If analogs of the amino acids arginine, methionine, phenylalanine and tryptophan are administered to drosophila larvae for anywhere from 4-24 hours, mean lifespan of the adult fly is less than that of control non-exposed. The same type of experiment was performed on 2 species of fungi but the conclusion was that the results were open to other interpretation as well as support of the error hypothesis; whereas they concluded that results with certain *Neurospora crassa* mutants fully support the error catastrophe hypothesis. It appears to me that as soon as one brings in mutants one is working with mutation theory rather than an extra-mutation theory of aging. It appears that Holliday's argument has become that altered proteins lead to aging and he seems to believe this to be Orgel's hypothesis. The Orgel hypothesis however was based on extra-mutational protein alterations. Again, in a recent paper Holliday and Tarrant (1972) report that old WI-38 fibroblasts contain 2 pentose phosphate pathway enzymes (glucose-6-phosphate dehydrogenase and 6-phospho gluconate dehydrogenase) having increased heat lability and cite this as evidence in support of the Orgel hypothesis. Again this deals with some event different from Orgel's hypothesis that the only long lasting effect and therefore aging effect must be in enzymes directly involved in the transcriptional-translational processes.

Both groups seem also to support generally Hayflicks' dictum that there is a finite lifespan for any cell—a programmed death. For a review of this subject see Holeckova, E. and Cristofalo, V., Editors, Aging in Cell and Tissue Culture (1970). In all of these studies, however, the critical test of the theories (actual measurement of altered proteins) has not been performed and survival has been the quantity measured.

Many studies have been concerned with determination of macromolecular concentration; enzyme activity or metabolic pathway potential as a function of age. Only a few of these will be mentioned. A. Zorzoli and J. B. Li (1967) reported no impairment in overall gluconeogenic ability of old mouse (20-26 months) compared with young adult mouse (5-7 months) kidney. However, for certain enzymes there were significant differences between the 2 groups and the following enzymatic activitiy was less in senescent than adult: Triosephosphate isomerase; lactate dehydrogenase; glucose-6-phosphatase (as well as in the citrate cycle enzyme, fumarase). However the ability of the old kidney to use oxaloacetate or succinate was unchanged from the adult; this was also true for the two key gluconeogenic enzymes: Fructose-1,6-diphosphatase and Phosphoenolpyruvate carboxykinase. R. C. Adelman (1970) has reported that 2 year old male and female Sprague-Dawley rats have a much slower return of liver glucokinase activity than do 2 month old Sprague-Dawley rats when both groups have been starved equally for 72 hours, then refed. Nevertheless the activity of the old rat liver glucokinase does eventually reach that of the young, and the premanipulated old level. From his data he concludes that the impairment of the old liver could be (1) less effective glucokinase enzyme, (2) impairment of the response to the control systems (eg. insulin stimulated activity), (3) impairment in production or release of the "messengers". Nevertheless there must be "a modification either in the rate or accuracy of protein biosynthesis, the rate of protein degradation, or of a specific biological activity."

H. E. Enesco (1967) reported a comparison of DNA concentration in Sherman male rats of 2 ages: Young (3 months) and old (27 months—the colony maximum is 29 months). There was no difference between the groups with respect to DNA of (1) molecular layer cells of cerebellum; (2)

proximal tubules of kidney; (3) diploid liver; (4) tetraploid liver cell nuclei. Within an age group, the brain DNA concentration did not differ from the kidney DNA concentration. The average nuclear diameter of the cerebellar molecular layer cells was significantly less in the old rats than in the young. This was not true of the kidney nor of the 2N or 4N liver.

There are many other approaches being made in gerontology. With as much effort as is now being expended in this area there is every reason to believe that sufficient insight will be gained to enable alleviation of at least some of the disability of aging very soon.

BIBLIOGRAPHY

Adelman, R. C. 1970. An Age-dependent Modification of Enzyme Regulation. *J. Biol. Chem. 245:* 1032-1035.

Behrens, L. B. 1972. NIH Headed for Institute on Aging. *Biomedical News III* 8/72 p.10. Washington, D. C.

Burnet, M. 1965. Somatic Mutation and Chronic Disease. *Brit. Med. J. 1:* 338-342.

Christensen, H. N. 1959. Decreasing Tissue Amino Acid Hunger with Age. *Geriatrics 14:* 429-432.

Christensen, H. N.; D. H. Thompson; S. Markel and M. Sidky. 1958. Decreasing Amino Acid Hunger of Human Muscle with Age. *Proc. Soc. Exp. Biol. Med. 99:* 780-782.

Curtis, H. J. 1963. Biological Mechanisms Underlying the Aging Process. *Science 141:* 686-694.

Curtis, H. J.; J. Tilley; C. Crowley and M. Fuller. 1966. The Role of Genetic Factors in the Aging Process. *J. Gerontol. 21:* 365-368.

Emerson, J. D. and G. M. Emerson. 1955. Failure of the Rat to Show Continuous Growth in Response to a Crude Alkaline Extract of Rat Pituitary Glands. *Amer. J. Physiol. 182:* 521-523.

Emerson, J. D. and G. M. Emerson. 1958. Skeletal Muscle Fiber Diameters in Normal Adult and Pituitary Giant Female Rats. *Fed. Proc. 17:* 42, pt. I, March (abstract).

Emerson, J. D. and G. M. Emerson. 1961. Effect of Growth Hormone Supplementation on Life Span of the Female Rat. *Fed. Proc. 20:* 188, pt. I, March (abstract).

Enesco, H. E. 1967. A Cytophotometric Analysis of DNA Content of Rat Nuclei in Aging. *J. Gerontol. 22:* 445-448.

Evans, H. M.; M. E. Simpson and C. H. Li. 1948. The Gigantism Produced in Normal Rats by Injection of the Pituitary Growth Hormone; Body Growth and Organ Changes. *Growth 12:* 15-32.

Haining, J. L. and W. W. Correll. 1969. Turnover of Tryptophan-induced Tryptophan Pyrrolase in Rat Liver as a Function of Age. *J. Gerontol. 24:* 143-148.

Harrison, B. J. and R. Holliday. 1967. Senescence and the Fidelity of Protein Synthesis in Drosophila. *Nature 213:* 990-992.

Harrow, B. 1946. TEXTBOOK OF BIOCHEMISTRY, 4th Ed., Philadelphia, W. B. Saunders, p. 571.

Holeckova, E. and V. J. Cristofalo, Eds. 1970. AGING IN CELL AND TISSUE CULTURE. Plenum Press, New York.

Holliday, R. 1969. Errors in Protein Synthesis and Clonal Senescence in Fungi. *Nature 221:* 1224-1228.

Holliday, R. and G. M. Tarrant, 1972. Altered Enzymes in Ageing Human Fibroblasts. *Nature 238:* 26-30.

Li, C. H.; I. Geschwind and H. M. Evans. 1949. Effect of Growth and Adrenocorticotropic Hormones on Amino Acid Levels in Plasma. *J. Biol. Chem. 177:* 91-95.

Orgel, L. S. 1963. The Maintenance of the Accuracy of Protein Synthesis and its Relevance to Ageing. *Proc. Nat. Acad. Sci. U.S.A. 49:* 517-521.

U. S. Department of Commerce, Bureau of the Census. 1971. POCKET DATA BOOK U.S.A. U. S. Government Printing Office, Washington, D. C. pp. 37, 41.

Van Slyke, D. D. and G. M. Meyer. 1913-1914. The Fate of Protein Digestion Products in the Body. III. The Absorption of Amino-Acids From the Blood by the Tissues. *J. Biol. Chem. 16:* 197-212.

Webster's New International Dictionary of the English Language Unabridged, 1955, 2nd Ed. W. A. Nielson, Editor-in-Chief. G. C. Merriam Company, Publishers, Springfield, Mass.

Walford, R. L. 1969. THE IMMUNOLOGIC THEORY OF AGING. Williams and Wilkins, Baltimore, Maryland.

Zorzoli, A. and J. B. Li. 1967. Gluconeogenesis in Mouse Kidney Cortex. Effect of Age and Fasting on Glucose Production and Enzyme Activities. *J. Gerontol. 22:* 151-157.

Editor's Comments
on Papers 27 Through 32

One consistent belief in gerontology is that along with genetic factors, diet is of tremendous importance to geriatric good health. At intervals during this century many papers have appeared from many nutritionists on the effect of caloric restriction and lifespan (Loosli, 1973; McCay et al., 1935). Robertson et al. (Paper 27) reported on mouse studies; from McCay's laboratory at Cornell came reports on some of the pathophysiology of restricted versus unrestricted rats (Papers 28 and 29). In yet another of these studies (Paper 30), Drs. A. J. Carlson and F. Hoelzel reported that intermittent fasting of rats appeared to prolong their lives. Although no clinical implication can be drawn from these studies, they make a large contribution to understanding of the aging process. The role of vitamins in human aging is covered in Papers 31 and 32 (see also Kirk and Chiefie, 1948). Vitamin supplementation of the geriatric diet has been a recurrent theme (see Pelton and Williams, 1958).

Reprinted from *Austral. J. Exp. Biol. Med. Sci.* **12**:33–45 (1934)

THE INFLUENCE OF INTERMITTENT STARVATION AND OF INTERMITTENT STARVATION PLUS NUCLEIC ACID ON THE GROWTH AND LONGEVITY OF THE WHITE MOUSE

by

T. BRAILSFORD ROBERTSON, HEDLEY R. MARSTON, AND
J. W. WALTERS

(From the Laboratory of the Division of Animal Nutrition of the Commonwealth
Council for Scientific and Industrial Research, at the University of Adelaide,
South Australia).

(Submitted for publication 22nd February, 1934.)

During the last two decades Robertson carried out many experiments in which he sought a clue that would provide a guide in the elucidation of the mysteries of the process of senescence.

The hypothesis which stimulated these researches was primarily based on the observation of Hertwig (1903), who showed that division occurs in any given species of cell when the ratio of the volume of the nucleus to the volume of the whole cell reaches a certain value.

It follows that if anything should happen to delay the growth of the nucleus in comparison with the growth of cytoplasm, so that the critical ratio would not be attained, then the division of the cells could no longer occur and stasis of growth in the cell community must result. The origin of the deterioration of animal tissues with age, and the consequent mortality of complex cell communities, might reside in such a gradual falling off of the nucleo-cytoplasmic ratio of certain tissue cells below the limits compatible with healthy function. The proportion of the nuclear materials in the cells is known to diminish throughout life —at first rapidly and later more slowly—(LeBreton and Schaeffer (1923), Dawbarn (1932)), and it seems not improbable that death, which supervenes on the impaired individual efficiency of all tissue cells, is the ultimate outcome of the process of growth.

If, then, duration of life is set by events and characteristics which are internal, and are attributable to progressive physico-chemical changes occurring in the tissues of the animal itself, it is conceivable that these changes might be modified, and if means could be found to accomplish this, then the duration of life of animals should be susceptible to control by experimental procedures.

Robertson exploited two main methods of attack in his attempts to alter the nucleo-cytoplasmic ratio of the growing animal. He tried to augment nuclear synthesis by increasing to an abnormal extent the nutriments known to be required for the elaboration of nucleic acid; he attempted, on the other hand, to diminish the growth of cytoplasm, whereby the decrease in the ratio with age would be arrested by preventing the progressive increase of the denominator of the fraction.

Feeding relatively massive doses of nucleic acid derived from thymus or from yeast resulted in some increase in the duration of life in the experimental animals, as did also ingestion of large doses of thyroid autocoid during pre-adolescence.

In the following experiments, which constitute the last of the series started by Robertson prior to his death in 1930, attempts were made to reduce the cytoplasmic mass by withdrawing food from the experimental animals two days in every seven, and hopes were entertained of supplying materials for nuclear synthesis by superimposing a daily dose of 25 mg. of yeast nucleic acid on the treatment.

Each experimental unit consisted of twenty-four mice, which were selected, cared for, and their behaviour tabulated as previously described (Robertson, 1925).

The results supervening on intermittent starvation of both males and females are contrasted with control groups of each sex, and the effect of adding 25 mg. of yeast nucleic acid to the daily ration are expressed in figs. 1-4.

During the two-day fasting periods the mice lost over 12 p.c. of their body-weight, but this was rapidly regained after they had access to food, and, while the immediate effect of intermittent starvation was to reduce the growth rate of all groups, the mean body-weight of the animals so treated sooner or later became greater than that of the controls, which continually received a superabundance of the same food. This effect was especially noticeable in the male animals. Feeding 25 mg. per day of yeast nucleic acid to the fasted animals had little further influence either on their growth or longevity.

While the periodic abstinence from food did not significantly increase the life duration, it is remarkable that such treatment certainly did not decrease the expectancy of life, and, furthermore, the significant increase in the body-weight of the male animals which followed such treatment is most striking when we consider the relatively high rate of energy consumption of the small rodent.

REFERENCES.

Dawbarn, M. C. (1932): Austral. J. exper. Biol., 9, p. 213.
Hertwig, R. (1903): Biol. Zbl., 22, p. 1.
Hertwig, R. (1903): Über das Wechselverhältnis von Kern und Protoplasma, München, 1903.
LeBreton, E. and Schaeffer, G. (1923): Trav. de l'Institute de Physiol., Faculté de Méd. le Strasbourg.
Robertson, T. Brailsford (1925): Austral. J. exper. Biol., 2, p. 91.

Table 1.

Control Males.

Number of animals.	Age in weeks.	Weight in gm.	Probable error of mean. + or −	Number of animals.	Age in weeks.	Weight in gm.	Probable error of mean. + or −
23	5	3·39	·16	20	62	29·90	·45
23	6	10·00	·23	20	64	30·05	·48
23	7	11·89	·31	20	66	30·35	·47
23	8	13·50	·31	20	68	30·00	·49
23	9	15·13	·28	20	70	29·60	·42
23	10	17·13	·33	19	72	30·00	·43
23	11	18·33	·31	19	74	30·00	·47
23	12	19·35	·34	19	76	29·89	·47
23	13	20·41	·41	19	78	29·00	·42
23	14	21·00	·36	18	80	29·86	·50
23	15	21·80	·38	18	82	29·89	·59
23	16	22·50	·37	17	84	30·00	·54
23	17	23·43	·39	17	86	29·82	·53
23	18	23·78	·34	16	88	29·97	·56
23	19	23·87	·30	16	90	30·09	·50
23	20	24·43	·29	16	92	29·75	·52
23	21	25·04	·32	15	94	29·60	·54
23	22	25·65	·33	15	96	29·33	·52
23	23	26·33	·32	14	98	29·32	·41
23	24	26·22	·34	14	100	29·28	·62
23	25	26·80	·34	13	102	29·00	·86
23	26	26·85	·35	12	104	29·12	·55
23	27	27·02	·35	12	106	29·04	·60
23	28	27·63	·40	10	108	28·85	·82
23	29	27·76	·44	9	110	29·94	·56
23	30	27·28	·46	9	112	29·16	·66
23	32	26·83	·39	8	114	28·18	·88
23	34	28·13	·44	8	116	28·81	·83
23	36	28·93	·48	7	118	29·00	1·11
23	38	28·61	·41	6	120	29·75	·98
23	40	28·26	·36	6	122	29·75	1·13
22	42	28·73	·43	6	124	29·16	1·23
22	44	28·68	·42	6	126	28·58	1·06
22	46	29·27	·42	4	128	30·25	—
21	48	28·88	·51	4	130	27·75	—
21	50	28·74	·45	2	132	28·25	—
21	52	28·67	·49	2	134	25·75	—
21	54	29·14	·46	2	136	27·00	—
21	56	29·62	·47	2	138	26·50	—
21	58	28·71	·40	2	140	24·50	—
20	60	29·12	·42	2	142	24·25	—

Table 2.

Males. Intermittent Starvation.

Number of animals.	Age in weeks.	Weight in gm.	Probable error of mean. + or −	Number of animals.	Age in weeks.	Weight in gm.	Probable error of mean. + or −
23	5	8·89	·21	23	9	13·39	·37
23	6	9·27	·26	23	10	14·96	·38
23	7	10·50	·29	23	11	16·19	·42
23	8	11·81	·30	23	12	17·30	·41

TABLE 2 (continued).

Males. Intermittent Starvation.

Number of animals.	Age in weeks.	Weight in gm.	Probable error of mean. + or −	Number of animals.	Age in weeks.	Weight in gm.	Probable error of mean. + or −
22	13	18·59	·38	19	72	31·68	·42
22	14	19·66	·33	19	74	31·39	·44
22	15	20·25	·35	19	76	30·87	·43
22	16	21·14	·35	19	78	30·47	·49
22	17	22·27	·36	19	80	30·29	·51
22	18	22·50	·36	19	82	30·32	·58
22	18	22·98	·39	19	84	29·95	·67
22	20	23·68	·33	18	86	30·11	·68
22	21	24·07	·30	17	88	30·00	·73
22	22	24·57	·29	16	90	29·50	·96
22	23	25·34	·36	15	92	30·16	·98
22	24	25·91	·29	14	94	31·39	·51
22	25	26·25	·28	13	96	31·15	·41
22	26	26·36	·32	13	98	30·69	·46
22	27	26·61	·37	13	100	31·27	·67
22	28	26·57	·32	12	102	30·79	·60
22	29	26·77	·34	12	104	31·58	·66
22	30	26·59	·34	12	106	30·62	·60
22	32	26·57	·39	11	108	29·64	·59
22	34	27·73	·47	11	110	28·50	1·05
22	34	27·73	·47	9	112	29·94	·79
22	36	28·66	·46	8	114	30·19	·93
22	38	28·82	·52	8	116	29·19	·91
22	40	28·98	·48	7	118	30·43	1·04
21	42	29·62	·39	7	120	29·93	1·20
21	44	30·02	·36	6	122	29·58	1·17
21	46	30·43	·45	5	124	30·10	·70
21	48	30·98	·40	5	126	29·50	·84
21	50	30·93	·37	5	128	29·60	·94
21	52	31·12	·40	5	130	28·70	·82
21	54	31·57	·42	5	132	28·50	1·36
21	56	31·76	·44	4	134	27·62	—
21	58	31·74	·40	2	136	28·75	—
20	60	31·72	·42	2	138	27·25	—
20	62	32·05	·41	2	140	27·25	—
20	64	31·87	·42	1	142	28·00	—
20	66	32·07	·44	1	144	26·00	—
19	68	32·00	·42	1	146	25·00	—
19	70	31·76	·41				

TABLE 3.

Males. Intermittent Starvation + Vegetable Nucleic Acid.

Number of animals.	Age in weeks.	Weight in gm.	Probable error of mean. + or −	Number of animals.	Age in weeks.	Weight in gm.	Probable error of mean. + or −
24	5	9·10	·17	24	11	15·33	·37
24	6	8·85	·18	24	12	16·31	·42
24	7	9·71	·26	23	13	17·69	·39
24	8	11·37	·30	23	14	18·69	·41
24	9	12·48	·36	23	15	19·83	·42
24	10	13·89	·39	23	16	20·52	·47

193

TABLE 3 (continued).

Males. Intermittent Starvation + Vegetable Nucleic Acid.

Number of animals.	Age in weeks.	Weight in gm.	Probable error of mean. + or −	Number of animals.	Age in weeks.	Weight in gm.	Probable error of mean. + or −
23	17	21·76	·43	22	72	31·27	·62
23	18	22·17	·41	21	74	31·76	·47
23	19	22·50	·44	21	76	31·14	·54
23	20	23·00	·42	20	80	30·60	·55
23	21	23·89	·40	19	82	30·76	·58
23	22	24·48	·47	19	84	30·34	·61
23	23	25·04	·43	19	86	30·47	·63
23	24	25·39	·42	19	88	30·26	·68
23	25	25·63	·39	19	90	29·89	·69
23	26	26·00	·43	18	92	30·11	·72
23	27	26·17	·39	18	94	30·25	·71
23	28	26·32	·43	18	96	29·63	·87
23	29	26·22	·42	17	98	30·76	·78
23	30	26·00	·48	16	100	30·93	·80
23	32	26·91	·51	15	102	31·13	·80
23	34	27·46	·51	14	104	31·25	·87
23	36	28·11	·54	14	106	31·50	·84
23	38	28·63	·49	12	108	32·96	·76
23	40	29·00	·56	11	110	31·55	·73
23	42	29·15	·59	10	112	31·75	·92
23	44	29·30	·53	10	114	31·40	·88
23	46	29·69	·52	10	116	31·40	·85
23	48	29·69	·57	10	118	30·80	1·00
23	50	29·95	·51	10	120	29·85	1·17
23	52	30·00	·53	8	122	28·94	1·24
23	54	30·69	·54	7	124	29·30	1·55
23	56	30·95	·54	6	126	29·41	1·23
23	58	31·15	·59	6	128	27·66	1·23
23	60	31·43	·60	5	130	27·20	1·26
23	62	31·61	·59	4	132	28·62	...
23	64	31·24	·58	3	134	26·83	—
23	66	31·24	·61	2	136	26·00	—
23	68	30·61	·76	1	138	28·50	...
22	70	31·25	·63	1	140	24·50	—

TABLE 4.

Control Females.

Number of animals.	Age in weeks.	Weight in gm.	Probable error of mean. + or −	Number of animals.	Age in weeks.	Weight in gm.	Probable error of mean. + or −
24	5	8·44	·16	24	15	19·22	·21
24	6	10·02	·28	24	16	19·50	·24
24	7	11·79	·26	24	17	19·93	·23
24	8	13·16	·24	24	18	20·20	·22
24	9	14·58	·24	24	19	20·54	·22
24	10	15·81	·27	24	20	21·08	·25
24	11	16·60	·24	24	21	21·31	·23
24	12	17·31	·22	24	22	21·66	·24
24	13	17·89	·22	24	23	22·12	·27
24	14	18·62	·21	24	24	22·43	·26

TABLE 4 (continued).

Control Females.

Number of animals.	Age in weeks.	Weight in gm.	Probable error of mean. + or −	Number of animals.	Age in weeks.	Weight in gm.	Probable error of mean. + or −
24	25	22·81	·27	21	82	27·09	·70
24	26	22·87	·27	21	84	26·73	·71
24	27	23·12	·29	21	86	26·80	·74
24	28	23·37	·29	21	88	26·45	·73
24	29	23·27	·28	21	90	25·45	·82
24	30	23·54	·32	19	92	26·55	·80
24	32	23·70	·36	18	94	26·50	·81
24	34	24·27	·36	18	96	25·72	·85
24	36	24·93	·37	16	98	26·47	·95
24	38	24·81	·38	16	100	26·87	·89
24	40	25·02	·43	14	102	26·78	·93
24	42	25·35	·42	14	104	26·53	·89
24	44	25·85	·44	13	106	26·00	·96
24	46	26·16	·47	12	108	26·58	·96
23	48	26·43	·57	12	110	26·87	1·00
23	50	26·54	·55	12	112	26·96	1·11
23	52	27·02	·52	12	114	26·46	1·05
23	54	27·56	·57	12	116	26·00	1·10
23	56	27·73	·59	12	118	25·71	·95
23	58	27·84	·65	11	120	23·95	1·06
23	60	27·91	·75	9	122	24·83	1·13
23	62	28·56	·73	9	124	24·00	1·12
23	64	28·80	·77	7	126	23·21	1·43
23	66	28·95	·79	5	128	24·30	1·37
23	68	29·22	·79	3	130	23·16	—
23	70	29·00	·77	3	132	23·33	—
23	72	28·54	·73	3	134	23·16	—
23	74	28·67	·83	2	136	19·75	—
23	76	28·65	·79	1	138	17·50	—
23	78	27·90	·67	1	140	15·50	—
21	80	27·50	·72				

TABLE 5.

Intermittent Starvation. Females.

Number of animals.	Age in weeks.	Weight in gm.	Probable error of mean. + or −	Number of animals.	Age in weeks.	Weight in gm.	Probable error of mean. + or −
23	5	8·83	·19	23	19	21·59	·30
23	6	9·30	·23	23	20	21·87	·30
23	7	10·78	·30	23	21	22·39	·27
23	8	12·30	·27	23	22	22·67	·30
23	9	13·48	·35	23	23	22·78	·31
23	10	14·72	·33	23	24	23·22	·33
23	11	16·04	·34	23	25	23·35	·28
23	12	16·65	·33	23	26	23·46	·28
23	13	17·67	·37	23	27	23·61	·26
23	14	18·56	·37	23	28	23·61	·27
23	15	19·48	·35	23	29	23·76	·31
23	16	19·89	·32	23	30	23·89	·30
23	17	20·87	·33	23	32	24·26	·32
23	18	21·09	·32	23	34	25·17	·33

TABLE 5 (continued).

Intermittent Starvation.   Females.

Number of animals.	Age in weeks.	Weight in gm.	Probable error of mean. + or −	Number of animals.	Age in weeks.	Weight in gm.	Probable error of mean. + or −
23	36	25·50	·32	17	98	29·05	·55
23	38	25·67	·32	15	100	28·53	·67
23	40	25·74	·33	15	102	28·83	·66
23	42	26·17	·37	15	104	28·07	·57
23	44	26·69	·33	15	106	28·10	·65
23	46	27·39	·37	14	108	28·50	·66
23	48	27·65	·40	14	110	28·32	·66
23	50	27·46	·39	14	112	28·18	·70
23	52	27·54	·37	14	114	27·43	·85
23	54	28·02	·40	13	116	28·07	·67
23	56	27·83	·44	13	118	28·19	·65
22	58	28·36	·43	13	120	28·15	·65
22	60	28·54	·41	13	122	26·54	·62
22	62	28·41	·40	13	124	25·69	·78
22	64	28·82	·43	13	126	24·38	·73
22	66	28·84	·38	10	128	25·25	·97
22	68	28·93	·44	9	130	25·61	·63
22	70	28·75	·45	7	132	25·57	·59
22	72	28·73	·41	7	134	23·42	·74
22	74	28·59	·44	6	136	22·50	1·01
22	76	28·14	·42	5	138	22·80	·73
21	78	27·69	·44	4	140	21·87	—
20	80	28·25	·41	2	142	20·75	—
20	82	28·17	·50	2	144	21·00	—
20	84	27·92	·45	1	146	21·50	—
20	86	27·82	·47	1	148	22·50	—
20	88	27·80	·53	1	150	22·00	—
20	90	27·77	·54	1	152	22·00	—
20	92	27·57	·57	1	154	24·00	—
18	94	28·22	·55	1	156	23·50	—
18	96	27·94	·63				

TABLE 6.

Intermittent Starvation + Vegetable Nucleic Acid.   Females.

Number of animals.	Age in weeks.	Weight in gm.	Probable error of mean. + or −	Number of animals.	Age in weeks.	Weight in gm.	Probable error of mean. + or −
24	5	8·89	·21	23	18	20·80	·32
24	6	8·98	·20	23	19	21·37	·28
24	7	10·12	·19	23	20	22·00	·30
24	8	11·25	·31	23	21	22·37	·29
24	9	12·29	·33	23	22	22·69	·29
24	10	13·54	·36	23	23	22·89	·30
23	11	14·80	·39	23	24	23·56	·27
23	12	16·06	·35	23	25	23·37	·30
23	13	16·78	·36	23	26	23·50	·29
23	14	17·87	·34	23	27	23·41	·30
23	15	18·83	·29	23	28	23·80	·24
23	16	19·50	·29	23	29	23·96	·28
23	17	20·15	·30	23	30	24·09	·31

TABLE 6 (continued).

Intermittent Starvation + Vegetable Nucleic Acid. Females.

Number of animals.	Age in weeks.	Weight in gm.	Probable error of mean. + or −	Number of animals.	Age in weeks.	Weight in gm.	Probable error of mean. + or −
23	32	24·56	·35	13	98	26·65	1·00
23	34	25·28	·33	12	100	27·16	·83
23	36	25·76	·30	11	102	27·86	·76
23	38	25·67	·32	11	104	27·95	·77
23	40	26·02	·31	10	106	27·80	·82
23	42	26·61	·35	10	108	26·70	1·13
23	44	27·33	·35	8	110	28·25	1·12
23	46	27·30	·34	8	112	28·18	·99
23	48	27·96	·33	8	114	28·87	1·26
23	50	27·67	·35	6	116	27·91	1·15
23	52	28·00	·35	6	118	27·74	1·11
23	54	27·93	·40	6	120	28·20	1·35
23	56	28·28	·39	5	122	27·40	1·46
23	58	28·39	·40	4	124	28·50	—
23	60	28·48	·37	4	126	28·22	—
23	62	28·80	·37	4	128	27·87	—
23	64	28·69	·42	4	130	27·87	—
23	66	28·93	·40	4	132	27·50	—
23	68	28·72	·39	4	134	26·66	—
23	70	28·65	·44	3	136	24·83	—
23	72	28·35	·41	3	138	25·50	—
23	74	28·33	·44	3	140	25·16	—
23	76	28·00	·52	2	142	23·25	—
23	78	27·74	·48	2	144	23·75	—
22	80	27·73	·53	2	146	21·50	—
22	82	27·48	·55	2	148	20·50	—
22	84	27·16	·55	1	150	28·00	—
22	86	26·79	·60	1	152	28·50	—
21	88	26·74	·69	1	154	28·00	—
20	90	26·87	·64	1	156	27·50	—
20	92	26·32	·71	1	158	26·50	—
17	94	26·00	·76	1	160	26·00	—
14	96	26·03	·96	1	162	26·00	—

TABLE 7.

Intermittent Starvation Experiment. Mortality Statistics.

Male Animals.				Female Animals.			
Age in Days.	Control.	Intermittent Starvation.	Intermittent Starvation + Nucleic Acid.	Age in Days.	Control.	Intermittent Starvation.	Intermittent Starvation + Nucleic Acid.
		Per cent. Survivors.				Per cent. Survivors.	
200	100	100	100	600	82·6	81·8	82·6
250	100	100	100	650	73·9	68·2	78·3
300	95·6	95·5	100	700	69·5	59·1	69·6
350	91·3	95·5	100	750	60·8	50·0	52·2
400	91·3	95·5	100	800	43·4	36·4	43·5
450	86·9	90·9	100	850	34·7	27·3	34·8
500	82·6	86·4	95·7	900	17·4	22·7	26·1
550	82·6	86·4	87·0	950	8·7	9·1	8·6

TABLE 7 (continued).

Intermittent Starvation Experiment. Mortality Statistics.

Male Animals.				Female Animals.			
Age in Days.	Control.	Intermittent Starvation.	Intermittent Starvation + Nucleic Acid.	Age in Days.	Control.	Intermittent Starvation.	Intermittent Starvation + Nucleic Acid.
		Per cent. Survivors.				Per cent. Survivors.	
1,000	8·7	4·5	—	600	87·5	87·0	95·7
1,050	—	—	—	650	79·2	87·0	87·0
1,100	—	—	—	700	66·7	65·2	52·2
1,150	—	—	—	750	50·0	60·9	43·5
1,200	—	—	—	800	50·0	60·9	34·8
200	100	100	100	850	37·5	56·5	21·7
250	100	100	100	900	20·8	44·0	17·4
300	100	100	100	950	8·3	26·1	13·0
350	95·8	100	100	1,000	· ·	8·7	8·7
400	95·8	95·7	100	1,050	—	4·3	4·3
450	95·8	95·7	100	1,100	—	—	4·3
500	95·8	95·7	100	1,150	—	—	—
550	91·7	91·3	100	1,200	—	—	—

Mean Duration of Life.

Males	Control	712 days.	Probable error 27·27 days.
	Intermittent Starvation	745 „	„ „ 26·75 „
	Intermittent Starvation + Nucleic Acid	769 „	„ „ 21·00 „
Females	Control	773 days.	Probable error 21·00 days.
	Intermittent Starvation	819 „	„ „ 24·7 „
	Intermittent Starvation + Nucleic Acid	763 „	„ „ 20·5 „

198

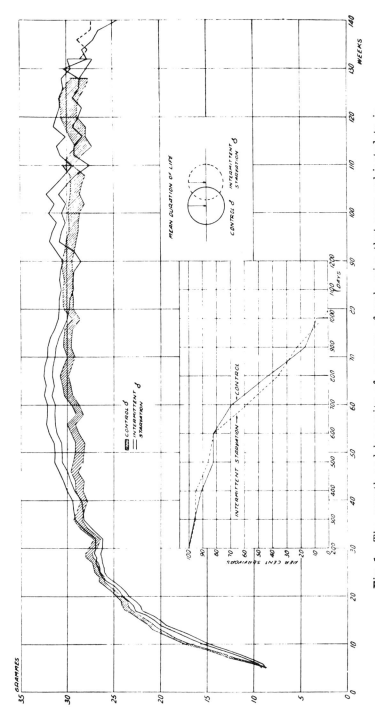

Fig. 1. The growth and longevity of a group of male mice that were subjected to intermittent starvation two days in each week throughout the complete life cycle is contrasted with that of normal male mice which were continually offered the same diet, *ad lib.*

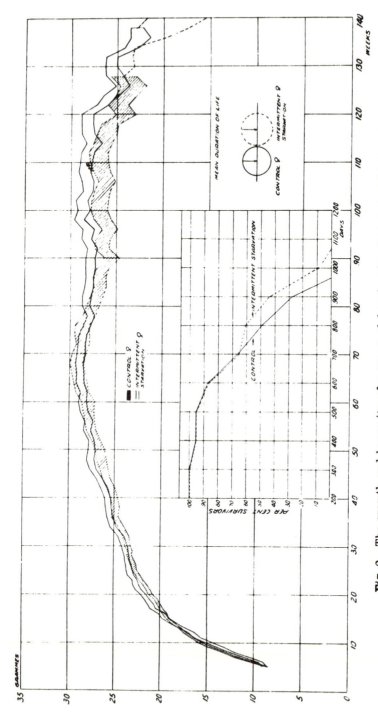

Fig. 2. The growth and longevity of a group of female mice that were subjected to intermittent starvation two days in each week throughout the complete life cycle is contrasted with that of normal female mice which were continually offered the same diet, *ad lib.*

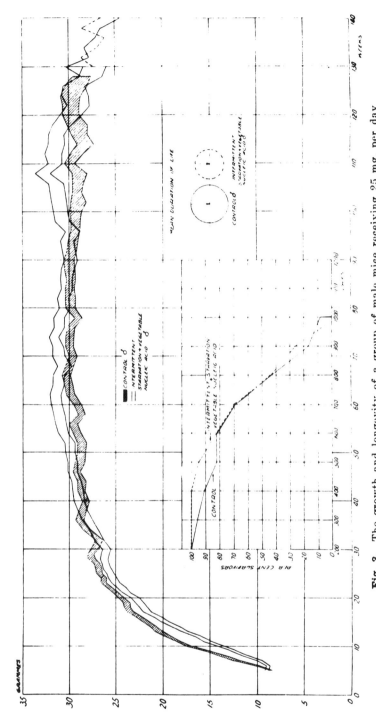

Fig. 3. The growth and longevity of a group of male mice receiving 25 mg. per day of yeast nucleic acid that were subjected to intermittent starvation two days in each week throughout life, is contrasted with normal male mice which were offered the same basal diet each day.

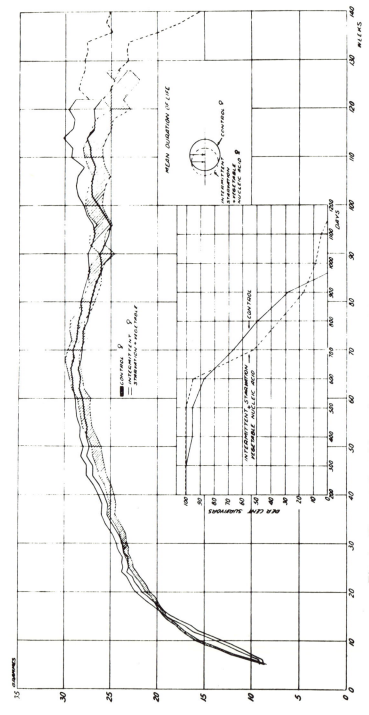

Fig. 4. The growth and longevity of a group of female mice receiving 25 mg. per day of yeast nucleic acid that were subjected to intermittent starvation two days in each week throughout life, is contracted with normal female mice which were offered the same basal diet each day.

28

1943 by Academic Press, Inc.
Reprinted from *Arch. Biochem.* **2**:469–479 (1943)

Growth, Ageing, Chronic Diseases, and Life Span in Rats

Clive M. McCay, Gladys Sperling, and Leroy L. Barnes

School of Nutrition, Cornell University, Ithaca, N. Y.

Received June 18, 1943

INTRODUCTION

The first purpose of the present study was to follow the development of chronic diseases in normal and retarded rats by killing samples of the population at regular intervals. The second purpose was to determine the effect of feeding an adequate basal diet supplemented with four sources of calories commonly eaten by man, namely starch, sugar, milk, and meat.

In the two preceding studies of retarded growth (1) (2) evidence was presented that retarded animals lived for longer periods because they were less subject to such diseases as those of the lungs that attack rats in middle life. Earlier observations had also indicated that retarded rats were usually free from tumors during the period of retardation. In the second of the preceding studies a small number of rats had been retarded for a thousand days without complete loss of the power to grow after realimentation. This observation justified extension to help determine the maximum period of retardation.

EXPERIMENTAL

This experiment started in March 1939 and terminated with the death of the oldest rat in the same month of 1943.

Five hundred rats were started on the experimental diets at the time of weaning. Three hundred of these were retarded in growth. Two hundred others were allowed to grow normally after being divided into four groups.

The same basal diet was fed to all. This consisted of a mixture in grams of cooked starch 20, cellulose 2, cod liver oil 8, lard 7, sucrose 5, alfalfa leaf meal 1, salt mixture 6, dry yeast 14, crude casein 27, and dry liver 10.

The rats retarded in growth were allowed a limited amount of this diet each day.   Individuals of the normal groups were given the same daily allowance of the basal diet as the retarded animals plus all they wished to eat of one of the following four supplements depending upon the group.

    I. Lard 10, Cooked starch 90;   Called "starch."
   II. Lard 10, Cooked starch 50, Sucrose   40; Called "sugar."
  III. Lard 10, Cooked starch 60, Dried whole milk 30; Called "milk."
   IV. Lard 10, Cooked starch 60, Dried pork liver 30; Called "liver."

In establishing experimental groups, attention was given to both sex and origin of litter.

Most of this experiment was run with the rats housed in an air conditioned room with the temperature at 23°C.   Humidity was kept as near 50 per cent as possible.   Natural light was excluded from the animal room.   Artificial lights were kept on for about an 8 hour working day for the first two years.   After this lights were kept on for twelve hours starting at 6 each morning.

Rats were started on the diet at weaning.   Retardation was not started until they weighed about 50 grams, each.   In general retarded rats were allowed to increase their body weight about 5 grams each 50 days.   This increase in weight was made by feeding a supplement of fresh beef liver and fresh lettuce.   All control animals were given an equal amount of the same supplement during the same period.

Representative rats from each experimental group were killed at intervals of about 100 days, starting in April, 1939.   The bodies of these rats were used for chemical and pathological studies to determine changes in composition and the rate of development of chronic diseases.   The results of some of these studies have been published by Lowry and Associates (3).   Other studies in this field will appear later by John Saxton, Jr.

In killing animals random selection was used.   Five rats of each sex were taken from the retarded animals and one of each sex from each of the four groups that grew normally.

Throughout the study extensive use was made of x-ray photographs for determining the size of the bones at given ages and also for noting the calcification of tissues as the rats grew older.

Starting at 300 days of age representative rats from the retarded group were given all the food they wished in order to allow them to resume growth.   This group, permitted to grow at 300 days, was divided into four sub-groups and fed the diets given the normal rats.   Fifty-six rats were used in this group.

After 900 days of retardation another group of twenty rats was allowed to resume growth.   At 1100 days, sixteen rats were likewise given an opportunity to resume growth.   The poorest rats in the retarded

TABLE I

Life Span of Normal and Retarded Rats

Groups	Mean span in days	Number	Span of three oldest in days
I. Normal "Starch"	Female— 722	19	1065—1103—1117
	Male — 595	19	783— 916— 933
II. Normal "Sugar"	Female— 733	19	932—1147—1154
	Male — 674	19	801— 850— 855
III. Normal "Milk"	Female— 610	19	725— 753— 836
	Male — 688	19	825— 853— 911
IV. Normal "Liver"	Female— 683	19	821— 912— 968
	Male — 531	19	682— 701— 827
Retarded 300 days	Female— 812	28	1147—1167—1196
	Male — 777	24	1023—1048—1054
Retarded 900 days	Female—1124	10	1214—1227—1249
	Male —1086	10	1173—1174—1190
Retarded 1100 days or more	Female—		1320—1368—1456
	Male —		1223—1261—1323
Retarded for entire life	Female—		1311—1320—1456
	Male —		1205—1210—1211

group at this age were selected to determine whether they had lost their power of growth.   Many of them died shortly after realimentation.

After 1150 days another small group of ten retarded rats was given adequate food for growth.

Basal metabolism studies were made by Mrs. L. C. Will upon retarded and normal rats in the course of this study.   These will be reported separately.

The mean span of life excluding rats sacrificed, from each group is shown in Table I.

The data of Table I indicate clearly the favorable effect of the retardation of growth. Beyond the 900 day period, however, retardation is less favorable. This accords with our earlier experience that 900 days is about the optimum period of retardation for the production of very old rats.

Five per cent of the rats that grew normally exceeded a thousand days in age. These were all females with no male attaining this age. Twenty-

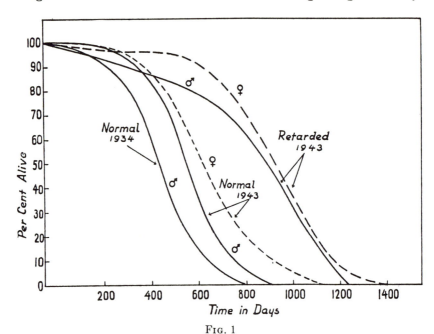

FIG. 1

Curves Showing the Per Cent of Normal and Retarded Rats Alive at
Different Ages

one per cent of the rats that were retarded for 300 days exceeded the age of 1000 days. Four of these were males and seven females. Of the rats retarded in growth more than 300 days, fifty per cent exceeded the age of 1000 days. Forty-seven of these were females and forty were males. The retardation of growth tends to equalize the life span of the opposite sexes. This accords with our earlier experience.

Among the eight groups of normal animals there were only three significant differences that may have been related to the diet. The females fed the "sugar" supplement differed from those given "milk."

206

The males given the "sugar" and also those given the "milk" supplements lived significantly longer than those fed "liver." In spite of statistical significance we doubt if these differences have real meaning. At least the groups fed the supplements of carbohydrates were not inferior in span of life.

The curves of survivors have been plotted in Fig. 1. The usual difference between the opposite sexes in the case of normal growth is evident. Quite the opposite is true for animals long retarded in growth. Finally the curve for male animals established a decade ago (4) affords comparison and indicates an improvement in survival for normal animals today.

Viability of Spermatozoa

In the course of these studies, when male rats were killed, samples of spermatozoa were examined under the microscope and viability recorded. Among the normal groups motile sperm were found in those individuals fed supplements of "starch" and "sugar," only through the 150 day period. In contrast the rats fed supplements of "milk" and "liver" showed motile sperm when the last group was killed at 620 days of age. Sperm motility persisted among the retarded males through the age of 750 days when this last group was killed.

These results were perplexing inasmuch as all rats received the same daily allowance of the basal diet which must have supplied the vitamin E. Inasmuch as those fed the carbohydrate supplements lost motility of sperm very early while those fed "milk" or "liver" did not, one might conclude that these latter supplements provided an essential supplement of vitamin E. The difficulty in this explanation is that the retarded males retained motility of sperm on the same level of vitamin E that produced sterility in those growing normally with a carbohydrate supplement. Possibly the smaller mass of body tissue in the retarded animals permitted a better economy in the use of vitamin E.

To determine whether the basal diets were deficient in vitamin E, an auxiliary experiment was run. Sixty rats of opposite sexes were fed the basal diet plus the "sugar" supplement. Half of these were given an additional allowance of wheat germ oil. Three hundred and sixty days later, one testis was removed from half of the males with and without wheat germ oil. Those receiving wheat germ oil had motile sperm while the others did not. This seemed to provide evidence that our basal diet was insufficient in vitamin E when the supplement for calories was composed largely of carbohydrates.

When the females from this auxiliary study were about one year old they were bred to normal males. In no case were there litters unless the female had been given the vitamin E supplement.

This experiment with vitamin E is of special interest inasmuch as early sterility in the male as a result of vitamin E deficiency had no effect upon total span of life. The animals from the auxiliary study were retained until the end of life. They also showed no significant differences in life span for the males as indicated in Table II. This is contrary to the common idea that early sterility and premature senility may run parallel, in the male. The females fed wheat germ oil exhibited values for the mean span of life significantly longer than the control group. This was not true in the data of Table I, however. The data are not strictly comparable since several other factors than vitamin E were involved.

TABLE II

Life Span of Rats With and Without Wheat Germ Oil as a Supplement

Variable	Rats No.	Mean life span in days	Mean P.E.
Males with wheat germ oil supplement.............	15	741	39
Males with no supplement.........................	15	703	24
Females with wheat germ oil supplement...........	14	840	33
Females with no supplement......................	15	694	26

Oestrous Cycle and Retarded Growth

Vaginal smears were made at intervals on all animals. These were usually made for a period of 21 days and those rats showing no cornified smears were considered anoestrous. As previously found (5) some of the controls showed continuously cornified smears at some time. Also the percentage of anoestrous smears increased gradually with age (Table III).

In the case of retarded rats the results also agree with the earlier ones. In some of the retarded rats (16 out of 48) the vagina did not open until between the 370–375th day.

Normal cycles were reestablished in rats realimented early in life (300 days) 100 per cent. After this it did not have so great an effect but as shown previously it did affect part of the animals.

Pathology Study

Since all pathological findings from this study will be published elsewhere by Dr. John Saxton, Jr., who was responsible for this part of the work, only brief summaries will be included here.

Inasmuch as typical animals were killed starting when relatively young, a picture of the development of the chronic diseases of rats at different ages was completed. Rats retarded in growth exhibited a much greater resistance to these diseases than those that grew normally. The diseases appeared ultimately, especially in those groups allowed to complete their growth. However, at a given age the incidence of chronic disease was much lower in retarded animals than in the controls that grew normally. This accords with our earlier experience. Furthermore, the development of tumors was negligible in rats that were retarded in growth until after they had been allowed to attain maturity.

TABLE III

Changes in the Oestrous Cycle

Controls

Age	Alive No.	Anoestrous per cent	Normal per cent	Partly corn per cent
1 year–1 year, 2 months.......	75	5	77	10
1 year, 7 months.............	54	33	46	15
2 years, 7 months............	6	50	50	—

Raised at 300 days

1 year–1 year, 2 months.......	28	0	85	—
1 year, 7 months.............	24	12.5	70	16
2 years, 7 months............	7	14	28	—

Retarded 900 days or more

1 year–1 year, 2 months.......	100	93	3	—
1 year, 7 months.............	94	100	—	—
2 years, 7 months............	51	17.6	41	—

(Ones not accounted for in the above were doubtful.)

The absence of early signs of the common chronic diseases that attack rats indicates the major reason for the extension of the mean span of life.

Two reviews have summarized recent evidence indicating that excess ingestion of nutrients may have an unfavorable effect in relation to disease resistance in animals. The first of these concerns resistance to inoculated tumors in studies such as those of Tannenbaum using low calory diets (6). The second deals with the studies of Claire Foster and others in showing decreased resistance of mice to poliomyelitis when fed a slight excess of vitamin B_1 (7) (8). Likewise these mice had greater resistance when fed low calory diets. These findings accord with our observations in all studies of retarded growth.

Several attempts have been made by us to learn more about the cause of the chronic lung disease that afflicts rats during the latter half of life. Some years ago we attempted to isolate specific organisms but failed. In the course of the present study an auxiliary experiment was run to determine whether either air conditioning of the rat quarters or the relative dustiness of the feed might affect the resistance of the lungs. Since this study will be described later by Dr. John Saxton, Jr., only a brief summary is included here.

Eighty rats were divided into four groups. Half of these rats were kept in air conditioned quarters and half in a room subject to the usual variable conditions in a laboratory. These rats were further subdivided so that half received a dry, rather dusty, mixture of stock diet while the other half had this same diet well moistened. These rats were autopsied after the experiment had been in progress for 500 to 600 days.

The males showed less resistance to the common lung disease then the females. This accords with the common experience that the females live longer. The difference in relation to the variables studied were not great enough to be significant. Therefore, it is unlikely that we have discovered factors responsible for the lung disease although animals retarded in growth are much more resistant than normal ones. Neither air conditioning nor the relative dustiness of the diet seems to be an important factor in producing diseased lungs.

Growth

In our earlier studies the resumption of growth after 900 days of retardation was achieved easily but after 1000 days some rats succeeded and part failed. Under the conditions of these experiments the thousand day period seems to be a crucial dividing line. In the present trials the ability to resume growth has been judged by changes in body weight and by measurements of bone length. These latter are based upon x-ray photographs taken at regular intervals throughout the experiment. Details will be presented in a later report.

In this study there was no question that growth was resumed at 900 days of age. The group retarded for 1100 days and then allowed to resume growth was selected from the rats in the poorest health since it was assumed if these could resume growth that the remainder of the group could do so. Since this poor group failed for the most part, a healthier fraction was chosen for realimentation at 1150 days of age. The response of this group in terms of weight increase is given in Table IV. This indicates clearly that some individuals but not all can resume growth after 1150 days of retardation.

TABLE IV

Changes in Retarded Rats Allowed to Grow after 1150 Days of Age

Rat No.	Sex	Wt. at 1150 days g.	Max. wt. attained g.	Tibia length at 1150 days cm.	Max. tibia length cm.
3	Fem.	162	176	3.27	3.29
96	Fem.	147	156	3.19	3.19
110	Fem.	160	165	3.19	3.20
120	Fem.	164	180	3.17	3.20
191	Fem.	161	197	3.30	3.32
12	Male	155	Died	3.43	—
128	Male	165	229	3.33	3.43
150	Male	161	166	3.29	3.30
154	Male	162	196	3.31	3.35
250	Male	160	198	3.30	3.34

TABLE V

Ultimate Body Size After Retarded Growth

Normal Growth	Supp.	No. of An.	Mean Max. Wt. Attained g.	Extremes of Max. Wt. Attained g.	Age of Max. Wt. days	Tibias No.	Mean tibia length at 348 days cm.
I. F.	Starch	19	277	192–359	473	6	3.55
M.		19	381	284–471	430	6	3.78
II. F.	Sugar	19	303	229–417	468	7	3.59
M.		19	445	305–543	458	6	3.89
III. F.	Milk	19	330	229–458	422	6	3.60
M.		19	515	399–677	454	—	4.06
IV. F.	Meat	19	324	217–521	472	6	3.63
M.		19	460	281–600	391	6	4.01
							At age 539 days
Retarded 300 days							
F.		28	270	168–373	594	10	3.44
M.		24	351	272–475	609	10	3.73
							At age 1050 days
Retarded 900 days							
F.		10	193	158–223	982	8	3.39
M.		8	248	219–283	1007	8	3.53

Ultimate Body Size

The rat seems to be the species least stunted permanently by long retardation of growth. In the past, however, evidence has accumulated that even the rat is somewhat dwarfed by a relatively short period of retardation. Some pertinent data from these trials have been assembled in Table V.

Definite conclusions can be drawn in regard to ultimate body size. The male exceeds the female even after 900 days of retarded growth with maintenance of the opposite sexes at about the same weight during retardation. The close correlation between the length of the tibia and the gross body weight indicates that the weight of the body is a better criterion of true size than is usually supposed. In other words the degree of fatness is less misleading or perhaps more constant than one imagines, when groups of rats are considered.

Response to a Dietary Regime After the Retardation of Growth

In the present study the group of rats allowed to resume growth after 300 days of retardation was divided into four sub-groups. These were placed upon the same major calory supplements allowed the four normal groups, namely "starch," "sugar," "milk," and "liver" as indicated at the beginning. The response as indicated in the growth curves which are not reproduced here was in the same order as that of the original groups of rats that had not been retarded in growth.

SUMMARY

In a third study of retarded growth in relation to ageing, rats were killed at regular intervals to determine the incidence of the common chronic diseases that usually terminate life prematurely. Retarded rats are much less subject to these diseases than those that grow normally when groups equal in age are considered.

Rats can be retarded as much as 1150 days and still resume growth when provided with adequate calories. This resumption of growth was followed by weight increases and x-ray photographs of bones.

Rats were allowed to grow normally with an adequate allowance of a good basal diet plus supplements of interest in human nutrition, namely milk, meat, starch, and sugar as additional sources of calories. It is doubtful if these four supplements modified the total span of life significantly. With equal amounts of vitamin E rats on the richer carbohydrate diets tended to become sterile early in life in contrast to retarded animals upon the same allowance. This premature sterility in the males had no effect upon the total span of life.

Rats retarded for 300 days responded to the four additional sources of calories in the same order as those allowed to grow normally from the beginning. Such rats were unable to attain the same body size as controls not subjected to retardation.

REFERENCES

1. McCay, C. M., Crowell, Mary F., and Maynard, L. A., *J. Nutrition* **10,** 63 (1935).
2. McCay, C. M., Maynard, L. A., Sperling, G., and Barnes, L. L., *J. Nutrition* **18,** 1 (1939).
3. Lowry, O. H., McCay, C. M., Hastings, A. B., and Brown, A. N., *J. Biol. Chem.* **143,** 281 (1942).
4. McCay, C. M., Ku, C. C., Woodward, J. C., and Sehgal, B. S., *J. Nutrition* **8,** 435 (1934).
5. Asdell, S. A., and Crowell, Mary F., *J. Nutrition* **10,** 13 (1935).
6. Tannenbaum, A., *Cancer Research* **2,** 460 (1942).
7. Foster, Claire, Jones, J. H., Henle, W., and Dorfman, F., *Science* **97,** 207 (1943).
8. Foster, Claire, Jones, J. H., Henle, W., and Dorfman, F., *Proc. Soc. Exptl. Biol. Med.* **51,** 215 (1942); *J. Am. Med. Assoc.* **121,** 1284 (1942).

29

Reprinted from *Arch. Biochem.* **2**:481–485 (1943)

Ageing, Basal Metabolism, and Retarded Growth

Lois Clise Will and C. M. McCay

Animal Nutrition Laboratory, Cornell University, Ithaca, N. Y.

Received June 18, 1943

INTRODUCTION

This study of the basal metabolism of the rats of the retarded growth experiment conducted by McCay and co-workers was undertaken to compare the heat production of rats retarded in growth with that of rats of the same age which had been allowed to grow normally. Since the rats studied were over 800 days of age, the data may also be useful as a supplement to the knowledge of the basal metabolism of old rats.

Ashworth and associates (1) in studies with retarded rats found that body weight was the most influential factor in limiting the metabolic rate and that age was relatively negligible. They suggested that the higher basal metabolism (per unit of weight) of underfed animals might be attributed to the fact that in such animals the viscera constituted a greater proportion of the body weight.

Horst and others (2) found that on the basis of surface area, retarded rats had a lower basal metabolism than either weight or age controls. These workers also observed that the basal metabolism of rats remained quite constant during the second and third years of life.

In a study with rats up to about 1100 days of age, Benedict and Sherman (3) noted a slight decline in total heat production during later life. Since body weight declined somewhat more than heat production there was an apparent increase in metabolism per unit of body weight.

Davis (4) found that the oxygen consumption of rats decreased throughout life, rapidly during the first four months and more gradually thereafter.

In 1939, Alex Black (5) observed a wide variation in the basal metabolism of a group of old male rats whose average age equalled 711 days. In comparisons between animals of equal weights, a higher basal metabolism was observed in the older animals.

EXPERIMENTAL

The plan of the retarded growth experiment and details have already been described in the preceding paper by McCay, Sperling, and Barnes. Basal metabolism determinations were made on a number of the experimental animals. Twenty-seven control rats were studied, 9 males and 18 females, between 800 and 900 days of age. Seven rats (4 males, 3 females) were observed which had been realimented after a retardation period of 900 days. Five animals (3 males, 2 females) were tested which had been realimented at 1150 days of age. The two last named groups were about 1200 days old at the time the metabolism measurements were made. Twenty-two retarded rats (11 males, 11 females) were studied between the ages of 800 and 900 days. Eleven retarded rats (5 males, 6 females) were observed after they had reached 1200 days of age. All animals studied appeared to be in good health at the time the tests were made.

It was planned to repeat the basal metabolism determinations on each individual until results were obtained which agreed within one calorie per square meter per hour. This checking was carried out for most of the animals, but some individuals became sick or died before the check determinations were made.

The metabolism apparatus employed was that described by Forbes, Kriss, and Miller (6). Temperature, light, and ventilation rate were maintained as uniformly as possible throughout the experimental period. By means of an automatic thermo-regulator, the air bath was kept at 30°C. which, according to the work of Swift and Forbes (7) is the critical temperature for the albino rat. The ventilation rate was maintained at 1 to 2 liters per minute. Bright illumination was used to discourage activity during tests.

The animals were brought to a post-absorptive state by a fast of 15–17 hours. The carbon dioxide and moisture production were measured over a six-hour period. The amount of activity was recorded hourly by means of a work adder attached to the respiration chamber. In calculating the average hourly carbon dioxide production, the carbon dioxide eliminated during the first hour was omitted. This procedure allowed the animals to become accustomed to the chamber. Thus, temperature equilibrium was established. This also allowed for accumulation of carbon dioxide in the chamber during the weighing period. If the work adder recorded unusual activity during some part of the test, the value for that hour was omitted.

Diack's formula (8) for the surface area of fasting albino rats was used for the retarded animals:

$$S = 7.64 \times wt.^{2/3}$$

For the surface area of the control rats and for the surface area of those rats which were allowed to grow normally after a certain period of retardation, Diack's formula for normal rats was used:

$$S = 7.47 \times wt.^{2/3}$$

In both normal and retarded animals no differences in basal metabolism related to sex were found.

TABLE I

Basal Metabolism of Normal and Retarded Rats at an Age of 800 to 900 Days

Group	Sex	No.	Mean Basal Metabolic Rate	
			cal./m.²/hr.	*cal./kg/hr.*
Retarded	Male	11	29.6 ± 0.67	4.50 ± 0.10
Control	Male	9	32.4 ± 0.69	3.41 ± 0.09
Retarded	Female	11	30.5 ± 0.69	4.63 ± 0.09
Control	Female	18	33.0 ± 0.35	3.83 ± 0.07
Retarded	Male and female	22	30.1 ± 0.47	4.57 ± 0.07
Control	Male and female	27	32.8 ± 0.32	3.69 ± 0.06

At about 850 days of age retarded rats had a higher basal metabolism than controls (Table I) in terms of calories per kilogram of body weight. The basal metabolism of retarded rats per unit of weight was significantly higher than that of animals retarded for 900 days and then realimented for a period of 300 days. The comparison was made when both were about 1200 days of age (Table II). Thus the same relation seems to exist that has been found when retarded rats are compared with normal ones much earlier in life. In contrast, those realimented at 1150 days, showed no differences from retarded animals. This was probably a reflection of the failure to achieve normal basal metabolism after this extreme period of retardation.

Retarded rats whose basal metabolism was measured at 850 and 1150 days of age gave the same values. In this case, therefore, there was no evidence for a change of basal metabolism related to age.

When calculations were based on surface area, the values for retarded rats at 850 days of age were significantly lower than those for controls. Also on this basis there was no difference between rats realimented at 900 or 1150 days of age and retarded animals of the same age. In contrast to data based upon body weight, those calculated to surface

TABLE II

Basal Metabolism of Retarded and Realimented Rats at 1200 Days of Age

Group (Males and Females)	No.	Mean Basal Metabolic Rate cal./m²/hr.	Mean Basal Metabolic Rate cal./kg./hr.
Retarded	11	33.1 ± 0.56	4.68 ± 0.08
Realimented at 900 days	7	32.5 ± 0.47	4.23 ± 0.08
Retarded	11	33.1 ± 0.56	4.68 ± 0.08
Realimented at 1150 days	5	35.8 ± 1.84	4.77 ± 0.26
Realimented at 900 days	7	32.5 ± 0.47	4.23 ± 0.08
Realimented at 1150 days	5	35.8 ± 1.84	4.77 ± 0.26

TABLE III

Basal Metabolism of Retarded Rats at Two Different Ages

Age Days	Sex	No.	Mean Basal Metabolic Rate cal./m²/hr.	Mean Basal Metabolic Rate cal./kg./hr.
850	Male	11	29.6 ± 0.67	4.50 ± 0.10
850	Female	11	30.5 ± 0.69	4.63 ± 0.09
1200	Male	5	32.6 ± 0.86	4.61 ± 0.12
1200	Female	6	33.6 ± 0.78	4.74 ± 0.11
850	Male	11	29.6 ± 0.67	4.50 ± 0.10
1200	Male	5	32.6 ± 0.86	4.61 ± 0.12
850	Female	11	30.5 ± 0.69	4.63 ± 0.09
1200	Female	6	33.6 ± 0.78	4.74 ± 0.11
850	Male and female	22	30.1 ± 0.47	4.57 ± 0.07
1200	Male and female	11	33.1 ± 0.56	4.68 ± 0.08

area show a lower basal metabolism for retarded rats at 850 than at 1200 days of age.

In general our values accord with those of others for rats of similar age. As far as we are aware these are the first measurements upon rats that have attained the age of 1200 days after long periods of retardation.

SUMMARY

1. Retarded rats at 850 days of age had a significantly higher heat production per unit of weight than normal rats; and a significantly lower heat production per unit of surface area than these controls.

2. Retarded rats at 1200 days of age had the same basal metabolism per unit of surface area as rats realimented at either 900 or 1150 days. Per unit of weight, retarded rats did not differ from rats realimented at 1150 days, but had a higher heat production that rats realimented at 900 days.

3. Retarded rats at 1200 days of age had a higher heat production per unit of surface area than retarded rats at 850 days. Heat production per unit of weight was not significantly different.

REFERENCES

1. ASHWORTH, U. S., BRODY, S., AND HOGAN, A. G., *Mo. Agr. Exp. Sta. Research Bull.* **176,** 32 (1932).
2. HORST, K., MENDEL, L. B., AND BENEDICT, F. G., *J. Nutrition* **8,** 139 (1934).
3. BENEDICT, F. G., AND SHERMAN, H. C., *J. Nutrition* **14,** 179 (1937).
4. DAVIS, J. E., *Am. J. Physiol.* **119,** 28 (1937).
5. BLACK, A., *J. Nutrition* **17,** 361 (1939).
6. FORBES, C. B., KRISS, M., AND MILLER, R. C., *J. Nutrition* **8,** 535 (1934).
7. SWIFT, R. W., AND FORBES, R. M., *J. Nutrition* **18,** 307 (1939).
8. DIACK, S. L., *J. Nutrition* **3,** 289 (1930).

30

Reprinted from *J. Nutrition* **31**:363–375 (1946)

APPARENT PROLONGATION OF THE LIFE SPAN OF RATS BY INTERMITTENT FASTING [1]

ANTON J. CARLSON AND FREDERICK HOELZEL

Department of Physiology, University of Chicago, Chicago

ONE FIGURE

(Received for publication October 4, 1945)

INTRODUCTION

When a sufficient amount of choice food is available, laboratory rats, like many humans, eat enough to become more or less obese. As a consequence, the life span of rats feeding ad libitum, like the life span of their human counterparts, is presumably shortened. This inference is supported by the repeated findings of McCay and his associates ('42 a, b; '43) that the life span of rats can be considerably prolonged by a drastic restriction in their allowance of food. The findings of McCay and his associates practically constitute an experimental confirmation of the claims of Cornaro (Butler, '05) who attributed a considerable prolongation of his life to a rigid restriction of his food intake. However, since the time of Cornaro (1464–1566) no similarly prolonged and rigid voluntary restriction of the human food intake appears to have been recorded. Obviously, Cornaro's prolonged practice of food restriction has not been widely followed because a normal appetite tends to impel its more or less complete appeasement at reasonably frequent intervals, when sufficient palatable food is easily obtainable. Only short periods of food restriction, such as the religiously interdicted periods of food restriction or fasting of the past, would seem to be practical.

[1] This research was aided by a grant from Swift & Co., Chicago.

In the future however, a periodic practice of food restriction or fasting is likely to depend mainly on experimental evidence of its value. It therefore seemed of interest to determine whether periodic or intermittent fasting would serve to prolong the life span of rats or reduce or prevent the shortening of the life span which is presumably produced by feeding ad libitum.

A study was already made by Robertson, Marston and Walters ('34) of the effect of intermittent fasting on the life span of mice. In that study, twenty-four male and twenty-four female mice were fasted 2 successive days in 7. The average life span of the fasted males was found to be 745 days while that of twenty-four controls was 712 days. The average for the fasted females was 819 days while that of twenty-four control females was 773 days. However, the prolongation of life was not regarded as significant by Robertson and his associates. One criticism of their study is that littermate mice were not used as controls. Hence the individual life spans apparently varied too much to make the results seem significant. Another criticism is that no observations appear to have been made to determine whether the fasted mice remained free from peptic erosion or ulceration of the stomach and duodenum. This has been found to occur in some mice (and young rats) after single periods of starvation of 36 hours or more (Sun, '27; Hoelzel and Da Costa, '37).

The effect and after-effect of intermittent fasting on some aspects of growth and nutrition were also studied by von Seeland on chickens (1887), by Morgulis on salamanders ('13), by Kopec and Latyszwski on mice ('32) and by Kellermann on rats ('39) but the effect on the life span was not determined in any of these studies.

Observations previously made in this laboratory showed that rats fasted every other day and fed a diet low in protein between fasts developed peptic ulcers in the forestomach within about 2 weeks (Hoelzel and Da Costa, '32). However, rats fed a diet adequate in protein between single-day fasts usually remained free from peptic ulcers. With the use of a diet relatively high in protein, no complication with peptic ulceration was therefore expected to develop in rats fasted 1 day in 3 or 4 but some doubts were still entertained whether rats could be fasted 1 day in 2 during prolonged periods without peptic lesions developing. In man, ulceration of the stomach is far less likely to occur while fasting because of an apparently lower fasting gastric acidity and the absence of the forestomach. Fasting 1 day in 2 or 3 by man also is apparently not the equivalent of fasting 1 day in 2 or 3 by the rat. However, in personal experiments, one of us (H.) found it impossible to maintain normal energy or remain free from nutritional edema while fasting every other day during periods of 2 to 5 months (Hoelzel, '43) but fasting 1 day in 3 immediately after having fasted 1 day in 2 during 5 months led to a recovery of energy and disappearance of nutritional edema. It was also found possible to recover fully from a 33-day fast in less than 33 days (Hoelzel, '44). Under these circumstances, it was deemed advisable to try various amounts of fasting in determining whether intermittent fasting would prolong the life span of rats.

In addition to various amounts of fasting, it also seemed advisable to try several diets. As a result, this study became somewhat complicated by the number of variables involved. The object of the present communication, however, is to report only the results of intermittent fasting on the life span of rats, independent of the specific effects of the different diets that were tried.

METHODS

In this study, 137 rats (60 males and 77 females), raised in the laboratory from rats obtained from The Wistar Institute, were used. These were all of the rats in seventeen litters with two or more of one sex or both sexes raised. The seventeen litters consisted of fourteen first litters and three second litters, with from two to thirteen raised rats in the individual litters. The rats were not weaned completely (separated from their mothers) until they were 35 days old.

Three omnivorous diets and one vegetarian diet were used. The omnivorous diets were a basic diet and two diets with 10% bulk-formers added to the basic diet. The basic diet consisted of 61.5% cooked and dried "whole veal," 31% corn starch, 2% powdered yeast, 1% cod liver oil, 1.5% inorganic salt mixture and 3% veal bonemeal. This diet provided approximately 35% proteins. The cooked and dried "whole veal" included practically all of the edible parts of calves, excepting excess fat and blood.[2] The first lot of this prepared veal contained 52% protein and 40% fat. Less fat was included in the preparation of subsequent lots but the composition of the original lot was approximated by adding fat when the diets were prepared. The second omnivorous diet consisted of the basic omnivorous diet plus 10% finely ground alfalfa stem meal. The third omnivorous diet consisted of the basic diet plus 5% psyllium seed husks and 5% specially prepared kapoc. The kapoc was mechanically cleaned, ground, boiled, washed, partly bleached, again washed and dried. The vegetarian diet consisted of 50% whole wheat flour, 10% peanut flour, 7% lima bean flour, 7% wheat gluten flour (containing 80% gluten), 7% corn gluten meal, 7% linseed meal, 5% powdered yeast, 5% alfalfa leaf meal and 2% NaCl. This diet provided approximately 30% proteins. Lettuce trimmings were supplied practically daily as a supplement to all of the diets. The control rats and the intermittently fasted rats while fed were kept continuously supplied with food.

Before the rats were 42 days old, all of them were supplied with the same food. This included some of each of the four experimental diets. When the rats became 42 days old, they were distributed so that some littermates of the same sex served in littermate tests of the effect of intermittent fasting or different amounts of intermittent fasting while other littermates served in tests of the effect of the different diets. Some rats with more than one littermate of the same sex consequently served as one of the littermates in 2 or more kinds of littermate tests. The intermittent fasting included fasting 1

[2] This was specially prepared for us by Swift and Co., Chicago.

day in 4, 1 day in 3 and 1 day in 2. The fasting was begun at the age of 42 days and was continued until the rats died.

RESULTS AND DISCUSSION

Effect of intermittent fasting on the life span

Figure 1 shows the distribution of the life spans of the individual control and fasted rats in 25-day periods. The life spans of rats with littermates only in the same group (but on different diets) are included. The average life spans of the

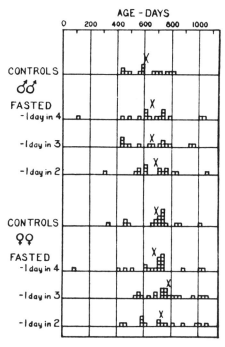

Fig. 1 Distribution of individual life spans of control and fasted rats in 25-day periods. Each square represents one rat. The average life span of each group is indicated by X. The life spans of rats with littermates only in the same group (but on different diets) are included.

groups are also indicated in figure 1 and in table 1. The results of the different amounts of fasting on littermates alone, with littermate controls fed identical diets ad libitum, are presented in table 2. Figure 1 and tables 1 and 2 show that, with the exception of the females fasted only 1 day in 4, the average life spans of all of the groups of fasted rats exceeded that of the controls. Moreover, the data in table 2 indicate that the prolongation of life by fasting was practically proportional to the amount of fasting and that the life spans of the males were, on the average, increased more than the life spans of the females. However, this may merely mean that the life spans of the males were shortened more than the life spans of the females by feeding ad libitum.

The effect of fasting on littermate rats is also indicated by comparisons between the life spans of rats fasted 1 day in 4 or 3 and littermates fasted 1 day in 3 or 2, respectively. Data thus obtained and combined with the data in table 2 yield a

TABLE 1

Average life spans of control and fasted rats. These averages include the life spans of rats with littermates only in the same group but on different diets. Figures in parentheses indicate number of rats in each group.

SEX	Controls	AVERAGE LENGTH OF LIFE IN DAYS			
		Fasted			
		1 day in 4	1 day in 3	1 day in 2	All degrees
Males	612 (14)	658 (16)	653 (15)	683 (15)	664 (46)
Females	688 (19)	675 (21)	781 (22)	733 (15)	730 (58)

total of thirty male littermate comparisons and show that the average life span of the males was increased 90 days by fasting. Similarly obtained data on females show that the average life span in forty-five littermate comparisons was increased only 23 days by fasting. It seems noteworthy that, in spite of the substantial increase in the average life span of the males by fasting, the life span of the fasted males only approximated that of the control females (fig. 1 and tables 1 and 2).

A more detailed analysis of the results suggests that fasting 1 day in 4 and 1 day in 2 were complicated more by some extraneous factors than fasting 1 day in 3 or feeding ad libitum. Thus, figure 1 shows that the earliest male and female deaths occurred in the groups fasted 1 day in 4 and the impression was that some of the other rats fasted 1 day in 4 also did not fare as well as most of the rats fasted 1 day in 3 or the controls. Perhaps the amount of food consumed in 3 days of feeding, with increased voracity but without proportionately increased capacity after 1 day of fasting, constituted a greater physiological overstrain than the amount of food consumed by the controls or by the rats fasted 1 day in 3. Figure 1 further shows that the males and females fasted 1 day in 2 also began dying earlier than the rats fasted 1 day in 3. Evidently fasting 1 day in 2 and beginning this at the age of 42 days was too much fasting for some rats. One of the females fasted 1 day in 2 apparently died of a hemorrhage from a chronic duodenal ulcer. Nothing like this was seen among over 2000 rats in a study of the production of peptic ulcers (Hoelzel and Da Costa, '37). More or less erosion and ulceration of the stomach was observed in other rats in this study but in most cases the lesions merely seemed to be due to premortal conditions, chiefly starvation due to loss of appetite associated with, or produced by, respiratory infections. (In about half of the rats with respiratory infections, no erosion or ulceration of the stomach occurs in spite of a complete loss of appetite or starvation and the usual postmortem changes in the intestines also are not seen. In such cases, all digestive secretions seem to be suppressed, excepting the secretion of a little bile.) Some erosion of the stomach may have occurred as a direct result of the experimental fasting among the rats fasting 1 day in 2 while they were still young. Moreover, female rats were previously found to develop more severe gastric lesions than males during prolonged starvation and a complication of this type may therefore explain why the females in this study did not benefit as much as the males from repeated single-day fasts. However, individual rats vary in their susceptibility to peptic erosion and ulceration and even some that were fasted 1 day in 2 evidently remained entirely free from such lesions. Both the male and the female that lived longest among the 137 rats (1057 and 1073 days, respectively) were rats fasted 1 day in 2. The optimum amount of fasting for the average rat in this study nevertheless appears to have been fasting 1 day in 3 and the data in table 2 show that with this amount of fasting the life span of the males was increased about 20% and that of the females about 15%.

Effect of intermittent fasting on growth

Table 2 shows that the average weights of the intermittently fasted rats at 300 days were always lower than the average weights of their littermate controls but no drastic retardation of growth was produced by the fasting. In some cases, the average femoral lengths of the fasted rats at death were greater than, or equal to, those of the controls and, in other cases, the rats were only a little smaller. In short, intermittent fasting seems to make it possible to increase the life span to some extent without stunting the rats. Tests are in progress

TABLE 2

Showing the effect of different amounts of fasting on the weight, size (length of femur at death) and life span of littermate rats. Littermate controls fed identical diets ad libitum.

AMOUNT OF FASTING	NUMBER OF PAIRS OF LITTERMATES	AVERAGE WEIGHT (GM)				AVERAGE FEMORAL LENGTH AT DEATH (MM)		AVERAGE LENGTH OF LIFE (DAYS)		
		At 42 days		At 300 days				Controls	Fasted	Difference due to fasting
		Controls	Fasted	Controls	Fasted	Controls	Fasted			
Males										
1 day in 4	7	149	149	449	413	39.1	39.3	681	768	+ 87
1 day in 3	7	133	133	397	339	38.7	36.7	557	667	+ 110
1 day in 2	4	118	127	356	265	38.1	36.0	527	666	+ 139
All degrees	18	136	138	408	357	38.7	38.1	599	706	+ 107
Females										
1 day in 4	12	117	123	280	248	34.6	35.1	721	685	− 36
1 day in 3	10	118	120	291	258	34.8	35.2	708	814	+ 106
1 day in 2	5	113	114	276	234	34.5	34.1	614	768	+ 154
All degrees	27	117	120	823	249	34.7	35.0	696	748	+ 52

to determine whether the size of fasted rats can be more fully maintained and life can still be prolonged by beginning the fasting at 100 or 200 days, instead of at 42 days, and fasting the rats no more than 1 day in 3.

Are the results of fasting due, in whole or in part,
to increased activity?

Tests made with rotary cages by Wald and Jackson ('44) revealed that rats run more when deprived of food, and Mc-Cay and his associates ('41) found that exercised rats lived longer than non-exercised rats. The activity of our fasting rats was largely limited to gnawing at the cages in attempts to escape. Many of the rats that were fasted 1 day in 4 or 3 seemed to become adapted to the fasting and remained at rest most of the time. The greatest unrest was manifested by some of the rats that were fasted 1 day in 2 but the life spans of the most restless rats were not the longest. The explanation seems to be that the greatest unrest or gnawing was manifested by the most voracious rats — the rats that apparently ate the greatest amounts of food between the days of fasting. The amount of food eaten may therefore have more than offset any possible benefit from increased exercise. In any event, the finding of McCay and his associates that rats subjected to forced exercise lived longer than non-exercised rats did not prove that the exercise per se increased the life span. The periods of forced exercise may merely have served to prevent the rats from eating as much as the controls in relation to their respective physiologic needs.

Influence of individual constitutions on the life spans

Constitutional similarities and differences among the individual rats, as determined by genetic factors and pre-experimental nutritional conditions, were obviously important factors determining the specific life spans. In the first place, a high degree of genetic uniformity in the Wistar strain evidently explains the death of 67% of the rats between the ages of 550 and 850 days and the death of 85% between the ages of 400 and 900 days in spite of the use of four different diets and four different regimens of feeding or fasting. Some littermate rats, after having been kept from 400 to 1000 days on widely differing nutritional regimens, died within 24 hours or a few days of one another. Four of the twelve rats that lived to be over 1000 days old belonged to one of the seventeen litters. The view that rats in small litters are likely to be in a superior condition is supported by the finding that two males that composed one of the two smallest litters not only lived longer than eight (all) other males on similar nutritional regimens but also lived longer than fourteen (all) females on similar nutritional regimens. In contrast to this, the average life span of thirteen rats that composed one of the three largest litters was the lowest of any of the seventeen litters. However, independent of the size of the litters from which the rats came, the life span was found to be influenced more or less by the pre-experimental nutritional status or weight attained by the age of 42 days, when the rats were started on the specific experimental regimens. That is, the rats that were heaviest at the age of 42 days tended to live longest among the rats on the same regimen but this again was less true of the rats that were fasted 1 day in 3 or 2 than of the control rats or those that were fasted only 1 day in 4. That is, the prolongation of life due to fasting 1 day in 3 or 2 tended to outweigh the apparent handicap of a poorer nutritional start in life, as indicated by a lower than average pre-experimental weight. The data in table 2 show clearly that the heaviest group of male control rats lived longer than the lighter male controls and that their fasted littermates had correspondingly long life spans.

Influence of intermittent fasting on the development of disorders leading to death

Saxton ('45) showed that the development of inflammatory, neoplastic and degenerative diseases was delayed by the restriction of calories which increased the life span of the rats in the experiments of McCay and his associates. Similarly, intermittent fasting seems to delay the development of the disorders which lead to death. Table 3 shows that a retardation of the development of mammary tumors, proportional to the amount of fasting, occurred in this study. These results support the observations previously made by Tannenbaum

TABLE 3

Development of mammary tumors in control and fasted rats.

	CONTROLS	FASTED		
		1 day in 4	1 day in 3	1 day in 2
Number of females developing tumors	7	6	8	1
Per cent of females developing tumors	37%	29%	36%	7%
Earliest age at which a tumor began developing	437 days	458 days	675 days	775 days
Average age at which tumors began developing	628 days	613 days	783 days	. .
Average life span of females with tumors	760 days	760 days	871 days	977 days
Weight of largest tumor	462 gm	220 gm	140 gm	26 gm
Average weight of tumors	193 gm [1]	67 gm [1]	36 gm	. .
Average rate of growth of tumors (gm gained per 100 days)	134 gm [1]	48 gm [1]	42 gm	13 gm

[1] The weights of the tumors in 2 control rats and in 1 rat fasted 1 day in 4 were not recorded and the weight of a tumor in another rat fasted 1 day in 4 was excluded because the tumor was dehydrated. It became dehydrated because it was torn loose by the rat after it apparently began to interfere with defecation.

('40; '42) concerning the relation between the food intake and the development of tumors in mice. However, genetic factors may explain the occurrence of mammary tumors in all of the (six) females in one of the seventeen litters and the occurrence of ten of the other sixteen tumor cases in five pairs of littermates. The larger tumors became responsible for the deaths of some of the females because of the tendency of the large tumors to ulcerate or become obstructive. The development of other types of tumors was apparently also retarded by intermittent fasting. The only tumor in the digestive tract, a fibrosarcoma in the forestomach, was found in the oldest control rat (a female 1012 days old). The tumor in the stomach was probably secondary to a tumorous condition of the uterus. Ulceration of the tumorous uterus evidently was responsible for the development of a fistula between the uterus and the ileum in this rat. Nothing comparable to this was seen among the fasted rats.

SUMMARY

Tests in which a group of thirty-three rats were allowed the same food ad libitum and groups of thirty-seven, thirty-seven and thirty rats were fasted 1 day in 4, 3 and 2, respectively, after the age of 42 days, showed that the apparent life span was increased by the intermittent fasting. The optimum amount of fasting appeared to be fasting 1 day in 3 and this increased the life span of littermate males about 20% and littermate females about 15%. However, the pre-experimental condition of the individual rats was also found to be an important factor determining the life spans.

No drastic retardation of growth was produced by the intermittent fasting but the development of mammary tumors was retarded in proportion to the amount of fasting.

LITERATURE CITED

BUTLER, W. F. 1905 The Art of Living Long. W. F. Butler, Milwaukee.

HOELZEL, F. 1943 Gastric acidity, nutritional hydration and appetite. Am. J. Digest. Dis., vol. 10, p. 121.

———— 1944 An explanation of appetite. Am. J. Digest. Dis., vol. 11, p. 71 and p. 101.

HOELZEL, F., AND E. DA COSTA 1932 Production of ulcers in the prostomach of rats by protein restriction. Proc. Soc. Exp. Biol. Med., vol. 29, p. 382.

———— 1937 Production of peptic ulcers in rats and mice by diets deficient in protein. Am. J. Digest. Dis. and Nutrition, vol. 4, p. 325.

KELLERMANN, J. H. 1939 The effect of intermittent starvation on calcification, food utilization and tissue composition. Onderstepoort J. Vet. Sci. and Animal Ind., vol. 12, p. 321.

KOPEC, S., AND M. LATYSZWSKI 1932 Untersuchungen über das Wachstum der Mäuse unter den Einfluss intermittierender Fütterung. II. Darreichung vollwertiger Nahrung, abwechselnd mit vollständiger Karenz. Biol. Generalis, vol. 8, p. 489.

MCCAY, C. M. 1942 a Nutrition, ageing and longevity. Trans. and Studies Coll. Physicians Philadelphia, 4 Ser., vol. 10, p. 1.

———— 1942 b Chemical aspects of ageing. Problems of Ageing, E. V. Cowdry, Ed., 2nd edition, p. 680. The Williams and Wilkins Co., Baltimore.

MCCAY, C. M., L. A. MAYNARD, G. SPERLING AND H. S. OSGOOD 1941 Nutritional requirements during the latter half of life. J. Nutrition, vol. 21, p. 45.

MCCAY, C. M., G. SPERLING AND L. L. BARNES 1943 Growth, ageing, chronic diseases, and life span in rats. Arch. Biochem., vol. 2, p. 469.

MORGULIS, S. 1913 The influence of protracted and intermittent fasting upon growth. Am. Naturalist, vol. 47, p. 477.

ROBERTSON, T. B., H. R. MARSTON AND J. W. WALTERS 1934 The influence of intermittent starvation and intermittent starvation plus nucleic acid on the growth and longevity of the white mouse. Aust. J. Exp. Biol. and Med. Sci., vol. 12, p. 33.

SAXTON, J. A., JR. 1945 Nutrition and growth and their influence on longevity in rats. Biological Symposia. Vol. XI. Jacques Cattell, Ed. Ageing and Degenerative Diseases. R. A. Moore, Ed., p. 177. The Jacques Cattell Press, Lancaster, Pa.

SUN, T. P. 1927 The effect of starvation and refeeding on the intestinal epithelium of the albino mouse. Chinese J. Physiol., vol. 1, p. 1.

TANNENBAUM, A. 1940 The initiation and growth of tumors. Introduction. I. Effects of underfeeding. Am. J. Cancer, vol. 38, p. 335.

———— 1942 The genesis and growth of tumors. II. Effects of caloric restriction per se. Cancer Research, vol. 2, p. 460.

VON SEELAND 1887 Ueber die Nachwirkung der Nahrungsentziehung auf die Ernährung. Biol. Centralbl., vol. 7, pp. 145, 184, 214, 246 and 271.

WALD, G., AND B. JACKSON 1944 Activity and nutritional deprivation. Proc. Natl. Acad. Sci., vol. 30, p. 255.

31

Reprinted from *Symposium on Problems of Gerontology*, Nutrition Symposium Series, No. 9, 59–72 (1954)

VITAMIN B_{12} AND AGING*

B. F. CHOW

The Johns Hopkins University
School of Hygiene and Public Health
Baltimore, Maryland

Introduction

The absorption of orally administered vitamin B_{12} appears to be relatively ineffective, since a major portion of the dose appears in the feces; almost no measurable activity is found in the urine[1]. Nevertheless, absorption can be demonstrated in animals from the appearance of radioactivity in the blood and tissues, such as kidneys and livers, of rats after feeding vitamin B_{12} labeled with Co^{60} [2]; and by determining the rise in the vitamin B_{12} activity in sera and, subsequently, in urine of dogs fed massive doses[3]. The early evidence of absorption by man was provided primarily by clinical experiences in the treatment of pernicious anemia either with a massive dose of this vitamin alone or with a small dose together with gastric juice[4].

Recently three methods for the measurement of absorption of vitamin B_{12} have been reported. According to one[5], a known amount of radioactive B_{12} is fed to a test subject and the unabsorbed B_{12} appearing in feces collected over a period of 10-14 days is determined. The difference between these two values is taken as a measure of absorption. It was reported that when small amounts of radioactive B_{12} ranging from 0.5 to 1.0 micrograms were fed to a clinically healthy subject only some 20% of the radioactivity appeared in the stool. The absorption

* This work was supported by a grant-in-aid from the Atomic Energy Commission, Merck & Co., Inc., the Sharp and Dohme Division of Merck & Co., Inc., The Upjohn Company and The National Vitamin Foundation.

was thus assumed to be 80%. If the test were performed on patients with pernicious anemia, the absorption was only 10-20%, but could be increased by simultaneous administration of gastric juice. The second method[6] involves the oral administration of two micrograms of radioactive vitamin B_{12} to a test subject who receives subcutaneously two hours later 1000 micrograms of unlabeled vitamin to flush out the absorbed vitamin. The radioactivity appearing in the urine specimen collected during the first twenty-four hours after the oral administration is taken as a measure of the absorption. According to this procedure as much as 0.2 micrograms of radioactive B_{12} (10% of the administered dose) could be detected in the urines of healthy individuals. However, no appreciable activity appears in the urine of pernicious anemia patients, unless an intrinsic factor preparation is given together with the radioactive B_{12}. In the third method[7] radioactive B_{12} is administered per os and the increase in radioactivity, as measured with a scintillation counter, over the liver of the test subjects five days after B_{12} feeding is taken as a measure of absorption. These three methods are useful not only for the estimation of absorption of B_{12} but for the detection of intrinsic factor activity, in spite of the difficulties involved in the quantitative collection of urine and particularly of feces from patients, or the uncertainties of relatively crude counting technics.

It is believed by some that absorption of vitamins and some other nutrients is impaired in the aged, though no clear cut demonstration of this has been reported. In our efforts to compare the absorptive capacities for vitamin B_{12} in the young and the old, we have developed a new oral tolerance test. It involves feeding a large dose of vitamin to test subjects from whom three blood specimens are drawn; shortly before, 1.5 and 3 hours after feeding.

233

The sera separated from these samples are assayed for vitamin B$_{12}$ activity according to the procedure developed in our laboratory. Previous experience indicated that in the young and the old populations alike a maximum rise in serum level was reached in two to three hours after administration. The magnitude of the increase in serum B$_{12}$ level is taken as a measure of the ability of the individual to absorb the vitamin. This test was used by us to compare the absorptive capacities of young and old individuals. The results of such a study will be presented in this communication.

Selection of Subjects:

A. Young Subjects: Unless otherwise stated, the subjects in this group were students or technical assistants from the School of Hygiene and Public Health in the age range 20-35. As far as could be ascertained, they were clinically healthy and free of any metabolic diseases such as diabetes, etc., at the time of test.

B. Old Subjects: Most of the old people studied were residents of one of three homes for the aged in Baltimore or New York City. The diet in each home was uniform. As an example, the diet in one of the homes consisted of 1,800 to 2,200 cal./day; 9 to 12 gm. N/day; 1.0 to 1.1 gm. phosphorus; 40 to 50 mEq. of K; 200 to 250 gm. carbohydrate, and 50 to 70 gm. fat per day. Meat, fish or eggs (100 gm./day) as well as milk (100 to 200 ml./day) were included in the diet. Another group of old individuals was drawn from the members of a club who lived with members of their own families in different parts of New York City and were of different economic levels. Although the diet history for this group has not been ascertained, it is assumed that considerable variation existed. All subjects were ambulatory and free from acute illness at the time of testing. Their age ranged from 60-90, with an average of about 75 years.

Experimental Design:

With very few exceptions, fasting blood samples (15 cc.) were drawn from the test subjects early in the morning. The desired amount of crystalline vitamin B_{12} solution was measured into a beaker containing approximately 20 cc. of water. The total content, as well as three subsequent rinsings, was administered to the subject orally. Blood samples were again drawn $1\frac{1}{2}$ and 3 hours after B_{12} feeding. All specimens were allowed to clot and the sera were collected with a capillary and assayed for vitamin B_{12} activity.

The Individual Variation of Vitamin B_{12} Levels in the Serum:

Estimates of the variability of serum levels in individuals were made from determinations of serum activity at desired time intervals. This study involved the use of seven young subjects over a period of ten days. One blood sample was drawn from each subject every other day. On two of these days, three samples were drawn; at 9 A. M., 2 P. M. and 5 P. M. The diets of these subjects during the test period included at least two pounds of steak per person per day and a liberal amount of milk. Thus, their intake of exogenous B_{12} is estimated to be above average. The daily variations of the mean values are given in Table I. ·The results indicate further that the maximum variation was not greater than 50 micromicrograms, and that the serum level of an individual is relatively consistent and does not fluctuate appreciably during the day, nor is it affected to any appreciable extent by the diet.

Table I

Daily Variation of B_{12} Serum Level of a Group of Seven Young Individuals.

Normal Diet	High Beef Diet			Normal Diet
Day 1	Day 3	Day 4	Day 7	Day 8
250 μmcg.	227 μmcg.	260 μmcg.	253 μmcg.	251 μmcg.

Morning fasting samples were used.

The Response of Young People to Various Doses of Vitamin B₁₂:

In a series of four experiments performed over a period of four months thirty different young individuals were used and three levels of vitamin B_{12}, 0 γ, 250 γ, and 1000 γ, tested. The results of the study are grouped in Table II. It can be seen that only 3 out of 9 young subjects responded to the 250 microgram dose whereas 11 out of 12 to the higher dose. Response is considered positive if the rise in serum level of B_{12} was 150 micromicrograms or more. This criterion is used hereafter.

Table II

Response of Young Individuals to Oral Tolerance Test for Vitamin B_{12}.

Dosage	Av. Change in μ mcg.	Range μ mcg.	Response #	%
0	57	26—92	0(10)*	0
250γ	92	14—173	3(9)	33
1000γ	330	84—>1000	10(11)	90

* = Number in parenthesis indicates total number of subjects tested.

The Response of Old People to Oral B$_{12}$ Test:

In order to test the response of old individuals to the same oral doses of vitamin B$_{12}$, forty-three old subjects were studied. They came from the four groups mentioned before. Their ages ranged from sixty-five to ninety with an average of seventy years. The results tabulated in Table III indicate that only 14 out of 35 old people responded to high dosages and none out of 8 to the 250 γ dose. Statistical analysis of the response of the young and the old by the Chi square method gave a value of 6.6 and the difference with age is significant at the one percent level.

Table III

Response of Old Individuals to Oral Tolerance
Test for Vitamin B$_{12}$.

Dosage	Av. Change in μ mcg.	Range μ mcg.	Response #	%
250γ	28	0—84	0(8)	0
1000γ	170	0—1300	14(35)	40

The B$_{12}$ Binding Power of Gastric Secretion From Young and Old Individuals:

The lower frequency response in the older population, as compared with the young group, at both dose levels, may be explained on the basis of a defective absorption mechanism or the desaturation of the tissues as a result of inadequate B$_{12}$ intake, or a peculiar intestinal flora which competes effectively for the administered vitamin B$_{12}$ because of greater affinity for this vitamin. The first possibility, which appears most likely, was explored more fully in the following experiments.

The absorption of vitamin B$_{12}$, at least by patients with pernicious anemia, is dependent to a large extent on the presence of Castle's intrinsic factor in the gastric juice[4]. Presently available technics do not permit the quantitative measurement of intrinsic factor with any degree of accuracy or convenience. Another property of gastric juice, its B$_{12}$ binding capacity, has been measured. "Binding" capacity has been variously determined by a number of investigators and this term therefore carries with it different meanings dependent on the technic employed. In this communication all measurements of binding capacity were made by the method previously reported from this laboratory[8]. Briefly, when a suspension of resting cells of L. *leichmannii* is added to a solution of vitamin B$_{12}$, the organisms adsorb the vitamin quantitatively and it can be removed completely from the solution by centrifugation. On the other hand, in the presence of a sufficient amount of gastric juice the adsorption onto the cells can be prevented. The decrease in the amount of B$_{12}$ adsorbed by the organisms bears a quantitative relationship to the quantity of gastric juice added. This observation then forms a quantitative basis for the determination of the so-called "binding power." In our earlier report we found that, when fresh gastric juice obtained without histamine or alcohol stimulation was electrophoresed on paper, the B$_{12}$ binding substance moves in the electrical field as a single component. These results and others lead us to believe that the intrinsic factor in gastric juice possesses the property of binding vitamin B$_{12}$. On the other hand, there are ample data in the literature to show that not all B$_{12}$ binding substances from gastric juice or hog stomach extract possess intrinsic factor activity as determined in pernicious anemia patients. Yet, the author is not aware of any report to the effect that a therapeutically active fraction is entirely devoid of binding capacity. Assuming that the measurement of binding power in the gastric juice bears a semi-quantitative relationship to intrinsic factor activity, we have determined the B_{12} binding substance in the gastric secretion of young and old individuals without achlorhydria. The results are shown in Figure I. It can be seen that the amount of vitamin B_{12} bound to each milligram of nitrogen in the gastric juice showed an agewise difference. The gastric secretion obtained from the old people has a mean binding power lower than that obtained from the young. It should be noted that the results are expressed in terms of millimicrograms of B_{12} bound per unit of nitrogen. Assuming the

Figure I

AVERAGE Mγ B₁₂* BOUND PER MG. GASTRIC

SECRETION NITROGEN

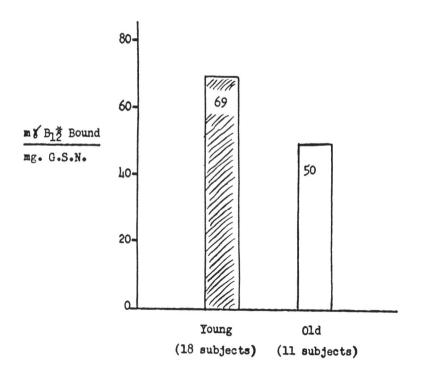

validity of reports in the literature to the effect that old individuals secrete less gastric juice with a lower concentration of nitrogenous substances[9], the total B$_{12}$ binding substance in the gastric juice of the old subjects must then be even less than would appear from the data in the table. This difference may account for the poor absorption of the aged. If this be true, one might expect to find a low B$_{12}$ reserve for the old, which might manifest itself in a lower serum level as well as low tissue saturation. To explore this possibility we have assayed for vitamin B$_{12}$ 80 samples of sera from individuals with an average age of seventy years, and thirty samples from young individuals in the student body of the School of Hygiene and Public Health.

The results of our analyses show a marked difference in the mean values for these two groups. They are 158±10.7 for the young and 108±8.2 for the old. The mean difference, 50, is highly significant (P < 0.01). Our data therefore confirm the findings of Mollin and Ross[10] who assayed by another microbial procedure the serum levels of a great variety of individuals and found a significantly lower mean B$_{12}$ value for the aged (P < 0.001). It is interesting to note that this relative difference exists among the population of this country as well as in England, despite differences in diets and environments.

The second consequence of poor absorption in the aged lies in the state of desaturation of the tissues. This deficiency in the tissue space can be measured by estimating the amount of injected B$_{12}$ retained by old individuals. To this end a group of 47 old subjects, drawn from the Baltimore City Hospitals, were injected with varying doses of vitamin B$_{12}$, namely 75, 50, 30 and 20 micrograms. The urinary B$_{12}$ collected in the eight hour specimen was measured. Similar studies were performed using a group of 50 young individuals drawn from our student population. The results of urinary excretion by the two groups of subjects are given in Figure II. It can be seen that at each dose of injected B_{12} the young people excreted approximated twice that of the old people. It is our belief that the greater retention of vitamin B_{12} reflects relatively greater desaturation of the tissue in accordance with the hypothesis which we have just postulated.

Figure II

THE URINARY EXCRETION OF VITAMIN B_{12} FOLLOWING PARENTERAL

ADMINISTRATION OF A TEST DOSE OF B_{12} TO YOUNG AND

OLD INDIVIDUALS

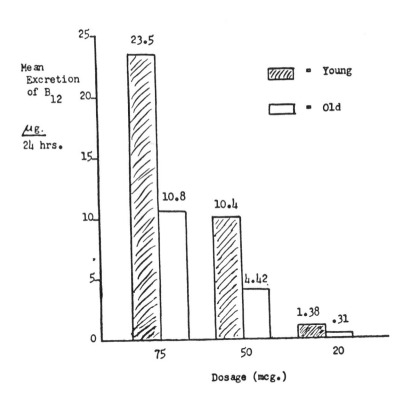

Discussion

Interest in the role of water soluble vitamins in the nutrition of the aged was aroused by the early reports of Stefenson and his associates who claimed that the addition of B vitamins and ascorbic acid to the dietary of old persons resulted in greater improvement (in general vitality and vigor)[11]. A greater need for ascorbic acid and the concept of the existence of a state of unsaturation with respect to thiamine in the aged have also been reported.[12] On this phase, we shall no doubt hear some more from Dr. Rafsky. However, extensive investigations by Horwitt, *et al.*, have revealed no differences in the excretion of thiamine or riboflavin between young and old subjects.[13] All these studies are complicated to a large extent by the necessity of measuring accurately the intake of the test vitamin present in food either as free or bound forms. The uniqueness of vitamin B_{12} for the excretion study has been brought out in previous communications from our laboratory.[1, 14] In the first place the B_{12} content in the ordinary diet of test subjects is unusually small, so as not to affect either the blood level or urinary excretion to any appreciable extent. Thus, this source of B_{12} will not interfere with the measurement. This observation will therefore make it unnecessary to control the diet of the test subjects shortly before or during the test. In the second place, the availability of radioactive vitamin B_{12} labeled with Co^{60} facilitates the differentiation of the administered B_{12} from that previously existing in the tissues.

Our knowledge of the stimulatory effect of vitamin B_{12} in child growth,[15] its involvement in various diseases such as diabetes,[16] and its therapeutic effectiveness in the treatment of various types of anemias[17, 18] makes it worthwhile to explore its absorption following oral administration to individuals of various ages and in various disease states. We are interested in old people as our test subjects since we believe that these individuals may also manifest biochemical symptoms of B_{12} deficiency. It is therefore of prime importance to ascertain whether their absorption mechanism has been impaired in the process of aging. While the poorer response of the older people to the oral feeding of vitamin B_{12} may be considered as a manifestation of a defective absorption mechanism, it is possible that the tissues of old people are "unsaturated" and that the absorbed B_{12} is taken up by the deficient organs; hence failure to see an increase in serum level. However, either mechanism demonstrates a lack of B_{12} in the aged. These data suggest that supplementary therapy for old people may be desirable to restore their B_{12} level to normalcy. Whether this has clinical significance can only be ascertained after more extensive clinical and biochemical evaluations are carefully and critically made.

Vitamin B_{12} now is accepted as essential to human nutrition. Its role in the therapy of pernicious and other megaloblastic anemias is universally acknowledged. The accumulated evidence of current biochemical and clinical investigations points more and more to the existence of other less spectacular but possibly more important roles. Future researches may be expected to develop a fuller picture of the utility of B_{12} by reevaluating current hypotheses, confirming and extending some, refuting others, and opening new ones yet unrealized. Whatever may come, there is no doubt that the appearance of B_{12} on the nutritional scene marks a significant step toward a fuller knowledge of human nutritional requirements and the roles of essential nutrients.

Bibliography

1. Chow, B. F., C. A. Lang, R. Davis, C. L. Conley and C. E. Ellicott: The Appearance of Vitamin B_{12} Activity in Urine After Oral and Intramuscular Administration to Man. Bull. J. Hopkins Hosp. *87*:156 (1950).

2. Chow, B. F., C. Rosenblum, R. H. Silber, D. T. Woodbury, R. Yamamoto and C. A. Lang: Oral Administration of Vitamin B_{12} Containing Co^{60} to Rats. Proc. Soc. Exp. Biol. Med. *76*:393 (1951).

3. Yamamoto, R. S., C. Barrows, Jr., C. A. Lang and B. F. Chow: Further Studies on the Absorption of Vitamin B_{12} Following Oral and Parenteral Administration. J. Nutrit. *45*:507 (1951).

4. Berk, L., W. B. Castle, A. D. Welch, R. W. Heinle, R. Ander and M. Epstein: Observations on the Etiologic Relationship of Achylia Gastrica to Pernicious Anemia. X. Activity of Vitamin B_{12} as Food (Extrinsic) Factor. New Eng. J. Med. *239*:911 (1948).

5. Heinle, R. W., A. D. Welch, V. Scharf, G. C. Meacham and W. H. Prusoff: Studies of Excretion (and Absorption) of Co^{60}-Labeled Vitamin B_{12} in Pernicious Anemia. Trans. Assoc. Am. Phys. *65*:214 (1952).

6. Schilling, R. F.: Intrinsic Factor Studies. II. The Effect of Gastric Juice on Urinary Excretion of Radioactivity After the Oral Administration of Radioactive Vitamin B_{12}. J. Lab. Clin. Med. *42*:860 (1953).

7. Glass, G. B. J., L. J. Boyd, G. A. Gellin and L. Stephanson: Test for Intrinsic Factor Activity: Measurement of Hepatic Uptake of Ingested Radioactive Vitamin B_{12}. Fed. Proc. *13*:54 (1954).

8. Chow, B. F. and R. L. Davis: Some Observations on Substances Combining with Vitamin B_{12}. *Recent Advances in Nutrition Research,* Nutrition Symposium Series, No. 5, Page 17, The National Vitamin Foundation, New York (1952).

9. Yamamoto, R. S. and B. F. Chow: A Rapid Method for the determination of B_{12} Binding Power in the Gastric Juice. J. Lab. Clin. Med. *43*:316 (1954).

10. Mollin, D. L. and G. I. M. Ross: The Vitamin B_{12} Concentrations of Serum and Urine of Normals and of Patients with Megaloblastic Anaemias and Other Diseases.   J. Clin. Path. *5*:129 (1952).

11. Stephenson, W., G. Penton and V. Korenchevsky: Some Effects of Vitamin B and C on Senile Patients.   Brit. Med. J. *2*:839 (1941).

12. Rafsky, H. A. and B. Newman: Vitamin B Excretion in the Aged.   Gastroenterol. *1*:737 (1943).

13. Horwitt, M. K., E. Liebert, O. Kreisler and P. Wittman: Investigations of Human Requirements for B-Complex Vitamins. Bull. Natl. Res. Council 116 (1948).

14. Conley, C. L., J. R. Krevans, B. F. Chow, C. H. Barrows and C. A. Lang: Observations on the Absorption, Utilization and Excretion of Vitamin B_{12}.   J. Lab. Clin. Med. *38*:84 (1951).

15. Chow, B. F.: Sequelae to the Administration of Vitamin B_{12} to Humans.   J. Nutrit. *43*:323 (1951).

16. Becker, B., C. A. Lang and B. F. Chow: Vitamin B_{12} Excretion and Diabetic Retinopathy.   J. Clin. Nutrit. *1*:417 (1953).

17. West, R.: Activity of Vitamin B_{12} in Addisonian Pernicious Anemia.   Science *107*:398 (1948).

18. Spies, T. D., L. G. Garcia, F. Milanese, T. R. Lopez and B. Culver: Observations on the Hematopoietic Response of Persons with Tropical Sprue to Vitamin B_{12}.   South. Med. J. *41*:523 (1948).

32

Reprinted from *Symposium on Problems of Gerontology*, Nutrition Symposium Series, No. 9, 73–94 (1954)

BLOOD AND URINE VITAMIN LEVELS IN THE AGED

J. E. KIRK

Washington University
School of Medicine
St. Louis, Missouri

The publications dealing with blood and urine vitamin levels in aged persons can be classed in two main groups. One group includes surveys on persons consuming a self-selected diet, and the other group, studies on institutionalized persons. The data obtained in population surveys will, to a great extent, reflect the dietary habits of the individuals, whereas the investigations conducted on persons consuming an institutional diet of known composition can be expected to give some information concerning the effect of age on the blood and urine vitamin levels.

Because of the high incidence of debilitating disease in institutionalized individuals it seems questionable whether results derived from nutrition studies on inmates of infirmaries can be applied directly to the non-institutionalized segment of the population. Since the chances for acquiring the cooperation of normal elderly individuals for nutritional balance studies are not favorable, conclusive information with regard to the effect of age on the blood and urine concentrations of various vitamins can probably not be obtained at the present time.

Surveys of individuals on a self-selected diet

Although several extensive nutrition surveys are available from recent years, comparatively few include observations on individuals above the age of 60.

246

A study of the carotene and vitamin A concentrations
of serum in a normal British population was carried out
by Campbell and Tonks[1] in 1947.   The survey included 133
individuals, 116 men and 17 women between 18 and 73
years, who resided in the Midlands District of England.
Twenty-five of the subjects were 60 years of age or older.
The vitamin A analyses were performed by the Carr Price
reaction.   The values observed by Campbell and Tonks are
presented in Figure 1 and fail to show any significant variation with age in the carotene and vitamin A serum levels.

Figure I

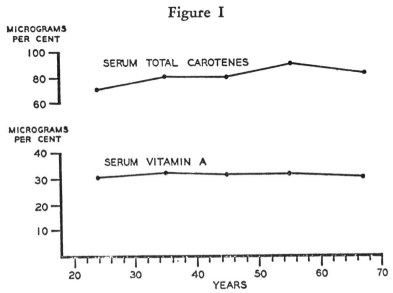

Carotene and vitamin A content of serum in 116 men and 17 women
residing in Midlands District of England.[1]

The results of a similar investigation on a healthy population group were reported in 1951 by Williams and his
associates.[28]   The individuals were residents of Groton
Township, New York.   Determinations of serum carotene,
vitamin A, and ascorbic acid were performed both during
the spring season and in the fall, using the micromethods

recommended by Bessey. An analysis of the diet consumed by the residents was carried out during the fall season and showed a high intake of both vitamin A and C. Although individual blood vitamin values are not given in the publication, it is possible from the reported data to calculate approximate mean serum values for subjects between 21 and 59 years and for persons 60 years and over. The results of these calculations are entered in Table 1 and show no certain difference between the serum vitamin levels for the two age groups, either during the spring or fall.

Table 1

Mean serum vitamin concentrations observed in Groton Township Study (28)

Sex	Season	Age group 21-59 years Number of subjects	Mean serum value	Age group 60 years and above Number of subjects	Mean serum value
		Carotene concentration in micrograms per cent			
Men	Spring	113	125	25	121
Women	Spring	132	130	23	127
Men	Fall	160	90	33	95
Women	Fall	193	91	30	105
		Vitamin A concentration in micrograms per cent			
Men	Spring	103	49	26	46
Women	Spring	132	40	23	46
Men	Fall	159	56	33	51
Women	Fall	192	46	30	58
		Total ascorbic acid concentration in milligrams per cent			
Men	Spring	114	0.82	24	0.83
Women	Spring	131	1.02	22	1.07
Men	Fall	162	0.84	33	0.76
Women	Fall	190	1.01	30	1.07

In contrast to the results obtained in the Groton Township Study, a survey conducted in 1940 by Trier[26] on the concentration of reduced ascorbic acid in serum shows a significant difference between young, middle-aged, and old adults. The investigation by Trier comprised 707 adults,

92 of whom were 65 years of age or older.   Blood for
serum ascorbic acid determination was collected in connection with the admission of the subjects to a hospital in
Copenhagen; the ascorbic acid analyses were performed by
the methylene blue method of Lund and Lieck.   None of
the individuals suffered from diseases known to be associated with changes in the serum ascorbic acid content.

Figure 2

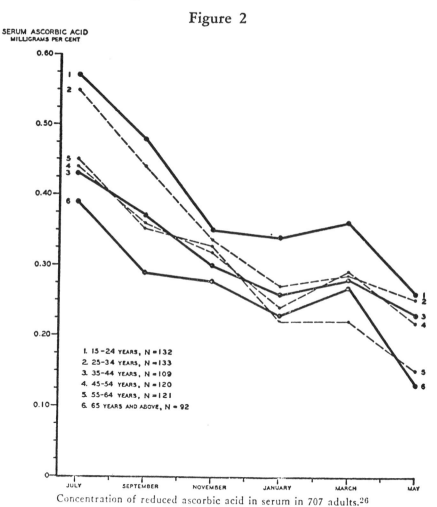

Concentration of reduced ascorbic acid in serum in 707 adults.[26]

The main data from Trier's publication are reproduced in Figure 2. It will be seen from the figure that the three graphs, which represent the mean values for young (15-34 years), and middle-aged (35-54 years), and old persons (65 years and older) do not overlap, the difference in serum ascorbic acid concentration being present throughout the year. The values for intermediate age groups, which are presented in the figure by dotted lines, show some degree of overlapping, but in general it can be concluded from Trier's data that the serum ascorbic acid concentration of this population group tends to decrease with advancing age. The persons included in Trier's study were representative of the Danish population with regard to economic status, but since they were admitted to the hospital because of some disease condition probably cannot be considered as representative of the healthy, active population.

An investigation of the content of reduced ascorbic acid in serum has further been carried out in 1940 by Difs[7] who studied 53 male residents of Uppsala, Sweden. The blood analyses were made during the months of May and June, at which season the ascorbic acid content of the Swedish diet is at a minimum. The determinations, which were made by the method of Farmer and Abt, show very low serum ascorbic acid values in both the young and old individuals (Table 2).

Table 2

Mean values of reduced ascorbic acid in serum as observed in nutrition survey by Difs (7)

Age group (years)	Number of subjects	Reduced serum ascorbic acid Mean mg. %	Range mg. %
17—39	11	0.16	0.03—0.47
40—49	18	0.14	0.05—0.48
50—59	16	0.10	0.02—0.16
60—82	8	0.10	0.05—0.24

The concentrations of free riboflavin, flavin adenine dinucleotide, and total riboflavin in serum were studied by Suvarnakich, Mann and Stare[25] in 141 normal American subjects, 82 men and 59 women, consuming a self-selected diet. The riboflavin analyses were performed by a modification of Burch, Bessey, and Lowry's method.

No significant difference in the riboflavin content of serum was observed between the men and the women. As seen from Table 3 an analysis of the data obtained in various age groups also fails to show any certain variation in the serum riboflavin content with age.

Table 3

Normal human serum riboflavin levels classified according to age (25)

Age group (years)	Number of subjects	Serum riboflavin in micrograms per cent		
		Free riboflavin	Riboflavin-adenine-dinucleotide	Total riboflavin
Below 20	15	0.78	2.36	3.14
20—29	30	0.86	2.17	3.03
30—39	26	0.90	2.25	3.15
40—49	28	0.63	2.39	3.02
50—59	19	0.86	2.43	3.29
60 and over	8	1.18	2.74	3.92

The results of a survey of the 24-hour urinary excretion of pantothenic acid have been reported by Schmidt[24] in Copenhagen. The study included 102 men and 85 women between the ages of 20 and 80 years. The subjects consumed a self-selected diet; 21 of the individuals were 60 years of age or older. The pantothenic acid determinations were performed by the method of Nielsen, Hartelius, and Johansen.

A summary of Schmidt's findings is presented in Table 4 and shows a moderate decrease in pantothenic acid excretion with age. A calculation of the coefficient of correlation age/pantothenic acid excretion gives an r value of —0.28 (t=3.01) for the men, and a value of —0.33 (t=3.19) for the women.

Table 4

24-hour pantothenic acid excretion in the urine (24)

Age group (years)	Men		Women	
	Number of subjects	Pantothenic acid excretion mg.	Number of subjects	Pantothenic acid excretion mg.
20—29	24	2.89	30	2.72
30—39	42	2.92	19	2.47
40—49	17	2.83	17	2.43
50—59	9	2.65	8	2.53
60—80	10	2.24	11	2.00

Studies of individuals on an institutional diet

Investigations on the blood vitamin concentrations of large groups of institutionalized individuals between the ages of 45 and 90 years have been carried out by Kirk and Chieffi during the last seven years. The studies have included measurements of carotene,[9] vitamin A,[9] thiamine,[10] diphosphopyridine nucleotide,[16] ascorbic acid,[14] and tocopherol.[4] The inmates from whom the blood samples were obtained were free from gastrointestinal disease (except gastric achlorhydria, hypochlorhydria, and constipation), and did not suffer from diseases known to be associated with' changes in the blood vitamin levels. None of the individuals had received vitamin preparations for several months before the blood analyses. The diet of the institution contained an average of 110 gm. of protein, 69 gm. of fat, and 265 gm. of carbohydrate daily, and had a total energy value of about 2150 calories. Chemical assays of the prepared food showed a mean daily content of about 10,000 I. U. of vitamin A, 1.5 mg. of thiamine, 45 mg. of ascorbic acid, and 39 mg. of tocopherol. The calculated nicotinic acid content was 14 mg. In the case of vitamin A, thiamine, and nicotinic acid the dietary vitamin values were above the recommended minimum intake for sedentary adults, whereas for ascorbic acid the content was somewhat lower. Determinations of the actual food consumption by the individuals were not made, but only persons who consumed the major part of the offered diet were included in the study. It was ascertained through measurements of the actual food intake by 15 elderly subjects over a two week period that an average of 83 per cent of the offered food was consumed by these individuals.

Blood samples for vitamin analysis were withdrawn from the fasting subjects. The carotene, vitamin A, thiamine, ascorbic acid, and tocopherol determinations were performed by standard macro procedures; the employed technique is described in detail in the bibliographic references listed in Tables 5 and 6. For determination of the DPN content of the red blood cells the fluorometric micro method of Lowry was used, employing a factor of 0.304 to convert F_2 values to DPN values.

A summary of the blood and plasma vitamin analyses is given in Figure 3 and Table 5 for the men, and in

Figure 4 and Table 6 for the women. Values for the pyruvic acid[10] blood concentration have likewise been entered in the figures and tables.

It will be seen from the presented data that a significant correlation between age and blood vitamin content was found only in the case of ascorbic acid in the male subjects, the correlation coefficient for this relation being —0.44 (t=3.20). In the women a decrease in blood ascorbic acid with age was also noticeable, but the reduction was not statistically significant.

With regard to the other vitamins listed in the tables the observed lack of a significant correlation between age and total carotene content of plasma, and between age and vitamin A plasma content, is in agreement with the findings reported by Yiengst and Shock[29] in a study of 126 institutionalized men between the ages of 40 and 90 years.

Although the graphs representing the blood thiamine concentration show no statistically certain decline with age, an analysis of the individual blood thiamine values obtained in the 218 middle-aged and old subjects included in the study shows that blood thiamine concentrations below 2 micrograms per cent were observed in 11 per cent of both the men and the women. In contrast to this, blood thiamine values below 2 micrograms per cent were not encountered in determinations on blood samples from 16-39 year old adults on a self-selected diet. It should be mentioned in this connection that a fairly high incidence of moderate vitamin B$_1$ deficiency in aged institutionalized persons has also been reported by Rafsky and Newman,[19] who observed urinary thiamine excretions below 50 micrograms / 24 hours in 18 per cent of the individuals studied.

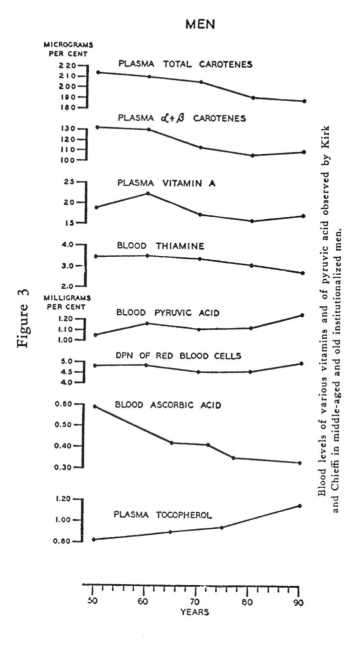

Figure 3

Blood levels of various vitamins and of pyruvic acid observed by Kirk and Chieffi in middle-aged and old institutionalized men.

255

WOMEN

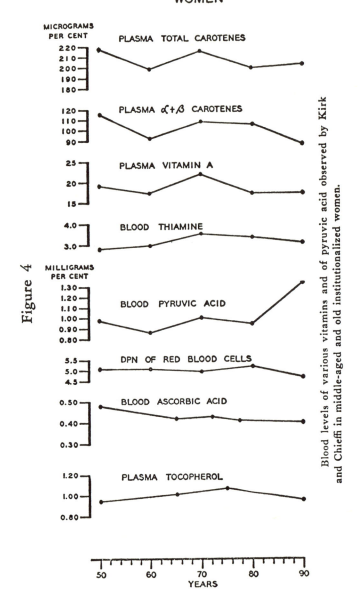

Figure 4

Blood levels of various vitamins and of pyruvic acid observed by Kirk and Chieffi in middle-aged and old institutionalized women.

256

Table 5

Correlations between age and blood and plasma concentrations of various vitamins and of pyruvic acid for institutionalized men aged 45 to 90 years

Compound	Material analyzed	Number of subjects	Mean value	r	t	Reference
Total carotenes	Plasma	66	203 micrograms %	—0.06	0.48	9
α + B carotenes	Plasma	66	118 "	—0.12	0.97	9
Vitamin A	Plasma	66	18 "	—0.12	0.97	9
Thiamine	Blood	115	3.3 "	—0.16	1.74	10
Pyruvic acid	Blood	71	1.13 mg. %	+0.01	0.08	10
DPN*	Red Blood Cells	78	4.8 "	—0.04	0.35	
Total ascorbic acid	Blood	61	0.41 "	—0.44	3.21	14
Tocopherol	Plasma	66	0.96 "	+0.23	2.05	4

* Total pyridine nucleotides expressed as DPN.

Table 6

Correlations between age and blood and plasma concentrations of various vitamins and of pyruvic acid for institutionalized women aged 45 to 90 years

Compound	Material analyzed	Number of subjects	Mean value	r	t	Reference
Total carotenes	Plasma	83	206 micrograms %	—0.01	0.05	9
α + B carotenes	Plasma	83	103 "	—0.09	0.82	9
Vitamin A	Plasma	83	18 "	—0.07	0.63	9
Thiamine	Blood	103	3.3 "	+0.02	0.18	10
Pyruvic acid	Blood	103	1.01 mg. %	+0.15	1.53	10
DPN*	Red Blood Cells	72	5.0 "	—0.07	0.59	
Total ascorbic acid	Blood	81	0.43 "	—0.05	0.45	14
Tocopherol	Plasma	96	1.01 "	+0.05	0.58	4

* Total pyridine nucleotides expressed as DPN.

With regard to pyruvic acid no statistically significant correlation was found in the studies by Kirk and Chieffi[10, 16] between the fasting thiamine and pyruvic acid values, nor between the fasting blood thiamine values and the pyruvic acid concentrations observed 90 minutes after peroral ingestion of 100 gm. of glucose.

An investigation of the ascorbic acid content of plasma in institutionalized persons was reported in 1940 by Westergaard.[27] Blood samples were obtained from 30 patients and 31 employees in an institution for the aged in Copenhagen. The age of the inmates ranged between 64 and 88 years; the mean age of the employees was 33 years. All the subjects received their food from the same hospital kitchen; an evaluation of the ascorbic acid content of the diet was not made. The ascorbic acid determinations were performed by Farmer and Abt's method.

The analyses, which were carried out during the month of March, showed a zero ascorbic acid concentration in plasma in 27 out of the 30 inmates. In contrast to this an average ascorbic acid level of 0.28 mg. per cent was observed in the young employees; only in three of these was ascorbic acid absent from the plasma.

A study from the same institution on the 24-hour urinary excretion of riboflavin was published in 1947 by Daubenmerkl.[6] His investigation included 20 elderly, apparently healthy inmates, and 25 young employees. All subjects received their food from the same hospital kitchen. The age of the inmates ranged between 63 and 89 years, that of the employees between 20 and 35 years. The riboflavin analyses in urine were carried out by a fluorometric method devised by Daubenmerkl. An evaluation of the riboflavin content of the diet was not made.

A summary of Daubenmerkl's findings is presented in Table 7. It will be seen from the data that a marked difference with regard to riboflavin excretion was found between the young and old subjects, the excretion in the elderly individuals being only about one-third of that observed in the young employees.

258

Table 7

24-hour riboflavin excretion in the urine for individuals on an institutional diet (6)

Age group (years)	Number of subjects	24-hour riboflavin excretion Mean Micrograms	Range Micrograms
20—35	25	810	316—1677
60—74	10	280	170—508
75—84	7	282	180—598
85—89	3	210	194—229

Discussion

Neither the population surveys nor the institutional studies have revealed any certain variation with age in the mean serum carotene and vitamin A values. It should, however, be noted that in 22 per cent of the institutionalized middle-aged and old individuals studied by Kirk and Chieffi plasma vitamin A levels below 10 micrograms per cent were found. These findings are in agreement with observations by Rafsky and his associates, who in two studies[22, 23] on institutionalized old persons reported serum vitamin A levels below 10 micrograms per cent in 7 and 29 per cent of the subjects.

The importance of these observations is difficult to evaluate since approximately the same incidence of hypovitaminemia A (17 per cent) was found by Kirk and Chieffi in studies on young, active individuals. Since the diet of the young subjects was not assayed for vitamin A it is possible that the low vitamin A plasma values for this group merely reflects a low vitamin A intake in the diet.

The pathogenesis of the low vitamin A plasma values found in the institutionalized persons is not clear, since the diet both in Kirk and Chieffi's and in Rafsky and Newman's studies[20] contained an adequate amount of vitamin A, and since the absorption of vitamin A in the aged seems to be essentially normal.[21, 29] In a significant number of the subjects studied by Kirk and Chieffi[2] the low vitamin A plasma values were associated with clinical signs of vitamin A deficiency. These signs in the majority of the cases disappeared following peroral administration of vitamin A and attainment of normal vitamin A plasma levels.[13] The fact that the vitamin A plasma values of these subjects quickly declined to subnormal levels after the vitamin A administration was discontinued might indicate that the cause of the hypovitaminemia A could be sought in a reduced ability of the liver to store or release vitamin A.

With regard to vitamin B_1 the studies have likewise failed to show a statistically significant correlation between age and blood thiamine content. The fact, however, that 11 per cent of the institutionalized middle-aged and old individuals were found to have blood thiamine values below 2 micrograms per cent, whereas such low levels were not encountered in young active adults, raises the question of the gerontological importance of hypothiaminemia. The finding by Kirk and Chieffi is in agreement with the observations of Rafsky and Newman on the occurrence of subnormal urinary thiamine excretion in institutionalized aged persons. It should be mentioned that a significant correlation was observed by Kirk and Chieffi[11] between the low blood thiamine content and the incidence of clinical signs of vitamin B_1 deficiency, and that treatment of the hypothiaminemic individuals with thiamine tablets consistently resulted in an increase of the blood thiamine level to normal and in the majority of the cases was followed by a disappearance of the deficiency symptoms.[3]

The pathogenesis of the hypothiaminemia in aged individuals has not as yet been established. It does not seem likely that an inadequate thiamine intake with the food was responsible for the low blood thiamine values in the majority of the cases, since the prepared diet in Kirk and Chieffi's study contained an average of 1.5 mg. of thiamine daily. A sufficient thiamine intake (0.81 mg. daily) was similarly recorded by Rafsky and Newman[20] for their group of individuals with low urinary thiamine excretion.

An increased utilization of thiamine by old individuals might account for the development of hypothiaminemia, but no support has been provided so far for this contention. On the contrary it has been demonstrated by Horwitt[8] that when young and old subjects, who for a while have been given diets supplemented with thiamine, are placed on a thiamine low diet, the curves representing the urinary excretion of thiamine during the subsequent 90 day period follow essentially the same course.

The possibility of an increased destruction of thiamine by the gastric juice must be considered since Chieffi and Kirk[5] in *in vitro* experiments found an average disappearance of 34 per cent of thiamine incubated for three hours at 37 C. with gastric juice from old individuals. The disappearance of thiamine was usually found to be higher with samples from achlorhydric individuals than with gastric juice of normal acidity. Against the contention, however, that a destruction of thiamine by the gastric juice is of major importance for the causation of hypothiaminemia is the fact that the same incidence of achlorhydria was noted by Kirk and Chieffi[11] for subjects with normal and subnormal blood thiamine values. In agreement with this

Rafsky, Newman, and Joliffe[23] found no correlation between gastric acidity and urinary excretion of thiamine in aged persons.

The action of the intestinal bacteria on thiamine may be a factor of importance in the production of hypothiaminemia. It is well known from the studies by Orla-Jensen, Olsen, and Geill[18] that the intestinal flora of old subjects is both qualitatively and quantitatively different from that of young adults, but no comparison has been made of the ability of the intestinal bacteria of old and young subjects to destroy thiamine. It has, however, been shown by Orla-Jensen and his associates that the feces in 30-35 per cent of persons over the age of 70 years contain more than 100 million *Streptoccoccus salivarius* bacteria per gram, whereas such high content of *Streptoccoccus salivarius* was never encountered in young adults. It may be of significance in this connection that *Streptoccoccus salivarius* is capable of utilizing thiamine, for which reason this organism has been employed by Niven and Smiley[17] for biological assay of the vitamin.

That incorporation of thiamine by the intestinal bacteria takes place to a considerable extent has been shown by Kirk and Chieffi,[12] who for persons on an ordinary diet observed a daily thiamine excretion in the stool of between 0.3 and 0.9 mg. The finding that the administration of thiamine tablets to hypothiaminemic individuals will produce a marked rise in the blood thiamine level may be explained by the fact that appreciable quantities of thiamine manage to escape the action of the bacteria when the thiamine is introduced in a concentrated form. Even under these circumstances, however, one-half to two-thirds of the dose of thiamine given can be recovered from the stool.

With regard to ascorbic acid the results obtained in the Groton Township Study differ markedly from those reported in the Scandinavian population surveys.   It is possible that this difference can be explained, at least partly, by the high vitamin C content of the American food and the low vitamin C content of the Scandinavian diet.   When the vitamin C content of the available food is low an insufficient intake of ascorbic acid is more likely to result in aged persons than in young adults because the total food consumption by the old subjects generally is smaller.   Under conditions, however, where the ascorbic acid content of the food is high, a lower food intake by aged persons may still be sufficient to insure an adequate supply of vitamin C.

Another explanation of the discrepancy between the American and Scandinavian investigation might be that there actually exists a tendency for the ascorbic acid serum concentration to decrease with age, similar to that observed in institutionalized persons.   Such tendency would be obscured in the case of a very high ascorbic acid intake (Groton Township Survey), but would become apparent when the ascorbic acid intake was moderate (Trier's investigation).   When the intake of vitamin C finally becomes very low (Difs' study) the difference in serum ascorbic acid concentration between old and young subjects would again tend to become eliminated.

The high incidence of hypovitaminemia C in institutionalized aged persons receiving a diet adequate with regard to ascorbic acid would suggest that a destruction of ascorbic acid in the intestinal tract may be a factor of importance.   Since only about three per cent of ingested ascorbic acid can be recovered from the stool of aged individuals[16] a simple incorporation of the vitamin by the intestinal bacteria would not seem to be a factor of major significance.   In connection with the discussion of hypovitaminemia C in old individuals it should be pointed out that some cases have been encountered by Kirk and Chieffi[15] in whom ascorbic acid given by mouth in large doses failed to produce a rise in the blood ascorbic acid concentration, whereas a normal increase occurred when the vitamin was administered parenterally. On the basis of these observations an impaired absorption of ingested ascorbic acid must be accepted as a possible cause of subnormal blood ascorbic acid values in the aged.

Although the significance of an inadequate vitamin intake as a cause of hypovitaminemia remains indisputable, the data presented in this review suggest that other factors often are operating. An important support for this concept is given by studies of Rafsky and Newman,[22] who performed simultaneous determinations of the blood content of various vitamins in old institutionalized persons consuming a diet of adequate vitamin content. In many instances low blood values of only one or two of the vitamins were found, whereas the concentration of the other vitamins was normal. It seems likely, therefore, that different conditions obtain for the absorption or utilization of the various vitamins, and the importance of a separate consideration of each vitamin must consequently be stressed in studies of the vitamin nutrition of the aged.

Summary

The publications on blood and urine vitamin levels for non-institutionalized and institutionalized old subjects are reviewed, and the values compared with those observed in young and middle-aged adults. The investigations have shown a tendency for the ascorbic acid blood concentration to decline with age in institutionalized men. A fairly high incidence of hypothiaminemia and subnormal urinary thiamine excretion have likewise been demonstrated in elderly individuals confined to institutions. The pathogenesis for the low blood and urine vitamin values is discussed.

Bibliography

1. Campbell, D. A. and E. L. Tonks: Vitamin A Total Carotenoids and Thymol Turbidity Levels in Plasma. Tests in Normal Subjects Residing in the Midlands during 1947. Brit. Med. J. 2:1499 (1951).

2. Chieffi, M. and J. E. Kirk: Vitamin Studies in Middle-Aged and Old Individuals. II. Correlation Between Vitamin A Plasma Content and Certain Clinical and Laboratory Findings. J. Nutrit. 37:79 (1949).

3. Chieffi, M. and J. E. Kirk: Vitamin Studies in Middle-Aged and Old Individuals. V. Hypovitaminemia B_1. Effect of Thiamine Administration on Blood Thiamine Concentration and Clinical Signs and Symptoms. J. Geront. 5:326 (1950).

4. Chieffi, M. and J. E. Kirk: Vitamin Studies in Middle-Aged and Old Individuals. VI. Tocopherol Plasma Concentrations. J. Geront. 6:17 (1951).

5. Chieffi, M. and J. E. Kirk: The Rate of Destruction of Thiamine by Gastric Juice of Old Individuals. J. Geront. 6(Suppl.):71 (1951).

6. Daubenmerkl, W.: Undersøgelser over Laktoflavinudskillelsen i Urin. E. Munksgaard, Copenhagen (1947).

7. Difs, H.: Beiträge zur Diagnostik der Vitamin-C-Mangelkrankheit. Acta med. Scandinav. Suppl. 110 (1940).

8. Horwitt, M.: Dietary Requirements of the Aged. J. A. D. A. 29:443 (1953).

9. Kirk, E. and M. Chieffi: Vitamin Studies in Middle-Aged and Old Individuals. I. Vitamin A. Total Carotene and $a + B$ Carotene Concentrations in Plasma. J. Nutrit. 36:315 (1948).

10. Kirk, E. and M. Chieffi: Vitamin Studies in Middle-Aged and Old Individuals. III. Thiamine and Pyruvic Acid Blood Concentrations. J. Nutrit. 38:353 (1949).

11. Kirk, J. E. and M. Chieffi: Vitamin Studies in Middle-Aged and Old Individuals. IV. Clinical Studies in Hypovitaminemia B_1. J. Geront. 5:236 (1950).

12. Kirk, J. E. and M. Chieffi: Effect of Oral Thiamine Administration on Thiamine Content of the Stool. Proc. Soc. Exptl. Biol. & Med. 77:464 (1951).

13. Kirk, J. E. and M. Chieffi: Hypovitaminemia A. Effect of Vitamin A Administration on Plasma Vitamin A Concentration, Conjunctival Changes, Dark Adaptation and Toad Skin. J. Clin. Nutrit. 1:37 (1952).

14. Kirk, J. E. and M. Chieffi: Vitamin Studies in Middle-Aged and Old Individuals. XI. The Concentration of Total Ascorbic Acid in Whole Blood. J. Geront. 8:301 (1953).

15. Kirk, J. E. and M. Chieffi: Vitamin Studies in Middle-Aged and Old Individuals. XII. Hypovitaminemia C. Effect of Ascorbic Acid Administration on the Blood Ascorbic Acid Concentration. J. Geront. 8:305 (1953).

16. Kirk, J. E. and M. Chieffi: Unpublished Data.

17. Niven, C. F. and K. L. Smiley: A Microbiological Assay Method for Thiamine. J. Biol. Chem. 150:1 (1943).

18. Orla-Jensen, S., E. Olsen and T. Geill: Senility and Intestinal Flora. Kgl. Danske Videnskab. Selskab. Biol. Skrifter. 3:1 (1945).

19. Rafsky, H. A. and B. Newman: Vitamin B$_1$ in the Aged. Gastroenterology 1:737 (1943).

20. Rafsky, H. A. and B. Newman: Nutritional Aspects of Aging. Geriatrics 2:101 (1947).

21. Rafsky, H. A. and B. Newman: A Study of the Vitamin A and Carotene Tolerance Tests in the Aged. Gastroenterology 1:1001 (1948).

22. Rafsky, H. A. and B. Newman: Interrelationship Among the Vitamins in the Aged. Geriatrics 4:358 (1949).

23. Rafsky, H. A., B. Newman and N. Jolliffe: A Study of the Carotene and Vitamin A Levels in the Aged. Gastroenterology 8:612 (1947).

24. Schmidt, V.: Pantothensyrestudier. E. Munksgaard, Copenhagen, (1949).

25. Suvarnakich, K., G. V. Mann and F. J. Stare: Riboflavin in Human Serum.   J. Nutrit. 47:105 (1952).

26. Trier, E.: C-Vitaminstudier Hos Syge Og Sunde.   E. Munksgaard, Copenhagen (1940).

27. Westergaard, E.: Staseprøven Og Dens Kliniske Betydning. E. Munksgaard, Copenhagen (1940).

28. Williams, H. H., J. S. Parker, Z. H. Pierce, J. C. Hart, G. Fiola and H. L. Pilcher: Nutritional Status Survey, Groton Township, New York. VI. Clinical Findings. J. A. D. A. 27:215 (1951).

29. Yiengst, M. V. and N. W. Shock: Effect of Oral Administration of Vitamin A on Plasma Levels of Vitamin A and Carotene in Aged Males.   J. Geront. 4:205 (1949).

Editor's Comments
on Papers 33, 34, and 35

33 SELYE et al.
A Progeria-like Syndrome Produced by Dihydrotachysterol and Its Prevention by Methyl-testosterone and Ferric Dextran

34 LANSING
Increase of Cortical Calcium with Age in the Cells of a Rotifer, Euchlanis Dilatata, a Planarian, Phagocata sp., and a Toad, Bufo Fowleri, as Shown by the Microincineration Technique

35 SIMMS and STOLMAN
Changes in Human Tissue Electrolytes in Senescence

Abnormalities in calcium metabolism were hinted at in some of the Part II papers. In this section, Dr. A. I. Lansing (Paper 34) shows the accumulation of intracellular calcium as a function of age in a number of animal forms. Drs. Simms and Stolman (Paper 35) evaluate the electrolyte changes in senescent (seventy years and older) man. Paper 33 is a report from Dr. Hans Selye's laboratory on attempts to produce an experimental model of senility by treating rats with dihydrotachysterol (DHT). In their words "It is a matter of everyday clinical experience that the avidity of various tissues for calcium increases with age." Summed, in the penultimate paragraph, are their findings, "All the changes that characterize the DHT-induced progeria-like syndrome are prevented by suitable treatment with methyltestosterone or ferric dextran (Fe-Dex), but treatment with a combination of both these agents reveals no synergism between them."

Selye et al. (Paper 33) found that as a consequence of administration of DHT certain changes mimic "senility" but that others do not; making this an imperfect model of premature aging.

33

Reprinted from *J. Am. Geriatrics Soc.* **11**(1):1–16 (1963)

A PROGERIA-LIKE SYNDROME PRODUCED BY DIHYDRO-TACHYSTEROL AND ITS PREVENTION BY METHYL-TESTOSTERONE AND FERRIC DEXTRAN

HANS SELYE, M.D., Ph.D., RALPH STREBEL, Ph.D.* and LADISLAV MIKULAJ, M.D.

Institut de Médecine et de Chirurgie expérimentales, Université de Montréal, Montréal, Canada

It is a matter of everyday clinical experience that the avidity of various tissues for calcium increases with age. This tendency manifests itself in the formation of gross calcification in the cardiovascular system, cartilaginous structures, tendons, periarticular tissues, and lens of the eye (cataracts), as well as the development of calcareous concretions in such areas as the pineal gland, prostate, and urinary passages. In addition to these macroscopically visible calcium deposits there occurs with age a gradual increase in the chemically detectable calcium content of various organs in members of the vertebrate kingdom. It is generally held that calcinosis is a secondary result of "decreased tissue vitality" and represents a "dystrophic" phenomenon; yet a review of the literature shows that several investigators have considered the possibility that an increase in tissue calcium concentration may be the cause of many of the changes characteristic of senility (1). The assumption of such a causal relationship had to remain purely speculative, however, since until recently it was not possible to demonstrate that prevention of gross calcification will in fact interfere with the development of other lesions characteristic of senility.

It has been known for more than thirty years that in the fetal or in the newborn rat, intoxication with an impure vitamin-D preparation (irradiated ergosterol) produces a kind of osteoporosis with spontaneous fractures, intense catabolism and loss of skin elasticity (2, 3), whereas in older rats, it tends to produce calcification in various soft tissues, especially in the arteries, heart and kidneys (3, 4). More recently, it was shown that a syndrome reminiscent of progeria can be produced by chronic overdosage with small doses of dihydrotachysterol (DHT) and that all the manifold manifestations of this experimental disease are inhibited when tissue calcification is prevented by simultaneous treatment with ferric dextran (Fe-Dex) (5), methyltestosterone (6) or 17-ethyl-19-nortestosterone (7).

The term "progeria" implies premature aging and it has been used to designate clinical (Hutchinson-Gilford syndrome) and experimental (x-ray damage) con-

* Fellow of the U. S. National Institutes of Health, Fellowship-No., MF-8987-C3.

ditions, in which organ changes reminiscent of senility develop at an early age. However, it should be clearly stated at the outset that we have no reliable objective indicator of "physiologic aging" and, hence, our assessment of premature senility must rest upon the demonstration in young individuals of changes that normally tend to occur only late in life. It is with these limitations in mind that we shall speak of progeria, but in order to underline even more clearly that the syndrome elicited by chronic DHT intoxication in the rat is not an accurate replica of senility, we shall refer to it only as "progeria-like."

In this communication, we wish to present a detailed morphologic study of the organ lesions that develop during chronic DHT intoxication in the rat and to report upon a series of experiments designed to determine the best procedures for the inhibition of these changes by means of ferric dextran and methyltestosterone.

MATERIALS AND TECHNIQUES

For the experiments that form the basis of this report we employed exclusively female rats of the Holtzman farms, with an initial body weight of either 100 gm. (range 90–110 gm.) or 200 gm. (range 190–210 gm.). We used 315 rats of the 100 gm., and 196 rats of the 200 gm. range to determine the optimal dose of methyltestosterone and ferric dextran (Fe-Dex) as well as to compare the efficacy of Fe-Dex with that of related drugs. However, we shall describe in detail only the eventually-perfected best technique for the production and prevention of the progeria-like syndrome; the procedures used in preliminary and complementary experiments will be briefly mentioned later in the text.

The main experiment was performed on 100 female Holtzman rats with a mean initial body weight of 103 gm. (range 98–110 gm.), which were divided into 5 equal groups and treated as indicated in Graph I. With the exception of the *untreated controls* of Group 1, all animals received *dihydrotachysterol* or DHT [Calcamin (Wander)] at a dosage level of 50 μg. in 0.5 ml. of oil by mouth daily, starting on the first day. Group 2 received no other treatment. Group 3 was given *ferric dextran* [Fe-Dex, Imposil (Benger)] in amounts equivalent to 2 mg. of metallic iron in 1 ml. of water, daily, intraperitoneally. Group 4 received injections of *methyltestosterone* [Oreton-M (Schering)] at a dosage level of 1 mg. in 0.2 ml. of water, daily, subcutaneously. Group 5 received *Fe-Dex + methyltestosterone* at the same dosage levels. All the treatments in Groups 3 to 5 were initiated five days prior to the beginning of DHT treatment and were continued until the termination of the experiment.

The rats were maintained exclusively with cubes of Purina Laboratory Chow (Purina Co. of Canada) and tap water during the first half of the experiment. However, after fifteen days of DHT administration, severe dental anomalies developed in the animals receiving no other treatment, and they were unable to chew the hard Purina cubes; therefore, during the second half of the experiment the ground Purina Laboratory Chow was given to the animals of all groups for the sake of uniformity. The rats were killed with chloroform on the thirtieth day and representative specimens of various soft organs were fixed in alcohol-formol (4 parts of absolute alcohol and 1 part of 10 per cent formaldehyde) for subsequent embedding in paraffin and staining with hematoxylin-phloxine (for general structure), the von Kóssa technique (for calcified foci), Gomori's aldehyde fuchsin (for elastic fibers), cresyl violet (for metachromatic material) and the Prussian-blue technique (for iron). In addition, some soft tissues as well as the bones and teeth were fixed and simultaneously decalcified in a solution containing 20 per cent formic acid and 10 per cent formaldehyde. These decalcified specimens were also embedded in paraffin and stained with the aforementioned techniques.

Clinical course

During the five days preceding the initiation of DHT treatment, the animals of all groups gained weight approximately at the same rate and showed no evident clinical manifestations of disease, except for a slight brownish discoloration of the skin (indicative of mild hemosiderosis) in the group treated with ferric dextran. Accordingly, the body-weight curves in Graph I follow a virtually identical course until the first day of DHT treatment. However, after this the growth of the rats receiving DHT alone soon fell behind that of the other groups, and beginning on the fifth day it declined rapidly, until at the end of the observation period it returned to the starting level. On the other hand, the rats treated with DHT + methyltestosterone continued to grow just as rapidly as the controls. Indeed, their final weight was slightly (though not significantly) above that of the untreated controls. Eventually the body weight of these rats was more than twice that of the rats given DHT alone. We may well speak of a complete abolition of the DHT-induced catabolism. Treatment with DHT + ferric dextran likewise inhibited DHT-induced weight loss, and at the end of the experiment

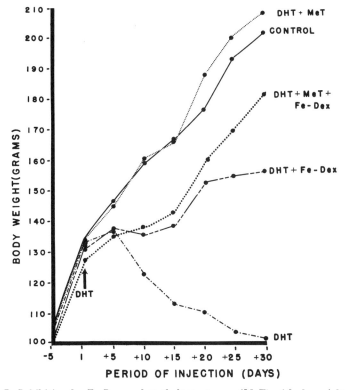

GRAPH I. *Inhibition by Fe-Dex and methyltestosterone (MeT) of body-weight depressing effect of DHT.*

271

the rats so treated weighed approximately 50 per cent more than those given DHT alone. Concurrent administration of methyltestosterone + ferric dextran did not result in a synergism between the anticatabolic effect of these two DHT antagonists; it caused a growth rate intermediate between that induced by ferric dextran and by methyltestosterone (Graph I).

As regards the general appearance of the rats treated with DHT alone, the outstanding changes were gradually progressing emaciation and muscular weakness, reaching such a degree that the rat can hardly lift its head from the floor (Fig. 1). At the same time the skin became dry, scaly and inelastic; it formed numerous wrinkles. A skin-fold picked up between the fingers remained in position, as does the skin of old people, whereas the skin of the treated animals snapped into place immediately because of its turgor and elasticity, as did that of the intact controls. The bones, and particularly the ribs, were clearly visible through the thin, fat-free skin of the emaciated rats treated with DHT alone, and the vertebrae formed a sharp kyphosis in the lower thoracic and upper lumbar region. This gibbus persisted even under anesthesia and could not easily be reduced by mechanical pressure upon the back. All these changes were prevented by ferric dextran alone (Fig. 1), and even more completely by ferric dextran + methyltestosterone, or methyltestosterone alone.

Apart from the brown pigmentation of the skin, there was no obvious clinical sign of disease in the rats treated with ferric dextran, except that the submaxillary lymph nodes were palpably enlarged and hard owing to suppuration. This curious side effect of ferric dextran treatment has been noted before (5), but it is not clear why only these lymph nodes are selectively affected.

Skeleton

Apart from the general stunting of growth, the most outstanding result of chronic DHT overdosage was an intense osteosclerosis affecting virtually every bone in the body. The sites of predilection were the spongiosa in the subepiphyseal regions of the long bones (femur, humerus, tibia). Presumably an inhibition of bone absorption primarily accounts for this form of osteosclerosis in which the trabeculae become unusually coarse and often lie so close together that the metaphysis contains virtually no marrow. The normal osteoclastic remodelling of the growing metaphysis is also inhibited on the periosteal surface; consequently, the metaphyseal portions of the long bones as well as the costochondral junctions of the ribs become broad and club-shaped. Similar changes of osteosclerosis were also noted in such areas as the wall of the mastoid bulla (Fig. 2), the vertebrae, and the surroundings of the costovertebral joints. The deformation was especially obvious in dissected preparations of the atlas (Fig. 3), wherever the bone is most exposed to mechanical forces.

All these changes could be prevented by administration of ferric dextran (Figs. 2 and 3), although they are quite unlike the osteoporosis characteristic of senility. Yet, DHT also produced calcification of the costal and tracheal cartilages—a condition which is typical of old age—and this change was likewise prevented by treatment with ferric dextran, methyltestosterone, or a combination of both.

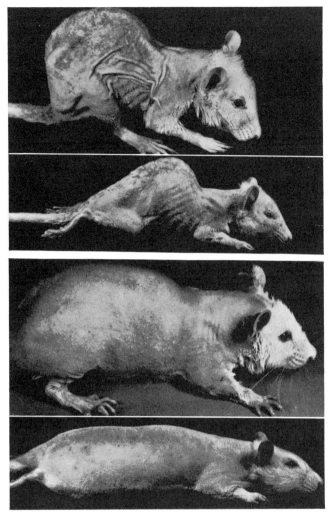

FIG. 1. *Inhibition by Fe-Dex of the catabolism, kyphosis and cutaneous atrophy produced by DHT.—Top:* DHT alone causes intense cutaneous atrophy with wrinkling of the skin, kyphosis and loss of weight. Under anesthesia (next picture), the kyphosis is seen to persist even when the hind legs are stretched back. The ribs protrude through the atrophic musculature. *Bottom:* All these changes are prevented by Fe-Dex.

Skin

Histologic examination of the skin of rats treated with DHT alone showed virtually complete disappearance of adipose tissue and severe atrophy of the dermal collagen and of the cutaneous musculature. The elastic fibers were but moderately affected; however, they tended to become fragmented. The cutaneous arteries had undergone calcification. The hair follicles and the sebaceous glands were atrophic.

A particularly striking change was seen in the mastocytes of the skin. These

273

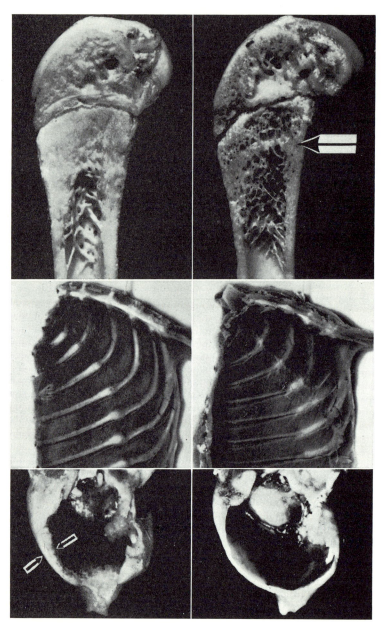

FIG. 2. *Inhibition by Fe-Dex of skeletal changes produced by DHT.—Top left:* Intense sclerosis of epiphysis and distal end of diaphysis as seen on cross section through femur of rat treated with DHT alone. Trabeculae in marrow cavity are coarse and the shaft comparatively thick. *Top right:* Essentially normal bone structure in similar section through femur of rat treated with DHT + Fe-Dex. The single band of osteosclerosis (arrow) which runs through the spongiosa parallel to the growth cartilage disc, presumably represents bone formed at the beginning of the experiment, when the amount of Fe-Dex stored was not yet fully sufficient to compensate for the DHT. *Middle left:* "Rosary-like" thickening of costrochondral junctions in a rat treated with DHT alone (sternum near upper margin). *Middle right:* Corresponding region of a rat given DHT + Fe-Dex. The ribs are of normal appearance. *Bottom left:* Intense thickening of mastoid wall (between arrows) in rat treated with DHT alone. *Bottom right:* Normal mastoid bone in rat treated with DHT + Fe-Dex.

6

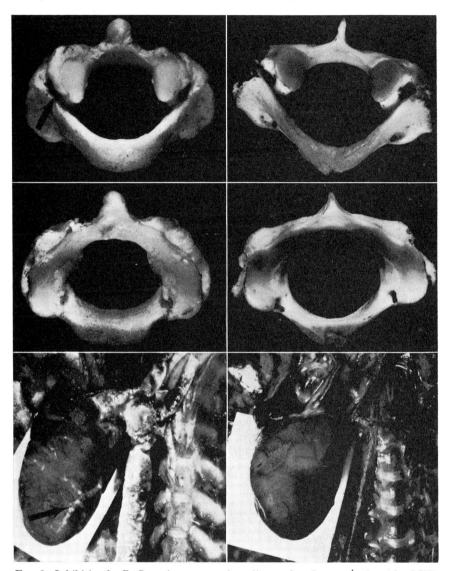

Fig. 3. *Inhibition by Fe-Dex of osseous and cardiovascular changes produced by DHT.*— *Top left:* Intense deformation of atlas with particularly pronounced broadening of the anterior tubercle. The groove for the vertebral artery and first cervical nerve is narrow and the foramen transversarium (arrow) within the transverse process is hardly visible at the bottom of this groove. Both anterior and posterior arches are thickened. *Top right:* Simultaneous treatment with Fe-Dex resulted in maintenance of normal vertebral structure. *Middle left and right:* Same vertebrae seen from below. *Bottom left:* Intense calcification of aorta and its major branches induced by DHT. The anterior descending branch of the left coronary artery is particularly conspicuous owing to calcification and dilatation (arrow). The intervertebral discs are narrowed and there are large exostoses on the ribs near the costovertebral joints. *Bottom right:* Essentially normal thoracic organs in a rat treated with DHT + Fe-Dex.

were very numerous but constantly discharging their metachromatic granules and the latter became diffusely distributed throughout the connective tissue, forming thick sheaths around the arteries. Except for this mastocyte discharge, all the cutaneous changes were prevented by ferric dextran, methyltestosterone or a combination of both.

The skin of the animals given ferric dextran alone or in combination with methyltestosterone contained large amounts of Prussian-blue-positive iron, both in the form of granules within phagocytes and as a diffuse impregnation of the dermal and subcutaneous collagen fibers.

The sebaceous glands of the rats treated with DHT + methyltestosterone not only failed to show the atrophy characteristic of treatment with DHT alone, but actually underwent hypertrophy and hyperplasia.

Cardiovascular system

It is well known that acute, heavy overdosage with DHT and other vitamin-D compounds produces a generalized metastatic calcification which affects not only the arteries but also the myocardium, the renal parenchyma, the gastric mucosa and some of the skeletal muscles, particularly those of the neck and shoulder region. This syndrome of systemic calcinosis is quite similar to that elicited by acute overdosage with parathyroid hormone. On the other hand, in the present experiments in which chronic overdosage with comparatively small amounts of DHT was produced, calcification was almost completely limited to the arteries. The aorta and its major branches as well as the coronary arteries were most severely affected, but the smaller arterial vessels throughout the body were likewise involved. Yet other soft tissues (with the exception of the stomach) remained virtually free of calcium deposits.

The histologic appearance of this "Mönckeberg type" of arteriosclerosis is sufficiently known, from the standpoint of both experimental and clinical medicine, to deserve no detailed discussion here. Suffice it to say that all manifestations of the DHT-induced calcinosis were greatly diminished or abolished by simultaneous treatment with ferric dextran and even more constantly by methyltestosterone (Figs. 3 and 4). However, here again the mastocytes, which surround the arteries and are particularly numerous around their smallest branches, exhibited unique behavior. They showed intense degranulation, both in the rats treated with DHT alone (in which there was calcification) and in those in which calcinosis was prevented by ferric dextran, methyltestosterone, or combined treatment with both these agents. Both in the skin and around the internal arterial vessels the mastocyte changes induced by DHT remained uninfluenced by the agents which prevent the calcinotic effect of this compound.

Other soft tissues

The large parenchymatous organs, particularly the liver and kidney, the lymphatic tissue of the thymus, lymph nodes and Peyer's plaques, as well as the connective and adipose tissue throughout the body underwent severe atrophy as a consequence of chronic DHT intoxication. In this respect ferric dextran and methyltestosterone again exhibited their usual prophylactic action. In the animals treated with ferric dextran, heavy Prussian-blue-positive iron deposits were seen throughout the connective tissue, the reticulo-endothelial system and, to a lesser extent, in the parenchymal cells of the kidney and liver. However, this siderosis is not an indispensable prerequisite for DHT antagonism since it did not occur in the methyltestosterone-treated rats, which were even better protected against the toxic actions of DHT.

Atrophy of the connective tissue with calcification frequently occurs in the laryngeal cartilages and vocal cords of senile individuals; hence, it is noteworthy that such changes also developed in our DHT-treated rats, except in those that received prophylactic treatment with methyltestosterone and/or ferric dextran (Fig. 4).

Teeth

The incisor teeth of the rat are particularly sensitive indicators of derangements in calcium metabolism. Dental anomalies are also common in senile rats. In these rats the incisors tend to spread apart, presumably because their alveolar processes weaken and then malocclusion results. When the continuously growing incisors of these rodents no longer face each other properly, normal growth cannot be checked by the wear and tear of mastication. In this case the incisors either become obliquely eroded (if they meet at an angle) or they continue to grow into huge, curved, tusk-like structures (if they do not meet at all). Similar changes were seen in the rats treated with DHT, unless they also received one or both of our prophylactic agents (Fig. 5).

Specificity of the prophylactic agents

The preceding description is based solely upon experiments performed with the most effective technique that we were able to devise so far for the prevention of chronic DHT intoxication. However, numerous other experiments had to be conducted first in order to arrive at this procedure and to assess its specificity. It would be redundant to describe all this preliminary work in detail, but a brief summary of it may help in the evaluation of the underlying mechanisms.

It is of special interest, for example, that *lower or higher dosages of methyltestosterone* (such as 100 µg. or 3 mg. per day, given subcutaneously to 100-gm. rats) were considerably less effective than the dosage of 1 mg. used in the standard arrangement of the experiments just described.

In otherwise similarly conducted, but *more prolonged experiments*, the rats receiving DHT alone all died by the end of the second month, whereas all those receiving ferric dextran, methyltestosterone or both these agents, survived. If combined treatment with DHT plus these prophylactic treatments was then interrupted, the protected animals continued to develop normally and showed no indication of delayed damage. Even after a rest period of three months, autopsy revealed no noteworthy organ changes except for remnants of hemosiderosis in the groups treated with ferric dextran. It is evident from these observations that the progeria-like syndrome induced by DHT is associated with a shortening of the life span and that this effect—as the organ lesions themselves—can be inhibited by ferric dextran and methyltestosterone. Furthermore,

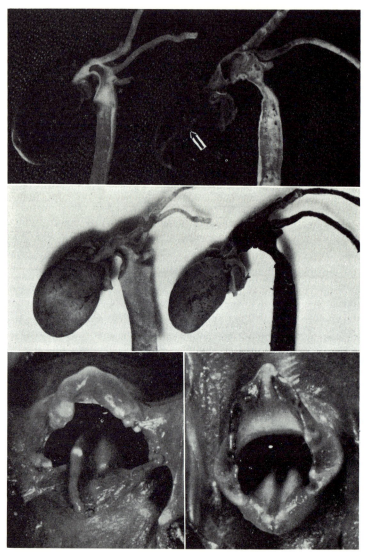

Fig. 4. *Inhibition by Fe-Dex of cardiovascular and laryngeal changes produced by DHT.*— *Top left:* Normal heart and vessels of rat treated with DHT + Fe-Dex. *Top right:* Calcification of aorta and its major branches as well as of descending branch of left coronary artery (arrow) in rat treated with DHT alone. *Middle left and right:* Same preparations following staining with AgNO$_3$. All calcified regions are stained black except the coronary artery which courses too deep in the muscle to be visualized with this technique. By contrast, small calcified foci in subepicardial muscle which were not visible without staining now appear as black lines. *Bottom left:* Marked deformation due to connective tissue atrophy and nodular calcification in epiglottis and vocal cords of rats treated with DHT alone. *Bottom right:* Normal appearance of these structures in rat given DHT + Fe-Dex.

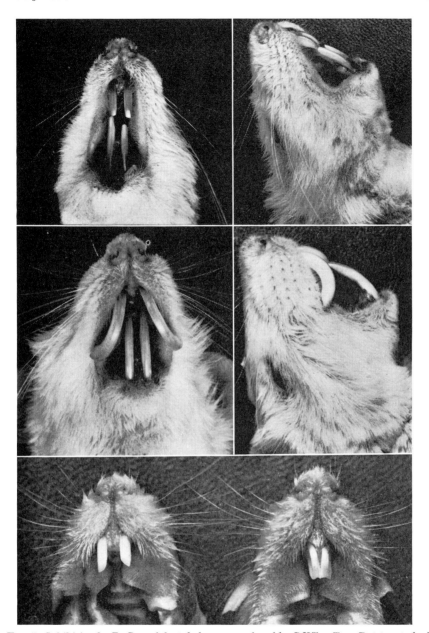

FIG. 5. *Inhibition by Fe-Dex of dental changes produced by DHT.—Top:* Rat treated with DHT alone. Frontal and lateral view of incisor teeth which have spread apart and are eroded owing to malocclusion in rat. *Middle:* Similarly treated rat. Here, the upper incisors form tusk-like structures because they have spread apart so far that they can no longer be eroded by the lower pair during the process of mastication. *Bottom left:* Rat treated with DHT alone. The upper incisors have spread far apart and their tips are obliquely eroded owing to malocclusion. *Bottom right:* Concurrent treatment with Fe-Dex results in the maintenance of normal dental structure.

animals protected in this manner while DHT is given, exhibit no adverse after-effects upon interruption of both the pathogenic and prophylactic treatments.

In general, experiments on growth and aging are best performed in young, rapidly growing animals because, in them, retardation of development and the appearance of changes characteristic of senility are particularly striking. That is why most of our work was performed on 100-gm. rats. However, essentially similar results were obtained on *older animals* (weighing 200 gm.) which, because of their greater sensitivity, received the standard amount of DHT (50 μg. per day) used in all experiments discussed in this paper.

Methyltestosterone was not tested on 200-gm. rats, but *ferric dextran (Fe-Dex)* (1 ml. containing 50 mg. of iron, injected intravenously or, even better, intraperitoneally every fifth day) definitely inhibited the DHT-intoxication syndrome, whereas *dextran* (1 ml. of a 6 per cent solution in 200-gm. rats, given intraperitoneally every fifth day) was quite ineffective. Apparently, *iron* is indispensable for the prophylactic effect of ferric dextran. It must be kept in mind, however, that a low molecular dextran is used in the manufacture of Fe-Dex, whereas the commercial dextran which we employed (Abbott) is a high molecular polymer. Still, the form in which iron is administered undoubtedly plays an important role since even much lower doses of Fe-Dex (*e.g.*, 1 ml. containing 2 mg. of iron, daily, intraperitoneally in 100-gm. rats) proved to be highly effective, whereas the same amount of iron given as *Fe-OS* [ferric oxide saccharate, Proferin (Merck, Sharp & Dohme)], *Fe-Din* [ferric dextrin, Ferrigen (ASTRA Södertälje, Sweden)] or *Fe-Sol* [Jectofer (ASTRA), an iron sorbitol citric acid complex prepared in the presence of dextrin] given in the same manner exhibited little if any prophylactic potency.

Fe-Dex causes intense iron storage in the reticulo-endothelial system; hence, control experiments were also performed with *carbon suspensions* (Higgin's American India ink, 50 per cent, 1 ml. every fifth day, intravenously or intraperitoneally in 200-gm. rats). Although a slight diminution of the DHT-induced catabolism could be seen in the rats receiving India ink intravenously, the difference was not statistically significant; intraperitoneal injections were entirely inert. Yet *Th-Din* [colloidal thorium dioxide stabilized with dextrin (Thorotrast, Testagar)] given intraperitoneally to 200-gm. rats every fifth day at a dosage level of 1 ml. containing 25 mg. of thorium dioxide did exhibit a slight, but statistically significant, protective action.

Egg white (2 ml. per day of a 10 per cent solution intraperitoneally) and *egg yolk* (2 ml. of a 10 per cent solution daily intraperitoneally) were ineffective when tested on 100-gm. rats against the usual dose of DHT.

The possibility that the prophylactic effect might be a secondary consequence of *stress* induced by the preventive agents was likewise considered but repeated bone fractures, causing considerable stress, were ineffective.

DISCUSSION

There can be no doubt that both methyltestosterone and ferric dextran are highly effective in protecting the organism against chronic intoxication with

DHT. It remains to be seen, however, whether this finding has any bearing upon the problem of aging. Rats receiving prolonged treatment with DHT do exhibit a number of changes characteristic of senility, and particularly of premature senility as manifested in man by the Hutchinson-Gilford syndrome or progeria. In this syndrome, atrophy and wrinkling of the skin and generalized arteriosclerosis (Mönckeberg type) with intense calcification of the arteries are combined with a shortened life span (8–10). In addition to these changes, our DHT-treated animals exhibited certain dental anomalies which commonly occur in old rats, as well as a deformation of the spinal column not unlike senile kyphosis. The generalized and progressive catabolism with atrophy of the liver, kidney, thymicolymphatic apparatus and skeletal musculature, as well as of the connective and adipose tissue throughout the body, is likewise common in advanced senility. Cataracts are comparatively rare in animals treated with DHT alone (5), but this compound sensitizes the rat for the production of changes in the crystalline lens by the subsequent administration of 5-hydroxytryptamine or isoproterenol (11).

Although the most constant skeletal change in senility is osteoporosis, our animals exhibited a greatly increased bone density. In man, excessive bone proliferation is rarely seen at an advanced age except in the form of "lipping" of the vertebrae in senile kyphosis and of localized bone proliferations around arthritic joints. However, generalized osteosclerosis in combination with diffuse arteriosclerosis of the Mönckeberg type may also be observed in clinical medicine, for example, in the osteitis deformans of Paget (12, 13) and in the marble-bone disease of Albers-Schönberg (14). Furthermore, in very immature rats, intoxication with vitamin-D compounds (including DHT) can produce osteoporosis with extreme fragility of the bones (2, 3, 15). It is not inconceivable, therefore, that incidental conditioning factors determine whether calcification of the arteries with progeria-like changes is associated with osteoporosis or with osteosclerosis.

A tendency toward soft-tissue calcification is undoubtedly a characteristic feature of senility. Several theories of aging are based upon the assumption that calcium plays some causative role in tissue aging (1); yet, it must be kept in mind that our model of progeria-like changes does not necessarily represent a true replica of premature aging. From our experiments we are entitled to conclude only that both methyltestosterone and ferric dextran are extremely efficacious in combatting the metabolic changes induced by chronic DHT intoxication.

Virtually nothing is known about the mechanism through which these prophylactic agents exert their protective effect and, indeed, methyltestosterone and ferric dextran do not necessarily act through the same mechanism. It has long been known that androgens exert an anabolic or anticatabolic effect, and that virilizing adrenocortical tumors may elicit the "infant Hercules" syndrome in children owing to excessive development of the musculature. Later, when synthetic testosterone became available, it could be shown by experiments on the rat that this hormone stimulates somatic growth (especially in females). Hence we concluded that the anabolic effect of virilizing tumors is presumably due to an excess production of some testosterone-like androgenic hormone (16). Methyltestosterone also has been shown to antagonize the catabolic action of various stressors in the rat: it significantly diminishes the body-weight loss induced by repeated injections of formaldehyde, estradiol or aminoacetonitrile. However, this androgen does not block the weight loss produced by any of these agents as actively as that of calcifying compounds such as DHT or vitamin D_2 (17).

Ever since the famous experiment of Brown-Séquard, who in 1889 claimed to have rejuvenated himself by subcutaneous injections of a dog testis extract, many investigators have maintained that sex hormones can exert a "rejuvenating" effect (for literature see reference 18). But all this work fell into disrepute because its interpretation was greatly complicated by the psychologic consequences of sexual stimulation. Unfortunately, it is difficult to obtain large numbers of homogeneous, senile experimental animals, but now that we have a reliable test for the inhibition of such objective changes as soft-tissue calcification, bone lesions, and catabolism in the rat, this "rejuvenating" action of the androgens should be re-examined in senile animals. Such experiments are desirable quite irrespective of whether the prevention of such changes as cardiovascular calcinosis, catabolism, dental abnormalities or cutaneous atrophy are, or are not considered indicative of senility.

The effect of ferric dextran is undoubtedly independent of androgenic stimulation since this compound possesses no hormonal activity. We were led to examine it as a possible anticalcinotic agent only because of its potent calciphylactic challenging action.

Calciphylaxis is a mechanism which enables the organism to deposit calcium selectively in certain areas. Thus, following pretreatment with parathyroid hormone or with DHT, various calciphylactic challengers (*e.g.*, ferric dextran, egg white, metals, 5HT) can induce selective calcification in the skin, muscles, cardiovascular system, pancreas, salivary glands or uterus. The phenomenon represents an induced hypersensitivity reaction to certain compounds not known to be antigenic in the usual sense (11).

It is not within the scope of this communication to discuss the mechanism of calciphylaxis in detail. Suffice it to say that calcium is attracted to the challenged area when this region is comparatively circumscribed. When extensive areas are impregnated with a challenger (as they are after repeated intraperitoneal injections of ferric dextran), an inverse response results. This is known as anacalciphylaxis and presumably depends upon the fact that under these conditions the challenger (*e.g.*, ferric dextran) does not cause any selective massive challenge and calcium fixation at the injection site. Instead, innumerable minute iron deposits are fairly evenly distributed throughout the body and compete successfully for the substrate (calcium, calcifiable matrix) with organs, such as the vascular system and the bones, which would normally attract calcium after DHT treatment. Thus, the protection offered by ferric dextran might be due to the formation of countless microscopic "calcium turnover-points" at sites where it is deposited. The minute dustlike granules of calcium could then be mobilized easily for subsequent excretion without the formation of massive unabsorbable deposits at any one point (5). It is possible that some of the other calciphylactic challengers tested in this series (*e.g.*, Th-Din) act through the same mechanism.

There is no apparent similarity between the classic pharmacologic actions of methyltestosterone and of ferric dextran. Hence, it was thought that the two agents might act through entirely unrelated mechanisms and that simultaneous treatment with both compounds could result in a potentiation of their anti-DHT effects. This did not prove to be the case under our experimental conditions. However, at the dosage level employed, methyltestosterone in itself was maximally active in that it blocked DHT intoxication completely. It is possible that a synergism could be demonstrated with threshold amounts of the two compounds.

SUMMARY

The histologic changes characteristic of the "progeria-like syndrome" induced in the rat by chronic intoxication with dihydrotachysterol (DHT) are described in detail.

It was found that under certain experimental conditions, DHT produces a Mönckeberg type of generalized arteriosclerosis with virtually no soft-tissue calcification in organs other than the arteries and the cartilaginous portions of the ribs, trachea and larynx. At the same time there is loss of body weight, atrophy of the liver, kidney, thymicolymphatic apparatus, fat and connective tissue, and loss of elasticity of the skin with a great tendency toward wrinkle formation. Dental anomalies develop, similar to those seen in senile rats, and the life span is greatly shortened. Cataracts are rarely observed, but pretreatment with DHT sensitizes the rat for the production of cataracts by other agents.

Whereas these changes are reminiscent of senility, the changes in the bones are not; in DHT-treated animals the bones undergo severe osteosclerosis. Under other circumstances DHT may produce osteoporosis with greatly increased bone fragility, but since this is not the case here, the "progeria-like syndrome" induced by chronic DHT overdosage cannot be considered an exact replica of premature senility.

All the changes that characterize the DHT-induced progeria-like syndrome are prevented by suitable treatment with methyltestosterone or ferric dextran (Fe-Dex), but treatment with a combination of both these agents reveals no synergism between them.

The possible clinical implications of these findings are briefly discussed.

Acknowledgments

This work was supported by grants from the National Institutes of Health, U. S. Public Health Service (Grants Nos. AM-01641-05, NB-02037-04 and H-6182), The John A. Hartford Foundation and The Gustavus and Louise Pfeiffer Research Foundation.

REFERENCES

1. LANSING, A. I.: Some physiological aspects of ageing, *Physiol. Rev.* **31:** 274, 1951.
2. SELYE, H.: Knochenveränderungen bei den jungen Vigantol-behandelter Tiere (Verein Deutscher Ärzte in Prag, 26. Okt. 1928), abstracted in *Med. Klin.* **25:** 167, 1929.
3. SELYE, H.: Morphologische Studie über die Veränderungen nach Verfütterung von bestrahltem Ergosterin (Vigantol) bei der weissen Ratte, *Krankheitsforsch.* **7:** 289, 1929.

4. KREITMAIR, H., AND MOLL, T.: Hypervitaminose durch grosse Dosen Vitamin D, *Münch. med. Wchnschr.* **75:** 637 & 1113, 1928.

5. SELYE, H., AND STREBEL, R.: Prevention by calciphylaxis of the progeria-like syndrome induced by chronic dihydrotachysterol overdosage, *Proc. Soc. Exper. Biol. & Med.* (in press).

6. SELYE, H.: Effect of various hormones upon the syndrome of dihydrotachysterol (AT-10) intoxication, *Acta endocrinol.* **25:** 83, 1957.

7. SELYE, H., AND RENAUD, S.: On the anticatabolic and anticalcinotic effects of 17-ethyl-19-nortestosterone, *Am. J. M. Sc.* **235:** 1, 1958.

8. COOKE, J. V.: The rate of growth in progeria with a report of two cases, *J. Pediat.* **42:** 26, 1953.

9. CUSHING, H.: Hyperactivation of the neurohypophysis as the pathological basis of eclampsia and other hypertensive states, *Am. J. Path.* **10:** 145, 1934.

10. SAPHIR, O.: A Text on Systemic Pathology. New York, Grune & Stratton, Vol. 1, 1958; Vol. 2, 1959.

11. SELYE, H.: Calciphylaxis. Chicago, The University of Chicago Press, 1962.

12. BARR, D. P.: Pathological calcification, *J. Missouri M.A.* **27:** 75, 1930.

13. EDHOLM, O. G.; HOWARTH, S., AND McMICHAEL, J.: Heart failure and bone blood flow in osteitis deformans, *Clin. Sc.* **5:** 249, 1945.

14. CLAIRMONT, P., AND SCHINZ, H. R.: Klinische, röntgenologische und pathologisch-anatomische Beobachtungen zur Marmorknochenerkrankung, *Arch. klin. Chir.* **132:** 347, 1924.

15. SELYE, H.: Experimental production of cutaneous calcinosis and sclerosis with dihydrotachysterol (AT-10), *J. Invest. Dermat.* **29:** 9, 1957.

16. McEUEN, C. S.; SELYE, H., AND COLLIP, J. B.: Effect of testosterone on somatic growth, *Proc. Soc. Exper. Biol. & Med.* **36:** 390, 1937.

17. SELYE, H., AND MISHRA, R. K.: On the ability of methyltestosterone to counteract catabolism in diverse conditions of stress, *Arch. internat. Pharmacodyn. & Thérap.* **117:** 444, 1958.

18. SELYE, H.: Textbook of Endocrinology. Acta Inc., Med. Publ., Montreal, Vol. 1, 1947; Vol. 2, 1949.

34

Reprinted from *Biol. Bull.* **82**:392–400 (1942)

INCREASE OF CORTICAL CALCIUM WITH AGE IN THE
CELLS OF A ROTIFER, EUCHLANIS DILATATA, A
PLANARIAN, PHAGOCATA SP., AND A TOAD,
BUFO FOWLERI, AS SHOWN BY THE
MICROINCINERATION TECHNIQUE [1]

ALBERT I. LANSING [2]

(*Department of Zoology, Indiana University, Bloomington*)

In the preceding study the writer (1942) demonstrated that the
amount of calcium in the cortex of the leaf cells of *Elodea* increases with
age. The following studies were conducted in order to discover whether
a similar increase in calcium content occurs in representative animal cells.

MATERIAL AND METHODS

Material for analysis was chosen so as to include both multiplying
and non-multiplying cells of diverse organisms. The rotifer, *Euchlanis
dilatata,* and the gastrocnemius muscle of the toad, *Bufo fowleri,* were
selected to provide examples of non-multiplying cells; the planarian,
Phagocata sp., provides within the same animal both multiplying and
non-multiplying cells.

Euchlanis dilatata

The stock of this rotifer was developed from a single animal found
in a pond near Bloomington, Indiana. The rotifers were cultured in
the laboratory on pyrex depression slides containing two drops of culture
fluid (Sonneborn, 1936). A number of newly-hatched rotifers were
isolated and 40 of these animals were removed and fixed for histochemical analysis. The remaining animals were cultured on the depression
slides throughout the entire life span. The animals were transferred
daily to fresh depressions and samples of 20 animals were taken each
day for chemical analysis. The last sample was taken at the end of
the fourth day at which time the rotifers manifested the characteristic

---

[1] Part of the dissertation submitted to the faculty members of the Graduate
School in partial fulfillment of the requirements for the degree, doctor of philosophy, in the Department of Zoology, Indiana University.

[2] Now at the Department of Anatomy, Washington University School of
Medicine, St. Louis.

changes of senescence. The maximum age of *Euchlanis dilatata* when grown at 30° C. is four to five days. This was determined in a number of experiments on the normal life cycle (unpublished data).

Phagocata sp.

Several hundred of the multipharyngeal planarian, *Phagocata* sp., were collected from a spring near Bloomington, Indiana, and brought into the laboratory. The planaria were examined with a dissecting microscope and measured while fully extended. The smallest animals found were 3 to 4 mm. in length; 25 of these small planaria were selected for chemical analysis. A second group of 25 animals 5 mm. in length and markedly broader than the preceding group of animals, was selected for analysis to represent the planaria of medium size, since these were most abundantly found. The largest animals were 10 mm. in length; 25 of these were selected at random for chemical analysis. On the basis of size it was assumed that the planarians 3 to 4 mm. in length were the youngest of the three groups and that the planarians measuring 10 mm. in length were the oldest. This conclusion was substantiated by a comparison of the degree of pigmentation of the animals. The smallest animals possessed the light gray pigmentation of young planaria while the large animals were a dense black, a characteristic of adult *Phagocata*.

Bufo fowleri

A collection of toads was made during the third week of August in the vicinity of Greenwood Lake, Indiana. All the animals were gathered from a relatively small area in order to reduce environmental variations to a minimum.

Six toads measuring 5.6 to 6.9 cm. in length (fully extended) were selected for analysis and pithed. The gastrocnemius muscles were carefully excised and were immediately put into absolute alcohol-formalin fixative. Six toads measuring 13.6 to 15.7 cm. were pithed and the gastrocnemius muscles excised and fixed as were the previous group. On the basis of the length measurements described above and the growth data of Hamilton (1934) whose work was done on the closely related toad, *Bufo americanus americanus* Holbrook, it was concluded that the toads measuring 5.6 to 6.9 cm. were four to five months old and that the toads measuring 13.6 to 15.7 cm. were two or more years old.

Microincineration Technique

The technique of microincineration employed in these experiments is essentially the same as that of Scott (1933a). Satisfactory results were obtained by the author (1938) with this technique in an analysis of the localization of calcium in *Paramecium caudatum*. The experimental material was fixed in absolute alcohol-formalin (9 pts. to 1 pt.), dehydrated, cleared in xylol, and imbedded in paraffin. The rotifers and planaria were sectioned at six micra and the gastrocnemius muscle of the toad was sectioned at eight micra. The sections were mounted on clean glass slides and placed in an electric furnace. As recommended by Scott, the initial temperature increase was effected slowly, 20 minutes being required to obtain a temperature of 100° C. The temperature was then raised to and kept at 600° C. for 30 minutes which was found to be adequate for complete volatilization of the organic substances. The slides were cooled very slowly and placed without cover glasses in clean slide boxes to make possible future chemical analysis of the incinerated material. No attempt was made to analyze other elements besides calcium although some measure of the iron content of the preparations could be obtained from inspection of the untreated slides. A reddish-yellow color in the untreated incinerated preparations indicated the presence of iron and the intensity of this color could be used as an index of the iron content.

Calcium was identified chiefly by means of the alizarin reaction. (Saturated aqueous sodium alizarin sulfonate reacts with calcium to form the red precipitate of calcium alizarinate.) Occasional checks on the alizarin reactions were made by means of the delicate gypsum reaction. The reagents used in this reaction were one microdrop of 0.1 N HCl followed by one microdrop of 0.1 N H_2SO_4 (Scott). The presence of calcium was indicated by the formation of needle-like crystals of calcium sulfate. Since there was a marked diffusion of salts following the HCl treatment, precise localization of calcium could not be effected by this reaction, and for that purpose the alizarin reaction was depended upon completely. There was no piling up of the granules of ash in the incinerated sections since the material was cut at six and eight micra; that is, the incinerated preparations were but one granule deep. Consequently, an increase in the number of granules which stain red after the alizarin treatment, and thus an increase in the intensity of the staining reaction could be taken to mean that the amount of calcium had increased. Similarly, an increase in the number of calcium sulfate crystals formed, using the alternative test, was taken as an index of an increase in the calcium content.

Slides of the various organisms were stained with Ehrlich's haematoxylin, and these preparations were compared with the incinerated material for the purpose of identifying structures. As will be brought out later in the paper, material stained with Ehrlich's haematoxylin may be used in direct determinations of the calcium content of the tissues with the intensity of staining as an index of the calcium content.

RESULTS

Bufo fowleri

The gastrocnemius muscle of the toad when incinerated furnishes a picture very similar to that obtained by Scott (1932) in his microincineration studies on striated muscle. The sarcolemma shows in young fibers as a very fine, white line of ash. The residual ash of the sarcolemma in many preparations is so slight as to be almost invisible. The ash of the sarcolemma in old muscle fibers is strikingly different from that of young tissue. Here the line of white ash is glaring and heavy. The striations show in young and old muscle fibers as parallel rows of discrete, small white granules. However, the granules in the striations of old muscle fibers are markedly larger than those in young muscle fibers. As observed by Scott, the isotropic bands or the J bands appear to be ash free. In these preparations no trace was found of the intermediate bands of the J striation, or the Z band, although Scott reports observing the ash skeleton of the Z striation in "favorable" material.

Tests with sodium alizarin sulfonate demonstrate that the nuclei of young and old muscle fibers are both rich in calcium. The large amounts of this cation present in the nuclei rendered it impossible to estimate quantitative differences between young and old muscle fibers. The sarcolemma of young muscle fibers after alizarin treatment shows the red color characteristic of calcium alizarinate and tests with the gypsum reaction reveal the needle-like crystals of calcium sulfate. Contrary to previous experience with other tissues it was possible to use the gypsum reaction for quantitative estimations of calcium because of the large size of the muscle fibers. The sarcolemma of old muscle fibers gives the same positive tests for calcium but consistently demonstrates a marked increase in calcium content, as indicated by an increase in the staining intensity with alizarin and an increase in the number of crystals formed in the gypsum reaction. Similarly, the striations of old muscles show a marked increase in the concentration of calcium over the striations of young muscle fibers. The nuclei of both young and old muscle fibers contain varying amounts of iron as indicated by the presence of reddish-yellow granules. Iron is also present in the striations of both young and old fibers and there appears to be an increase in the iron content of the striations with age.

Phagocata sp.

Incinerated preparations of this multipharyngeal planarian show an interesting variation in the total ash content of the various tissues. The epithelial lining of the body is richest in inorganics. The pharynges show a markedly low total inorganic content in contrast to the high salt content of the epithelium (Fig. 1). The ash in the pharynges is a dull bluish-white and is uniformly scant in the various tissue layers of these organs. However, the cell membranes of the cells lining the lumina of the pharynges contain considerably more ash than other regions of these organs. Throughout all the tissues and organs that were examined

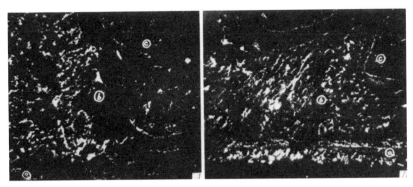

FIG. 1. Photomicrographs of incinerated preparations of *Phagocata*. Sections cut at 6 micra. (*A*) Young animal showing relatively large amounts of ash in the interstitial cells and small amounts of ash in the pharynges. (*B*) Old animal showing the increase in the ash content of the interstitial cells and the epithelial cells. Ash outline of some of the cells of the pharynges can be distinguished. Epithelium (*a*), Interstitial cells (*b*), Pharynx (*c*). Eastman "Contrast Process Panchromatic" film; 500-watt projection lamp; 15-second exposure, 200 magnification.

there was an increase in the total amount of ash with age. The basal membrane of the epithelial lining of the body in young animals is very thin and difficult to detect, but in old specimens the basal membrane is a glaring white line of ash. The increase in total ash content of the cell membranes of epithelial, interstitial (Fig. 1), and nerve cells is apparent. There appear to be no detectable changes in the total ash content of the rhabdites or the nuclei in the epithelial layer with age. This may be due to the fact that even young preparations are very rich in inorganics in these structures and an increase would be difficult to detect. The tissue layers of the pharynges, which as previously stated contain relatively little ash, show little or no increase with age in total ash content (Fig. 1).

Application of the chemical tests for calcium demonstrates that calcium increases with age in all the cells studied. The epithelial layer is rich in calcium in young as well as old specimens, but there is a marked increase in the calcium content of the cell membranes of the epithelial cells and basal membrane with age. There is an increase in the calcium content of the nuclei and cell membranes of the cells of the pharynges with age, but the change here is far less than it is in the epithelial layer. Repeated tests for calcium in the cells of the pharynges confirm this slight change with age in the calcium content. The cilia of the lining of the pharynges are apparent in most of the preparations but no changes in their calcium content could be observed. The most marked increase in calcium content with age in the cells of the pharynges occurs in the cell membranes of the cells lining the lumina. A pronounced increase in the calcium content of the interstitial and nerve cells was observed. Calcium increases with age in the nuclei, cytoplasm, and particularly the cell membranes of these cells.

Examination of the untreated incinerated slides indicates that the epithelial and interstitial cells, and the rhabdites are richest in iron content. The epithelial and nerve cells show no increase in iron content with age. The interstitial cells reveal an inconsistent fluctuation in iron content with age. The cytoplasm of these cells, in some preparations, shows an increase in iron content with age while in other preparations there was no perceptible difference in the iron content of young and old specimens.

The picture obtained in the animals of medium size was very similar to that found in the group of large planaria. However, the concentration of calcium in the various cells of the large planaria was somewhat greater than that found in the cells of the medium group.

Euchlanis dilatata

Incinerated preparations of this rotifer manifest the same age changes that were observed in *Phagocata*. There was no significant difference in the amount of total ash in the cells of the one- and two-day-old specimens. However, the three-day-old rotifers contained much more ash than did the younger material, and the amount of total ash increased still further in the four-day-old material.

Tests with sodium alizarin sulfonate and the gypsum reaction showed that the increase in the calcium content of the rotifers paralleled the total ash increase. Thus, the first indication of an increase in calcium content was observed in the three-day-old material and a further increase was found in the four-day-old rotifers. Difficulty was experienced in identifying the skeletons of the various cells in this rotifer and only the cells of the brain, gut, and ovary showed clearly in the incinerated preparations. This may be due to the fact that the animals contract some-what during the fixation process. Tests indicated that calcium increased markedly in the nuclei, cytoplasm and cell membranes of these cells in the three- and four-day-old rotifers. The cell membranes of the one- and two-day-old rotifers showed as thin rings delicately tinted with a red color after they were stained with alizarin. The cell membranes of the three- and four-day-old rotifer material showed as heavy rings of ash which were stained a deep red with the alizarin.

The iron content of the cells of *Euchlanis* appeared to vary some-what with age, but the iron changes were not as consistent as in *Phago-cata*. There was a distinct increase in the iron content of some of the four-day-old specimens over the younger material. On the other hand, specimens were found in which the iron content was higher in the two- and three-day-old material than it was in the four-day-old material. The iron was found to vary most in the nuclei and cell membranes.

Ehrlich's Haematoxylin

It was earlier stated that control slides were prepared which were stained with Ehrlich's haematoxylin. Routine checks made with these slides on incinerated preparations revealed a striking relationship be-tween the intensity of haematoxylin staining of the various cell types and the calcium distribution and content of these cells. In agreement with Scott (1933) it was found that structures rich in calcium as deter-mined by microincineration invariably stained a dark purple with the haematoxylin, and structures with a low calcium content stained but lightly. Thus, the cells of the pharynges of *Phagocata* were delicately stained with haematoxylin in contrast to the other body tissues of *Phago-cata* which stained heavily. As observed previously, the pharynges were very low in calcium content. The basal membrane of the epithelial layer of *Phagocata*, which analysis for calcium following microincineration proved to be rich in calcium, stained a dense purple with the haema-toxylin. Similarly, the cell membranes of the epithelial and interstitial cells which were demonstrated to be rich in calcium also stained very heavily with the haematoxylin. A comparison of stained slides of young and old planarian and toad material revealed that the old material under the same staining conditions invariably stained more heavily than did the young material, and that the regions that stained more heavily corre-sponded to those regions which manifest an increase in calcium content with age. This relation between the intensity of staining with Ehrlich's haematoxylin and the calcium content has been frequently observed by the author in various types of material.

The use of haematoxylin as an indicator for calcium has been criticized by Lison (1936) in his excellent book on histochemical methods. He states that the color reaction between haematoxylin and calcium is dependent upon the presence of aluminum, chromium or gold in the fixatives used. However, despite the fact that the reaction is indirect, the close correlation between the calcium content of a structure and the intensity of haematoxylin staining of that structure justifies the use of this simple staining procedure for the identification and localization of calcium in cells and tissues.

CONCLUSIONS

The present studies demonstrate that a calcium increase with age, observed in the cortex of *Elodea* cells (Lansing, 1942), occurs similarly in the cells of two invertebrates and in the muscle tissue of a vertebrate. The widespread occurrence of this localized calcium increase with age suggests that it is a general characteristic of the aging process.

Further development of the relation between calcium and aging from both a descriptive and experimental point of view will require an objective quantitative method for the determination and localization of calcium in cells. Further, since it has been demonstrated that calcium increases with age in many tissues and organs of mammals (Lansing, 1942), it would be pertinent to determine whether the calcium increase with age in mammals also takes place in the cell membranes.

SUMMARY

A rotifer, *Euchlanis dilatata*, a planarian, *Phagocata* sp., and toad, *Bufo fowleri*, were selected for an analysis of calcium localization and of possible calcium increase with age. Samples of animals of different ages were sectioned, incinerated and examined with a darkfield microscope. Calcium was identified by means of sodium alizarin sulfonate and the gypsum reaction. It was demonstrated that calcium increased with age in the cell membranes of all the cells studied. Calcium also increased with age in the nuclei and cytoplasm of nerve and interstitial cells of *Phagocata* and the cells of *Euchlanis*. Because of the large amounts of calcium present in the nuclei it was difficult to determine the degree of calcium increase.

The iron content of the various cells appeared to vary considerably but inconsistently with age.

Control slides stained with Ehrlich's haematoxylin showed a correlation between the intensity of staining of structures and the calcium content of those structures. The suggestion was made that Ehrlich's haematoxylin may be used as an indicator for bound calcium in cells.

LITERATURE CITED

HAMILTON, W. J., 1934. The rate of growth of the toad, Bufo americanus americanus Holbrook, under natural conditions. *Copeia,* No. 1, 88–90.

LANSING, A. I., 1938. Localization of calcium in Paramecium caudatum. *Science,* 87 : 303–304.

LANSING, A. I., 1942. Increase of cortical calcium with age in the cells of Elodea canadensis. *Biol. Bull.,* 82 : 385–391.

LISON, L., 1936. Histochimie Animale. Paris.

SCOTT, G. H., 1932. Distribution of mineral ash in striated muscle cells. *Proc. Soc. Exp. Biol. and Med.,* 29 : 349–351.

SCOTT, G. H., 1933a. The localization of mineral salts in cells of some mammalian tissues by micro-incineration. *Amer. Jour. Anat.,* 53 : 243–279.

SCOTT, G. H., 1933b. A critical study and review of the method of microincineration. *Protoplasma,* 20 : No. 1, 133–151.

SONNEBORN, T. M., 1936. Factors determining conjugation in Paramecium aurelia. I. The cyclical factor: The recency of nuclear reorganization. *Genetics,* 21 : 503–514.

35

Reprinted from *Science* 86:269–270 (1937)

CHANGES IN HUMAN TISSUE ELECTROLYTES IN SENESCENCE[1]

Henry S. Simms and Abraham Stolman
Columbia University Medical School

THERE are many reports of chemical alterations as animals increase in age up to maturity, but there have been few studies in which senescent animals have been compared with younger mature animals. We consider an animal to be senescent when it has lived three fourths of its maximum life span (taking one hundred years as the life span of humans) and that the younger mature animals used for comparison should be at least twice the age of sexual maturity.

For the analyses of human tissues which are reported in this paper two principal age groups were selected. The senescent group was seventy years old, or over, with an average of seventy-five years. The younger group, which served as a standard for comparison, consisted of individuals from thirty to forty years old, with an average of thirty-five years.

Tissues were obtained from autopsies, some from accident cases and others from pathological cases. These will be discussed separately. The accident cases[2] were people who appeared to have been in good health until killed suddenly by automobiles, by falling or by murder. Only those cases were analyzed where there had been a quick death uncomplicated by poisoning or intoxication. The analyses of eleven accident cases between the ages of thirty to forty years, with an average of thirty-five years, were taken as a standard for comparison with senescent tissues.

Table I represents the changes found in senescence. Tissues from six accident cases over seventy years old, having a mean age of seventy-five, were analyzed. Each value in Table I is the per cent. deviation from the standard values for younger tissues. It will be noted that, except for the heart water, there was an increase in water, chloride, total base, sodium and calcium. Furthermore, there was a decrease in potassium, magnesium, phosphorus, nitrogen and ash in all the tissues except the liver.[3]

[1] This investigation has been aided by a grant from the Josiah Macy, Jr., Foundation.

[2] The tissues from accident cases were obtained with the cooperation of Dr. Milton Helpern and other members of the Medical Examiner's Office of New York City.

[3] The values in Table I are calculated on a wet weight basis. When converted to a dry weight basis the positive values became even more significant, while the negative values became less significant. The nitrogen and ash did not decrease on a dry weight basis.

TABLE I
PER CENT. DIFFERENCES IN ANALYSES OF HUMAN TISSUES FROM ACCIDENT CASES OVER SEVENTY YEARS OLD RELATIVE TO TISSUES FROM ACCIDENT CASES THIRTY TO FORTY YEARS OLD

Constituent	Kidney	Liver	Spleen	Psoas muscle	Heart	Average of tissues
H_2O	+ 2.6	+ 1.7	+ 2.8	+ 0.8	– 1.4	+ 2. XH
Cl*	+(2)	+(18)	+(12)	+(56)	+(25)	+(23)
Total Base.	+ 3.	+ 12.	+ 4.	+ 6.	+ 7.	+ 7.
Na	+ 5.	+ 15.	+ 21.	+ 62.	+ 0.3	+ 20.
Ca	+60.	+ 4.	+ 14.	+ 33.	+ 31.	+ 28.
K	–19.	+ 6.	– 13.	– 7.	– 9.	– 12. XL
Mg	– 9.	+ 17.	– 10.	– 11.	– 2.5	– 8. XL
P	–13.	– 0.1	– 8.	– 12.	– 2.	– 9. XL
N	– 9.	+ 8.5	– 13.	– 3.	– 4.	– 7. XL
Ash	–11.	+ 1.	– 8.	– 1.	0.	– 5. XL

* The chloride values are less accurate than the other values in this table.
XH signifies that the average for the tissues does not include the heart.
XL signifies that the average for the tissues does not include the liver.

These changes in senescence were corroborated by our data on pathological cases obtained from autopsies in this department. Tissues from people over seventy years old were compared with tissues from people between thirty to forty years, all of whom died of disease. Eighty per cent. of the changes were in the same direction as those found with accident cases (Table I). These tissues were from patients who had died from the following diseases: carcinoma, nephritis, leucetic aortitis, brain abscess, arteriosclerosis and partial ileus. Pneumonia was a complication in three cases. Cases with severe infections or marked wasting were not taken and pathological organs were avoided as far as possible.

Partial further corroboration of the senescent changes was obtained by comparing another group of five pathological cases which were from sixty-five to seventy years old, with the young pathological cases. At this age only part of the changes were found, namely, those of total base, calcium, phosphorus and ash, with a moderate increase of chloride. On the other hand, these sixty-five to seventy year cases did not show significant changes of water, sodium, potassium, magnesium or nitrogen.

We do not consider these differences between old and young pathological tissues as being significant, except in so far as they substantiate the changes in old age found by the analyses of tissues from accident cases (Table I). In order to determine the effect of disease on the tissues the young pathological and accident cases were compared. Except for calcium, which was lower in the pathological tissues, there was a tendency toward changes in disease similar to those found in senescence. The magnitude of the changes in disease was less than in senescence, except in the case of magnesium. The present data do not warrant further comparisons. Extensive studies of tissue changes in selected diseases should be instructive. However, it is necessary to determine whether the differences found in tissues from patients dying of disease were produced progressivly with the advancement of the pathological condition or whether they arose in the terminal state preceding death.

These preliminary results are presented with no attempt to interpret their significance. Detailed analyses will be published after more data have been obtained. Only minor modifications of the average values for accident cases are to be expected as more tissues are analyzed. On the other hand, we do not claim that the analyses of pathological tissues are representative, but we feel that further work in that field would be profitable.

Summary

Analyses of tissues from people over seventy years old who died from accidents were compared with analyses of tissues from thirty to forty-year-old people who also died from accidents. The old tissues contained more water, chloride, total base, sodium and calcium; and they contained less potassium, magnesium, phosphorus, nitrogen and ash than the younger tissue.

Tissues from pathological cases of the same two age groups showed the same changes after seventy years. Only part of these changes were found in tissues sixty-five to seventy years old.

Tissues from young pathological cases when compared with accident cases of the same age were found to have undergone changes similar to those found in senescence, but to a lesser degree. Calcium formed an exception.

Editor's Comments
on Papers 36 Through 40

Since the enzymes (proteins) are central to metabolism of any organism, a large number of studies have been directed toward the question of alteration of enzyme activity with age.

In studies enumerated by Finch (1969, 1972) a number of different investigators have measured specific enzyme activities of livers and kidneys of olds rats or old mice. On balance, there is no consistent definitive alteration of the enzyme activities measured with age. Finch makes the point that significant change in enzyme activity may occur at any time in the lifespan and therefore to determine if a change is due to aging rather than due to growth or maturation, testing throughout the lifespan is required. An example from Finch's work: a liver enzyme activity in the fasting mouse decreased 40 percent between nine and sixteen months of age but did not change between sixteen and twenty-six months. If instead of getting this much information, that particular enzyme had been measured in nine-month-old and twenty-six-month-old animals, a difference would have been found (a decrease), but this alteration actually occurred during maturation rather than during aging! However, Finch did report finding a response lag, after application of an in vivo stimulus, in attaining the same degree of enzyme activity in old rats' livers compared with young rats' livers. This lag is due to extra-hepatic factors, said Finch; hormonal factors come into play later in the old organism than in the young. "These demonstrations . . . imply that the liver in a senescent mammal consists of cells, indifferent in age, which manifest changes during senility because of senescence in the regulation of extra-hepatic factors."

In Paper 36, R. C. Adelman also found that old tissues lag, in their response to perturbation, behind young tissues due to hormonal factors. However, Dr. Adelman's findings, contrasted with Dr. Finch's results, consist of a linear decline in the activity of the enzyme he studied as a function of age in the rat from two to twenty-four months (approximately equivalent to a study on six-year-old up to sixty-five-year-old humans). In summing the reports, Finch stated that there appear to be two different classes of age-related enzyme changes: *continuous* and *discontinuous*.

Here, again, many twentieth century investigators are concluding from their studies of basic metabolism that hormonal changes occurring in aging account for differences between young and old animals—basic features of aging lie within some selected small population of cells responsible for the production and release of hormones.

Medvedev (1962) related various studies and findings in the USSR indicating that regenerative ability while remaining high is slowed in rate in old tissues. He believes that for a given metabolic task, more energy is expended in old tissues. Many of Medvedev's experiments were on plants, which go in the same direction as animal tissues during the course of aging.

Perhaps surprising to some is the regenerative ability of the livers of old rats (25–26 months) when stimulated by partial hepatectomy, as reported by Drs. Bucher and Glinos (Paper 37). "The old rats equaled the adults in ability to regenerate liver mass but lagged behind somewhat in cell production." Here again the slower rate in older members of the population is noted and a later report from Dr. Bucher's laboratory gave the time course of the restoration of liver activity after the partial hepatectomy.

Paper 38 reports on one experimental test of ability to evoke shortened lifespan in the rat by procedures calculated to produce autoimmune disease.

Dr. W. S. Bullough compared mitotic activities in male mice of different ages and strains (Paper 39). His summation is, "It was discovered that, when judged from the point of view of mitotic activity the life of a male mouse consists of four ages. During the immature age the animals are still growing and their mitosis rate is generally high, . . . During the mature age which lasts from about the 3rd to the 12th month the mitosis rate is lowered. During the middle age which follows the mitosis rate increases, but in senility it is again reduced."

Ability of yet another system to respond was tested in healthy young and old humans (some of the patients were eighty years or greater in age) by an Australian group (Paper 40). Their findings support some impairment of the thymus dependent arm of the immune system in aging. Their findings also suggest that perhaps one measure of physiological age may be the immunological responsiveness of the individual.

36

Reprinted from *Nature* **220**:1005–1006 (1970)

REAPPRAISAL OF BIOLOGICAL AGEING

Richard C. Adelman

LIVING systems depend on adaptive regulation, deterioration in which leads eventually to death. The incidence of most disease increases with increasing age, which suggests that progressive impairment of adaptive response is associated with many illnesses common to advanced age. One biochemical expression of this impairment is the age-dependent increase in the time required to initiate certain enzyme inductions after administration of the appropriate inducing stimulus[1,2] (Table 1).

This biochemical parameter of ageing may provide a unique opportunity to investigate a sequence of events responsible for a particular ageing phenomenon. Recent evidence demonstrated that newly regenerated liver cells in ageing animals exhibit enzyme induction patterns characteristic of untreated animals of the same age[2,10]. So either the age-dependent modification of hepatic enzyme regulation must arise from a genetic alteration of the liver cell which is copied during the cell division induced by partial hepatectomy, or it is not inherent in the liver cell. Two independent observations suggest that the latter is the case. The induction of mouse liver tyrosine aminotransferase by exposure to cold, considered an adrenal steroid mediated process, exhibited an age-dependent lag period, whereas enzyme induction after

Table 1. REPORTED AGE-DEPENDENT ENZYME INDUCTIONS

Enzyme	Source	Inducing agent	Ref.
Glucokinase	Rat liver	Glucose	1
NADPH : cytochrome *c* reductase		Phenobarbital	2,3
NADPH oxidase			3
NADPH: neotetrazolium reductase			3
Cytochrome *P*-450			3
Aminopyrine *N*-demethylase			3
Hexobarbital hydroxylase			3
Aniline hydroxylase			3
p-Nitrobenzoic acid nitroreductase			3
Tyrosine aminotransferase	Mouse liver	Exposure to cold	4
Phosphoenolpyruvate carboxy-kinase	Rat adipose tissue	Fasting	5
NADPH : malate dehydrogenase		Fasting and refeeding	*
Citrate cleavage enzyme			*
Glucose 6-phosphate dehydrogenase			*
6-Phosphogluconate dehydrogenase			*
Glucose 6-phosphatase	Rat liver	Dexamethasone	6
Fructose 1,6-diphosphatase			6
Phosphofructokinase	Rat prostate, seminal vesicles	Testosterone	7
Tryptophan pyrrolase	Rat liver	Tryptophan	8
Tryptophan pyrrolase	Rabbit liver	Cortisol	9

* Unpublished results of R. W. Hanson.

Richard C. Adelman

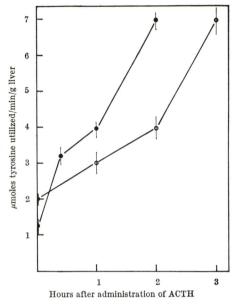

Fig. 1. The age-dependent induction of rat liver tyrosine aminotransferase. Tissue was prepared and enzyme activity assayed as described previously[14]. Each value represents the mean ±s.e. for at least four rats. The intraperitoneal dosage of ACTH was 2·5 units per 100 g of body weight. ●, 2 months old; ○, 18 months old.

administration of cortisol was independent of age[4]. Similarly, induction of rat liver glucokinase by glucose feeding, an insulin mediated process, exhibited an age-dependent lag, but enzyme induction by administration of insulin was independent of age (R. C. A., unpublished). Thus the ability of liver cells to respond to hormonal stimulation, unlike that of other cell-types such as adipose cells[11], is not an age-dependent phenomenon[2].

The role of endocrine function in the age-dependent modification of hepatic enzyme regulation is not clear. According to Finch *et al.*[4], the production of corticosterone by the adrenal glands in response to exposure to cold is not influenced by age. So the ageing modification involving tyrosine aminotransferase must occur between adrenal steroid production and hepatic enzyme induction. But the procedures available for accurate determination of functional serum hormone levels are questionable at best. An alternative approach recently developed by Adelman (R. C. A., unpublished) entails stimulation of the appropriate endocrine source and determination of circulating, functional hormone production as expressed by the time course of hepatic enzyme induction. Adrenal corticotrophic hormone (ACTH) administration resulted

300

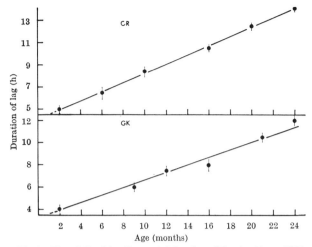

Fig. 2. The relationship of lag period duration of the glucokinase (GK) and NADPH : cytochrome *c* reductase (CR) inductions to chronological age of the rat. Tissue was prepared and enzyme activities assayed as described previously[1,2]. Each value represents the mean ±s.e. for at least four rats.

in a rapid, age-dependent increase in hepatic tyrosine aminotransferase activity (Fig. 1). Eighteen-month old rats required approximately twice as much time as 2 month-old rats to respond similarly to the same body-weight dosage of ACTH. If this enzyme induction was hormone mediated, then the endocrine function in question is influenced by age. It seems unlikely, however, that this induction was mediated by adrenal steroid. Whereas tyrosine aminotransferase activity peaked 4–5 h following administration of cortisol, the ACTH effect was observed in as little as 1 h and terminated after 3 h (R. C. A., unpublished). When the endocrine role in the age-dependent modification of hepatic enzyme regulation is resolved, the influence of sympathetic and parasympathetic innervation and of pituitary and hypothalamic function can be examined.

This general approach not only localizes the tissue of origin of the age-dependent modifications, but also contributes to comprehension of the ageing process(es). The unknown modification which is expressed as an increased lag period of hepatic enzyme induction was observed throughout the entire lifespan of the rat[2]. Looking at the chronological origin of this modification (Fig. 2), it is apparent that the briefest lag period for the inductions of glucokinase[1] and NADPH : cytochrome *c* reductase[2] coincides with the development of adult levels of these enzymes, approximately 15–30 days after birth[12,13]. It is tempting to speculate that the ageing phenomena which are expressed in adult liver and perhaps other tissues are the consequence of developmental phenomena in the foetal neuroendocrine regulatory system.

I thank Miss Kathleen Blasiak for technical assistance, and acknowledge the research support of the National Institutes of Health and the American Cancer Society.

RICHARD C. ADELMAN

Fels Research Institute and Department of
Biochemistry,
Temple University School of Medicine,
Philadelphia, Pennsylvania 19140.

Received June 24; revised August 17, 1970.

[1] Adelman, R. C., *J. Biol. Chem.*, **245**, 1032 (1970).
[2] Adelman, R. C., *Exp. Gerontol.* (in the press).
[3] Kato, R., and Takanaka, A., *J. Biochem.*, **63**, 406 (1968).
[4] Finch, C. E., Foster, J. R., and Mirsky, A. E., *J. Gen. Physiol.*, **54**, 690 (1969).
[5] Reshef, L., Hanson, R. W., and Ballard, F. J., *J. Biol. Chem.*, **244**, 1994 (1969).
[6] Singhal, R. L., *J. Gerontol.*, **22**, 77 (1967).
[7] Singhal, R. L., *J. Gerontol.*, **22**, 343 (1967).
[8] Haining, J. L., and Correll, W. W., *J. Gerontol.*, **24**, 143 (1969).
[9] Wu, S. Y., and Rosenthal, H. L., *Proc. Soc. Exp. Biol. Med.*, **122**, 414 (1966).
[10] Adelman, R. C., *Biochem. Biophys. Res. Commun.*, **38**, 1149 (1970).
[11] Rudman, D., and DiGirolamo, M., *Adv. Lipid Res.*, **5**, 35 (1968).
[12] Walker, D. G., and Holland, G., *Biochem. J.*, **97**, 845 (1965).
[13] Conney, A. H., *Pharmacol. Rev.*, **19**, 317 (1967).
[14] Singer, S., and Mason, M., *Biochim. Biophys. Acta*, **110**, 370 (1965).

Reprinted from *Cancer Research* **10**(5):324–332 (1950)

The Effect of Age on Regeneration of Rat Liver*

NANCY L. R. BUCHER, M.D., AND ANDRÉ D. GLINOS, M.D.

*(From the Medical Laboratories of the Collis P. Huntington Memorial Hospital of Harvard
University, at the Massachusetts General Hospital)*

Because cancer is frequently associated with aging, and with the processes of chronic injury and repair, it is important to estimate the type and amount of response to an effective growth stimulus that can occur in aging tissue. Accordingly, we have undertaken a study of the effects of age upon a regenerating tissue.

Rat liver was chosen for this purpose, because it can readily be induced to proliferate by means of partial hepatectomy. During the first 3 days after operation, it grows far faster than most neoplasms. In addition, its restorative capacity can be accurately measured.

It has usually been considered that the ability of tissues to regenerate decreases with age, and, as far as the liver is concerned, this concept has been borne out by the work of previous investigators. Norris, Blanchard, and Povolny (12) found that the rate at which liver mass was restored was far greater in young than in old rats. Marshak and Byron (10), studying the effect of age on mitosis, found that the interval between partial hepatectomy and the maximum mitotic count increased directly with the age of the animal. We have attempted to expand their findings by determining the rate of hepatic cell regeneration in rats of different ages.

METHOD

The present investigation is based upon the fundamental studies on liver regeneration initiated in this laboratory by Brues and his co-workers. Their procedure has been followed, with minor modifications (3).

Three groups of male and female albino rats of accurately known ages were used: (a) young rats, 4–6 weeks old, (b) adult rats, 4–8 months old, and (c) old rats, 21–30 months old (averaging $25\frac{1}{4}$ months). Most of the latter manifested emaciation, loss of hair, inertia, and other changes indicative of senility. The young rats weighed an average of 45 gm. (ranging from 25 to 78 gm.), the adult rats 233 (134–349), and the old rats 268 (170–488) gm.

Rats were starved for approximately 24 hours

* This work was supported by a grant from the American Cancer Society. This is publication No. 699 of the Harvard Cancer Commission.

Received for publication, January 21, 1950.

(18–26) before operation or autopsy. They were anesthetized with ether, and the median and left lateral lobes were removed. These were assumed to constitute 68.4 per cent of the total liver. This value is based upon the data of Brues *et al.* and confirmed by our own determinations on thirteen six-month-old rats, which yielded a mean value of 68.3 per cent $\pm$ 2.5. The animals were killed by exsanguination under ether anesthesia at intervals of 30 hours, 3, 7, and 14 days after operation. One set of results was expressed as per cent of original liver mass restored:

Per cent regeneration

$$= \frac{\text{weight of liver at autopsy}}{\text{weight of main lobes} \div 68.4 \text{ per cent}} \times 100.$$

These results were corrected for changes in the body weight of the rat during the period of regeneration. Tissues were fixed in Zenker's fluid and stained with eosin and methylene blue, or in Bouin's fluid and stained with hematoxylin and eosin. From counts of the nuclei of hepatic parenchymal cells in a measured area, in sections of known thickness cut from tissue blocks of known mass and volume, the number of such nuclei in the entire liver was estimated. Such counts were made on normal and regenerating livers, and a second set of results was expressed as per cent of the original number of hepatic nuclei restored.

Water content was estimated by drying small pieces of liver to constant weight in an oven at 95° C. In some instances it was also determined by means of an Abderhalden's drying pistol *in vacuo* at 78° C.

RESULTS

Restoration of liver mass.—The values for per cent restoration of liver mass in each age group are shown in Table 1. Following partial hepatectomy, all our rats consistently lost weight. The return of the two older groups of rats to their initial body weight level was variable and in many instances still incomplete at 14 days. Old rats were slower than adults; the former showed a mean loss of 6.2 per cent of their original weight by the end of the second week, and the latter a mean loss of 3.2 per cent. The young, growing rats, on the other hand, had returned to their original weight in 7 days. During the second week they gained tremendously —the increment amounting to an average of 39.3 per cent of their initial weight. For purposes of reasonable comparison between growing and non-growing animals, a correction for changes in body

the ratio to be 6.6 per cent for 50-gm. male rats and 6.08 per cent for 75-gm. rats. A correction for this additional factor would serve to exaggerate further the superior capacity of young rats to restore liver mass. The estimated magnitude of this correction in the young rats, based on Webster's

TABLE 1

PER CENT OF ORIGINAL LIVER MASS RESTORED

The standard deviations* and number of rats in each group are given at intervals after partial hepatectomy.

TIME AFTER OPERATION	YOUNG RATS		ADULT RATS		OLD RATS		YOUNG	ADULT	OLD
	No. of rats	Per cent restored (uncorr.)	No. of rats	Per cent restored (uncorr.)	No. of rats	Per cent restored (uncorr.)	Per cent restored (corrected for change in body weight)		
16 hrs.			7	36 ± 5	7	41 ± 10		38 ± 5	42 ± 11
30 hrs.	10	48 ± 8	7	46 ± 8	6	43 ± 7	56 ± 10	50 ± 10	45 ± 7
3 days	9	72 ± 10	11	60 ± 8	7	72 ± 7	78 ± 7	68 ± 10	75 ± 9
7 days	27	99 ± 22	21	82 ± 16	15	80 ± 11	98 ± 17	90 ± 16	86 ± 12
14 days	14	157 ± 21	16	89 ± 13	11	85 ± 9	113 ± 18	92 ± 14	91 ± 12

*Standard deviation: $s = \sqrt{\dfrac{\Sigma(x - \bar{x})^2}{n - 1}}$.

Where x is the individual observation, $\bar{x}$ is the mean and n is the number of rats.

weight during the period of regeneration seemed necessary. In order to treat the data uniformly, the correction was applied to the nongrowing as well as to the growing rats. Both uncorrected and corrected values are shown in Table 1. The correction caused no important alteration in the two older groups of rats, nor in the young rats, except at 14 days after operation, when body growth was very rapid. At the end of the second week of regeneration, correction for the tremendous weight gain in these young rats lowered the value from 157 to 113 per cent of original liver mass restored (Table 1). These results are summarized graphically in Figure 1. The old rats ran very close to the adults in rate of restoration of liver mass; no significant difference was demonstrable. The young rats, however, had a consistently higher rate throughout, finally reaching 113 per cent, as compared to 92 per cent for the adults. There was considerable variation among the individual rats in each group, as shown by the magnitude of the standard deviations (Table 1 and the vertical arrows in Fig. 1 at 7 and 14 days). In spite of this great variability, the difference between the young rats and the others seems to be a significant one, since the two older groups lagged behind throughout. On the basis of Fisher's formula for t (7), P was found to be less than 0.10 for the magnitude of the difference between young rats and adults at 7 days and less than 0.01 at 14 days.

The ratio of liver weight to body weight decreases as the rat grows (Webster *et al.* [16], and our own data in this experiment). Webster found

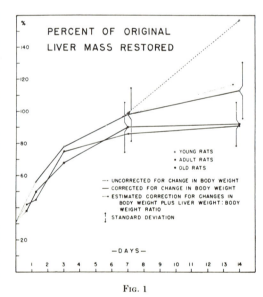

FIG. 1

data, is shown by the incomplete dotted line in Figure 1.

Restoration of hepatic cells.—The per cent restoration obtained in terms of the number of hepatic nuclei is shown in Table 2. Since endothelial, bile duct, and other cells were not counted, these values represent the ratio of the number of liver cell nuclei in the restored liver to the number in the original liver.

The correction for changes in body weight during the period of regeneration has not been applied to these data for two reasons: first, the total number of hepatic cells in a nongrowing rat is assumed to be relatively constant, and, unlike the liver mass, would not be expected to fluctuate with alterations in the animal's body weight and concomitant shifts in hepatic glycogen, fat, or protein

Table 2 shows that, within the limitations of the method, during the first 3 days no significant differences were demonstrable in the rate of replacement of hepatic nuclei. However, by the seventh day the adults and, particularly, the old rats had begun to lag behind the young ones. Since the young rats had just returned to their initial body

TABLE 2

PER CENT OF ORIGINAL NUMBER OF HEPATIC NUCLEI RESTORED

The standard deviation* and number of rats in each group are shown at intervals after partial hepatectomy.

TIME AFTER OPERATION	YOUNG RATS		ADULT RATS		OLD RATS	
	No. of rats	Per cent restored (uncorr.)	No. of rats	Per cent restored (uncorr.)	No. of rats	Per cent restored (uncorr.)
30 hrs.	4	28 ± 4	6	26 ± 3	6	24 ± 7
3 days	6	42 ± 8	10	45 ± 8	5	46 ±11
7 days	16	74 ±18	18	62 ± 7	14	51 ± 9
14 days	13	96 ±15	13	74 ±14	11	63 ± 7

* See footnote Table 1 for standard deviation.

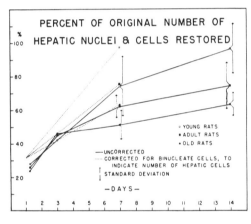

FIG. 2

storage; second, although the total number of liver cells does increase as the rat grows, this increment is not in direct proportion to the body weight. This second point may be clarified by the following considerations: the livers of the young rats contained approximately half as many hepatic cell nuclei as those of the adults. (We found a mean total of 326×10^6 hepatic parenchymal cell nuclei in the livers of young rats as compared to 651×10^6 in adults and 745×10^6 in old rats). On the other hand, the young rats had more than twice as many of these nuclei in proportion to their body weight (725×10^6/100 gm body weight as compared to 280×10^6 in the adults and 278×10^6 in the old rats). Thus, a simple correction for growth factors on a weight basis would not be justified.

weight at this point, growth factors did not have to be considered, and the lead they manifested can be considered valid. On the basis of Fisher's formula for t, the differences between young and adult, and adult and old rats, are all statistically significant ($P < 0.01$). By the fourteenth day, the young rats had still further increased their lead, having attained 96 per cent restoration as compared to 74 per cent for the adults and 63 per cent for the old rats. However, since the second postoperative week was a period of very rapid growth for these young animals, 96 per cent is undoubtedly too high a figure and should be corrected downward. Unfortunately, sufficient data are not available for arriving at an estimate of the true value.

These results are summarized by the solid lines in Figure 2, which represent rates at which hepatic nuclei are restored to their original numbers in each age group. These do not provide a satisfactory index of the rate of increase of hepatic cells, however, since in the young rats there are about twice as many binucleate cells as in the others.

Table 3 shows the incidence of binucleate cells in liver before and during regeneration. The results, based on random counts of 500–1,000 cells, were found to be quite consistent within each age group. There was a striking decrease in their numbers in all of the regenerating livers, as previously noted by Sulkin (15).

Since the values in Table 3 are derived from counts performed on histological sections, they are only relative. It is obvious that the true numbers of binucleate cells would be considerably higher, because the diameters of single nuclei (6–12μ) are greater than the thickness of the slice (6 μ), and, accordingly, many of the pairs will be separated by the sectioning process. Furthermore, the larger the cells, the less chance there is of including both nuclei in a section of uniform thickness; thus, an error is introduced because of variations of cell size, both with age and with the process of regeneration.

62 per cent for adults, and 51 per cent for old rats, they then become 97 per cent, 75 per cent, and 63 per cent, respectively, and are shown by the dotted lines in Figure 2.

With respect to restoration of hepatic cells, then, it may be said that, as in the case of liver mass, the adult rats are inferior to the young in regenerative capacity. In addition, the lag appears

TABLE 3

PER CENT OF BINUCLEATE CELLS

Relative percentages of binucleate cells in resting and regenerating livers of rats in three age groups, showing standard deviations* and number of rats in each group. These figures are based upon counts made on sections cut at 6 μ and are approximately ⅓ of the true values (St. Aubin and Bucher, unpublished).

TIME AFTER OPERATION	YOUNG RATS		ADULT RATS		OLD RATS	
	No. of rats	Per cent	No. of rats	Per cent	No. of rats	Per cent
0	23	22.4 ± 5.6	25	9.3 ±1.8	21	12.0 ± 2.7
30 hrs.	4	10.9 ± 2.3	5	6.6 ±0.42	5	6.2 ± 1.6
3 days	6	2.4 ± 1.9	8	2.2 ±0.97	6	5.8 ± 1.5
7 days	5	7.8 ± 3.2	6	2.1 ±0.76	4	4.9 ± 1.9
14 days	8	10.4 ± 2.9	9	5.9 ±2.9	7	5.9 ± 1.8

* See footnote Table 1 for standard deviation.

On the basis of an entirely different technic, by which whole liver cells are separated and then examined for the number of nuclei (St. Aubin and Bucher, unpublished), it was found that the actual percentages of binucleate cells were approximately 3 times the relative values shown in Table 3.

These later studies, which are still incomplete, indicated that in resting livers the incidence of binucleate cells was 58 per cent for young rats, 31 per cent for adult rats, and 35 per cent for old rats. The percentages remained unchanged, while no increased mitoses occurred during the first 24 hours after partial hepatectomy; but as mitosis became active they decreased abruptly. The percentages in regenerating liver had dropped to 16 per cent, 10 per cent, and 13 per cent, respectively, after 7 days.

If these percentages are applied to the values for the total number of hepatic nuclei in each liver, the total number of liver cells can readily be calculated. The rate of restoration in terms of actual cells will then be found to increase somewhat in all groups, since binucleate cells are more numerous in resting than in regenerating liver. The young rats, however, will exhibit a far greater increment than the others, so that in terms of cell restoration they will again far surpass both the other groups. To demonstrate the magnitude of this factor, the results have been calculated from average values for all three groups at the seventh day after partial hepatectomy; instead of 74 per cent for young rats,

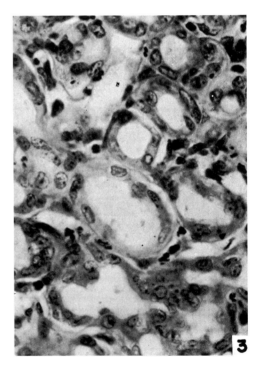

FIG. 3.—Cluster of hyperplastic bile ducts in the liver of a 1¾-year-old rat. (Zenker's fix. Eosin-methylene blue stain) ×700.

to be even more pronounced in the old rats. It should be noted that the old rats often had tumors and other conditions tending to debilitate them, as well as a much higher incidence of histological abnormalities in their livers. Nevertheless, the results suggest that advancing age produces at least some degree of additional impairment in the capacity to restore hepatic cells.

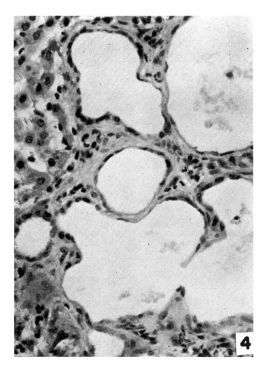

FIG. 4.—Cysts in the liver of a 2-year-old rat. (Zenker's fix. Eosin-methylene blue stain) ×350.

Histological findings.—The resting livers of the old rats showed no definitive characteristics by which they could invariably be recognized. However, certain abnormalities, which were never seen in the young and which were rare and of minor degree in the adult, were found to be relatively common among the old rats. These changes consisted chiefly of hyperplastic clusters of small, round bile ducts, and of single or multiple thin-walled cysts which were surrounded by fibrous stroma (Figs. 3 and 4).

No marked alterations, such as the nuclear inclusions found in senile mice by Andrew, Brown, and Johnson (1), or the syncitial cords seen by MacNider (9) in old dogs, were found to develop in the parenchymal cells with aging. The livers of the young rats, on the other hand, were distin-

guishable by the smaller size of the parenchymal cells, large numbers of which were binucleate (Figs. 5 and 7).

Occasional aggregations of cells occurred in the periportal areas in rats of all ages—infrequently in the young and often in the old. These infiltrations seemed to consist of leukocytes and mononuclear cells, including macrophages sometimes laden with pigment, fibroblasts, lymphoid cells, etc., in variable numbers and proportions (Fig. 9). Periportal infiltrations of connective tissue cells and lymphocytes were found by Andrew, Brown, and Johnson (1) to be characteristic of senile mouse livers.

The changes taking place in the histological appearance of the liver during regeneration have been carefully described by numerous investigators (13, 6, 3, 4, 2, 15, and many others). There is

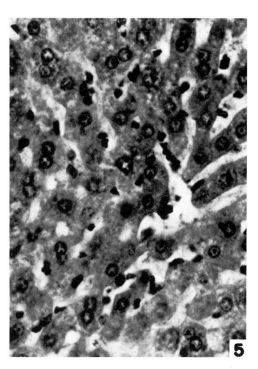

FIG. 5.—Resting liver of a 5-week-old rat. Note small size of cells and nuclei, and large number of binucleate cells. (Zenker's fix. Eosin-methylene blue stain) ×700.

a variable but marked increase in cell and nuclear size, which is apparent late in the first day. The liver cells fill with fat globules, especially in the periportal areas. After 24 hours, mitotic figures appear, scattered throughout the lobules. The increase in cell size and number soon leads to a crowding and irregularity in the alignment of the parenchymal cells that is characteristic of regenerating liver, although the fundamental architecture of the lobule is preserved. The basophilia of the liver cell cytoplasm deepens markedly. Binucleate cells, normally common, become scarce. Figures 6 and 8 show such changes in the regenerating liver of a young rat and an old rat, respectively.

As the hyperplasia progresses, the regenerative changes gradually recede, so that, after 2 weeks, they are much harder to observe.

The alterations just described were found to occur in all three age groups in our series, and no essential differences in the over-all pattern of regeneration were observed in most rats. The abnormalities that did occur were found occasionally in the old rats, seldom in the adults, and almost never in

our series, because the regenerative rate did not seem to be greatly altered in the rats having these lesions. With one exception they all fell within the same ranges as corresponding rats with histologically normal livers.

The average nuclear diameters which were found in resting liver and at intervals after operation are shown in Table 4. The young rats had

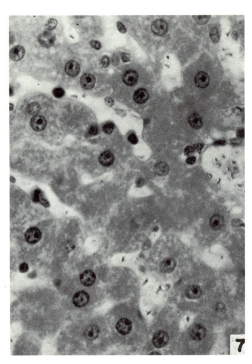

FIG. 7.—Resting liver of a 2½-year-old rat. Note larger size of cells and nuclei as compared with Fig. 5. (Zenker's fix. Eosin-methylene blue stain) ×700.

definitely smaller nuclei throughout. A marked relative increase in diameter was found in all three groups at 30 hours after operation, and, although somewhat diminished, this enlargement still persisted at 14 days. There was close agreement between the old rats and the adults.

The average number of hepatic nuclei per cubic millimeter of tissue is shown in Table 5. A marked decrease occurred in all groups during the period of regeneration. According to Stowell (14), who applied Chalkley's method of tissue analysis to this problem, the area occupied by vascular tissue is greatly diminished in regenerating liver. This finding no doubt reflects the crowding-in of newly formed liver cells upon the sinusoids, which is a striking feature of the microscopic picture. At any rate, the decrease in the number of hepatic nuclei

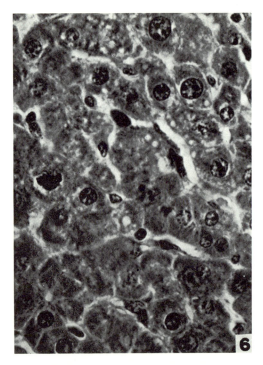

FIG. 6.—Regenerating liver from 5-week-old rat, 3 days after partial hepatectomy. Note cellular and nuclear enlargement and scarcity of binucleate cells. Numerous fat droplets. Mitotic figure at left. (Zenker's fix. Eosin-methylene blue stain) ×700.

the young. They consisted of scattered focal necroses and periportal infiltrations of cells which spread out to invade the surrounding parenchyma (Fig. 10). Tiny focal necroses with collections of wandering cells have occasionally been found in resting livers of supposedly normal rats in our laboratory. These animals were not discarded from per unit volume of tissue does not represent a mere dilatation of sinusoids, but, rather, it reflects both the increase in cell size and the decrease in binucleate cell content which occur during regeneration. The adult and old rats were closely parallel except at 7 days when the old rats also exhibited the

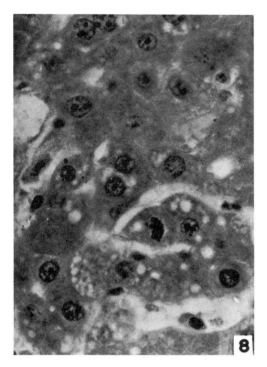

FIG. 8.—Regenerating liver from 2½-year-old rat 3 days after partial hepatectomy. Note numerous fat globules, marked nuclear enlargement, and mitotic figure. Changes are similar to those shown in Fig. 6. (Zenker's fix. Eosin-methylene blue stain) ×700.

greatest lag in cell restoration, as noted above. By 14 days, they were both approaching normal. The young rats, with smaller cells, many more of which were binucleate, showed higher values throughout. The persistence of cell enlargement in the young rats at 14 days is probably partly a result of the increase in cell size that occurs with body growth.

The determinations of wet and dry weight of tissue yielded no data suggesting that changes in water content were of any importance in producing the major differences in regeneration between the three groups.

DISCUSSION

Our results differ in some respects from those of previous investigators. With regard to restoration of liver mass, Norris, Blanchard, and Povolny (12), using weight of the rat as an index of age, found that young rats (under 100 gm.) responded with an excessive overgrowth, their livers increasing to 145 per cent of the original weight in 7 days. Large rats (over 250 gm.) showed a slow rise to only 95 per cent in 9 days, while intermediate rats reached a peak of 120 per cent at 8 days. No corrections were made for changes in body weight during the period of regeneration. The exceedingly rapid regeneration exhibited by young rats, in their experiment, was also found to occur in our series; this finding persisted, although in a lesser degree, even after our data were corrected for body growth (Fig. 1).

In our colony, where body weight was not found a reliable criterion of age, we did not find significant differences in restoration of liver mass between

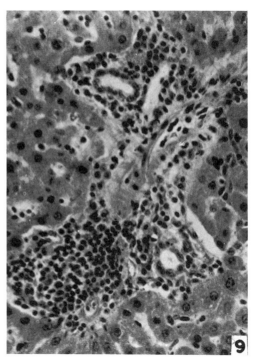

FIG. 9.—Periportal cellular infiltration in the resting liver of a 2⅓-year-old rat. (Zenker's fix. Eosin-methylene blue stain) ×350.

adult and old rats, although the average age of our old rats exceeded 2 years. It is well known that under highly favorable conditions albino rats can survive for over 3 years, but this is not usual in our climate (5). McCay (11) cites the mean life span of the albino rat as 600 days, and this approximates the usual duration of life in our colony. The old rats used in this present investigation represent survivors of a much larger group, many of which died, apparently of old age, during the several months preceding the experiment. Hence, it seemed justifiable to consider our rats as old.

With respect to the ability to regenerate new liver cells, our findings indicate a definite decrease with age. Adult rats are greatly inferior to young ones, and old rats even more so (Fig. 2). It is not

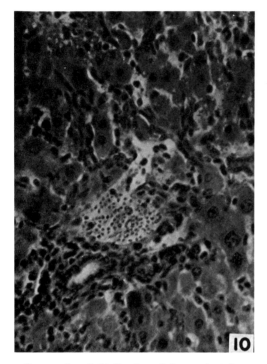

FIG. 10.—Spread of infiltrating cells from periportal areas into surrounding parenchyma. Atypical pattern occasionally seen in certain areas of regenerating livers of old and adult rats. This is from a 2½-year-old rat, 2 weeks after partial hepatectomy. (Zenker's fix. Eosin-methylene blue stain) ×350.

clear whether the superior capacity of the young animals in this regard is related to the fact that, since they are already in a state of active growth, the added factor of regeneration produces a kind of summation of stimuli, or whether there is merely a progressive decline with age. Possibly, the finding of Marshak and Byron (10) supports the latter idea. They found that age increasingly delayed the initiation of mitosis in regenerating livers. Similarly, Glinos (8), working with tissue cultures of normal rat liver, found a progressive decline in growth capacity with age. On the other hand, he also found that, although resting liver of old rats failed to grow in such cultures, regenerating liver from the same animals grew fully as well as that of young controls. This astonishing increase in proliferative capacity in old rats could still be demonstrated at 45 days after partial hepatectomy, which was many weeks after vigorous mitotic activity had ceased. These findings suggest that certain conditions may arise in a growing liver that enable it to respond more effectively than a resting liver to an additional growth stimulus.

The regenerative capacity may be appraised in various ways. Measurement of restoration of tissue mass does not differentiate between deposition of substances in cells and true growth. The mitotic count provides an index of growth activity at any single moment, but since growth may proceed in waves, the count does not necessarily represent the over-all rate at which a given liver is actually regenerating. The increase in the total number of nuclei during a certain period of time provides more specific information on this latter point; growth is then defined in terms of functional biological units, rather than simple mass. Estimation of regeneration of whole cells is a further refinement of this concept.

The part played by binucleate cells is obscure. They are remarkable for the constancy with which their number characterizes each age group and the

TABLE 4

AVERAGE NUCLEAR DIAMETER (MICRA)

Average nuclear diameters in resting and regenerating livers of rats in three age groups, showing standard deviations* and number of rats in each group.

TIME AFTER OPERATION	YOUNG RATS		ADULT RATS		OLD RATS	
	No. of rats	Nuclear diameter (micra)	No. of rats	Nuclear diameter (micra)	No. of rats	Nuclear diameter (micra)
0	42	6.0 ±0.42	45	7.3 ±0.48	35	7.2 ±0.44
30 hrs.	4	8.0 ±0.28	6	9.0 ±0.59	6	8.9 ±0.92
3 days	6	7.6 ±0.79	10	9.0 ±0.62	5	8.8 ±0.66
7 days	18	7.3 ±0.36	18	8.2 ±0.41	14	9.0 ±1.35
14 days	13	7.6 ±0.57	13	8.4 ±0.45	11	8.4 ±0.72

* See footnote Table 1 for standard deviation.

drastic reduction which occurs in all groups during the process of regeneration. Whatever their significance, it should be noted that the ability to restore liver, by rats of different ages, varies considerably, depending on whether nuclei or cells are regarded as the basic functional unit by which the degree of regeneration is to be evaluated. The trend appears to be in the direction of restoration, not only of the original cell number, but also of the original degree of binuclearity.

SUMMARY AND CONCLUSIONS

Regeneration of the liver following partial hepatectomy has been studied in three groups of rats: young, adult, and old. The livers of the young rats exhibited smaller cells and a much higher degree of binuclearity. Those of the old rats were often indistinguishable from the adults, although they did

REFERENCES

1. ANDREW, W.; BROWN, H. M.; and JOHNSON, J. B. Senile Changes in the Liver of Mouse and Man, with Special Reference to the Similarity of the Nuclear Alterations Am. J. Anat., 72:199–221, 1943.
2. BEAMS, H. W., and KING, R. L. The Origin of Binucleate and Large Mononucleate Cells in the Liver of the Rat. Anat. Rec., 83:281–97, 1942.
3. BRUES, A. M.; DRURY, D. R.; and BRUES, M. C. A Quantitative Study of Cell Growth in Regenerating Liver. Arch. Path., 22:658–73, 1936.
4. BRUES, A. M., and MARBLE, B. B. An Analysis of Mitosis in Liver Restoration. J. Exper. Med., 65:15–27, 1937.
5. FARRIS, E. J. The Rat in Laboratory Investigation, p. 4. Edited by J. Q. Griffith, Jr., and E. J. Farris. Philadelphia: J. B. Lippincott Co., 1942.
6. FISHBACK, F. C. A Morphologic Study of Regeneration of the Liver after Partial Removal. Arch. Path., 7:955–77, 1929.
7. FISHER, R. A. Statistical Methods for Research Workers. 10th ed. Edinburgh: Oliver & Boyd, 1946.

TABLE 5
AVERAGE NUMBER OF HEPATIC NUCLEI × 10³ PER CUBIC MILLIMETER

Average number of hepatic nuclei × 10³ per cubic millimeter of fixed tissue in resting and regenerating livers of rats in three age groups, showing standard deviations* and number of rats in each group.

TIME AFTER OPERATION	YOUNG RATS		ADULT RATS		OLD RATS	
	No. of rats	Nuclei (×10³)	No. of rats	Nuclei (×10³)	No. of rats	Nuclei (×10³)
0	42	267 ± 62	47	135 ± 32	36	138 ± 21
30 hrs.	4	122 ± 11	6	71 ± 10	6	80 ± 19
3 days	6	169 ± 36	10	87 ± 13	5	89 ± 14
7 days	18	162 ± 44	18	144 ± 18	14	83 ± 19
14 days	13	156 ± 34	13	109 ± 14	11	102 ± 20

* See footnote Table 1 for standard deviation.

frequently show certain abnormalities which were rare in the younger animals. During regeneration, the changes in the histological picture were similar in all three groups.

In young rats, regeneration was superimposed upon the normal process of body growth; hence, this group was not strictly comparable to the others. When corrections were made for the various factors associated with growth, however, it seemed that these rats still greatly exceeded the others, in ability both to restore liver mass and to form new cells.

The old rats equaled the adults in ability to regenerate liver mass but lagged behind somewhat in cell production.

ACKNOWLEDGMENTS

We are grateful to Dr. Joseph C. Aub for advice and encouragement in this work, to Mrs. Marie Scott for assistance in performing nuclear counts, and to Mr. Peter Thomson for wet and dry weight determinations on tissues.

8. GLINOS, A. D. The Effect of Regeneration on the Growth Capacity of Rat Liver *in vitro*. Anat. Rec., 103:456, 1949, and unpublished data.
9. MACNIDER, W. DEB. Problems of Aging, pp. 670–79. Ed. by E. V. Cowdry. Baltimore: Williams & Wilkins Co., 1942.
10. MARSHAK, A., and BYRON, R. L., JR. The Use of Regenerating Liver as a Method of Assay. Proc. Soc. Exper. Biol. & Med., 59:200–202, 1945.
11. MCCAY, C. M. Problems of Aging, p. 684. Ed. by E. V. Cowdry. Baltimore: Williams & Wilkins Co., 1942.
12. NORRIS, J. L.; BLANCHARD, J.; and POVOLNY, C. Regeneration of Rat Liver at Different Ages. Arch. Path., 34:208–17, 1942.
13. PONFICK, E. Über Leberresection und Leberrecreation. Verhandl. d. deutsch. Gesellsch. f. Chir., 19:28–30, 1890.
14. STOWELL, R. E. Nucleic Acids and Cytologic Changes in Regenerating Rat Liver. Arch. Path., 46:164–78, 1948.
15. SULKIN, N. M. A Study of the Nucleus in the Normal and Hyperplastic Liver of the Rat. Am. J. Anat., 73:107–25, 1943.
16. WEBSTER, S. H.; LILJEGREN, E. J.; and ZIMMER, D. J. Organ: Body Weight Ratios for Livers, Kidneys and Spleens of Laboratory Animals. I. Albino Rat. Am. J. Anat., 81:477–513, 1947.

38

Reprinted from *Ala. J. Med. Sci.* **10**:281–284 (1973)

Is Aging An Autoimmune Disease? Failure To Decrease Lifespan Of The Female Rat By Long Term Intermittent Adjuvant Administration

J. D. Emerson* and G. M. Emerson**

ABSTRACT

A lifespan study of six month old female rats was conducted. Forty-four rats were treated with various antigens and adjuvant components at several intervals throughout the remainder of their lifespan whereas 70 non-injected controls were followed for comparison. No life shortening effect of the treatments was observed and there was no alteration of pathology present at post-mortem examination. One treated group (emulsion controls) had a greater lifespan than the controls and the other treated groups (P=0.012 and less). We concluded that these experiments fail to reveal an autoimmune basis of aging.

INTRODUCTION

One theory of aging holds that senility is a disseminated type of autoimmune disease (Walford, 1969; Ram, 1967; and Blumenthal and Berns, 1964). If this be the case, then use of potent adjuvants such as Freund's in human therapy or prophylaxis would be potentially hazardous in that it would accelerate aging. Such adjuvant techniques are now used in allergic de-

#Supported in part by American Cancer Society Grant T-302 A and in part by U.A.B. Private Donations Fund 55-7922; 97-7922.

*Professor of Physiology and Biophysics. Deceased September 22, 1971. (Correspondence should be addressed to GME).

**Department of Physiology & Biophysics and Department of Biochemistry, University of Alabama in Birmingham, Medical Center, Birmingham, Alabama 35294.

sensitization and offer promise for use in cancer immunotherapy, active immunization against viruses, bacteria and bacterial toxins. For this reason, as well as providing a means of testing the autoimmune theory, we undertook this study to determine whether or not administration of adjuvants, and the individual components of adjuvants, accelerated the aging process. We report the lifetime study of female rats repeatedly injected from young adulthood with homologous tissue in mycobacteria containing adjuvants. Others have reported serious and often fatal autoimmune disease following injection of heterologous, homologous and isologous homogenates of brain, kidney, or thyroid in potent adjuvants (Olitsky and Lee, 1953; Levine and Wenk, 1963; Shaw, et al., 1964; Heyman, et al., 1959; Weigle, 1965; Lee and Schneider, 1962; and Rose, et al., 1965). In our study, as detailed below, we failed to find acceleration of the aging process.

MATERIAL AND METHODS

Experimental animals: One hundred fourteen young nulliparous female rats, of mean age 179 days, were divided into 5 groups as set forth in Table I. These were a substrain of Long-Evans rats maintained in our closed colony laboratory for 20 years. The animals were housed under conditions necessary for doing lifetime studies. Table II below sets forth the treatment regimen of these animals which occured during a period of 456 days. All animals were followed from onset until the last animal died 1034 days after the first injection initiating the project for this population of 114 rats. Each animal was allowed to die of "natural" causes. Whenever the condition of the carcass permitted, an autopsy was performed. Calculation of lifespan and pathology present at death were performed and statistically evaluated by group comparison and Chi Square analysis. During their lifetime, joints of these animals were evaluated since adjuvant arthritis has been observed following treatment of animals with mycobacterta in oil, during pertussis produced lymphocythemia, even without antigen (Waksman, et al., 1960; Pearson, et al., 1963; and Klamer, 1965).

Adjuvant and other materials: Old Tuberculin (O. T.) was used as purchased from the Pharmacy. Group 4 animals received 0.1 ml. intradermally, containing 10 mg., as pre-treatment and Group 2 and 3 received the same dose on the same date as Group 4. *Bacillus Calmette Guerin* (BCG) live, 3 mg. wet weight equivalent (7.2 x 10^6 viable organisms), was injected intraperitoneally into Group 3 rats as pre-treatment. This BCG was kindly supplied by Dr. Sol R. Rosenthal, Tice Laboratory, University of Illinois Institution for Tuberculosis Research. *Mycobacterium Smegmatis* (MS) heat killed, pulverized and suspended in oil, was injected into Group 2 rats at a dose of 0.3 mg. per rat, pre-treatment. This was the mycobacterial component of the adjuvant because of its reported superior potency (Shaw, et al., 1964 and Freund, et al., 1948) and its extensive use in Freund's adjuvant in man without acute ill effects (Graham and Graham, 1962). *Oil* used to suspend the mycobacteria is a light mineral oil, Humble Oil Company product Bayol 55 (or Bayol F). *Arlacel A,* Atlas Powder Company product, was the emulsifier used. *Antigens* consisted of all those macromolecules present in a fibroadenoma removed from a colony rat. The tissue had been homogenized, frozen and thawed a number of times until no intact cells remained. Additionally, a pituitary mammotrophic tumor, originating in

TABLE I.   Treatment Groups and Mean Age

Group Number and Description	Number in Group	Age (days) at Onset Mean ± Std. Error
1. Control No treatment	70	179 ± 0.92
2. Mycobacterium smegmatis pre-treatment (M.S.)	13	182 ± 1.6
3. Bacillus Calmette Guerin pre-treatment (B.C.G.)	13	175 ± 3.0
4. Old Tuberculin pre-treatment (O. T.)	15	177 ± 2.5
5. Emulsion Controls. No pre-treatment	3	184 ± 0.0

TABLE II.   Injection Protocol

Group	Day 0	19	48	54	95	101	124	308	313	397	402	456
1	Nil	Nil	Nil	Nil	Nil	Nil	Nil	Nil	Nil	Nil	Nil	Nil
2	M.S.	O.T.	Pert.	Emul.	Pert.	Emul.	Pert.	Pert	Emul.	Pert.	Emul.	Pert.
3	BCG	O.T.	Pert.	Emul.	Pert.	Emul.	Pert.	Pert	Emul.	Pert.	Emul.	Pert.
4	Nil	O.T.	Pert.	Emul.	Pert.	Emul.	Pert.	Pert	Emul.	Pert.	Emul.	Pert.
5	Nil	Nil	Nil	Emul.	Nil	Emul.	Nil	Nil	Emul.	Nil	Emul.	Nil

Groups are identical to those set out in Table I. Abbreviations are as given in Table I.

Dosages are: M. S. 0.3 mg. in 0.1 ml. Bayol 55.

O. T. 10 mg. Old Tuberculin, as packaged.

Pert. USP aqueous Pertussis Vaccine: day 48, 0.5 ml.; day 95, 0.4 ml.; day 124, 0.4 ml. all further treatments were with 10 times the concentration of the commercially packaged material and this was purchased directly from Lilly (Eli Lilly & Company, Indianapolis, Indiana): day 308, 0.3 ml.; day 397, 0.3 ml.; day 456, 0.3 ml.

Emulsion 0.3 ml.

another rat strain but which had been passaged through our rats a number of generations, was used and was prepared by the identical procedure as above to render it cell free. *Emulsion* consisted of M.S. suspended in 5 parts mineral oil/ 1 part Arlacel A. An equal volume of mixed homogenate was added. Emulsification was achieved by ultrasonic vibration with a cold probe (-50°C) serving as heat sink. The final composition was: 5 mg. M.S./ 60 mg. tissue per milliliter. Dosage was 0.3 ml. of emulsion. *Pertussis*, USP aqueous vaccine, was used as purchased from the Pharmacy except for injections during the latter part of the experiment. The last 3 injections consisted of a specially prepared (by Eli Lilly and Company) Pertussis vaccine which was 10 times the usual concentration.

RESULTS

During the lifetime of the animals, approximately 50% (6/13) of the M.S. group had joint enlargement following their initial injection. However, it subsided and no further swelling was seen in this group for the duration of their lifetime. No joint enlargement was seen in the other groups during their lifetime. Evaluations were made at least every other day for the duration of the experiment. No long term

residual effect of any treatment regimen was seen. As evidenced in Table III, there was no life shortening effect in any of the treatment groups compared with the controls. The group 5 animals (emulsion controls) actually exceeded the lifespan of all other groups, including the controls (P = 0.012 and less). There was no significant differences in the pathology present at autopsy in any of the groups. Therefore we conclude that these experiments fail to substantiate a universal autoimmune etiology of aging.

DISCUSSION

The experiments reported were instituted in female rats, approximately 180 days of age. It is possible on the basis of one's concept of aging to suggest that some other age would have been more appropriate. However, if one considers the question by comparison of rat age to human age, giving a ratio of 1 year of rat life to 30 years of human life, most would agree that starting the injections in these rats at an age approximately equivalent to 15 years in the human, would cover the span during which most aging changes are exhibited. This would be the period of life when overall anabolism had ceased and maintenance of the adult organism had begun. These were our reasons for choos-

TABLE III.   Lifespan and Pathology Present at Death

Group	Lifespan (days) Mean ± S. E. M. (Range)	Joint Enlargement	Pathology Present At Autopsy Tumor	Ventricular Dilatation
			number with/number autosied	
1	935 ± 23 (230 to 1218)	15/68	38/68 (45 tumors)	42/68
2	875 ± 47 (486 to 1078)	0/12	3/12 (3 tumors)	7/12
3	876 ± 54 (484 to 1120)	1/13	7/13 (8 tumors)	8/13
4	888 ± 43 (494 to 1094)	2/13	6/13 (7 tumors)	5/13
5	1077 ± 58 (999 to 1163)	1/3	2/3 (2 tumors)	3/3

ing this age of 180 days to institute these injections.

Injection of homologous normal and altered tissue (fibroadenoma should contain many normal and some altered macromolecules) in potent adjuvants and under conditions presumed to increase the immunologic reactivity of the recipients should provide a clearcut answer as to a general autoimmune etiology of aging. Additionally, autologous antigens should have been tested under the circumstances of these experiments since the adjuvant components would have come into intimate contact with many surface antigens of the recipients. There has been fear of using potent adjuvants of the Freund type and especially in conjunction with pertussis vaccine for various human immunizations because of the possibility of autoimmune disease resulting from interaction of the adjuvant at the injection site with the normal tissue of the recipient. The experiments herein reported demonstrate that under these conditions, no such effect results. These are especially interesting because the recipients were female rats and in the human population incidence of autoimmune disease is higher in females. Our experiments should have accelerated the generalized pathology of old age and decreased life span if normal aging results from the development of some immunologic reaction to the individual's own tissue during the course of life. By any mechanism advanced to date to account for autoimmune phenomena, these experiments failed to substantiate autoimmune etiology of aging. Furthermore, they indicate that under analogous conditions to those herein reported, use of such adjuvants can safely be made without incurring autoimmune disease.

CONCLUSION

Injection of potent adjuvants over the lifespan of a group of female rats failed to give increased incidence of autoimmune

disease or shortened lifespan. We feel therefore that the autoimmune theory must be rejected as the etiologic basis of aging.

REFERENCES

Blumenthal, Herman T. and Aline W. Berns, 1964. Autoimmunity and Aging. *Advances in Gerontological Research*, 1:289-342.

Freund, Jules; K. J. Thompson; H. B. Hough; H. E. Sommer; and T. M. Pisani, 1948. Antibody Formation and Sensitization With The Aid of Adjuvants. *J. Immunol.*, 60:383-398.

Graham, John B. and Ruth M. Graham, 1962. Autogenous Vaccine in Cancer Patients. *Surg. Gyn. Obst.*, 114:1-4.

Heymann, W.; D. B. Hackel; S. Harwood; S. G. F. Wilson; and Janet L. P. Hunter, 1959. Production of Nephrotis Syndrome in Rats by Freund's Adjuvant and Rat Kidney Suspension. *Proc. Soc. Exp. Biol. and Med.*, 100:600-604.

Klamer, B., 1965. Immunoelectrophoretic Characteristics of Plasma From Rats With Adjuvant Arthritis. *Experientia*, 21:529-530.

Lee, Johanna M. and Howard A. Schneider, 1962. Critical Relationships Between Constituents of the Antigen-Adjuvant Emulsion Affecting Experimental Allergic Encephalomyelitis In A Completely Susceptible Mouse Genotype. *J. Exp. Med.*, 115:157-168.

Levine, Seymour and Eugene J. Wenk, 1963. Allergic Encephalomyelitis: Rapid Induction Without The Aid of Adjuvants. *Science*, 141:529-530.

Olitsky, P. K. and Johanna M. Lee, 1953. Biological Properties and Variation of Reactions of the Encephalitogenic Agent in Nervous Tissue. *J. Immunol.*, 71:419-425.

Pearson, Carl M.; Fae D. Wood; E. G. McDaniel; and Floyd S. Daft, 1963. Adjuvant Arthritis Induced in Germ-Free Rats. *Proc. Soc. Exp. Biol. and Med.*, 112:91-93.

Ram, J. S., 1967. Aging and Immunological Phenomena—A Review. *J. Gerontol.* 22:92-107.

Rose, N. R.; J. R. Kite; T. K. Doebbler; R. Spier; F. R. Skelton; and E. Witebsky, 1965. Studies on Experimental Thyroiditis. *Ann. N. Y. Acad. Sci.*, 124 (I) :201-230.

Shaw, C. M.; E. C. Alvord; W. J. Fahlberg; and M. W. Kies, 1964. Substitutes For The Mycobacteria in Freund's Adjuvants in the Production of Experimental "Allergic" Encephalomyelitis in the Guinea Pig. *J. Immunol.*, 92:28-40.

Waksman, Byron H.; Carl M. Pearson; and John T. Sharp, 1960. Studies of Arthritis and Other Lesions Induced in Rats by Injection of Mycobacterial Adjuvant. *J. Immunol.*, 85:403-417.

Walford, R. L., 1969. THE IMMUNOLOGIC THEORY OF AGING. Copenhagen, Ejnar Munksgaard.

Weigle, W. O., 1965. The Induction of Autoimmunity in Rabbits Following Injection of Heterologous or Altered Homologous Thyroglobulin. *J. Exp. Med.*, 121:289-308.

AGE AND MITOTIC ACTIVITY IN THE MALE MOUSE, *MUS MUSCULUS* · L.

By W. S. BULLOUGH, *University of Sheffield*

(*Received* 18 *February* 1949)

(With Six Text-figures)

I. INTRODUCTION

In earlier analyses of mitotic activity in the male mouse (Bullough, 1948*a*, *b*) it was shown that the routine of waking and sleeping determines the form of the diurnal mitosis cycle, and that changes from the normal in this routine result immediately in changes from the normal in the mitosis cycle. The opinion was then expressed that factors such as the age and sex of the animals, and the habits of the laboratory staff, might be expected to influence the daily round of exercise and rest, and so to affect the form of the mitosis cycle.

Opportunity has now been found to discover the effect of age on the daily routine and mitotic activity of the mouse, and the following paper is a review of conditions in the male.

II. MATERIAL AND METHODS

(1) *The mice*

As in previous work, the observations were all made on mice of two pure line strains, Kreyberg's white label albinos and Strong's *CBA* agoutis. In the younger mice no differences were found between the strains, but with increasing age marked differences developed in both habits and mitotic activity. It is therefore unfortunate that so many of the mice of the older age groups were of one strain, the Strong's *CBA* agouti. This was due to the fact that these males rarely fight, and are therefore far more easily kept for long periods than are the more irritable Kreyberg's mice.

The results took about 12 months to collect, and thus represent mice examined at all seasons of the year. However, apart from unavoidable variations in the length of day, conditions were kept as uniform as possible. The room temperature was maintained at 20° C., and the mice received a regular diet of rat cake, dog biscuit, oats or flaked maize, and chopped carrots. Invariably they were given their food between 09.00 and 10.00 hr., and always it was given in excess so that at no time were they without something to eat.

(2) *The times of day*

The times of day recorded in the various experiments sometimes represent Greenwich mean time, sometimes British summer time, and occasionally double British summer time. In practice it was found unnecessary to record which of these systems was in operation when an experiment was performed, since the animals quickly adapted themselves to a change of the clock. It thus became abundantly clear that the daily habits of the animals were adjusted to the time of feeding, and they took only a few days to become accustomed to an hour's change either way.

(3) *The earclip technique*

This has already been described in detail by Bullough (1948*a*). Small pieces of ear were removed at intervals by means of a conchotome, and were fixed in Bouin's alcoholic fluid. After sectioning at a thickness of 7μ, the mitoses were counted in section lengths of 1 cm. From each earclip ten such counts were made, and from these an average figure was obtained. As each experimental group usually consisted of clips from ten mice, ten average figures were available from which to derive the mean and standard error. The latter was calculated by the method for small samples recommended by Simpson & Roe (1939).

(4) *The colchicine technique*

As a check on the results obtained by the earclip technique, mice were killed and examined after their mitoses had been arrested by means of colchicine. To each adult animal, weighing about 25 g., 0·1 mg. of colchicine dissolved in 0·25 c.c. of water was injected subcutaneously, but juvenile animals received proportionately less according to their weight. After 12 hr. the mice were chloroformed, dissected widely open, and fixed whole in Bouin's alcoholic fluid.

Half of each group of animals was injected at 09.00 hr. and killed at 21.00 hr., while half was injected at 21.00 hr. and killed at 09.00 hr. Thus it was planned that a complete period of 24 hr. should be covered by each experiment. However, after the experiments had been completed and the stock of mice used up, it became evident that colchicine not only arrests mitosis in the metaphase, but that it also depresses the number of resting cells which enter the prophase. A separate investigation of this point was then made (Bullough, 1949*b*), and as a result it had to be concluded that the colchicine experiments as recorded here do not reveal as much as was hoped of the degrees of mitotic activity typical of the different age groups.

(5) *Spontaneous bodily activity*

For comparison with the differences observed in the mitotic activity of the different age groups, the spontaneous bodily activity of the mice was also studied. For this purpose, five mice at a time were kept in a box containing two compartments connected by a small hole. In the hole was a hinged door which was pushed aside each time an animal passed, the movement being communicated to a spring arm and recorded on a revolving smoked drum.

Each group of mice remained in the apparatus for 20 days at a time, so that for each hour of the day and night twenty figures were obtained representing the spontaneous activity of the five mice. From these twenty sets of figures, averages and standard errors were calculated.

III. OBSERVATIONS

(1) *Monthly analyses of epidermal mitotic activity*

A study was first made of the mitosis cycles of normal male mice during each of the first 20 months of life. At the age of 20 months mice can be considered old, although there are great variations in this respect between different strains. Thus 20-month-old Strong's *CBA* mice are usually in good condition and, if carefully tended, they may live for another year or more, while 20-month-old Kreyberg's white label mice are usually thin and feeble and, in the best of conditions, they have only a short expectation of life. Difference in what has been termed the physiological age may also be induced by the conditions in which the mice live during their first 20 months, and by the diseases which they may have. In the experiments recorded here all the mice were subjected to the same conditions, and all were free from disease.

It appeared that the most satisfactory way to study the mitotic activity in each month of life would be to follow the cycle through a complete period of 24 hr., and then to repeat the experiment at a later date as a check on the first results. However, the effort required, and especially the numbers of mice needed, proved too great for this to be done. Consequently only those variations occurring between 08.00 and 20.00 hr. were analysed. This 12 hr. interval covered the feeding period between 09.00 and 10.00 hr. when the mice were always disturbed, the early afternoon sleep period during which the animal room was always quiet with all age groups resting, and the evening period of activity in which, by 20.00 hr., all animals were observed to be fully awake once more. Thus the interval 08.00–20.00 hr. could be expected to begin and end with periods of low mitotic activity, and to contain somewhere within it a period of high mitotic activity. During this time seven earclips were taken at 2 hr. intervals, and, since all of these could easily be obtained from one ear, it was possible to conserve the other ear for use in a subsequent month.

Whenever possible the results for each month were confirmed by a second experiment performed at a different time with different mice. Because of the limited supply this was not always possible, but it was usually found that confirmation of the results for any one month was provided by the results for the months which preceded and followed it.

It quickly became obvious that striking changes in the mitotic activity of the ear epidermis do occur with advancing age, and it was possible to distinguish four types of cycle which differed from one another in amplitude and often also in timing. These four ages of the mouse can be named as follows:

The immature age	From 1 to 3 months
The mature age	From 3 to 12 months
The middle age	From 13 to 18 months or later
The senile age	From the end of the middle age to death

The differences in mitotic activity between these various ages are clear cut, and an analysis of them is given below.

The immature age

In this period of life the animals are still actively growing, and they range in weight from under 10 g. to just over 20 g. Sections of the testes showed that at 1 month spermatozoa were forming but had not yet been released into the epididymis. By 2 months the epididymis was full of spermatozoa, and the animals were presumably in breeding condition. When given the opportunity, mice of these strains have been known to breed at an age of 5 or 6 weeks.

The characteristics of the epidermal mitotic activity of these young animals are indicated in the following Table 1.

Table 1. *The variations in the average numbers of mitoses present in unit section lengths (1 cm.) of the ear epidermis in groups each of ten immature male mice*

Time of day	Strong's CBA mice aged 1 month	Strong's CBA mice aged 2 months	Kreyberg's white label mice aged 2 months	Strong's CBA mice aged 3 months
08.00	3·7 ± 0·19	4·0 ± 0·28	3·9 ± 0·26	3·1 ± 0·21
10.00	2·4 ± 0·17	2·7 ± 0·43	1·8 ± 0·15	2·7 ± 0·19
12.00	4·3 ± 0·55	4·1 ± 0·37	4·0 ± 0·23	3·9 ± 0·31
14.00	5·3 ± 0·51	5·0 ± 0·20	5·5 ± 0·21	5·0 ± 0·14
16.00	1·7 ± 0·17	3·6 ± 0·25	3·1 ± 0·27	3·5 ± 0·22
18.00	2·1 ± 0·23	1·0 ± 0·14	1·4 ± 0·12	1·4 ± 0·18
20.00	2·0 ± 0·27	2·1 ± 0·17	2·7 ± 0·14	1·2 ± 0·13
Totals	21·5	22·5	22·4	20·8

Important points to notice in this table are that the peak of mitotic activity was at 14.00 hr., and that the highest average number of mitoses observed per unit section length of 1 cm. was only about 5. Further, it will be noticed that the total of the average numbers of mitoses in each group of observations was about 22, and that there were no differences between the Strong's *CBA* males and the Kreyberg's white label males.

The mature age

This age apparently begins quite abruptly when a mouse ceases to grow actively on reaching a weight of about 25 g., the testes then being fully active. This usually seems to happen some time about the beginning of the third month of life, and the first example, given in Table 2 below, is of a group of mice of that age. The mature age continues until the mouse is about a year old, and during that time little or no variation in the mitosis rate was found. The characteristics of the mitotic activity of this age can be seen from the Tables 2 to 4.

A survey of these tables indicates that between the ages of 3 and 12 months the time of maximum mitotic activity commonly remains, as in the immature animals, at about 14.00 hr. However, in these mature animals the maximum number of mitoses per unit section length of 1 cm. has risen from the immature figure of 5 to a new figure of about 8. Similarly, the totals of the average numbers of mitoses observed has risen from the immature figure of about 22 to a new figure of about 30.

Thus the mature age is characterized by an apparent rise in the mitosis rate. The question of whether this increase is real or illusory is dealt with in a later section.

Table 2. *The variations in the average numbers of mitoses present in unit section lengths (1 cm.) of the ear epidermis in groups each of ten mature male mice*

Time of day	Kreyberg's white label mice aged 3 months	Kreyberg's white label mice aged 4 months	Strong's CBA mice aged 5 months	Kreyberg's white label mice aged 6 months	Strong's CBA mice aged 7 months
08.00	5·1 ± 0·21	4·1 ± 0·24	4·2 ± 0·21	3·6 ± 0·29	3·1 ± 0·12
10.00	3·2 ± 0·13	2·5 ± 0·19	3·1 ± 0·29	2·5 ± 0·16	2·1 ± 0·18
12.00	5·4 ± 0·19	6·4 ± 0·42	5·5 ± 0·47	5·6 ± 0·37	4·6 ± 0·28
14.00	7·4 ± 0·32	8·2 ± 0·46	8·9 ± 0·31	9·8 ± 0·47	8·2 ± 0·32
16.00	6·4 ± 0·31	5·5 ± 0·33	5·1 ± 0·26	5·3 ± 0·26	5·6 ± 0·24
18.00	5·9 ± 0·16	2·9 ± 0·15	2·3 ± 0·19	2·8 ± 0·22	3·7 ± 0·13
20.00	1·6 ± 0·10	1·7 ± 0·07	1·2 ± 0·11	1·4 ± 0·15	1·7 ± 0·05
Totals	35·0	31·3	30·3	31·0	29·0

Table 3. *The variations in the average numbers of mitoses present in unit section lengths (1 cm.) of the ear epidermis in groups each of ten mature male mice*

Time of day	Strong's CBA mice aged 8 months	Kreyberg's white label mice aged 9 months	Strong's CBA mice aged 9 months	Kreyberg's white label mice aged 10 months	Strong's CBA mice aged 10 months
08.00	4·7 ± 0·23	8·6 ± 0·34	5·2 ± 0·16	5·1 ± 0·18	8·9 ± 0·54
10.00	3·5 ± 0·34	2·0 ± 0·24	2·3 ± 0·14	2·1 ± 0·17	1·6 ± 0·29
12.00	3·0 ± 0·28	1·1 ± 0·16	4·1 ± 0·21	2·2 ± 0·24	3·6 ± 0·32
14.00	7·0 ± 0·41	7·4 ± 0·32	7·5 ± 0·32	7·1 ± 0·30	4·0 ± 0·20
16.00	5·2 ± 0·43	5·0 ± 0·22	5·5 ± 0·28	5·4 ± 0·35	9·2 ± 0·24
18.00	4·2 ± 0·17	3·1 ± 0·24	4·6 ± 0·27	5·2 ± 0·21	4·1 ± 0·27
20.00	2·7 ± 0·20	3·4 ± 0·33	2·9 ± 0·12	2·8 ± 0·11	1·1 ± 0·17
Totals	30·3	30·6	32·1	29·9	32·5

Table 4. *The variations in the average numbers of mitoses present in unit section lengths (1 cm.) of the ear epidermis in groups each of ten mature male mice*

Time of day	Kreyberg's white label mice aged 11 months	Strong's CBA mice aged 11 months	Kreyberg's white label mice aged 12 months	Strong's CBA mice aged 12 months
08.00	5·3 ± 0·33	5·4 ± 0·25	5·5 ± 0·38	4·7 ± 0·22
10.00	2·6 ± 0·16	7·1 ± 0·31	1·7 ± 0·25	3·6 ± 0·17
12.00	3·4 ± 0·18	5·3 ± 0·26	2·9 ± 0·30	7·3 ± 0·36
14.00	7·3 ± 0·26	4·2 ± 0·21	7·0 ± 0·24	5·0 ± 0·31
16.00	4·3 ± 0·27	1·9 ± 0·17	3·9 ± 0·14	4·1 ± 0·18
18.00	3·1 ± 0·15	2·1 ± 0·23	4·0 ± 0·20	2·3 ± 0·18
20.00	2·2 ± 0·14	2·5 ± 0·18	4·2 ± 0·14	1·9 ± 0·13
Totals	28·2	28·5	29·2	28·9

A further point of interest also emerges from these tables. It can be seen that while the Kreyberg's white label mice continued with great regularity to develop maximum mitotic activity at 14.00 hr., the Strong's CBA mice did not. While these latter mice maintained their mitosis rate apparently unchanged, they tended after the age of about 10 months to develop maximum mitotic activity at an earlier hour. As will be seen in the following section, this tendency towards an earlier peak of mitotic activity is continued during middle age in mice of this strain.

The middle age

The next change in the mitosis rate was apparently abrupt, and was observed in 13-month-old Strong's *CBA* mice. About this time the animals seemed to be entering into what, by human analogy, can be called middle age. They usually appeared quieter and lazier, but the only positive sign of metabolic change was their increasing weight. The mature males had a steady average weight of about 25 g., but at 12 or 13 months almost all the animals began to lay down deposits of fat. This process was particularly marked in Strong's *CBA* mice, some of which reached weights of over 50 g. at an age of about 16 months. There was no other external sign of advancing age, and the fur remained glossy and thick. Internally, apart from the fat deposits, there was also no apparent change. The testes remained indistinguishable from those of younger mice, and, with one exception, all the middle-aged males examined showed active spermatogenesis with the epididymes full of spermatozoa. The single exception, a Strong's *CBA* mouse aged 16 months, had two shrivelled testes and lacked any spermatozoa. It was undoubtedly abnormal.

However, if it was difficult to point to any other feature which could be used as a positive sign that the middle-aged condition had been reached, the change in the mitosis rate at this time appeared to be certain and complete. This is brought out in the Tables 5 and 6 for Strong's *CBA* mice from which the characteristics of this middle-age period can be readily perceived.

For an understanding of the peculiarities of mitotic activity in the middle-age period, the figures of the 13- and 14-month-old mice are the most valuable. They show a sudden apparent increase in the mitosis rate, so that the maximum number of mitoses per unit section length of 1 cm. rose from an earlier figure of about 8 to the new figure of about 14. Similarly, the total of the average numbers of mitoses observed during the 12 hr. period rose from the earlier figure of about 30 to the new figure of about 47. The question of whether this increase is real or not is dealt with in a later section.

The other obvious change in the mitosis cycle shown by these tables is the steady shift of the period of maximum mitotic activity from 12.00 to 10.00 hr. and then from 10.00 to 08.00 hr. Further, it was observed that by the age of 16 months almost all the mitoses counted at 08.00 hr. were in the telophase. This was also true in the 17- to 20-month age groups, and it is therefore obvious that in all these cases the period of maximum mitotic activity had passed before the observations were commenced at 08.00 hr. This explains the lower total numbers of mitoses observed in these older groups.

It is also interesting to note that when the main peak of mitotic activity moved forward to 08.00 hr. or earlier, a small secondary burst of activity developed sometime between 12.00 and 16.00 hr. This was perhaps clearer in the sections themselves than it is in the tables because, while up to 12.00 hr. the mitoses were mainly in the ana- and telophases, in the early afternoon pro- and metaphases predominated. These in turn gave place to telophases by 16.00 and 18.00 hr.

Table 5. *The variations in the average numbers of mitoses present in unit section lengths (1 cm.) of the ear epidermis in groups each of ten middle-aged male mice*

Time of day	Strong's CBA mice aged 13 months	Strong's CBA mice aged 14 months	Strong's CBA mice aged 15 months	Strong's CBA mice aged 16 months
08.00	4·2±0·25	5·9±0·36	14·9±0·65	14·0±0·22
10.00	9·1±0·51	13·1±0·62	5·6±0·31	5·7±0·23
12.00	14·9±0·57	10·7±0·49	3·8±0·22	3·8±0·20
14.00	9·3±0·32	6·7±0·27	4·7±0·23	4·5±0·18
16.00	4·0±0·27	5·6±0·40	3·5±0·38	2·0±0·16
18.00	2·7±0·19	3·1±0·16	2·2±0·26	0·9±0·14
20.00	2·8±0·18	2·3±0·19	3·1±0·41	2·2±0·18
Totals	47·0	47·4	37·8	33·1

Table 6. *The variations in the average numbers of mitoses present in unit section lengths (1 cm.) of the ear epidermis in groups each of ten middle-aged male mice*

Time of day	Strong's CBA mice aged 17 months	Strong's CBA mice aged 18 months	Strong's CBA mice aged 19 months	Strong's CBA mice aged 20 months
08.00	13·9±0·43	14·0±0·47	13·9±0·33	12·6±0·45
10·00	6·3±0·31	11·5±0·64	9·4±0·30	5·9±0·37
12.00	4·0±0·23	3·7±0·28	5·4±0·32	2·9±0·39
14.00	4·5±0·25	4·0±0·29	4·6±0·18	5·0±0·41
16.00	5·2±0·31	1·7±0·22	3·2±0·31	6·3±0·49
18.00	1·7±0·12	2·9±0·29	1·2±0·19	6·6±0·35
20·00	2·5±0·15	2·0±0·19	1·6±0·21	1·2±0·24
Totals	38·1	39·8	39·3	40·5

Table 7. *The variations in the average numbers of mitoses present in unit section lengths (1 cm.) of the ear epidermis in groups of middle-aged male mice*

Time of day	Eight Kreyberg's white label mice aged 14 months	Five Kreyberg's white label mice aged 15 months	Seven Kreyberg's white label mice aged 16 months	Ten Kreyberg's white label mice aged 18 months
08.00	5·5±0·19	7·5±0·36	9·4±0·31	6·8±0·36
10.00	3·7±0·23	4·0±0·21	3·6±0·21	9·1±0·48
12.00	14·8±0·44	8·7±0·31	3·7±0·33	12·6±0·45
14.00	7·6±0·28	16·2±0·63	5·5±0·66	9·7±0·53
16.00	7·1±0·43	12·1±0·51	18·2±0·58	5·1±0·30
18.00	4·0±0·24	4·6±0·26	10·8±0·56	4·2±0·31
20.00	3·5±0·22	3·9±0·18	8·9±0·72	3·0±0·24
Totals	46·2	57·0	60·1	50·5

These results for the Strong's *CBA* mice have been described separately since they differ somewhat from those obtained with the Kreyberg's white label mice. These latter results are given in Table 7.

322

In the first place it may be stressed that these figures for the Kreyberg's mice confirm the fact that an apparent increase in the mitosis rate accompanies the transition to middle age. Compared with the maximum figures of about 8 mitoses obtained for mature mice, the new maximum lies between about 12 and 18. Similarly, the total of the average numbers of mitoses observed during the 12 hr. period of the experiment has risen in middle age from the earlier figure of about 30 to a new figure of between 46 and 60.

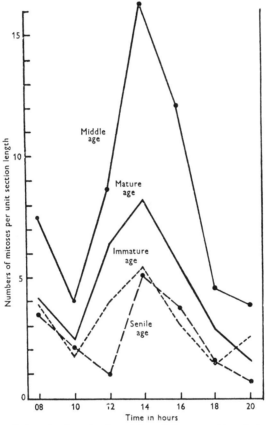

Fig. 1. The diurnal variations in the mitosis activity of the ear epidermis in groups of Kreyberg's white label males of various ages.

However, it will be seen that the Kreyberg's white label mice differed markedly from the Strong's *CBA* mice in that the period of maximum mitotic activity remained at about 14.00 hr. as in younger animals. The timing of this period of maximum mitotic activity was certainly more irregular than in the younger mice, but there is no evidence of any progressive forward shift.

The general conclusions can therefore be reached that the period of middle age, which begins at about 13 months, is characterized by an apparent rise in mitotic activity, and that, according to the strain of mouse used, this change may or may not be accompanied by changes in the timing of the mitosis cycle.

The senile age

Relatively few data are available for the senile age, which is characterized by feebleness and great loss of weight. In the Kreyberg's white label mice these changes were apparent before the age of 20 months, but in the Strong's *CBA* mice they were not. The Kreyberg's mice of 19 and 20 months, on which Table 8 is based, were emaciated with weights of less than 20 g. Their backs were permanently arched, and their fur was thin and poor. They were extremely feeble, and they spent almost all their time lying quietly in a corner.

Table 8. *The variations in the average numbers of mitoses present in unit section lengths* (1 *cm.*) *of the ear epidermis in groups of senile male mice*

Time of day	Ten Kreyberg's white label mice aged 19 months	Seven Kreyberg's white label mice aged 20 months
08.00	4·1 ± 0·30	3·5 ± 0·28
10.00	1·7 ± 0·31	2·1 ± 0·13
12.00	5·3 ± 0·27	1·0 ± 0·20
14.00	3·0 ± 0·22	5·1 ± 0·24
16.00	3·6 ± 0·30	3·8 ± 0·26
18.00	1·2 ± 0·14	1·6 ± 0·22
20.00	0·5 ± 0·10	0·7 ± 0·15
Totals	19·4	17·8

In these old animals the mitosis rate apparently fell to a slightly lower level than that seen in the immature males (Table 1). The time of maximum mitotic activity remained at about 14.00 hr., but at that time the average number of mitoses per unit section length of 1 cm. was only about 5 as compared with almost 13 in the 18-month-old Kreyberg's mice. A similar fall is seen in the total of the average numbers of mitoses observed during the 12 hr. period of the experiment. In these senile mice the figure was only about 18 or 19 as compared with about 50 for the 18-month-old animals.

(2) *Analyses of full diurnal cycles*

Following this preliminary survey, the observations were checked and extended by a study of each type of cycle in greater detail. The ages so examined were 2, 6 and 17 months, these being typical respectively of the immature, mature, and middle ages. Each experiment covered a full period of 24 hr., and the earclips were taken at 2 hr. intervals from 08.00 hr. on one day to 08.00 hr. on the next. It is unfortunate that no senile Kreyberg's mice were available for this experiment. Because of this the senile age group was omitted altogether, and the observations were restricted to Strong's *CBA* mice.

The immature age

The results obtained with the 2-month-old males are recorded in Table 9 and shown graphically in Fig. 2. They afford still further confirmation of the results previously obtained with immature males (Table 1). They also indicate that, in the conditions of the experiment, an immature male experiences periods of maximum mitotic activity at 04.00, 08.00 and 14.00 hr., and periods of minimum mitotic activity at 06.00, 10.00 and 22.00 hr.

It can also be seen that in none of the periods of maximum activity did the average numbers of mitoses present per unit section length of 1 cm. rise above 5·8, while the lowest recorded figure at 10.00 hr. was 1.4. The total of the average numbers of mitoses observed between 08.00 hr. on the first day and 06.00 hr. on the second day was approximately 40.

The mature age

The second group of males, ten Strong's *CBA* mice aged 6 months, gave the figures recorded in Table 9 and in the graph in Fig. 2.

Table 9. *The diurnal variations in the average numbers of mitoses present in unit section lengths (1 cm.) of the ear epidermis in groups each of ten male mice*

Time of day	Strong's CBA mice aged 3 months	Strong's CBA mice aged 6 months	Strong's CBA mice aged 17 months
08.00	4·5 ± 0·20	4·3 ± 0·18	15·3 ± 0·49
10.00	1·4 ± 0·13	2·7 ± 0·26	5·1 ± 0·34
12.00	4·8 ± 0·26	5·1 ± 0·34	4·4 ± 0·19
14.00	5·8 ± 0·18	8·6 ± 0·40	6·1 ± 0·16
16.00	3·2 ± 0·13	6·8 ± 0·24	5·0 ± 0·31
18.00	2·7 ± 0·16	5·7 ± 0·25	2·7 ± 0·18
20.00	2·8 ± 0·25	2·2 ± 0·11	2·6 ± 0·28
22.00	1·5 ± 0·17	3·9 ± 0·15	4·7 ± 0·22
24.00	2·3 ± 0·22	4·5 ± 0·12	13·5 ± 0·30
02.00	3·6 ± 0·19	4·9 ± 0·19	9·0 ± 0·39
04.00	5·6 ± 0·26	5·1 ± 0·32	3·6 ± 0·22
06.00	1·6 ± 0·13	9·1 ± 0·37	8·6 ± 0·48
08.00	4·2 ± 0·26	5·5 ± 0·23	14·8 ± 0·35
Totals	44·0	68·4	95·4

These results are in confirmation of those recorded above for mature males (Tables 2–4). Compared with the immature animals, there were only two periods of maximum mitotic activity at 06.00 and 14.00 hr., and two periods of minimum activity at 10.00 and 20.00 hr., and hour by hour the mitosis rate was on a higher level. The greatest average number of mitoses present per unit section length of 1 cm. was 9·1 and the lowest was 2·2. These figures can be compared with 5·8 and 1·4 respectively in the immature animals. As a final point of contrast, it should be noted that the total of the average numbers of mitoses observed between 08.00 hr. on the first day and 06.00 hr. on the second was about 63, which represents a rise of approximately 55% over the figure for the immature animals.

The middle age

Table 9 and Fig. 2 also include an analysis of the mitosis counts from the group of ten Strong's *CBA* males aged 17 months. Once again confirmation is provided for the results given earlier (Tables 5 and 6), and it is very clear that the diurnal mitosis cycle of these older males differs from that of the younger males both in its timing and in its amplitude. The main periods of maximum mitotic activity were at 08.00 and 24.00 hr., and there was a lesser burst of activity at 14.00 hr. on which comment has already been made. The maximum average number of mitoses present per unit section length of 1 cm. reached the high level of 15·3, while the minimum number fell no lower than 2·6. The total of the average numbers of mitoses observed between 08.00 hr. on the first day and 06.00 hr. on the second was about 80, which is an increase of about 30 % over the figure for the mature males and of about 100 % over the figure for the immature males.

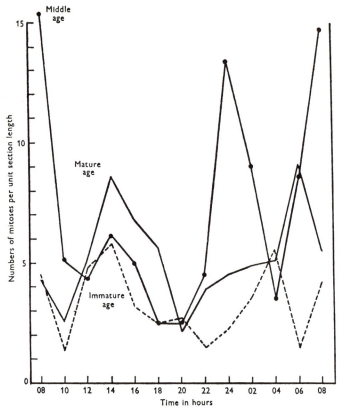

Fig. 2. The diurnal variations in the mitotic activity of the ear epidermis in groups of Strong's *CBA* males of various ages.

(3) *Experiments with colchicine*

From all the experiments recorded above it can safely be concluded that the diurnal cycles of epidermal mitotic activity in Strong's *CBA* males differ in timing in the immature, mature and middle ages, while in Kreyberg's white label males the timing of the cycles of mature, middle-aged, and senile animals is essentially the same.

However, the most important point still remains obscure. This is the question of whether in fact the ear epidermis of the immature male has a lower mitosis rate than that of the mature male, and whether this in turn has a lower mitosis rate than that of the middle-aged male. While all the evidence suggests that this is so, the conclusion is so unexpected that other explanations must be sought. The most obvious alternative possibility is that the results obtained may be due to age changes in the speed at which each division is completed. If in a mature animal the speed of completion of a mitosis is less than in an immature animal, then it might be expected that the former would show more mitoses at any given moment than would the latter. Again, if the speed of completion of a division is still further reduced in middle age, then the numbers of mitoses visible at any given moment might be expected to rise once more.

However, in the case of the senile animal it can hardly be supposed that a sufficient increase in the speed of division could occur to account for the fall in the numbers of mitoses observed, and it appears reasonable to draw the immediate conclusion that this age is in fact characterized by a real reduction in the mitosis rate.

An attempt to answer this whole question was made with the use of colchicine, which is considered to arrest all mitoses at about the metaphase. The theory underlying these experiments was that by means of a single injection all the mitoses beginning during the subsequent 12 hr. period could be arrested, so that, after sectioning and counting in the manner already described, a fairly accurate estimate could be obtained of the numbers of mitoses which normally occur during this period. In this way any complication due to the speed of completion of the divisions could be eliminated, and, with two experiments, the full period of 24 hr. could be covered and an estimate made of the total number of mitoses which occur daily.

In practice, however, difficulties were encountered which are best discussed after a consideration of the results. These difficulties made it necessary to consider the Kreyberg's mice separately from the Strong's mice, as is done in Tables 10 and 11. The mice concerned were injected with colchicine at 09.00 hr. and killed at 21.00 hr. to cover the 12 hr. of day, or injected at 21.00 hr. and killed at 09.00 hr. to cover the 12 hr. of night. Each adult mouse received 0·1 mg. of colchicine dissolved in 0·25 c.c. of water which was injected subcutaneously. Each immature mouse, being approximately half the weight of an adult, received only 0·05 mg. of colchicine in 0·125 c.c. of water.

Table 10. *The average numbers of mitoses arrested by colchicine in 12 hr. in unit section lengths (1 cm.) of the ear epidermis in groups each of ten Kreyberg's white label males*

Age of mice	Period 09.00–21.00 hr.	Period 21.00–09.00 hr.
1 month	4·8 ± 0·16	4·1 ± 0·21
5 months	10·3 ± 0·48	5·7 ± 0·32
16 months	15·4 ± 0·55	12·8 ± 0·71

From Table 10 it would appear that the total numbers of mitoses occurring in a period of 24 hr. in each cm. length of sections of ear epidermis cut 7 μ thick was in immature males about 9, in mature males about 16, and in middle-aged males about 28. While this affords strong confirmation that real increases in the mitosis rate do occur with increasing age, all these figures are considerably smaller than would be expected from the other tables given above. Thus a doubt immediately arises as to the accuracy of the method, and this doubt is increased by a consideration of the results from the Strong's *CBA* mice given in Table 11.

Table 11. *The average number of mitoses arrested by colchicine in 12 hr. in unit section lengths (1 cm.) of the ear epidermis in groups each of ten Strong's CBA males*

Age of mice	Period 09.00–21.00 hr.	Period 21.00–09.00 hr.
1 month	3.7 ± 0·31	4·5 ± 0·26
4 months	12·2 ± 0·67	6·8 ± 0·33
6 months	10·8 ± 0·61	6·0 ± 0·35
14 months	9·4 ± 0·73	7·6 ± 0·52
15 months	14·7 ± 0·81	5·6 ± 0·22
16 months	11·7 ± 0·54	5·5 ± 0·38
20 months	13·0 ± 0·62	8·5 ± 0·48

From this table it is evident that the results for the immature males, with a daily mitosis total of about 8, and for the mature males, with a daily mitosis total of about 18, are similar to those obtained with the Kreyberg's mice. The difference is seen in the middle-aged males, which in this table show little or no increase over the mitosis rate typical of the mature animals. The daily mitosis totals of the middle-aged Strong's males lie between about 17 and 21, and so do not approach the middle-aged Kreyberg's males' figure of 28.

From all these colchicine results a strong suspicion arises that the drug not only arrests mitosis in the metaphase, but that it also slows down the rate at which the resting cells enter the prophase. If this is so, then the results obtained cannot be regarded as an indication of normal conditions, and in order to clear up this point it was necessary to carry out an investigation into the action of colchicine using the earclip technique (Bullough, 1949b). This investigation showed that only for a period of about 5 hr. after the injection of 0·1 mg. of colchicine does the epidermal mitosis rate remain normal. After 5 hr. a depressing effect rapidly develops, and after 6 hr. mitosis stops altogether. Thus, in the colchicine experiments recorded in Tables 10 and 11, the mitoses observed were those which developed during only the first 5 hr. of the 12 hr. period.

With this in mind, the results can be interpreted as follows. In all the three age groups of Kreyberg's mice injected at 09.00 hr., the colchicine must have arrested in or about the metaphase those mitoses which developed during the period up to 14.00 hr., the usual time of maximum mitotic activity associated with the afternoon sleep period. Thus these three sets of figures are strictly comparable, and it can be concluded that the numbers of mitoses which are involved in the rise to maximum activity in immature, mature, and middle-aged animals are in the approximate proportion of 1:2:3.

In the same way, the figures for the immature and mature Strong's *CBA* males injected at 09.00 hr. are also comparable, and are in the same approximate proportion of 1 : 2. It is the figures for the middle-aged Strong's males which cannot be compared, since it is evident from Tables 5, 6 and 9 that in this strain the period 09.00–14.00 hr. is not a time of greatly increasing mitotic activity. Instead, the maximum activity is passed before 08.00 hr., and the increased activity which has been noted at about 14.00 hr. is slight by comparison.

Of the figures obtained for the period 21.00–09.00 hr., little can be said except that in general they support the evidence provided by the figures for the period 09.00–21.00 hr. It is important to bear in mind that the mitosis cycle is less regular during the night, probably because of the lack of a feeding time by which it can be stabilized.

While admitting the generally unsatisfactory nature of these colchicine experiments, it is legitimate to conclude that they offer the strongest evidence that a real increase in the mitosis rate of the ear epidermis occurs between the immature and mature ages, and again between the mature and middle ages. As stated earlier, it is also reasonable to conclude that the senile age is characterized by a reduction in mitotic activity to a level slightly below that of the immature mice. It is not yet possible to state accurately the sizes of these increases and decreases, but, judging from all the figures available, they are perhaps in the approximate proportions of immature, 1; mature, 2; middle age, 3; senile, 1.

(4) *Analyses of spontaneous bodily activity*

An attempt was also made to account for the observed changes in the timing of the diurnal mitosis cycles in the different age groups. Since these changes in timing were most pronounced in the Strong's *CBA* strain, all the experiments were performed with these animals.

In view of earlier results (Bullough, 1948 a, b), which related the diurnal changes in the mitosis rate to the periods of waking and sleeping, it was immediately suspected that the age changes in the diurnal mitosis cycles were merely reflexions of age changes in the animal's daily habits. A study was therefore made of activity and rest in immature, mature, and middle-aged mice. All the experiments were conducted in the same way. In each case five males were put into a box with two compartments connected by a small hole, and, by means of a recording device, it was possible to discover the number of times which the five animals passed through the hole in each hour of the day and night. In each experiment the five animals remained in the box for 20 consecutive days, so that twenty sets of figures were obtained from which the averages and standard errors were calculated.

Immature age

The five males used were 4 weeks old at the beginning of the experiment, and 7 weeks old at the end, and the results which they gave are expressed in Table 12 and in Fig. 3. In the figure the results are represented for convenience by a line graph, instead of more correctly by a block graph, and superimposed is the graph of the diurnal mitosis cycle of immature Strong's *CBA* males (Table 9). It is evident that these young animals were never still for long, so that even in the quietest hour of the day there was an average of about eleven passages through the hole. However, it is clear from the graphs that the quieter periods at about 04.00, 08.00 and 14.00 hr. were also the times of maximum mitotic activity, while the periods of greatest bodily activity at about 06.00, 10.00 and 21.00 hr. were the times of minimum mitotic activity. Of these periods of greatest bodily activity, that at about 10.00 hr. coincided with the daily feeding time, while those at 06.00 and 21.00 hr. approximately coincided with dawn and dusk respectively.

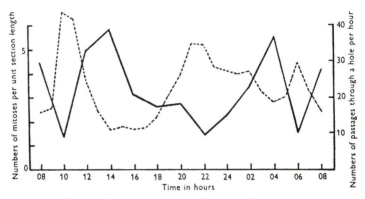

Fig. 3. The diurnal variations in the mitotic activity of the ear epidermis (solid line) as compared with the diurnal variations in the spontaneous bodily activity (broken line) of immature Strong's *CBA* males.

For later comparisons it should also be noted that the total of the average numbers of times which the five animals passed through the hole each day was approximately 565.

Mature age

The Strong's males examined in this experiment were 5 months old, and the results are given in Table 12 and in Fig. 4.

Like the immature animals, these males become extremely active at about 10.00 hr., when they were in the habit of being fed, and were inactive at 14.00 and 15.00 hr., when they observed an afternoon rest period. They became active again in the evening, and they maintained a moderate degree of activity throughout the night. However, unlike the immature males, they did not show any increased activity about dawn, but instead they observed several hours of rest until feeding time.

These points are illustrated in Fig. 4 to which, for comparison, a graph of mitotic activity has been added (Table 9). Once again it is obvious that the times of high bodily activity are also the times of low mitotic activity, while the times of low bodily activity are the times of high mitotic activity.

It should also be noticed that the mature males indulge in less spontaneous bodily activity than do the immature males. Their rest periods are longer and more pronounced, and the total of the average numbers of times which they passed through the hole each day was only about 460 as compared with about 565 for the younger animals.

Table 12. *The spontaneous bodily activity of groups of five male mice expressed as the average numbers of passages through a hole per hour*

Hour ending	Strong's *CBA* mice aged 1 month	Strong's *CBA* mice aged 5 months	Strong's *CBA* mice aged 17 months
09.00	16·6 ± 1·88	10·9 ± 1·35	4·2 ± 1·03
10.00	46·4 ± 3·02	49·6 ± 5·11	5·3 ± 1·21
11.00	43·9 ± 3·00	44·7 ± 3·27	11·8 ± 1·77
12.00	25·0 ± 2·41	24·9 ± 2·70	5·1 ± 1·44
13.00	15·8 ± 2·11	13·4 ± 2·78	4·6 ± 1·10
14.00	11·1 ± 1·86	7·1 ± 1·83	4·4 ± 1·00
15.00	12·2 ± 1·73	5·0 ± 1·08	3·4 ± 0·71
16.00	11·5 ± 0·87	8·5 ± 1·52	2·4 ± 0·62
17.00	11·8 ± 1·43	14·8 ± 2·16	3·5 ± 0·53
18.00	14·5 ± 1·35	26·2 ± 3·52	13·3 ± 1·91
19.00	20·6 ± 1·52	30·1 ± 2·97	23·9 ± 2·32
20.00	27·6 ± 1·27	29·6 ± 2·60	21·8 ± 1·79
21.00	35·0 ± 2·93	24·9 ± 3·16	19·5 ± 1·93
22.00	34·5 ± 3·09	21·3 ± 2·55	15·5 ± 1·62
23.00	28·7 ± 2·38	18·4 ± 2·13	15·0 ± 1·59
24.00	27·0 ± 2·77	21·5 ± 2·59	13·9 ± 1·97
01.00	26·1 ± 1·84	16·8 ± 1·44	16·3 ± 2·98
02.00	27·3 ± 1·92	18·1 ± 1·10	15·1 ± 3·30
03.00	22·4 ± 2·10	17·3 ± 2·12	22·4 ± 2·95
04.00	19·4 ± 1·73	17·0 ± 1·02	16·8 ± 2·70
05.00	20·7 ± 2·04	14·8 ± 2·31	13·3 ± 0·97
06.00	29·4 ± 2·34	10·2 ± 1·17	14·2 ± 5·00
07.00	21·1 ± 1·51	6·3 ± 0·85	8·2 ± 2·78
08.00	15·8 ± 2·76	8·9 ± 1·09	4·0 ± 0·85
Totals	564·4	460·3	277·9

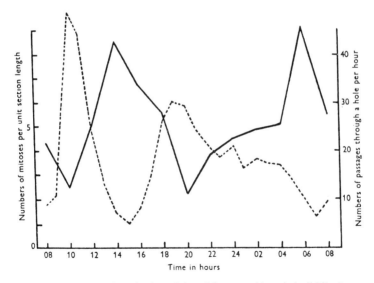

Fig. 4. The diurnal variations in the mitotic activity of the ear epidermis (solid line) as compared with the diurnal variations in the spontaneous bodily activity (broken line) of mature Strong's *CBA* males.

331

Middle age

The third experiment was performed with 17-month-old males, and the results are also shown in Table 12. They are illustrated graphically in Fig. 5.

The differences between this cycle of spontaneous activity and those of the younger animals are considerable. In the first place it can be seen that the middle-aged mice were not greatly disturbed when the food was put into their box at about 10.00 hr., so that the early morning rest period became almost continuous with the

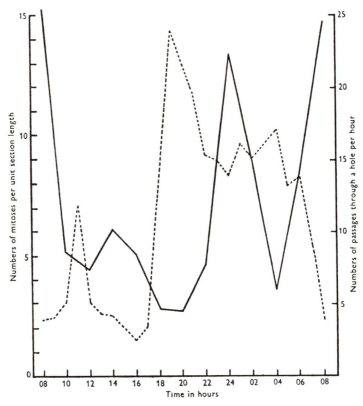

Fig. 5. The diurnal variations in the mitotic activity of the ear epidermis (solid line) as compared with the diurnal variations in the spontaneous bodily activity (broken line) of middle-aged Strong's *CBA* males.

afternoon rest period. The animals were closely watched at their feeding time, and it was found that they ate very little and quickly returned to rest. Thus their daily routine was a simple one with almost continuous rest during the 12 hr. period 06.00–18.00 hr., and almost continuous activity during the 12 hr. period 18.00–06.00 hr.

Another point of difference from the younger males was that at no time did these animals develop such a high rate of activity. The highest average number of passages through the hole in 1 hr. was only 23·9, as compared with 49·6 for the mature males and 46·4 for the immature males, while the lowest number of passages was 2·4, as compared with 5·0 and 11·1 respectively. This drop in the spontaneous activity of the middle-aged mice is most clearly shown by the total of the average numbers of passages through the hole per day. This figure was only about 280, as compared with 460 for the mature males and 565 for the immature males.

In Fig. 5 the comparison is made between the bodily activity (Table 12) and the mitotic activity (Table 9) of middle-aged Strong's *CBA* males. Once again the usual inverse relationship is demonstrated. The beginning of the early morning rest period coincides with a rise in the mitosis rate, and the beginning of the evening activity coincides with a fall. In the night there is a slackening of bodily activity about midnight which is accompanied by a second rise in the mitosis rate, and an increase in activity about 04.00 hr. which is accompanied by a second fall. In addition, there are minor fluctuations in bodily and mitotic activity between 10.00 and 18.00 hr. which also show an inverse relationship.

However, these times of minor fluctuations by night and by day are particularly interesting since they provide an apparent contradiction. It can be seen that the rest period between 10.00 and 17.00 hr. is the longest and most clearly defined in the whole day, and yet it is accompanied by only relatively slight mitotic activity. By contrast, the reduction in bodily activity between 22.00 and 02.00 hr. is negligible, but the increase in the mitosis rate which accompanies it is great. This curious state of affairs has considerable theoretical importance, and it is dealt with in some detail in the next section.

With this apparent anomaly set aside, the general conclusions emerging from these results can be summarized as follows. In all age groups high bodily activity is associated with a low rate of mitosis, while rest or sleep is associated with a high rate of mitosis. Thus the differences observed in the timing of the diurnal mitosis cycles of immature, mature and middle-aged Strong's *CBA* males are related to, and apparently dependent on, differences in the timing of the diurnal cycles of spontaneous activity. Finally, it might appear to be significant that the immature animals which have the highest rate of bodily activity have also the lowest rate of mitotic activity; that the mature animals which have a lower rate of bodily activity have a higher rate of mitotic activity; and that the middle-aged animals which have the lowest rate of bodily activity have the highest rate of mitotic activity.

(5) *Mitosis during sleep in middle-aged mice*

As described above, the cycle of mitotic activity in the ear epidermis of middle-aged Strong's *CBA* males offers an apparent modification of the general rule. While the animals observed 12 continuous hours of almost uninterrupted rest, this did not result in 12 continuous hours of high mitotic activity. The mitosis rate rose to a very high level at the beginning of this rest period, but by 10.00 hr., when the mice were fed, it fell to a relatively low level. After the insignificant disturbance due to feeding, the mitosis rate rose only slightly at 14.00 hr., and then fell steadily until the end of the rest period. With the beginning of the evening period of wakefulness it fell still further.

In a previous publication (Bullough, 1949 a) the tentative conclusion was reached that the critical factor which allows the development of a high rate of mitosis is probably the high glycogen content of the tissue concerned, and further that such a high glycogen content is normally developed with the onset of sleep because of the deposition of blood sugar which takes place at that time. However, it may be surmised that the greatest deposition takes place only at the beginning of sleep while the blood sugar level is actually being lowered, so that the process is not a continuous one. Consequently it may well be that if sleep is unduly prolonged, so that the glycogen content of the tissue becomes depleted, the mitosis rate must fall. In a younger mouse the sleep period does not normally last for more than a few hours at a time, and it appears that sufficient energy is stored in the epidermis to maintain a high level of mitotic activity until the animal wakes. In a middle-aged mouse the sleep period is apparently too long for this to happen, and the slight disturbance at about 10.00 hr. is seemingly followed by only slight further deposition of sugar so that the mitosis rate shows only a slight recovery at 14.00 hr. After 14.00 hr. the fall in the mitosis rate is continuous until after the next burst of activity and of feeding. Then the relatively slight period of rest about midnight is accompanied by the development of a very high rate of mitotic activity.

If this theory is correct, it should be possible to cause an almost immediate rise in the mitosis rate of a sleeping middle-aged male by supplying extra carbohydrate by injection, since it could be expected that this carbohydrate would be taken up by the blood stream and deposited in the tissues. The following series of experiments was performed to test this. Sleeping Strong's *CBA* males, all middle-aged, were injected subcutaneously with starch solution using the technique developed by Bullough (1949*a*). This was done at 11.00 hr. when it was anticipated that the mitosis rate would be low, and each mouse received 20 mg. of starch dissolved in 0·4 c.c. of normal saline. Earclips were taken from these mice, and from saline-injected controls, at intervals from 08.00 to 20.00 hr., and it was observed that neither the injections nor the removal of the earclips caused any significant disturbance of the rest period. The results of four separate experiments are shown in Tables 13 and 14.

All the results were essentially similar. A single injection of 20 mg. of starch induced an immediate rise in the epidermal mitosis rate, so that between 1 and 3 hr. later a rate of cell division similar to that normally seen at about 08.00 hr. was

Table 13. *The effect of the injection of 20 mg. of starch at 11.00 hr. on the average numbers of mitoses present in unit section lengths (1 cm.) of the ear epidermis in groups each of ten sleeping, middle-aged, Strong's CBA males.*

Time of day	Mice aged 15 months		Mice aged 16 months	
	Injected with saline	Injected with starch	Injected with saline	Injected with starch
08.00	15·2±0·58	14·7±0·79	14·1±0·32	12·7±0·35
10.00	4·5±0·31	3·9±0·30	5·4±0·23	4·9±0·30
12.00	3·7±0·13	8·3±0·39	3·9±0·21	8·1±0·33
14.00	4·6±0·20	12·4±0·44	4·7±0·25	11·1±0·45
16.00	3·5±0·13	4·3±0·32	2·4±0·18	5·1±0·33
18.00	2·7±0·16	2·1±0·22	1·1±0·24	2·7±0·18
20.00	3·2±0·28	2·9±0·23	2·0±0·16	1·2±0·26

Table 14. *The effect of the injection of 20 mg. of starch at 11.00 hr. on the average numbers of mitoses present in unit section lengths (1 cm.) of the ear epidermis in groups each of ten sleeping, middle-aged, Strong's CBA males*

Time of day	Mice aged 17 months		Mice aged 20 months	
	Injected with saline	Injected with starch	Injected with saline	Injected with starch
08.00	13·3 ± 0·37	13·6 ± 0·52	13·6 ± 0·41	13·4 ± 0·65
10.00	5·4 ± 0·35	8·2 ± 0·39	6·3 ± 0·39	7·6 ± 0·48
12.00	3·9 ± 0·13	10·2 ± 0·59	3·1 ± 0·19	13·8 ± 0·68
14.00	5·2 ± 0·18	12·0 ± 0·41	5·5 ± 0·21	9·6 ± 0·55
16.00	4·9 ± 0·23	4·1 ± 0·22	4·8 ± 0·23	5·4 ± 0·25
18.00	2·9 ± 0·09	4·6 ± 0·35	3·7 ± 0·15	4·5 ± 0·32
20.00	2·6 ± 0·15	5·5 ± 0·28	1·2 ± 0·16	1·0 ± 0·20

induced. This is in agreement with the theory that an exceptionally long sleep period results in a depletion of the carbohydrate content of the ear epidermis with a consequent drop in the rate of cell division.

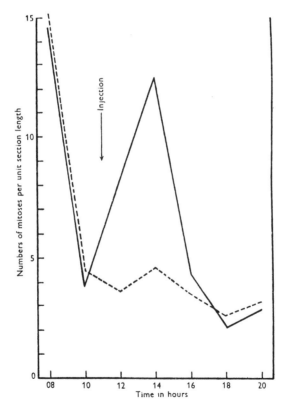

Fig. 6. The variations in the mitotic activity of the ear epidermis in resting, middle-aged, Strong's CBA males following the injection at 11.00 hr. of 20 mg. of starch in normal saline (solid line) and of normal saline alone (broken line).

(6) *Mitosis in other tissues*

Throughout this investigation it was found convenient to concentrate on conditions in the ear epidermis, but it is obviously of the greatest importance that an attempt should be made to discover whether the results obtained are also typical of other tissues. It was hoped that precise and detailed information on this point would become available from a study of the colchicine injected animals, but the difficulties encountered in the use of this drug have already been described. However, valuable, if limited, information was obtained from some of the tissues of the Kreyberg's white label mice which had given the most reliable results for the ear epidermis.

The first tissue to be examined from these mice was the epidermis of the antero-dorsal region of the back, the region above the scapulae. This was done in order to determine whether the conditions already found in the ear epidermis could be considered as typical of the epidermis as a whole. The mitoses were counted in unit lengths of 1 cm. of sections cut 7 μ thick, and the results, given in Table 15, are therefore directly comparable to those already obtained from the ear.

Table 15. *The average numbers of mitoses arrested by colchicine in 12 hr. in unit section lengths (1 cm.) of the antero-dorsal epidermis in groups each of ten Kreyberg's white label mice.*

Age of mice	Period 09.00–21.00 hr.	Period 21.00–09.00 hr.
1 month	48·5 ± 2·41	22·9 ± 1·13
5 months	39·8 ± 1·52	17·3 ± 1·08
16 months	44·5 ± 2·70	20·5 ± 1·21

In this table there is one result which is strikingly different from anything which has been described before, namely that the highest mitotic activity occurred in the 1-month-old mice. All the results obtained with the ear epidermis have shown that low mitotic activity is typical of the immature age group, and it follows that, in this particular at least, the ear epidermis cannot be taken as typical of the epidermis as a whole. However, the results for the middle-aged mice confirm those already obtained with the ear epidermis in showing an increase in mitotic activity over that recorded for the mature mice.

The second tissue examined was the stratified epithelium lining the oesophagus. Sections, 7 μ thick, were cut transversely in the region just anterior to the diaphragm, and the numbers of mitoses were counted in unit section lengths of 1 mm. The results are given in Table 16.

Table 16. *The average numbers of mitoses arrested by colchicine in 12 hr. in unit section lengths (1 mm.) of the stratified epithelium of the oesophagus in groups each of ten Kreyberg's white label males*

Age of mice	Period 09.00–21.00 hr.	Period 21.00–09.00 hr.
1 month	15·7 ± 0·53	12·6 ± 0·91
5 months	9·1 ± 0·49	6·7 ± 0·36
16 months	20·0 ± 0·98	16·4 ± 0·63

Again the immature mice gave a mitosis count which was considerably higher than that given by the mature mice, and again the middle-age period was characterized by a sharp rise in the mitosis rate.

The third tissue examined was that of the salivary gland. This was cut into sections 7μ thick, and the mitoses were counted in unit section areas of 0·5 mm.². The results are shown in Table 17.

Table 17. *The average number of mitoses arrested by colchicine in 12 hr. in unit section areas (0·5 mm.²) of the salivary gland in groups each of ten Kreyberg's white label males*

Age of mice	Period 09.00–21.00 hr.	Period 21.00–09.00 hr.
1 month	3·5 ± 0·22	1·6 ± 0·08
5 months	1·3 ± 0·06	0·7 ± 0·05
16 months	2·0 ± 0·07	1·1 ± 0·06

Once again the results are similar with a relatively high mitosis rate in the immature and middle-age groups.

The final tissue examined was the epithelium lining the tubules of the epididymis. This was chosen as a representative of the accessory sexual organs, and the counts were made on sections, cut 7μ thick, of that region of the caput epididymis in which the epithelial cells have a particularly tall columnar form. For the present purpose the tissue was regarded as homogeneous, and the numbers of cell divisions were estimated in unit section areas of 0·5 mm.². They are recorded in Table 18.

Table 18. *The average numbers of mitoses arrested by colchicine in 12 hr. in unit section areas (0·5 mm.²) of the epididymis in groups each of ten Kreyberg's white label males*

Age of mice	Period 09.00–21.00 hr.	Period 21.00–09.00 hr.
1 month	11·4 ± 0·41	5·9 ± 0·21
5 months	0·9 ± 0·11	0·7 ± 0·06
16 months	2·1 ± 0·15	1·6 ± 0·13

In spite of the fact that these figures do not really represent the numbers of mitoses occurring in a period of 12 hr., two conclusions emerge the validity of which can hardly be doubted. The first is that the ear epidermis is abnormal in developing fewer mitoses in the immature stage than in any other stage except the senile. The results for the other tissues indicate unanimously that mitotic activity is greater, and sometimes far greater, in the immature than in the mature male.

The second conclusion is that these results do not contradict the evidence of the ear epidermis that a rise in mitotic activity is typical of middle age.

IV. DISCUSSION

The main conclusion arising from the foregoing data is that, when judged from the point of view of mitotic activity, there are four distinct ages in the life of a male mouse. Of these it seems generally true to say that the first is characterized by a high rate of cell division, and, since the animals are actively growing at this time, this is what would be anticipated. The second age begins when the adult body size has been attained. Then there is an abrupt change to a lower rate of mitosis, which is maintained at a remarkably steady level until the age of about 12 or 13 months when a further change marks the onset of middle age. This third age is characterized by an increased mitosis rate, the precise degree of increase apparently varying from tissue to tissue. The final change occurs with the onset of senility, and, although fewer data are available concerning it, it is probably true, and certainly logical, to say that it is characterized by a mitosis depression which affects the whole body.

Apart from the evidence of the mitosis rate, the difficulty of defining these four ages is considerable. The state of the reproductive system is of no assistance, and no other internal criterion has been discovered except the size of the fat deposits. Externally it is often possible, and with practice usually possible, to distinguish the four ages by the size and general appearance of the animals. Thus immature mice have not yet reached their full stature, while middle-aged mice have exceeded it by the deposition of quantities of fat. Coincidentally, the immature animals are excitable and active, while the middle-aged animals are placid and quiet. The senile animals are feeble and shrunken with arched backs and poor fur, so that they are particularly easily distinguished.

This general vagueness of definition makes it difficult to suggest any obvious basis for the changes in the mitosis rate, and the curious fact that the change from age to age is apparently quite sudden adds to the difficulty. It is extraordinary how the transition from the immature to the mature plan of mitotic activity is accomplished in no more than a week or two, and the same phenomenon is evident in Kreyberg's mice during the transition from middle age to senility. The change from maturity to middle age is perhaps equally abrupt, but this is not yet certain.

Approximately coincident with these changes in the mitosis rate are the changes in spontaneous bodily activity. These can be regarded as furnishing a complete explanation for any alteration in the timing of the mitosis cycle, as, for instance, that between the immature and mature ages, and again that between the mature and middle ages in the Strong's *CBA* mice. However, in spite of the general inverse relationship which exists between bodily activity and mitotic activity, it seems unlikely that changes in spontaneous bodily activity alone can account for the observed alterations in the mitosis rate. The transition from mature to middle age is characterized by a great reduction in spontaneous bodily activity and by an increase in the mitosis rate, but, while the one may assist in the development of the other, it appears probable that it is not solely responsible for it. It is interesting to notice here that during pregnancy in the rat the spontaneous bodily activity is also greatly reduced (Wang, 1925). Again the reduction in muscular activity might be expected to favour the development of a high rate of mitosis, but obviously this reduction cannot be held solely responsible for the raised mitosis rate. Further, it must be remembered that immature mice are very active and restless and yet have a high mitosis rate, while conversely senile mice spend almost the entire day lying at rest and yet only develop a low mitosis rate.

The conclusion seems inescapable that the age changes in the mitosis rate are due mainly to some factor other than that of exercise. In analysing this point it is obviously important to discover whether these changes, which are so abrupt in the ear epidermis, are equally abrupt and have the same timing in all other tissues. Such evidence as is available at the moment suggests that this may be so, and, if this is proved, then perhaps the critical factor or factors may lie not in the tissues themselves but in some discreet part of the body. In this case, a critical change in the composition of the blood might be suspected, and here it is of interest to recall the tendency for both the blood-sugar level and the renal threshold to rise with increasing age (see review by Cannon, 1942). From previous results on the effects of the blood-sugar level on mitotic activity (Bullough, 1949a), it would be expected that any such rise would be accompanied by an increase in the mitosis rate, and this might perhaps furnish some explanation for the condition in middle age. Of course, as already mentioned, the reduction in the spontaneous bodily activity during middle age may also assist in the development of excessive reserves of sugar, and the deposition of fat at this time might be taken as evidence that such an excess does, in fact, develop.

An interesting side issue which may be mentioned here is the effect on mitotic activity of the prolonged rests of the middle-aged animals. That rest and sleep are favourable to mitotic activity is now well known (Bullough, 1948a, b), but the present results show clearly that full stimulation is achieved only during the first few hours. Thereafter the mitosis rate falls unless more carbohydrate is added to the system for deposition into the tissues. This happens if the animal wakes, eats and sleeps again, or if carbohydrate is injected.

The fact that middle age is characterized by an increase in mitotic activity which is apparently general throughout the body is of particular interest. While male mice do not usually develop spontaneous tumours, it may be said of mice generally that the cancer age begins at about 12 months. If it should now transpire that an increase in the mitosis rate is normal during mammalian middle age, when spontaneous tumours are especially liable to develop, it may be a matter of considerable importance. Mottram (1944), and others working on experimental carcinogenesis, have distinguished between the blastogenic action of a carcinogen in producing cancer cells, and the developing action of non-carcinogenic factors which, by inducing hyperplasia, assist in the formation of a tumour. Thus Berenblum & Shubik (1947) have insisted that the initial action of a carcinogen is to induce a sudden and irreversible change whereby a few normal cells are converted into 'latent tumour cells' which then lie dormant. The development of these 'latent tumour cells' is an altogether different process which can be assisted by any treatment causing hyperplasia, and, in the absence of such treatment, many of these cells would never receive the stimulus to develop. Thus, while the development of a raised mitosis rate in middle age would not of itself be expected to cause, or even assist in, the formation of cancerous cells, it might be expected to increase the chances of development of any latent cancer cells which were already present.

It would follow from this that if the high mitotic activity of middle age could be reduced, a reduction in the incidence of spontaneous tumours might also result. In this connexion it is now known that underfeeding has a powerful effect in reducing cancer incidence. The reviews of Tannenbaum (1947) and Boyland (1948) include evidence that a reduction in the diet of a mouse to two-thirds of what it would eat if it fed *ad lib.* markedly reduces the incidence of a variety of tumours, both spontaneous and induced, and also retards the time of appearance of those which do form. It has now been shown (Bullough, unpublished) that such starvation has the effect of causing an immediate and pronounced reduction in the mitosis rate of the ear epidermis of the male mouse, and thus it is evident that a restriction of diet acts in an opposite manner to that of a developing agent which induces hyperplasia.

It may therefore be suspected that any factor which restricts mitotic activity in middle age, and so induces what can be called hypoplasia, will also hinder the formation of tumours. At the moment the most potent restricting agents known are starvation and insulin, both of which act by lowering the blood-sugar level, and a similar effect can be induced by phloridzin, which acts by reducing the availability of whatever sugar is present in the body (Bullough, 1949 a). While work on these lines is still in progress, preliminary results have already indicated that mice kept phloridzinized during middle age are considerably less liable to develop spontaneous tumours than are the controls. In view of these results it appears highly significant that, in the experiments reported by Tannenbaum concerning the effect of restrictions of diet on carcinogenesis, it is the carbohydrate fraction of the food which is the most important. A reduction in the protein fraction has no effect on tumour development, while a reduction in the fat fraction produces irregular results.

V. SUMMARY

1. A study has been made of the mitosis rate and of the diurnal cycles of male mice during each of the first 20 months of life. The mice used belonged to the Kreyberg's white label and the Strong's *CBA* strains. Most of the observations were made on the ear epidermis, but some attention was also given to other tissues.

2. It was discovered that, when judged from the point of view of mitotic activity, the life of a male mouse consists of four ages. During the immature age the animals are still growing and their mitosis rate is generally high, although the ear epidermis provides an exception to this rule. During the mature age which lasts from about the 3rd to the 12th month the mitosis rate is lowered. During the middle age which follows the mitosis rate increases, but in senility it is again reduced.

3. Coincident with these changes in the mitosis rate are changes in the spontaneous bodily activity. The mice are most active during immaturity and maturity. In middle age their activity is reduced by about half, and in senility they spend almost the whole time resting. Particularly in the Strong's *CBA* mice there are also changes in the timing of the diurnal cycle of spontaneous bodily activity, and these are immediately mirrored by changes in the timing of the diurnal cycle of mitotic

activity so that throughout life a general inverse relationship between bodily activity and mitotic activity is maintained.

4. In middle-aged Strong's *CBA* males the daily rest period extends almost without interruption from 06.00 to 18.00 hr. However, the most active cell division develops only at the beginning of this period, and it is evident that in prolonged sleep a lack of some vital factor develops. It is shown that subcutaneous injections of starch overcome this lack in sleeping mice and result almost immediately in the redevelopment of a high mitosis rate. Thus it would appear that sugar is the vital factor involved, and that the sugar content of the tissues is quickly used up during high mitotic activity.

5. These results are discussed particularly in relation to the problem of carcinogenesis.

REFERENCES

BOYLAND, E. (1948). *Nature, Lond.*, **161**, 106.
BERENBLUM, I. & SHUBIK, P. (1947). *Brit. J. Cancer*, **1**, 383.
BULLOUGH, W. S. (1948a). *Proc. Roy. Soc.* B, **135**, 212.
BULLOUGH, W. S. (1948b). *Proc. Roy. Soc.* B, **135**, 233.
BULLOUGH, W. S. (1949a) *J. Exp. Biol.* **26**, 83.
BULLOUGH, W. S. (1949b). *J. Exp. Biol.* **26**, 287.
CANNON, W. B. (1942). *Problems of Ageing*, Ch. 22. Edited by E. V. Cowdry, Baltimore.
MOTTRAM, J. C. (1944). *J. Path. Bact.* **56**, 181.
SIMPSON, G. G. & ROE, A. (1939). *Quantitive Zoology*, New York.
TANNENBAUM, A. (1947). In *Approaches to Tumor Chemotherapy*. Published by the American Association for the Advancement of Science, Washington.
WANG, H. (1925). *Amer. J. Physiol.* **71**, 736.

40

AGEING, IMMUNE RESPONSE, AND MORTALITY

IAN C. ROBERTS-THOMSON   SENGA WHITTINGHAM
URIWAN YOUNGCHAIYUD   IAN R. MACKAY

*Clinical Research Unit, Walter and Eliza Hall Institute
of Medical Research and Royal Melbourne Hospital,
Melbourne, Victoria 3050, Australia*

Summary   In aged as compared with young people T-cell immune responses tested by three different systems were significantly depressed; in the aged (more than sixty years) compared with the young (less than twenty-five) the number of positive delayed-type hypersensitivity reactions to five ubiquitous antigens was significantly lower; the lymphocyte response to the mitogen phytohæmagglutinin was significantly lower; and the presumed T-cell-dependent late IgG response to 5 μg. of monomeric flagellin was significantly lower. Furthermore, the mortality of very old people (over eighty), who were hyporesponsive in tests for delayed hypersensitivity, was significantly greater over a two-year period than that of comparable people who were not hyporesponsive.

Introduction

THE probable role of an immunological component in ageing and senescence has attracted the attention of biologists,[1] immunologists,[2] and gerontologists.[3] Lymphoid organs may be expected to " age " pari passu with other tissues, but there is the additional possibility that lymphoid failure of itself accelerates senescence by predisposing to infection and degenerative diseases. There are numerous studies on immunological aspects of ageing in animals, but relatively few in man. Our investigations in elderly people, using three different test systems, give clear evidence for impaired function of the immune system, especially thymus-dependent cell-mediated responses. Also, notably, hyporeactive responses were associated with higher mortality.

342

Participants and Methods

Participants

199 adults were studied and, excluding those over eighty years, all considered themselves healthy in so far as they did not feel the need to consult a doctor. For delayed-type hypersensitivity (D.T.H.) cutaneous responses to five ubiquitous antigens, 20 healthy people under twenty-five years of age were compared with 68 healthy people over sixty years of age. For lymphocyte responses to phytohæmagglutinin (P.H.A.), 20 healthy people under twenty-five years of age were compared with 20 healthy people over sixty. For responses to immunisation with the antigen monomeric flagellin from *Salmonella adelaide,* 27 healthy people under twenty-five years of age were compared with 44 healthy people over sixty. Finally, the mortality over a two-year period of 52 people over eighty years of age was correlated with their D.T.H. responses to five ubiquitous antigens. These people, 14 men and 38 women, were in homes for the aged because of their inability to live alone. Although some were diagnosed as having "degenerative" diseases such as cerebrovascular disease, ischæmic heart-disease, osteoarthritis, diabetes mellitus, and Parkinson's disease, all were ambulant, cooperative, and well-nourished, and none had cancer or immunopathic disease. Information on death and its presumed cause was available in all cases, but post-mortem examinations were not performed.

D.T.H. Skin Tests

The five antigens used were *Candida* (Bencard), mumps skin-testing antigen (Eli Lilly), trichophyton (Bencard), tuberculin 1/1000 strength (Commonwealth Serum Laboratories, Melbourne), and streptokinase 10 units/ streptodornase 2·5 units ('Varidase', Lederle). Each antigen, 0·1 ml., was injected intradermally; the procedure and criteria for positivity were as described by Toh et al.[4] Healthy people react to two or more antigens[4]; hence the aged people of this study were grouped according to their reactivity to 0–1 or 2–5 of the antigens used.

Lymphocyte Response to P.H.A.

Lymphocytes were separated from heparinised blood by an 'Isopaque-Ficoll' gradient. Triplicate cultures containing 10^6 lymphocytes per ml. were exposed to 5, 20, and 100 μg. of P.H.A. and the degree of transformation which occurred was measured by liquid scintillation counting of incorporated tritiated thymidine. The method used was that described by Toh et al.[4] except that cultures were prepared in a serum-free culture medium containing RPMI 1640 and Hepes buffer.[5] The results were expressed in disintegrations per minute.

Immunisation with Flagellin

Polymeric flagellin was prepared from *S. adelaide*, strain SW 1338, as described by Ada et al.,[6] and depolymerised from the polymeric to the monomeric state as described by Rowley and Mackay.[7] 5 µg. was injected subcutaneously into the forearm. Blood was withdrawn from each subject for the measurement of serum antibody to flagellin before injection and one, two, six, and ten weeks after injection. Sera containing total antibody and antibody remaining after the treatment of serum with 2-mercaptoethanol for one hour at 37°C, presumably IgG,[8] were titrated in doubling dilutions and tested by the tanned sheep-red-cell hæmagglutination reaction.[8,9] The late IgG antibody is presumed to be the thymus-dependent component of the response.

Statistical Methods

The mean values of disintegrations per minute of thymidine after transformation of lymphocytes by P.H.A. at various doses, and the mean titres of antibody to flagellin for the groups of young and old subjects, were compared by Student's *t* test after logarithmic conversion. Differences in the distribution of scores of D.T.H. reactions in young and old subjects and incidence of death according to D.T.H. reactions among subjects over 80 years were tested by chi squared.

Results

D.T.H. Reactions

The number of positive D.T.H. reactions in young and old people is recorded in table I. No-one less than twenty-five years of age had less than two positive reactions while 39 or 68 (57%) over sixty years of age had no or only one positive reaction. These differences between young and old were statistically significant (P<0·001).

TABLE I—D.T.H. SKIN REACTIONS IN YOUNG AND OLD PEOPLE

No. of positive reactions	No. of people age < 25 yr.	No. of people age > 60 yr.
0	0 } 0%	24 } 57%
1	0	15
2	2 } 100%	17 } 43%
3	6	8
4	8	4
5	4	0
Total	20	68

Lymphocyte Response to P.H.A.

A significantly higher response to 5, 20, and 100 μg. P.H.A. was demonstrated in young as compared to old people (P<0·001 for each concentration of P.H.A.) (fig. 1).

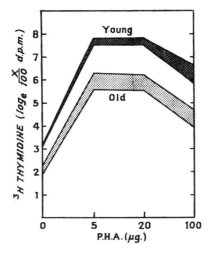

Fig. 1—Lymphocyte response to P.H.A. in young and old people.

The mean lymphocyte response (±standard error) to various concentrations of P.H.A. was significantly less in old people than in young people under twenty-five years of age.

Antibody to Flagellin

As was anticipated, natural antibody was higher in young people than in old people and was predominantly IgM [10] (fig. 2). After immunisation the levels of total antibody at two weeks (peak titre) and six and ten weeks were similar in the young and old (fig. 2). However, in old people the titres of IgG

TABLE II—SKIN REACTIONS AND DEATHS OVER 2 YEARS IN PEOPLE >80 YEARS OF AGE

No. of positive reactions	No. of people	No. dead after 2 years	
0	21	17	80%
1	14	11	
2	10	2	
3	3	2	35%
4	4	2	
5	0	0	
..	52	34	

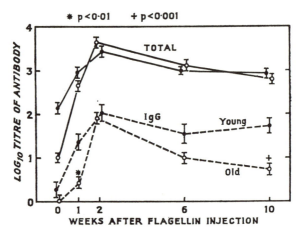

Fig. 2—Antibody response to flagellin in young and old people.

The geometric mean titre of total antibody (±standard error) was similar in young and old people. Titres of IgG antibody in old people were lower before and after the peak titre, and there was a more rapid fall-off with time.

antibody were generally lower (fig. 2), and at ten weeks there was a highly significant difference (P<0·001).

Survival According to D.T.H. Reactions

The number of positive D.T.H. reactions and the number of deaths among participants over eighty years are recorded in table II; those with less than two positive reactions had a significantly greater mortality over the two-year period of study (P<0·005) than those with two to five positive reactions. This latter finding was independent of sex and age in that the mean age at the time of testing was 85·1 years for survivors and 85·9 years for non-survivors, while the mortality over the two-year period was 50% for males and 71% for females. Bronchopneumonia, cerebro-vascular accident, and cardiac failure were the most commonly recorded causes of death; no deaths were attributed to cancer.

Discussion

The depression of D.T.H. responses to ubiquitous antigens with advancing age has been reported from this unit [4,11] and by others.[12,13] There are, however, few studies correlating mortality in old people with failure of cell-mediated immunity as shown by D.T.H. reactions, except in the case of cancer where mortality was greater in those anergic to dinitrochloro-benzene.[14,15] This increased mortality associated with impaired D.T.H. responses, whether in old age or in cancer, is unexplained. One possibility is predisposition to more numerous and more frequently fatal infections, especially illnesses associated with seasonal epidemics due to new types or strains of bacterial or viral pathogens. The lymphocyte response to P.H.A., presumed to be dependent on T cells, was clearly diminished in our elderly participants, and this finding supplements previous reports of impaired responsiveness of human lymphocytes to P.H.A. with ageing.[16-20] The humoral response to monomeric flagellin was also impaired in old people, the major defect being an inability to sustain IgG antibody production. This defect with ageing could be explained by a deficiency in helper T cells. In mice, the immune response to flagellin, particularly the IgG response, requires the collaborative activity of T cells.[21]

We suggest that cell-mediated immune functions deteriorate greatly with age, and that mortality is higher in old people with impaired D.T.H. responses. The defects of cell-mediated immunity in ageing could be explained by inadequate numbers of T cells or by a functional impairment of T cells. Weksler and Hütteroth[20] found that the absolute number of peripheral-blood lymphocytes and the percentages of T cells assessed by rosette formation with sheep erythrocytes, and of B cells assessed by membrane-bound immunoglobulin, were the same in old and young persons. On the other hand, Carosella et al.[22] reported a significant fall in rosette-forming T cells in blood occurring between forty-six and sixty years of age. It is uncertain whether the peripheral blood accurately reflects the " T cell mass " of the body, and whether T cells become functionally less effective with age. We conclude that whilst the thymus may not necessarily be the " life-span controller ",[23] the integrity of the thymus-derived component of the immune system could be an important determinant of longevity.

We thank Dr I. J. Wood for reviewing the manuscript, Mr J. Buckley for help with the statistical procedures, and Mrs Julie Matthews and Mrs Jennifer Leydon for excellent technical assistance. S. W. and I. R. M. worked with the aid of a grant from the National Health and Medical Research Council of Australia. U. Y. was a visiting Colombo Plan fellow.

Requests for reprints should be addressed to I. R. M.

REFERENCES

1. Burnet, F. M. *Pathology*, 1974, **6**, 1.
2. Walford, R. L. The Immunologic Theory of Ageing. Copenhagen, 1969.
3. Comfort, A. *Lancet*, 1963, ii, 138.
4. Toh, B. H., Roberts-Thomson, I. C., Mathews, J. D., Whittingham, S., Mackay, I. R. *Clin. exp. Immun.* 1973, **14**, 193.
5. Youngchaiyud, U., Coates, A. S., Whittingham, S., Mackay, I. R. *Aust. N.Z. Jl Med.* 1974 (in the press).
6. Ada, G. L., Nossal, G. J. V., Pye, J., Abbot, A. *Aust. J. exp. Biol. med. Sci.* 1964, **42**, 267.
7. Rowley, M. J., Mackay, I. R. *Clin. exp. Immun.* 1969, **5**, 407.
8. Rowley, M. J., Wistar, R., Mackay, I. R. *Immunology*, 1972, **22**, 475.
9. Wistar, R. *Aust. J. exp. Biol. med. Sci.* 1968, **46**, 769.
10. Rowley, M. J., Buchanan, H., Mackay, I. R. *Lancet*, 1968, ii, 24.
11. Mackay, I. R. *Gerontologia*, 1972, **18**, 285.
12. Waldorf, D. S., Wilkens, R. F., Decker, J. L. *J. Am. med. Ass.* 1968, **203**, 831.
13. Forbes, I. J. *Aust. N.Z. Jl Med.* 1971, **1**, 160.
14. Eilber, F. R., Morton, D. L. *Cancer*, 1970, **25**, 362.
15. Wells, S. A., Burdick, J. F., Joseph, W. L., Christiansen, C. L., Wolfe, W. G., Adkins, P. C., Durham, N. C. *J. thorac. cardiovasc. Surg.* 1973, **66**, 557.
16. Pisciotta, A. V., Westring, D. W., DePrey, C., Walsh, B. *Nature*, 1967, **215**, 193.
17. Heine, K. M., Stobbe, H., Klatt, R., Sahi, K., Herrmann, H. *Helv. med. Acta*, 1969–70, **35**, 484.
18. Conrad, R. A., Demoise, C. F., Scott, W. A., Makar, M. *J. Geront.* 1971, **26**, 28.
19. Hallgren, H. M., Buckley, C. E. III, Gilbertsen, V. A., Yunes, E. J. *J. Immun.* 1973, **111**, 1101.
20. Weksler, M. E., Hütteroth, T. H. *J. clin. Invest.* 1974, **53**, 99.
21. Miller, J. F. A. P. *Ann. N.Y. Acad. Sci.* (in the press).
22. Carosella, E. D., Mochanko, K., Braun, M. *Cell. Immun.* 1974, **12**, 323.
23. Burnet, F. M. *Lancet*, 1970, ii, 358.

Editor's Comments
on Paper 41

41   HAMILTON
Relationship of Castration, Spaying, and Sex to Survival and Duration of Life in Domestic Cats

Probably one of the best known and most sharply delineated features of human aging is the female climacterium. An excellent discussion of the variability among women during the time of cessation of ovarian function is given by Dr. Helen Zern (1973), who believes the difference among women lies in adrenal cortical function; in those syndrome-free women, adrenal estrogen takes over when ovaries cease. Failure of such endogeneous replacement therapy by the adrenals results in the syndrome.

Investigations into the relationship of the gonads to aging have been carried out by James B. Hamilton. Dr. Hamilton raised the question of whether or not the greater survival of the female mammal was due to the presence of the Y chromosome in the male or to some specific function of the male gonads. In a study (Paper 41; Hamilton et al., 1969), Hamilton compared lifespan in a large number of domestic cats raised in households of his area, finding clearly that in the male castration appears to prolong lifespan. In another paper (Hamilton and Mestler, 1969), Dr. Hamilton compared survival of eunuchs with survival of intact men and women and again found eunuchs survived for a greater period of time. From these reports varied interpretations are possible. They contrast sharply with reports in the previous sections.

41

Reprinted from *J. Gerontology* **20**:96–104 (1965)

Relationship of Castration, Spaying, and Sex to Survival and Duration of Life in Domestic Cats

James B. Hamilton, Ph.D.[1]

CASTRATION has been practiced since antiquity but only recently have attempts been made to ascertain if duration of life may be affected by removal of the testes or ovaries. To supplement an investigation currently in progress in man, the present study was undertaken to assess the effects of gonadectomy upon duration of life in another species which does not die at sexual maturity and has not been bred for a specific function, such as to win races or to produce wool, milk, or meat. Of the various domesticated animals the house cat seemed to be particularly suitable for the present study. Few sublines of cats have been developed and these are stated not to differ from one another to a marked extent (Mellen, 1940). This is in contrast to the numerous and distinctive sublines in many domesticated species, for example, in horses, sheep, cattle, dogs, rabbits, and fowl. Distinctive sublines may differ in duration of life, as observed in dogs and mice (Comfort, 1956b; Mühlbock, 1959).

Cats which are house pets are usually well cared for and are commonly permitted to live to old age. In New York City, many cats of known age are brought to veterinary hospitals when ill, old, or dead; the sex and age of the animal upon terminal illness or death are recorded, along with information as to whether the cat had been castrated or spayed. Therefore, it was possible to compare the duration of life in intact and in gonadectomized males and females brought to these hospitals.

Examination of articles listed in *Biological Abstracts, Index Medicus, Index Veterinarius,* and the *Index Catalogue of the Library of the Surgeon-General's Office* revealed little data on the effect of gonadectomy upon duration of life and only two brief descriptions of maximal longevity of house cats based on questionnaires answered by owners (Mellen, 1940; Comfort, 1956c).

MATERIALS AND METHODS

Selection of animals.—Data were obtained for 533 cats from the records of two veterinary hospitals in Manhattan, those in Series 1 from the American Society for the Prevention of Cruelty to Animals (ASPCA) for the period of March, 1962, to May, 1964, inclusive, those in Series 2 from the Animal Medical Center, chiefly for 1963.

Records were utilized if they specified the type of cat, sex, age at death, and endocrine status, i.e., if the cat was intact, castrated, or spayed. Cats subjected to trauma, as from falls, were included, since accidents may bear a relationship to such matters as locomotion, equilibrium, and osteoporosis. Cats were excluded if death was known or suspected to have been due to poisoning or occurred as a consequence of parturition or elective surgery, such as gonadectomy. Cats were also excluded if their owners requested euthanasia, in the absence of known disease, when the animals were less than three years of age.

Data.—Records were rejected if the owners were somewhat vague about the age of the cat. The stated age of the cats at death was only approximate, however, since it was based upon information provided by the owners. Age was calculated to the nearest year, unless an exact statement warranted tabulation to the nearest half-year.

The attributed causes of illness and death were recorded by veterinarians at or immediately prior to death of the cats. In most instances these diagnoses were not based upon exhaustive studies during life nor upon findings at autopsy. The suspected causes of death or

[1] Department of Anatomy, State University of New York College of Medicine at New York City, Brooklyn, New York.

disposal of the cats were most reliable for conditions recognizable upon physical examination.

The age of the animal at removal of the testes or ovaries was recorded infrequently but, when stated, was usually 6 to 12 months. In order to increase the comparability of gonadectomized and intact groups, cats were included in the present study only if they had lived at least one year, i.e., to an age when most recorded orchiectomies and ovariectomies had been done.

The great majority of the cats were of the domestic short-haired, tailed type known popularly as alley or tabby cats and are referred to as common cats in the present communication. Data were examined separately for two other categories of cats: (a) Siamese and (b) long-haired animals. Most of the latter were Persian but a few were Angora and one a Maine coon cat.

These cats lived in many different households and were probably subjected to a greater variety of environments than animals raised in a single laboratory.

The percentage of intact females that had been pregnant could not be ascertained, but it may be presumed that measures were employed to prevent unplanned matings in view of the problems posed by the care of litters in cramped housing quarters of a large city.

Fighting with other cats seems to have been of little consequence, since there was only one record of serious injury sustained in this manner. It seems likely that information of this type would have been recorded, since there were many references to other forms of trauma.

Maximal longevity of the species is not to be judged from the fact that only 0.4% of the cats lived more than 18 years. Of the 14 cats which were longest-lived in their groups, 11 were subjected to euthanasia because of senescence when apparently neither moribund nor ill with a specifically recognized pathological state.

RESULTS

Sources of error.—The cats selected for study represented a privileged category of house pets belonging to owners who expended time, and in many instances money as well, in bringing the animals to hospitals. Even so, when euthanasia was employed, it was not always pos-

sible to distinguish moribund animals from those which were senescent or ill but could have lived longer. Animals known to have been sacrificed when they were well are represented in the figures by the symbol ($>$).

A few animals were known to have been gonadectomized after one but before two years of age. These cats would not have been in the operated groups until they had survived part of the second year of life, an age at which many felines die. Withholding of operations until cats were more than one year old was not a source of substantial error, however, since the trends to be reported in the entire series of animals were also observed in cats which lived a minimum of two, three, or five years (Table 1).

Common Cats.—The data for the two hospitals showed many similar trends but were analyzed separately, since the age at death of intact and castrated males was earlier in Series 1 than in Series 2 and the age at death of intact females tended to be slightly later in Series 1 than in Series 2. The reasons for the earlier deaths of males in Series 1 than in Series 2 remain uncertain. Conceivably, males brought to a private hospital might also be guarded in other ways, with less freedom and exposure to danger than cats brought to the ASPCA. The differences between the two series were not due solely to unequal use of euthanasia, since

Table 1. Duration of Life in Common Cats as Analyzed Separately for Animals Which Survived a Minimum of One, Two, Three, or Five Years.

Group	Min. No. Yrs. Surv.	Series 1			Series 2		
		No. of Cats	Age at Death		No. of Cats	Age at Death	
			Mn$\pm\sigma_{mn}$	Median		Mn$\pm\sigma_{mn}$	Median
Castrated males	1	60	6.8$\pm$0.58	5.25	77	8.5$\pm$0.56	9.1
	2	54	7.4$\pm$0.59	6.0	73	8.9$\pm$0.55	9.0
	3	52	7.6$\pm$0.60	6.0	64	9.8$\pm$0.54	10.25
	5	35	9.6$\pm$0.66	9.0	52	11.2$\pm$0.48	11.0
Intact males	1	65	3.2$\pm$0.34	2.0	51	6.1$\pm$0.66	5.25
	2	42	4.3$\pm$0.45	3.0	42	7.2$\pm$0.69	6.5
	3	27	5.6$\pm$0.56	4.0	33	8.6$\pm$0.69	8.0
	5	13	8.0$\pm$0.68	7.0	27	9.7$\pm$0.68	8.0
Spayed females	1	28	9.2$\pm$0.88	11.0	45	8.4$\pm$0.71	8.25
	2	26	9.8$\pm$0.84	11.0	44	8.5$\pm$0.71	8.0
	3	25	10.1$\pm$0.81	11.0	39	9.3$\pm$0.71	8.5
	5	21	11.3$\pm$0.70	11.0	32	10.6$\pm$0.66	10.0
Intact females	1	58	7.7$\pm$0.68	7.5	50	7.4$\pm$0.72	7.0
	2	50	8.7$\pm$0.69	8.5	43	8.3$\pm$0.74	8.0
	3	44	9.6$\pm$0.68	10.0	38	9.2$\pm$0.73	9.25
	5	36	11.0$\pm$0.62	10.5	30	10.7$\pm$0.70	10.5

they were also present in data for cats which died "spontaneously."

a. *Comparisons of castrated and intact males.*—Mean and median ages at death were higher for castrated than for intact males in

Table 2. Differences in Survival of Cats.

Difference Between	Min. No. Yrs. Surv.	Series 1 Mn Age at Death	Series 1 P	Series 2 Mn Age at Death	Series 2 P
Castrated and	1	+3.6	<.001	+2.4	.008
intact males	2	+3.1	<.001	+1.7	.06
	3	+2.0	.04	+1.2	.19
	5	+1.6	.18	+1.5	.08
Spayed and	1	+1.5	.20	+1.0	.34
intact females	2	+1.1	.36	+0.2	.85
	3	+0.5	.65	+0.1	>.90
	5	+0.3	.75	−0.1	>.90
Intact males and	1	−4.5	<.001	−1.3	.10
females	2	−4.4	<.001	−1.1	.29
	3	−4.0	<.001	−0.6	.57
	5	−3.0	.01	−1.0	.30
Castrated males and	1	−0.9	.31	+1.1	.22
intact females	2	−1.3	.15	+0.6	.51
	3	−2.0	.03	+0.6	.50
	5	−1.4	.13	+0.5	.55
Castrated males and	1	−2.4	.02	+0.1	>.90
spayed females	2	−2.4	.02	+0.4	.68
	3	−2.5	.02	+0.5	.57
	5	−1.7	.10	+0.6	.46

both Series 1 and 2 (Tables 1 and 2; Figs. 1 and 2). Differences in mean age at death were marked at one year of age, but also tended to be higher in castrated than in intact males among cats which survived a minimum of two, three, or five years (Table 2). Therefore, the longer life of castrated than of intact males was partly but not solely attributable to improved survival in the years immediately after the age for sexual maturation (Table 2) which is stated to be 9 to 12 months (Mellen, 1940).

The percentage of long-lived animals tended to be greater in castrated than in intact males in both series, but the differences were not significant (Table 3).

For most of the commonly assigned causes of death or disposal of cats, the analyses of combined data for all cats showed that the age at death was later in castrated than in intact

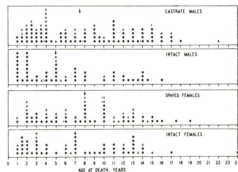

Fig. 2. Age at death of cats brought to the Animal Medical Center. ● = common cats; △ = Siamese cats; ▲ =long-haired cats. > indicates euthanasia of cats which were known not to be ill or senile:

Table 3. Percentage of Cats Which Lived to 14 or More Years of Age.

Group	Common Cats Series 1 Total No.	Series 1 No.	Series 1 %	Common Cats Series 2 Total No.	Series 2 No.	Series 2 %	Cats of All Types Total No.	No.	%
	Animals Which Survived At Least One Year								
Castrated males	60	4	6.7	77	15	19.5	171	23	13.5
Intact males	65	1	1.5	51	5	9.8	134	7	5.2
Spayed females	28	6	21.4	45	8	17.8	103	15	14.6
Intact females	58	10	17.1	50	4	8.0	125	16	12.8
	Animals Which Survived At Least Five Years								
Castrated males	35	4	11	33	15	29	105	23	22
Intact males	13	1	8	14	5	19	49	7	14
Spayed females	21	6	29	18	8	25	72	15	21
Intact females	36	10	28	18	4	13	75	16	21

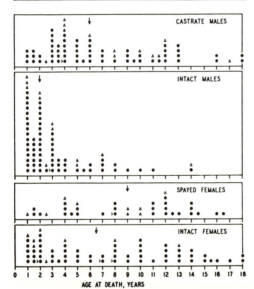

Fig. 1. Age at death of cats brought to ASPCA veterinary hospital. ● = common cats; △ = Siamese cats; ▲ =long-haired cats. > indicates euthanasia of cats which were known not to be ill or senile.

Table 4. Commonly Assigned Reasons for Death or Disposal of All Cats in Series 1 and 2 for Which Such Information Was Available.

Assigned Reason for Death or Disposal	Group[a]	1	2	3	4	5	6	7	8	9	10	11	12	13	14	15	16	17	18	Mean	Median	No.	%
Urinary retention	C	2	4	9	8	6	5	2	1	2										4	4	39	25
	M	10	11	5	1	4	1	2	2											3	2	36	33
External trauma	C		1					1									1			8	7	3	2
	M	6	4		1								1							3	1-2	12	11
	S	2	1		2	1								1						4	4	7	9
	F		2	1										1						5	2-3	4	4
Constipation and ingested foreign objects	C		1	1		1	1					1	1				1			8	6	7	4
	M		1																	—	—	1	1
	S		3		1				1		1									5	2-4	6	7
	F	2	1	1	1		1													3	2-3	6	6
Jaundice and hepatitis	C		1				1		1	1	1		1	1						9	9	7	4
	M	1								1										—	—	2	2
	S				1	1									1					—	—	3	3
	F	1																		—	—	1	1
Pneumonia and pneumonitis	C	1			1			1				1	1							7	7	5	3
	M	1			1	2		1												4	5	5	4
	S						1		2											--	—	3	2
	F	1	1					1			1									—	—	4	4
Nephritis and uremia	C			1		1	1	1		3		3	4	2		2	2	1		11	12	21	13
	M		1		1	3		2			1	1				1				7	5-7	10	9
	S			2						2		2		1		1	1			10	10	9	11
	F	2			1		1			1									1	7	4-7	6	7
Tumors, other than mammary	C		2	3	3	2	1	2	1	2	2	2	1	2	2	1	1	1		8	8-9	28	17
	M			2			1					2	1		3					10	11	9	8
	S			1	1	1				1	3	2		4	3	2	3	2		10	11	23	26
	F			1	2		2	2	1	1		1	1	1	3	2	1		1	10	9-10	19	16
Tumors, mammary	S													1						—	—	1	1
	F				1			1	1	1		1	1	2	3	1	2	1	1	12	10-13	16	14
Pyometra	F		1			1	1	2	2	2		1	2							8	8	12	10

[a]C=castrated male. M=intact male. S=spayed female. F=intact female.

males (Table 4). This was so whether the incidence of the pathological state in castrated males was similar to, or was greater or less than, that in intact males.

A pathological condition which occurred later in castrated than in intact males in both Series 1 and 2 was retention of urine, with or without bladder stones. In the combined data for both series the mean recorded age was 4.5 years in 39 castrated males and 3.1 years in 36 intact males ($P = .007$).

With regard to external trauma as a cause of death or destruction, there was a suggestion of later occurrence in castrated than in intact males ($P = .06$).

Higher mortality rates in intact than in castrated males did not arise solely from the greater incidence and earlier occurrence of a single pathological condition. After exclusion of deaths from trauma and from urinary retention, to which death or disposal of one-third of the males was attributed, the duration of

Table 5. Age at Death of Male Cats of All Types, Exclusive of Animals in Which the Assigned Cause of Death Was Urinary Retention or External Trauma.

Group	Series 1		Series 2	
	No. of Cats	Mean Age at Death	No. of Cats	Mean Age at Death
Castrated males	46	8.2[a]	70	8.8
Intact males	41	3.8	21	7.7

[a]Difference between castrated and intact males $P<.001$.

life was still significantly shorter in the intact than in the castrated males of Series 1 (Table 5). In Series 2 there was a similar trend, which was not significant, perhaps in part because the cause of death was omitted in many of the abstracted records made available. This happened to be particularly true for cats which died at a young age when the difference in mortality rates between intact and castrated males was particularly pronounced.

Nephritis, with or without a statement as to

the presence of uremia, tended to be recorded as a cause of death at a later age in castrated than in intact males ($P = .02$). Nephritis was somewhat more commonly reported in castrated than in intact males (Table 4) but the difference in incidence was slight (15 vs. 12%) in data restricted to cats which lived at least two years, i.e., to the age when the first instance of nephritis in males was noted.

The mean age at which tumors were recorded as the cause of death or disposal of cats was no later in castrated than in intact males. Tumors were the assigned cause of death or euthanasia in a somewhat higher percentage of castrated than of intact males (Table 4), but the difference in incidence was smaller (18 vs. 12%) in data restricted to males which lived at least two years, i.e., to the earliest age at which a tumor was recorded in males.

Testicular functions also exerted deleterious influences apart from any acceleration of senescence. The survival of intact males, compared with that of females or castrated males, was particularly poor during the years immediately following the age for sexual maturation. The increase in percentage of long-lived cats, when the data were restricted to animals which had lived five years instead of one, was almost threefold in intact males (cf. values for all cats in Table 3).

b. *Comparisons of spayed and intact females.*—Mean and median ages at death were slightly higher in spayed than in intact females in Series 1 and 2 but the differences were not significant (Table 2, Figs. 1 and 2). The differences were even smaller in animals which survived a minimum of two, three, or five years (Table 2).

Survival in terms of the percentage of long-lived cats, also showed trends to greater viability of spayed than of intact females (Table 3).

Breast tumors and pyometra were common in intact females but there was only one instance of mammary tumor and none of pyometra as the recorded cause of death in spayed females (Table 4). In intact females the mean age for deaths attributed to pyometra was comparable to that for deaths in general, whereas the mean age for deaths attributed to mammary tumors tended to be higher (Tables 1 and 4).

None of the other items listed in Table 4 oc-

curred significantly earlier nor more frequently in spayed than in intact females.

c. *Comparisons of intact males and females.*—Mean and median ages at death tended to be higher in females than in males (Table 2; Figs. 1 and 2). The difference was significant in Series 1. Cats which survived at least two, three, or five years also showed a significantly higher mean age at death in females than in males in Series 1 and a similar but statistically insignificant trend in Series 2.

A trend to greater viability of females than of males was also shown by the percentage of each group that was long-lived (Table 3).

The better survival of females than of males was marked at one or two years of age, a phenomenon also observed in dogs (Comfort, 1956b).

The chief reasons given for death or disposal of the animals were urinary retention in males, tumors in females. Data were too few to warrant analysis of possible sex differences in the age at which death was attributed to pathological conditions common to both sexes.

d. *Comparisons of castrated males and intact or spayed females.*—In the different series and categories of cats there was no consistent difference between castrated males and either intact or spayed females in duration of life or in age at death attributed to pathological states common to both sexes (Tables 1-4).

Siamese cats and long-haired cats.—Some of the values and trends resembled those in common cats (Table 6). The most consistent trend was to longer duration of life in orchiectomized than in intact males.

Table 6. Age at Death of Siamese and of Long-Haired Cats Which Survived One or More Years. (Data for Series 1 and 2 Combined.)

	No.	Mean	Median
Siamese Cats			
Castrated males	23	7.3±0.92[a]	7.0
Intact males	13	4.8±1.01	5.0
Spayed females	21	6.8±0.86[b]	6.0
Intact females	12	4.6±1.35	2.75
Long-Haired Cats			
Castrated males	11	7.6±1.93	9.0
Intact males	5	3.8±1.16	3.0
Spayed females	9	9.6±1.40	11.0
Intact females	5	10.5±1.80	12.0

[a]Difference between castrated and intact males, $P=0.10$.
[b]Difference between spayed and intact females, $P=0.16$.

DISCUSSION

The data in Series 1 and 2 were collected in separate hospitals staffed by different personnel. They provide independent confirmation that the duration of life was longer in castrated than in intact males. The agreement on this point seems especially noteworthy since the span of life in males was greater in Series 2 than in Series 1.

The longer life of common cats brought to the private hospital than of those taken to the ASPCA, a difference which was pronounced in males, is presumed to be due in part to differences in economic status of their owners and the care which they provided. This assumption is strengthened by the facts (a) that the proportion of common cats which were subjected to the costly operations of orchiectomy or spaying tended to be higher in animals brought to the private hospital than in those taken to the ASPCA (Table 1) and (b) that the duration of life in animals brought to the two hospitals tended to be more similar among Siamese and among long-haired cats than among domestic cats; the financial investment tended to be greater for these special categories than for common cats.

Attitudes of owners.—It is conceivable that intact animals, and perhaps males in particular, might be more troublesome than gonadectomized animals and therefore be discarded at an early age. Several lines of evidence demonstrate that this possibility was not completely responsible for the shorter life of intact males than of intact females or castrated males. First, euthanasia before ten years of age was requested in the absence of illness for only ten cats in the two series combined; five had been gonadectomized, three were intact females, and two were intact males. Second, the possibility of preferential disposal for any reason was largely eliminated in data for cats which died "spontaneously," i.e., without euthanasia and not as a result of elective surgery. In these cats the duration of life tended to be shorter in intact males than castrated males or intact females of Series 1 (Table 7) and a similar trend was observed in the smaller number of cats in Series 2 known to have died "spontaneously."

A third line of evidence was revealed in data for animals which lived at least two, three, or five years, and were presumably not especially troublesome, since they had not been disposed of at an early age. Values for these animals exhibited the same trends observed in data which included cats that died at one year of age (Table 1). As further evidence it may be noted that the magnitude of the difference between castrated and intact males, with regard to mean duration of life, was approximately the same in the common cats as in the Siamese and long-haired cats, even though the latter two categories of cats represented more costly investments than common cats and may have received special care.

The following additional evidence also cautions against speculation that the relatively short life of intact males was due to disaffection by their owners or that the long life of gonadectomized cats was due to sheltering by their owners: (a) the span of life is shorter in males than in females of most species that have been studied in this regard and this difference characterizes wild as well as domesticated animals (Hamilton, 1948); and (b) sheltering of human celibates in religious orders did not erase or materially change the lesser viability of males than of females (Madigan, 1957).

Effect of orchiectomy on life span.—The old and apparently-prevailing view is that orchiectomy does not prolong life and may predispose to premature aging (Verzár, 1963; Comfort, 1956a; Heriot, 1956; Pittard, 1934; Viecki, 1932; Korsakow, 1898; Merschejewsky, 1876). In outbred species, documentation in support of this view is slender. The largest number of cases was reported in psychotic men by Bremer (1959), who intimated that castration decreased viability. Unfortunately, Bremer did not utilize a control group of intact psychotic men. Korenchevsky (1952) stated that "deficiency of sex hormones . . . accelerates and intensifies processes of aging . . . ," but he did not study the duration of life in his series of rats. Data have been reported by Slonaker

Table 7. Comparison of Mean Age of Death for Total Deaths and Spontaneous Deaths Only.

	Age at Death (Years)			
	"Spontaneous" Deaths		All Deaths	
	No. of Cats	Mean	No. of Cats	Mean
Castrated males	42	5.7[a]	72	7.0[a]
Intact males	42	3.0	77	3.3
Spayed females	18	8.1[b]	37	8.7[c]
Intact females	24	4.6	66	7.3

[a]Difference between castrated and intact males, $P < 0.001$.
[b]Difference between spayed and intact females, $P < 0.05$.
[c]Difference between spayed and intact females, $P < 0.001$.

(1930) but for small groups of eight castrated and ten intact male rats in which the mean duration of life was 770 and 788 days, respectively.

Castrated males do not outlive intact males in some inbred species: mealmoths (Hamilton & Johansson, 1955) and DBA mice (Mühlbock, 1959). Duration of life tends to be decreased by inbreeding (Mühlbock, 1959; Smith, 1959), however, and sex differences in viability are small in some inbred strains of mealmoths (Hamilton & Johannson, 1955), mice (Mühlbock, 1959), and flies (Smith, 1959). Effects of castration upon duration of life may also be small in animals which lack hybrid vigor. A further complication in certain species and strains of animals, such as DBA mice, is the fact that removal of the gonads leads to hypertrophy and hyperplasia of the adrenal cortices, which then secrete large amounts of sex hormones (Woolley, Dickie, & Little, 1953).

Effects of ovariectomy on life span.—As with orchiectomy, the prevailing view seems to be that the effects of ovariectomy upon duration of life are nil or detrimental (Verzár, 1963; Williams & Novak, 1963; Comfort, 1956a; Slonaker, 1930). In outbred species, however, controlled studies have been meager. The largest number of Ss have been women who underwent operation, not at random to test the effect of oöphorectomy, but because of suspected pathology (Society of Actuaries, 1954).

Among inbred animals, oöphorectomized females outlived intact females in C_3H mice (Mühlbock, 1959). Fruit flies with vestigial ovaries survived better than intact females, an effect attributed to non-production of the large quantities of eggs characteristic of this species (Smith, 1959). This hypothesis would not explain the long life upon spaying of mice which produce small eggs in limited numbers, or upon mating of mosquitoes since they then lay eggs (Lavoipierre, 1958).

Gonadal function and survival.—It seems that gonadal functions may hamper full expression of the potential length of life in cats, since castration permits the ordinarily less-favored male to attain the range characteristic of intact females. Proof of deleterious effects by testicular functions stands in contrast to more speculative claims that the generally lesser viability of males than of females is due chiefly to heterogeneity of the sex chromosomes in males of most species (Lenz, 1923; Geiser,

1924-1925; Schirmer, 1929). Even in embryonic and immature animals, there is evidence that testes and ovaries play the major role in directing development of the secondary sex organs and of many other sex-differing characteristics observed in later life.

The relatively dormant status of sex genotype, once the embryonic gonads have differentiated into testes or ovaries in accordance with sex differences in chromosomes, has been emphasized by Yamamoto (1963). He and Humphrey (1948) have shown that in certain fish and amphibia the gonads can be experimentally induced to develop into testes in genetic females and into ovaries in genetic males. These testes and ovaries were functional and fertile in their sex-reversed form even though the sex chromosomes of their gametes conformed to the original genotype of the animal, which was female in animals with sperm and male in animals with ova. As early as the 16th day in female human embryos, one of the sex chromosomes acquires a hyperchromatic appearance, which is believed to represent a largely inactive state (Hirschhorn & Firschein, 1964).

The data at hand are preliminary and incomplete for any species, but the relationship of gonadal functions to survival seems to involve many variables. The effects of gonadectomy may differ under various circumstances, at different periods of life, and with individuals, strains, species, and sex. In general the intact male is less able to benefit from conditions favorable to survival and longevity and is more vulnerable to many hazards than the intact female. In recent decades sanitation, public health measures, and improved medical care have been associated with a greater mean duration of life in *Homo sapiens*, but less so in males than in females (Scheinfeld, 1958). Outbreeding and hybrid vigor are probably examples of favorable conditions which may augment sex differences in viability. Examples of conditions which are more hazardous to males than to females are obesity and feeding *ad libitum* without obesity (Berg & Simms, 1961).

Individuals, strains, and species vary in their response to gonadectomy. Some, but not all castrated cats are long-lived. Running activity is affected by gonadectomy in domestic but not in wild rats (Richter, 1954.) In some, but not all strains of mice, gonadectomy results in hyperfunction of the adrenals and early death. In certain strains and species even the usual sex differences in viability are not marked (Smith, 1959; Hamilton, 1948).

An urgent question pertains to the manner in which gonadal function might induce earlier death in intact than in gonadectomized animals and in males than females. Gametogenesis may be considered first, since duration of life may be adversely correlated with the male sex and with production of gametes in plants and invertebrates (Hamilton, 1948), organisms in which little is known about the presence and actions of sex hormones of the types known in higher forms of life. In dioecious forms of spinach, removal of the gamete-producing structures prolongs the life of male or female plants (Leopold, 1960). In the fruitfly, although not in some other poikilothermic forms, females with vestigial ovaries are exceptionally long-lived (Smith, 1959). It is interesting that ingestion of hen's eggs was carcinogenic in mice and chicks (Szepsenwol, 1961).

Sex hormones deserve the greatest consideration. They stimulate development of the reproductive systems and other structures. Androgens in particular exert potent effects beyond the confines of the reproductive system and are known to cause common pathological states like acne and male pattern baldness in individuals hereditarily predisposed to these conditions (Hamilton, 1941, 1942).

The poorer survival of intact males than of females and castrated males involves more than acceleration of senescence, since the number of deaths in intact male cats was especially high in the years immediately after sexual maturation. In this same period of life, death rates are also much higher for intact males than females in humans and dogs (Bowerman, 1950; Comfort, 1956b). Intact male cats which survived these critical years had a much improved chance to be long-lived (Table 3). When the deleterious effects of testicular functions were eliminated by castration, the percentage of long-lived cats was as large in males as in females.

SUMMARY

Data from two veterinary hospitals provided independent evidence that castrated male cats lived significantly longer than intact males. This difference in viability was not wholly attributable to early disposal of intact males by their owners, since orchiectomy prolonged the life of animals not subjected to euthanasia and mortality rates tended to be lower in castrated than in intact males throughout life.

Several of the assigned causes of death, or for disposal of the animals, were recorded at a later age in castrated than in intact males, but survival also tended to be better in castrated than in intact males during the years immediately after the age for sexual maturation.

In intact animals the duration of life was greater in females than in male cats brought to one hospital. A similar trend, although not statistically significant, was observed in cats taken to the other hospital.

The fact that castration can be associated with extension of life in male cats to a range characteristic of females suggests that in some organisms the lesser viability of intact males than of intact females may be due more to testicular functions than to differences in sex chromosomes.

The author is indebted to Drs. Philip McEnerny and Robert Tashjian of the Animal Medical Center and Dr. John Whitehead and Mr. Donald J. Schroeder of the Manhattan ASPCA. The writer is also indebted to Mrs. James Hamilton and Gordon E. Mestler for aid in the collation and analysis of data. Financial support was provided in part by the Harris McLaughlin Foundation and by an unrestricted grant made to this school by the U.S.P.H.S.

REFERENCES

Berg, B. N., and H. Simms: Nutrition and longevity in the rat. II. Food restriction beyond 800 days. *J. Nutrit.*, 74: 23-32, 1961.

Bowerman, W. G.: Annuity mortality. *Trans. soc. Actuar.*, 2: 76-102, 1950.

Bremer, J.: *Asexualization.* Macmillan Co., New York, 1959, 366 pp.

Comfort, A.: *The biology of senescence.* Rinehart, New York, 1956(a). 257 pp.

Comfort, A.: Longevity and mortality of Irish wolfhounds. *Proc. zool. Soc. Lond.*, 127: 27-34, 1956.(b)

Comfort, A.: Maximum ages reached by domestic cats. *J. Mammal.*, 37: 118-119, 1956.(c)

Geiser, S. W.: The differential death rate of the sexes among animals. *Wash. Univ. Stud. sci. Ser.*, 12: 73-96, 1924-1925.

Hamilton, J. B.: Male hormone substance. A prime factor in acne. *J. clin. Endocrinol.*, 1: 570-592, 1941.

Hamilton, J. B.: Male hormone stimulation is prerequisite and an incitant in common baldness. *Amer. J. Anat.*, 71: 451-480, 1942.

Hamilton, J. B.: The role of testicular secretions as indicated by the effects of castration in man and by studies of pathological conditions and the short lifespan associated with maleness. *Recent Prog. hormone Res.*, 3: 257-322, 1948.

Hamilton, J. B., and M. Johansson: Influence of sex chromosomes and castration upon lifespan: Studies of meal moths, a species in which sex chromosomes are homogeneous in males and heterogeneous in females *Anat. Rec.*, 121: 565-578, 1955.

Heriot, A.: *The castrati in opera.* Secker & Warburg, London, 1956, 243 pp.

Hirschhorn, K., and I. L. Firschein: Genetic activity of the X-chromosome in man. *Trans. N.Y. Acad. Sci., 26:* 545-552, 1964.

Humphrey, R. R.: Reversal of sex in females of genotype WW in the axolotl (Siredon or *Ambystoma mexicanum*) and its bearing upon the role of the Z chromosomes in the development of the testis. *J. exp. Zool., 109:* 171-185, 1948.

Korenchevsky, V.: Endocrines and aging. *In:* T. C. Desmond (Chairman), *Age Is No Barrier.* N.Y. State Joint Legis. Commit. on Prob. of Aging, Legis. Doc. No. 35, 1952, pp. 121-128.

Korsakow, W.: Die Eunuchen in Peking. *Dtsch. med. Wschr., 24:* 338-340, 1898.

Lavoipierre, M. M. J.: Biting behavior of mated and unmated females of an African strain of *Aedes aegypti. Nature, Lond., 181:* 1781-1782, 1958.

Lenz, F.: Übersterblichkeit der Knaben im Lichte der Erblichkeitslehre. *Arch. Hyg., Berl., 93:* 126-150, 1923.

Leopold, A. C.: Senescence of plants and plant organs, *In:* B. L. Strehler (Editor), *The Biology of Aging.* Amer. Inst. Biol. Sci., Washington, 1960, pp. 207-209.

Madigan, F. C.: Are sex mortality differentials biologically caused? *Milbank mem. Fd. quart. Bull., 35:* 202-223, 1957.

Mellen, I.: *The science and mystery of the cat.* Charles Scribner's Sons, New York, 1940, 275 pp.

Merschejewsky, W. O.: Einfluss der Verschneidung auf die Entwickelung des männlichen Organismus "Beilage." *In:* E. Pelikan (Editor), *Gerichtlich-Medicinische Untersuchungen über das Skopzenthum in Russland.* J. Ricker, Giessen, 1876, pp. 15-22.

Mühlbock, O.: Factors influencing the lifespan of inbred mice. *Gerontologica, 3:* 177-183, 1959.

Pittard, E.: *La castration chez l'homme.* Masson & Co., Paris, 1934, 327 pp.

Richter, C. P.: Effects of domestication and selection on the behavior of the Norway rat. *J. nat. Cancer Inst., 15:* 727-728, 1954.

Scheinfeld, A.: The mortality of men and women. *Sci. Amer., 198:* 22-27, 1958.

Schirmer, W.: Über den Einfluss geschlechtsgebundener Erbanlagen auf die Säuglingssterblichkeit. *Arch. Rass.- u. GesBiol., 21:* 353-393, 1929.

Slonaker, J. R.: The effect of the excision of different sexual organs on the development, growth and longevity of the albino rat. *Amer. J. Physiol., 93:* 307-317, 1930.

Smith, J. M.: The rate of ageing in *Drosophila subobscura. In:* G. E. Wolstenholme & C. M. O'Conror (Editors), *Ciba Foundation Colloquia on Ageing. Vol. 5. The Lifespan of Animals.* Little, Brown & Co., Boston, 1959, pp. 269-285.

Society of Actuaries. *Impairment Study;* 1951. Peter F. Mallon, Inc., Long Island City, N. Y., 1954, 300 pp.

Szepsenwol, J.: The effects of various diets upon sexual maturity in mice. *Nature, Lond., 191:* 1112-1113, 1961.

Verzár, F.: *Lectures on experimental gerontology.* Charles C Thomas, Springfield, Ill., 1963, 128 pp.

Viecki, V.: The sexual life of man and its relation to longevity. *Urol. cutan. Rev., 36:* 17-19, 1932.

Williams, T. F., and E. R. Novak: Effect of castration and hysterectomy on the female cardiovascular system. *Geriatrics, 18:* 852-859, 1963.

Woolley, G. W., M. M. Dickie, and C. C. Little: Adrenal tumors and other pathological changes in reciprocal crosses in mice. II. An introduction to results of four reciprocal crosses. *Cancer Res., 13:* 231-245, 1953.

Yamamoto, T.: Induction of sex reversal in sex differentiation of YY zygotes in the medaka, *Oryzias latipes. Geriatrics, 48:* 293-306, 1963.

REFERENCES

Aslan, A. 1957. Neue Erfahrungen über die verjüngende Wirkung des Novocains (Stoff H₃) nebst experimentellen, klinischen und statistischen Hinweisen. *Therapiewoche* **8**(1):3.

Aslan, A. 1958. Zur Wirkung des Novocain, Die Wirkung des H₁-Vitamins (PAB) und des Novocain (Stoff H₃) auf die Vermehrung tierischer Zellen. *Arzneimittel-Forschung* **8**:11.

Aslan, A. 1962. The therapeutics of old age—the action of procaine. In *Medical and Clinical Aspects of Aging*, Vol. 4, H. T. Blumenthal, Ed., Columbia University Press, New York, p. 272.

Chebotarev, D. F., and V. V. Frolkis. 1975. Research in experimental gerontology in the USSR. *J. Gerontology* **30**:441.

Finch, C. E. 1972. Enzyme activities, gene function and aging in mammals (review). *Exp. Geront.* **7**:53.

Finch, C. E., H. S. Huberman, and A. E. Mirsky. 1969. Regulation of liver tyrosine aminotransferase by endogenous factors in the mouse. *J. General Physiol.* **54**:675.

Finch, C. E. 1973. Catecholamine metabolism in the brains of aging male mice. *Brain Res.* **52**:261.

Hamilton, J. B., R. S. Hamilton, and G. E. Mestler. 1969. Duration of life and causes of death in domestic cats: Influence of sex, gonadectomy, and inbreeding. *J. Gerontology* **24**:427.

Hamilton, J. B., and G. E. Mestler. 1969. Mortality and survival: Comparison of eunuchs and intact men and women in a mentally retarded population. *J. Gerontology* **24**:395.

Kirk, E., and M. Chiefie. 1948. Vitamin studies in middle-aged and old individuals. *J. Nutrition* **36**:315.

Korenchevsky, V. 1950. Rejuvenative, or eliminative and preventative treatment of senility as suggested by experiments on rats. *Rev. Med. de Liege* **5**:687.

Loosli, J. K., 1973. Clive Maine McCay (1898–1967)—A biographical sketch. *J. Nutrition* **103**:3.

McCay, C. M., M. F. Crowell, and L. A. Maynard. 1935. The effect of retarded growth upon the length of lifespan and upon the ultimate body size. *J. Nutrition* **10**:63.

Medvedev, Zh. A. 1962. Aging at the molecular level and some speculations concerning maintaining the functioning of systems for replicating specific macromolecules. In *Biological Aspects of Aging*, Vol. 3, N. W. Shock, Ed., Columbia University Press, New York, pp. 255–266.

Pelton, R. B., and R. J. Williams. 1958. Effect of pantothenic acid on the longevity of mice. *Proc. Soc. Exper. Biol. Med.* **99**:632.

Robinson, D. S. 1975. Changes in monoamine oxidase and monoamines with human development and aging. *Federation Proceedings* **34**: 103.

Romanoff, L. P., C. W. Morris, P. Welch, R. M. Rodriguez, and G. Pincus. 1961. The metabolism of cortisol 4-C^{14} in young and elderly men. I. Secretion rate of cortisol and daily excretion of tetrahydrocortisol, allotetrahydrocortisol, tetrahydrocortisone and cortolone (20 α and 20 β). *J. Clinical Endocrinology Metabolism* **21**:1413.

Thomas, L. 1974. The future impact of science and technology on medicine. *Bull. American College Surgery* **59**:29.

Wilder, S. 1971. Prevalence of selected impairments, United States. (Data from the National Health Survey: Series 10, no. 99). DHEW Publication, No. (HRA)75, 1526.

Zern, H. Z. 1973. *Hormone Therapy of the Menopause and Aging.* Charles C. Thomas, Springfield, Ill.

ADDITIONAL READINGS

Brody, H., D. Harman, and J. M. Ordy, eds. 1975. *Clinical, Morphologic, and Neurochemical Aspects in the Aging Central Nervous System, Aging*, Vol. 1. Raven Press, New York.

Bromley, D. B. 1964. *Psychology of Human Ageing*. Penguin Books, Baltimore, Md..

Brues, A. M., and G. A. Sacher. 1965. *Aging and Levels of Biological Organization*. University of Chicago Press, Chicago.

Bullough, W. S. 1973. Ageing of mammals. *Z. Alternsforsch.* **27**:247.

Campbell, S. 1976. *The Management of the Menopause and Post-Menopausal Years*. University Park Press, Baltimore, Md.

Cowdry, E. V. 1939. *Problems of Ageing: Biological and Medical Aspects*. Williams & Wilkins, Baltimore, Md.

Garn, S. M. 1972. The course of bone gain and the phases of bone loss. *Orthopedic Clinics of North America* **3**:503.

Goldman, R., and M. Rockstein, eds. 1975. *The Physiology and Pathology of Human Aging*. Academic Press, New York.

Kohn, R. R. 1971. *Principles of Mammalian Aging*. Prentice-Hall, Englewood Cliffs, N.J.

Korenchevsky, V. 1961. *Physiological and Pathological Aging*. S. Karger, Basel.

Lansing, A. I., ed. 1952. *Cowdry's Problems of Ageing*. Williams & Wilkins, Baltimore, Md.

Linn, B. S. 1975. Chronologic vs. biologic age in geriatric patients. In *The Physiology and Pathology of Human Aging*, R. Goldman and M. Rockstein (eds.). Academic Press, New York, pp. 9–18.

McCay, C. M., and M. F. Crowell. 1934. Prolonging the life span. *Sci. Monthly* **29**:405.

Metchnikoff, E. I. I. 1907. *The Prolongation of Life: Optimistic Studies*. Chalmers Mitchell, trans. Heineman, London.

Osborne, T. B., and L. B. Mendel. 1915. The resumption of growth after long continued failure to grow. *J. Biol. Chem.* **23**:439.

Pearl, R. 1928. *The Rate of Living*. A. M. Knopf, New York.

Pearl, R., and R. deW. Pearl. 1934. *The Ancestry of the Long Lived*. Johns Hopkins University Press, Baltimore, Md.

Robertson, T. B., and L. A. Ray. 1920. On the growth of relatively long lived compared with that of relatively short lived animals. *J. Biol. Chem.* **42**:71.

Sherman, H. C., and H. L. Campbell. 1934. Rate of growth and length of life. *Science* **80**:547.

Steinberg, F. U., ed. 1976. *Cowdry's the Care of the Geriatric Patient*, 5th ed. C. V. Mosby, St. Louis.

Stieglitz, E. J. 1943. *Geriatric Medicine: Diagnosis and Management of Disease in the Aging and in the Aged*. W. B. Saunders, Philadelphia.

U. S. Department of Health, Education and Welfare, Public Health Service, National Institutes of Health, Division of General Medical Science, Center for Aging Research translation from the Russian. *Second Conference on Gerontology and Geriatrics*. Moscow. 1960.

Winick, M., ed. 1976. *Nutrition and Ageing*. Wiley, New York.

AUTHOR CITATION INDEX

SUBJECT INDEX

About the Editor

GERALDINE M. EMERSON is Assistant Professor of Biochemistry, Medical Center, University of Alabama in Birmingham (UAB). She obtained her medical science education at this Medical Center with primary emphasis in physiology, minoring in biochemistry, pharmacology, and neuroanatomy. She received the Ph.D. degree in 1960 and was appointed instructor in physiology and biochemistry; in 1961, in biochemistry alone.

Dr. Emerson is active in community service. She has served on the Advisory Council of the Jefferson County (Alabama) Retired Senior Volunteer Program (RSVP), an Action agency sponsored locally by Positive Maturity. She is completing her second year as Chairman of the RSVP Advisory Council. She serves on the Affirmative Action Committee of the School of Dentistry and the University of Alabama in Birmingham. She has held many offices in the UAB Chapter of Sigma Xi and is currently serving as President. Dr. Emerson is a fellow of the AAAS and AIC, having served in various offices of the Alabama Chapter of the American Institute of Chemists and is also a member of the American Physiological Society, the Gerontological Society, the New York Academy of Sciences, and the Alabama Academy of Sciences.

Her career lifetime interest in neurophysiology, growth, and aging are reflected in her publications.